The

CHRISTIAN REVIEW

VOLUME I (1844)

Edited by
TOLBERT FANNING
JAMES C. ANDERSON
WILLIAM H. WHARTON

Charleston, AR
COBB PUBLISHING
2021

The Christian Review: Volume I (1844)
is published in the United States of America by:
ISBN: 979-8-3303-8741-0

Cobb Publishing
704 E. Main St.
Charleston, AR 72933
CobbPublishing@gmail.com
www.CobbPublishing.com
479.747.8372

CHRISTIAN REVIEW.

VOL. I.   NASHVILLE, JANUARY, 1844.   NO. 1.

"THE CHRISTIAN REVIEW."

In presenting a new work to the public for patronage, many, doubtless, will be disposed to question the utility of another publication devoted to religion in the west, and particularly in Nashville, Tennessee. The question as to the propriety of commencing the REVIEW, will enable the Conductors to give such reasons for the step as they trust, will be satisfactory to all intelligent, high- minded persons.

1st. It is well known, the sentiments and practices of the Church with which the proprietors of this Journal are associated, are but imperfectly understood, woefully misrepresented, and perverted throughout the length and breadth of the land, and therefore, the momentous importance of a work in this country to disabuse the public mind. True, there are other publications devoted, in part, to this subject, but none of them have a circulation so extensive in the south-west, as it is hoped the REVIEW will have. Publications in opposition to our teaching, are constantly being issued from the sectaries around us, and something for self-defense, is absolutely required.

2d. Believing, as we devoutly do, that the Christian religion is not fully taught or practiced by any party of the age, and that myriads of our contemporaries, who earnestly desire to know the truth, are blinded by the "doctrines and commandments of men," and that there is great lack of deep and godly piety in the human institutions, which have spread as a mighty flood over this fairest portion of the Almighty's dominions, we feel that it is but a work of benevolence, to call our countrymen to the word of God, as alone containing "all things that pertain to life and Godliness."

3d. From the fact also, that the churches of Christ are not generally, fully and scripturally organized; and that consequently, the disciples of Christ are not, as a whole, as intelligent, spiritual, and zealous, and do not exert the beneficial influence they otherwise might, we send the REVIEW forth, hoping the saints will gain instruction and become much more successful in the advocation of truth and righteousness.

4th. The plan of the CHRISTIAN REVIEW, is one which, it is believed, is better calculated to enable brethren in different and distant sections of country, to become acquainted, than is usual in religious periodicals. Corresponding and Reporting Editors have been selected in different States, for the purpose of giving religious intelligence in every section of the country. Thus, in a small compass, and at little cost, those who wish to know the progress of truth, can do so by taking this publication. These are a few out of the many reasons, which might be offered, for commencing the CHRISTIAN REVIEW.   EDITORS.

OUR POSITION IN REFERENCE TO THE DIFFERENT RELIGIOUS DENOMINATIONS.

We are well aware, the various religious communities around us, are not altogether friendly to the religion we profess, and therefore, we expect all we say, to be closely and rigidly scrutinized. We are also assured the greatest exertions will be made, to create and perpetuate prejudices with all parties, and that all heartily unite in declaring we are wrong in religious sentiments. It is further true, that from various causes many esteem us as persons of warlike temper, and as unkind to all except our brethren. These suggestions afford ample room for giving our true position in reference to all mankind.

I. From the word of God, we are constrained to believe, there are two great divisions in the human family—saints and sinners. Whosoever is not on the Lord's side, is opposed to him, and he that "gathereth not" with the Savior, "scattereth abroad." Of course, we speak of such only as are capable of reflection, willing, and choosing a course to pursue through life. Those who believe understandingly, and heartily yield themselves, soul and body, to the Lord, are his elect; destined, by perseverance and well doing, to more exalted climes; and the rest of mankind are not the adopted sons and daughters of the Most High.

2. In most of the religious sects of the age, we see pious and God-fearing persons, whose sole desire is, to be prepared for another mode of existence. With all such, we heartily sympathize, and are willing to unite in seeking the "straight and narrow path." That there are Christians in confusion, we doubt not, from the declaration "come out *of her my people, that ye be not partaken of her plagues."*

3. We entertain not the least unkindness towards mortal creature on the earth; and although we are far from believing the different sectaries, as societies, meet the Divine approbation, we can charitably hope many are sincere, and therefore, we wish to treat none as enemies, but regard all with ourselves as erring mortals, and whatever we think wrong, we shall claim the privilege, as patriots and advocates of truth, to point out clearly. We suppose no good man can object to this course. While we have the Bible, we can see no authority or plausible reason for the existence of any Church not designated and portrayed in the New Testament, and consequently, we consider ourselves called of Heaven, to state our reasons in a friendly and courteous manner for such a conclusion. We desire no angry wars with those who differ from us; but if we could, as occasion might offer, examine each other's foundation, with meekness, and with a solemn regard for truth, many and great might be the beneficial results.

Our motto is, *Union and peace on the Bible alone;* but for our lives, we can unite on no other system. If we depart from this blessed volume, we are willing to bear the blame; but if it be found we are the only people on earth, who *profess* to believe, the Bible alone is all-sufficient for present salvation and government, we pray others not to think us presumptuous. To conclude this hasty article, we declare ourselves friendly to all mankind, and although we cannot think the religious parties of the day, authorized by the great Law-giver, we acknowledge the piety of many of their members, and we desire above all things to pursue a quiet, peaceable and respectful course towards all the world.

RELIGION.

Amongst all subjects, national, ecclesiastical, and political, which have agitated the world, none has ever been of so exciting a character as that of religion. It matters not, as to the kind of religion, so far as excitement is concerned, whether it be Pagan, Mohamedan, Jewish or Christian;—for any creed mankind will zealously contend, and suffer the loss of all things. But perhaps, in no country have persons manifested *more feeling* for their respective religions than in Protestantism. In North America, the people, by the constitution, are permitted to choose any kind of religion they may desire, and from this cause, more inquiries are made, and more intelligence generally abounds than in any other country of the globe. This is a fortunate feature in our form of government, and one which every citizen should take great delight to defend.

Still, even in this favored land, there is just reason to doubt whether the great mass are able to define the "pure and undefiled religion" of the Bible. It may be said alas! in too many instances, multitudes worship, they know not what. The reason of this is too obvious. Not a few are made religious without knowing the reasons why they are so, or the objects of it. The overwhelming majority from infancy are inducted into a sect, and grow up with inveterate prejudices against all the world, except their own party. Hence the manifest disposition to condemn others without any reason but that of their indomitable hatred.

Others again, are trained without considerable prejudices for any particular religion, and on arriving at mature years, by the merest casualty, they are made to profess, or "get religion," not knowing the foundation of a Gospel hope, or perceiving, clearly, the great truths so essential to the conversion and salvation of man, and under these circumstances, they are folded by a party, and soon their prejudices to all but their peculiar sect, are strong and unyielding.

Others again, study the Bible, understand the "power of God" in their conversion, and become intelligent Christians, and it is to such, a few words of enquiry and admonition may not be entirely inappropriate.

I do not wish to become censor in morals, and it is by no means an envious office to examine into the conduct of others, but without such a course, improvement cannot be anticipated. It can be no harm, at least, to ask a few civil questions, and give a little wholesome advice.

Are all who profess to be members of the church of Christ, truly spiritual and pious persons? The response cannot be favorable. The customs of society, I regret to think, are adverse, in too many instances, to true and genuine piety. Men profess their faith, join the church, and in most other respects, conform to the corrupt maxima and giddy fashions of the world. The struggle is to gain wealth and honor, and consequently the concerns of the present world, have more attention than those of another.

Do all who profess to be religious, consider themselves "not their own;" this world a mere preparatory stage for another, and do all make religion the most important matter in the every day affairs of life? It is also true, that few seem to think "the earth, and the fullness thereof are the Lord's," and assuredly all religionists do not *feel* and *act* with the fear of a just God before the mind. Truly pious and religious persons, are known by their gravity, sincerity, holy conversation, and love for the practices of the Christian graces. The lightness, irreverence, and love for vain and foolish pursuits, so manifest in society, are subversive of Godliness, and the refinements   of

Christianity.

Let every professor be a living monument of the truth and benefits of Christianity, and the influence will be felt and acknowledged. Let the love of the Lord be the chief theme of meditation by day and night, and let us not think, speak or act, but with the fear of God before us; and we shall thereby "grow in grace and the knowledge of the truth," and "others seeing our good works will glorify our Father who is in heaven." If, brethren, we cannot live for the Lord, we should throw off the mask, lest we prove stumbling blocks to others.   T. F.

CHURCH ORDER.

As the brotherhood, generally, think and speak of the subject of church organization as a matter of deep interest to the cause of truth, it cannot be amiss to call particular attention to it, at the earliest opportunity. In the present No. no discussions are intended, but we solicit brethren from all parts, to give us their light on the subject; for evidently, it is either dark and mysterious, or few have made it a matter of careful, and patient investigation.

A few suggestions however in relation to the importance of order may not be out of place. In all the sublime operations of nature, order and harmony prevail. Not a star in the vast canopy of heaven, varies the least in a thousand ages, and were one to leave the path marked by the God of all, the whole universe would be thrown into confusion and disorder. Light, heat, and moisture are necessary to the vegetation of seed, and the growth and health of every plant on the wide earth, and unless these agents act harmoniously, the seed perishes, or the plant withers and dies. Light, water or heat alone, will destroy the life of the plant, but all combine in the order of Heaven's decree, and they mutually assist each other.

In all well-regulated machinery, order is observed in every part. Disorder in he least wheel, screw, pulley, or pin, in machinery, may cause sad confusion.

The human frame is God's most perfect workmanship, and yet there are ten thousands of influences, parts and agencies, all of which must observe order and harmony, for the well being of man. The derangement of the least muscle, or fiber, may cause great distress and ultimate death. And does the Bible teach, the body of man is a fit representation of the church of God? Suppose the members of this body do not act, properly, their part, or the least one becomes sickly, are we not to fear disease will ensue throughout the body, without a speedy remedy?

Unless the acts of a church are performed in the order Heaven has ordained, are we not to fear they will not be acknowledged in a coming day?

Does the New Testament contain a perfect model of church order? If so, who will aid in presenting it to the public?   T. F.

PURE SPEECH.

Nothing contributes so much to clear views of the word of God, as to express our sentiments in scriptural language. Every idea in the Bible may be presented in the words of the Bible, and if we have an idea for which we cannot find words in the scriptures, we should take it for granted it is unauthorized by the spirit.   T. F.

CHAPTER ON FAITH.

"All men have not faith" (2 *Thee.* 3: 2.)

No man can come to God, or enjoy the least benefit of the Christian religion, without faith. It is the foundation of hope and all spiritual experience. As faith is the first step towards heaven, and the main spring of all our joys, I am disposed to treat the subject somewhat methodically.

1. WHAT IS FAITH?

"Faith is the confidence of things hoped for, the assurance of things not seen." (He. 11: 1.) An inspired definition is worth all the speculations of men. The Gospel faith is not a *mere* cold, formal admission, that the Bible is true, but it is the full, and hearty confidence, which lays hold of, and appropriates the promises of God to ourselves. It is the living, soul-stirring and animating principle of the heart, which hastens its possessor forward to obedience.

2. HOW DOES FAITH COME?

"Faith comes by hearing, and hearing by the word of God." (Ro. 10: 17.) To confide in the word of man, is the means of gaining human faith, and to receive the word of God into an honest and understanding heart, is the only plan to obtain Gospel faith. The difference of faith, consists not in the manner of believing, but in the character of the evidence, and abject of faith. As the all powerful word of God, must enter the heart to beget faith, it is preposterous to think of obtaining it without a knowledge of the great facts of revelation. He that understands the fundamental truths on which the Christian fabric stands, and rests his hope of salvation upon them, is a believer in the Biblical sense of the word; and others who have wept, dreamed, and prayed themselves into a "comfortable persuasion" they are believers, are, to say the least, egregiously bewildered and deceived,

3. WHAT IS THE END OF FAITH?

"Receiving the end of your faith, the salvation of your souls." (2 Pet. 1: 9.) By faith we are justified, the heart is purified, and the soul saved from sin. "Whosoever believeth that Jesus is the Christ (*gegennetai*) is begotten of God." "Who is he that conquers the world, but he that believes that Jesus is the Son of God." "He that believeth on the Son hath everlasting life."

By faith in the promises, the heart is changed, and the affections taken from the love of iniquity to the love of righteousness. The Jews on Pentecost, heard the words of the Spirit uttered by Peter, understood, and believed them; and thereby were converted from scoffers to humble suppliants. Their full confidence in the truth induced them to exclaim "what shall we do"? This is the invariable effect of faith.

4. IS THERE BUT ONE FAITH?

"One Lord, one Faith, one Baptism."—PAUL.

As no one would infer, when the apostle affirms there is one Lord, and one body, that there are more lawgivers and churches, than he acknowledges, it would be most futile to imagine there are more faiths than one. Yet marvelous to record, the inventive and speculative genius of man, has originated as many faiths, as the beast has names, and indeed there seems a pride that there shall be as many faiths as there are sectaries, and almost as many as there are human beings. This error arises mainly from the fact, that most persons do not discriminate between faith and speculations.

To say a man *believes* a speculation, which he does not pretend to understand, is too ludicrous for the nineteenth century. No one can assert with any degree of propriety, *he believes* the dogma of the "trinity," "total depravity that all will be saved "irrespective of character," that none will be saved but such as were "particularly elected before the foundation of the globe," or in "getting religion," for these are but inferences about which the Bible says not a syllable. But it is in perfect keeping with revelation, and reason, to say, we believe God made the world, Jesus is the Christ the Son of God, and that he that believes and is baptized shall be saved; for upon these points, we have abundant testimony. All who receive the scriptures, believe these truths, and it is impossible to differ in reference to them, without denying the word. Thus, it is obviously an easy matter to see all mankind, who believe at all, have precisely the same faith. How can they differ, believing the same facts communicated by the same words! Suppose two persons were to commence reading the New Testament, both avowing belief and they were to reach this passage. "In those days came John the Baptist in the wilderness of Judea saying, repent, for the kingdom of heaven is at hand." On examination, the words convey the same ideas to both, and now the question is; can they have different faiths, entertaining the same ideas? One might say, he "did not believe the kingdom of heaven was at hand," for it had been in existence in all ages. Here is a difference, but it is not about what is said, for one has denied the plain word of God, and therefore, is an unbeliever. This rule would hold good in reference to every prominent feature of the Bible. Long since have I seen it was impossible for any one to believe in a mystical speculative system of religion, and the emphatic, clear teaching of the Spirit at the same time. It does not then require a philosopher to see, the controversies of the age, are not about faith, but concerning opinions, and empty speculations. On this point I have more in reserve.

5. ARE THE DISOBEDIENT BELIEVERS?

"He that believeth on me hath everlasting life." (Jno. 6: 47.)

It is a popular, but very dangerous error, to conclude the mass of mankind, in what is termed Christendom, believe the word of God. It is an error, because with the idea that all the world believe, Scripture cannot be reconciled with itself; and it is dangerous, because so long as persons suppose they believe when they do not, they will rest in their sins, waiting for a miracle to be performed, to make them religious. It is possible for persons to think sincerely they do believe, when if they were to examine themselves, they know not what to believe, and therefore, are mistaken. Although the Jews said they wore Moses' disciples, Christ informed them they did not believe Moses, "for" said he, Moses "wrote of me, but ye believe not his writings."

The proof the Jews did not believe the writings of Moses, was demonstrated by the fact, that his teaching did not influence their conduct, in reference to the Savior. And is it unreasonable to conclude, many in this age have some vague notion the Bible is a good book, without knowing its teaching, or believing what is written? Thousands no doubt, have some indistinct idea the Bible is true, and religion "a good thing," from current report, and yet as to the truths of religion, they have no clear views, and consequently disregard its requirements. If a strict examination could be instituted infidelity, might be found not in the world only, but the religious communities would be convicted of skepticism and downright unbelief. Can men in the church believe a virtuous life, and zeal for God, the only means of securing present and eternal happiness, and still remain lukewarm and indifferent to their own interests? Impossible. Neither can I suppose the unconverted, careless part of the human race believe the truths of revelation.

Anciently, when individuals believed the Gospel, they were moved to flee for refuge, sought the Way of righteousness, and became obedient to the faith. The coaxing, praying, and threatening with damnation, to induce persons to become religious, which we now witness, were not practiced by the Apostles, as the teachers of this age do. The great truths of the Gospel were stated, and when men believed them they obeyed them; and so it is to this day, with those who become Christians.—The subject of faith is exhaustless; and hoping there will be space for more in future Nos., for the present I must conclude. T. F.

CONTROVERSY AND INTERROGATORIES.

"And the priests, the sons of Levi, shall come near; for them the Lord thy God hath chosen to minister unto him, and to bless in the name of the Lord: and by their word shall every CONTROVERSY be tried. (Deu. 21; 5.)

"Jehoshaphat set the Levites for *controversy.*" (2 Chron. 19; 8.)

"The Lord hath a *controversy* with the nations." (Jer. 25; 31.)

"The Lord hath a *controversy* with his people." (Mi. 6; 2.)

Plato and Franklin, were both benefactors of mankind, and the greatest luminaries of their respective ages; and yet most of their teaching was by questions and answers. With the examples of such men, I see some propriety in attempting to imitate their example. It is well known, there are abiding prejudices in this age, against religions controversy; and believing, as I do, that all that is valuable in science; government, and religion, is the result of rigid investigation, I will propound a few interrogations on this subject for the thoughtful.

1. Did not God in olden times proclaim decisions with nations, and his people, after controverting their errors?

2. Did not the Almighty particularly choose the priests for controversy?

3. Was not the life of the Messiah spent in controversy, first with the devil, and secondly, with his agents—the false religionists, and rebellious of his time?

4. Did not the Savior lose his character, with the great mass, and finally his life, for controverting the religious errors of his times?

5. Is it not fair to presume, if the Lord Jesus had not controverted the delusions on the earth when he appeared, he would have been most popular with all sects?

6. Did not the Apostles devote their lives to controverting error, and the sins resulting therefrom?

7. Did they not lose their lives for controverting false religions?

8. Did not most of the primitive Christians sacrifice their characters, and many of them their fortune and lives, by controverting error?

9. Did not Luther, Calvin and Wesley, effect their reformations by comparing truth with error, or controversy?

10. Why is it the followers of these great men generally declare themselves opposed to controversy?

11. Can a man who desires to know the truth, oppose investigation?

12. Do not partisans of every order, delight to controvert *their* own peculiarities, in opposition to others?

13. If the leaders were willing to know the truth, and disposed to let their followers know it, would they not court investigation?

14. Is not controversy the best means of eliciting the truth on the great questions which divide the religious world?

15. Can a man judge of the truth of any proposition, who does not know the arguments *pro* and *con?*

16. Have not many of the prejudices against public, and fair investigation, originated in an unwillingness to know the truth, and from the personal abuse of many debaters, and very unbecoming behaviour of disputants?

17. Should not the bitter abuse of some of our brethren, and the calumny and detraction of many partisans, in what are called "doctrinal sermons," and "controversies," be discountenanced by all God-fearing persons?

18. As investigations in reference to the various sciences are conducted with calmness and decorum, is it not a reproach upon religionists that they do not generally act likewise?

19. Is it not an indication of a contracted mind and corrupt heart, to abuse and slander one who differs from us in sentiment?

20. Should not Christians exert themselves publicly and privately to controvert error and sin?

21. Is not all profitable preaching controversy?

22. Should not all controversy be conducted with the reverence and solemnity, which the Savior manifested when he wept over Jerusalem, on account of the errors of its inhabitants?

23. If this course were pursued, would not all persons desirous of knowing the truth of God, anxiously seek investigation for their own good?

24. Is it not highly criminal for preachers to seek controversy for the purpose of exposing an opponent; to gratify pride; or for the purpose of acquiring fame as a debater?

T. F.

EDUCATION.

In every age of the world has the education of man been a subject of the deepest concern. No topic in the states of Europe at this day, is demanding such attention as the training of the young. Believing education indispensable to good society, and genuine happiness in time and eternity, it is intended to be a theme of frequent discussion in the "Christian Review."

At present, I care not to define the subject, or pursue it in its important details, but its momentous utility might be suggested with strict propriety, and general attention directed to it. When it is remembered there are about five thousand human beings of adult age in Tennessee, and many more in other and older States, who can neither *read* nor *write,* no benevolent man can think of the degradation of his countrymen without deep emotions of commiseration. To be deprived of the liberty of reading the word of God for ourselves, is a misfortune unequalled by few, if any others. Most individuals, to be sure, have opportunities of hearing something in relation to the scriptures, but so certain as that most eminent of Roman poets said, "once seeing is better than ten times hearing," those who cannot examine for themselves, must labor under the greatest inconveniences through life.

To occupy the stations the Author of all things designed, each individual should be educated; but with the present organization of society and systems of instruction, this seems impossible.

In future Nos. it is my intention to define education as fully as I am capable, and offer such a plan as I may think best suits the present state of society, and the circumstances with which we are surrounded. Will the readers of the Review prepare themselves to discuss this great matter?

T. F.

THE DEBATE BETWEEN A. CAMPBELL AND N. L. RICE.

There are but few persons, if any, who have heard of the late debate with A. Campbell of Virginia, and N. L. Rice of Kentucky, who do not feel more or less favorable to the religion of one or the other gentlemen. Reports have been variant and conflicting. To believe the friends of Bro. Campbell, who were present, we must conclude, that he was far the better disputant, had the better cause, and triumphed gloriously on every point: but to credit the letters and reports of Mr. Rice's friends, we should be induced irresistibly to admit, that Mr. Rice had all the talent, tact, learning and truth on his side; and that he not only vanquished his opponent, but either confounded and overwhelmed with his arguments, all the disciples of Christ present, or drove them from the field-

A stranger to religious controversy and sectarian prejudice can adopt but one mode of ascertaining the truth; that is, to read the book. No doubt zealous efforts have been made, and are still making, to create a partiality in the public mind, in favor of the arguments of Mr. Rice, and perhaps, some efforts have been made, to prejudice the community in favor of our teaching. Every expression to weaken or strengthen either gentleman's arguments, should be uttered with great cautiousness. The future happiness of the world is very intimately connected with the subjects debated, and it should be the sincere desire of every one to know and practice the truth.

The book should be read as if neither gentleman's sentiments had before been published, and with a determination to see, and feel the force of each man's arguments. Not a few individuals wished me to have a correspondent at Lexington, that I might hear of the matter as the debate progressed; but this was by no means desirable, and for at least three good reasons.

1st. I was aware it was next to impossibility for any one to give both the disputants' arguments fully and fairly.

2d. I did not wish my mind trammeled in the least when the time should arrive, that I might have the pleasure of reading the debate for myself.

3d. I knew both the men well, have heard them both discuss religious subjects to the utmost of their ability, and indeed on the very points in debate, and therefore, what a hundred of the best and wisest men of the age would say of their powers, or the success or failure of either, would not change my mind the least iota. After the debate shall have been read, it is my intention to speak of the debaters and their efforts, as each deserves; but till then "witness deposeth not."

T. F.

We publish the following letter, written some time since by a zealous brother, then resident in Alabama, to the Editor of a well-known religious print, issued not a hundred miles from the Capital of Virginia, in order to show the difficulties and obstructions our brethren have frequently to encounter and overcome that the Truth "may have free course and be glorified," in the conversion of our fellow men:

DEAR SIR:—I must request the favor of you to erase, for the future, my name from your subscription list. It is almost needless to state my reasons for this wish; I will do so, however, hoping you will have leisure to read them.

I am convinced, sir, that you are, it may not be designedly, but actually, opposing the Gospel of the Son of God: or at least mistaken something else for it, for although I was a member of your church, a reader of your "Telegraph," a believer in your creed, it was not till a short time since that I discovered from the New Testament, what that Gospel really is. I can now lay my hand upon my heart and say, I do most truly and, sincerely believe all that is written in the Law, in the Prophets, and in the Psalms, of the Old Testament; all that is written in Matthew, Mark, Luke and John, in the Acts, and the Epistles, of the New. I make this candid expose of my faith, for fear you should think that, in discarding the Calvinistic theory of Religion, I had discarded religion itself, along with it—and in giving up the speculations and opinions of the Westminster Assembly of Divines, as contained in their Catechisms, Confessions and Creeds, I had given up too, all hope of Glory, Honor and Immortality, at the resurrection of the Just; no sir, I have but removed myself from the sandy foundation of human traditions, and built upon the divine foundation of the Apostles and Prophets, Jesus the Messiah, being the chief corner stone.

But let me proceed. About twelve months gone I was induced to read the New Testament, again and again; I endeavored to bestow upon it the most profound attention; to study with the deepest interest, the rising glories of God's most wonderful Son—from his conception and birth through his life, to his death, to his resurrection and exaltation at the right hand of the Majesty on high. I thought much of the glad-tidings with which his message to earth was fraught; of its blessed hopes and precious promises; of its divine precepts and rich instructions; full of wisdom, and goodness, and love; especially the gracious words he uttered just before he blessed them and was parted from them, how that it was necessary he should have suffered and been raised again from the dead, in order that *Repentance* and Remission of Sin, should be preached in his name to all nations, beginning at Jerusalem. Here in imagination, I lingered with the disciples, until the great and notable day of the Lord came, the ever-memorable and eventful morning of Pentecost, when the little band were gathered together. The rushing wind, the forked tongues, the various gifts of speech, the holy zeal and heroic boldness of the fishermen of Galilee, astonished me, as it did the multitude when they came together. I listened to the explanation of the marvelous and amazing scene by Peter, heard him quote the Prophets in proof of the resurrection of Messiah; heard him appeal to the living and present apostles in attestation of the same fact. Peter spoke by the impulse of the Holy Spirit, whose demonstrations and whose power were manifested to the eyes and ears of the startled and astonished crowd, who had gathered about him, and they were no longer thoughtless and heedless before the Holy Apostles; they were convinced, convinced that Jesus was the Lord Messiah from Heaven, that they had sinned, deeply sinned, in murdering the Lord of Life and Glory; what were they to do, they appealed to the Holy men of God;. Peter answered, Repent and be Baptized every one of you in the name of Jesus Christ for the Remission of Sins, and you shall receive the gift of the Holy Ghost.

This sir, is the Gospel which you are opposing, you call it "Campbellism," "Heresy," and other evil names. I believe it in my heart, and have obeyed it from the heart, and am now enjoying its blessings in Peace of Conscience and joy in the Holy Spirit. In proclaiming it to others, I have been shut out from your 'churches,' have had to betake myself to Court-houses, to *Theatres,* and to the shady Groves of the Forest, that I might make known the Pardon, Salvation and Life, which our King hath purchased for my fellow men with his own blood.

In the limits of a sheet, it is impossible to say how far the leaders and teachers of modern times have strayed from the simplicity that was in Christ; how far they should reform their opinions and their practices in relation to his Kingdom; but sure, am I, that those who from deep and thorough conviction contend for reformation both in the world and in thee I have been greatly misrepresented, slandered, persecuted and abused! And from the unjust decisions which have been pronounced against them on Earth, they appeal with confidence in the rectitude of their intentions and the purity of their motives, as well as in the Truth for which they contend, to the high tribunal of Heaven, where the persecuted and the persecutor shall finally appear to meet the awards of the Great Judge. May the Lord himself forgive you the part you are acting, is my prayer.   W.

REVIEW

Of a "Treatise on Christian Baptism, collated from divert authors, with original notes and criticisms, being a review of Campbellism, by T. W. HAYNES."

As an observer of the sayings and doings of men, in manners, morals, and particularly in religion, I happened to open a pamphlet published in Nashville recently, with the above very classical and *kind* cognomen, a few days since, and noticing that the "general views" were endorsed and "recommended" by my friend Mr. R. B. C. Howell, and the *"copy-right secured,"* I concluded it must treat of subjects of considerable moment, and, therefore, I determined to examine it. I did so; and I have determined to give it a short and friendly notice.

As we have to take men as we find them in this world, great and small, as they present themselves, I think it not inappropriate to lengthen the preface to this review a little.

In the first place, I must state, that this notice is not prompted by the least unfriendly feeling towards the Baptist as a denomination, or the gentlemen who bind themselves for the truth of the doctrines of this pamphlet. My chief object is to seize upon this opportunity to present the true sentiments of the disciples of Christ on some points, in reference to which the great mass of the current writers and speakers seem not to understand us. As to Mr. Haynes as a man, or Baptist preacher, I have not a word to say; but as the "general views" are recommended by Mr. Howell, who is a man of more weight than any other of his denomination in this section of country, it might be considered negligence to leave a work of such a denomination unnoticed.

On taking this pamphlet in hand, the first thing Which caught my attention was the phrase *"Christian* Baptism." What, thought I, is the meaning of this? Is it possible my Baptist friends teach that Baptism is an ordinance for Christians to perform? I looked at the definition of the term Christian, and saw it was "a follower of Christ," "one who is in Christ," and I asked myself the question again, if a man can follow Christ, or be in Christ, without being "baptized into Christ," as the Galatians were? Gal. 3: 27.

Next, I was irresistibly led to enquire if the Baptists are becoming contradictory? I opened Mr. Howell's book on communion, at pa. 117, and read "Christian Baptism is the *only* authorized mode of entrance into the visible church." This was enough, I looked no further. If by the phrase "visible church," Mr. Howell meant the church of Christ; then as baptism is the "only mode" of entrance, those not baptized in obedience to God, are not in Christ, and of course must be in the other state. This will do. Next, in glancing my eye further over the title page, I saw the expression REVIEW OF CAMPBELLISM; and the thought occurred to me, that this was a time of extreme indulgence. This is a free country, men can accuse each other as they please, but there is a day coming for righteous retribution. Because it was popular, a profane Jew could contemptuously assert the Saviour "cast out devils by Beelzebub," and pronounce the disciples "Nazarenes," as if a sweet morsel had rolled on the tongue; and should it be surprising that those who advocate the Bible and its practices alone, in religion, should be denounced as heretics, Campbellites and devils? I speak the sentiment of my heart, and in the fear of God, when I declare, that I do not believe any humble Christian, who acts with an eye to the fear of his Maker, will attempt to fasten an *opprobrious* epithet on his fellow creature. All intelligent men know that we disdain "Campbellism," and only wish to honor the Lord whose we are, and for whose NAME we suffer, and are willing to suffer the loss of all things. This glaring behavior cannot last. Intelligence is on the wing, and will soon reach the better portion of the community.

In the third place, I looked at the bottom of the title page, and saw this expression *"copy-right secured."* Well, thought I, copy-rights are secured to men for their own productions. So, I opened to the first page. I began to read. The style was manly, spirited, classical, clear and Scriptural. I proceeded to the 23d page, more than half the matter for which Mr. Howell had endorsed. This is all very good said I. Is there no mark of quotation for this? I could find none. What learned Baptist, said I, has done this? I could think of none who wrote on this wise. Do not be astonished kind reader, when I inform you, that I opened Campbell and Walker's debate, and in the Appendix at page 153, I began to read, and found this endorsed matter word for word, to the 23d page, from the pen of A. Campbell of Bethany, Virginia. "Copy-right secured," mind, and that of my Bro. Campbell's writing. On this page the pamphlet seems to have taken a different turn, another subject is introduced, and A. Campbell is quoted by name. I continued through the "forty pages" for which Mr. Howell had endorsed, and found more than two thirds of it from Bro. Campbell. Pretty well, thought I, when Mr. Howell can "cheerfully recommend" the writings of Alexander Campbell to his "friends." I hope they will read and profit by them.

Having said so much in reference to the title page, and the "copy-right" of A. Campbell's works, I will notice but one item in the body of this work. The debate of Campbell and Walker is quoted p. 210, where Bro. C. says:

"The commission to baptize believers, or disciples, prohibits the baptism of others," and the "Christian System," p. 198, where Bro. C. says: "immersion was essential to discipleship," to show a contradiction. In the same manner, I can make Paul and Peter contradict each other in a hundred places. It is certainly true that the Greek verb, *Mathetuo,* used in the commission and translated by the word "teach," means to *disciple* or make disciples. Mind, this is before baptism, and without this discipleship. Baptism is worse than useless. It is said of the Saviour, *he* "*made* and *baptized* more disciples than John." The idea is very clear that Christ discipled before he baptized. But those who believed and were baptized were also denominated disciples. Is there not a contradiction here? Just as much as there is with Bro. C. Is the idea in the New Testament, that there are two kinds of disciples mentioned, one in *word only,* and the other, in both *word* and *deed!* If so, Bro. Campbell is correct, in asserting "The commission for converting the world, teaches that immersion was essential to discipleship." I have already shown that Jesus "mode" the disciples before baptism. I will next give one instance of disciples first in *word,* and secondly, by obedience, they were disciples in both *word* and *deed.* It is said, John 8: 30, 31: "As he spake these words, many believed on him. (Now they are the taught, believers, and disciples in word.) Then said Jesus to those Jews who believed on him, if you continue in my word, then are ye my disciples indeed." More on this point would be unnecessary, and a more lengthy review of the pamphlet under consideration, would be irksome too.

T. F.

LETTER FROM W. S. SPEER.

Dear Bro. Fanning;—Having just completed a tour of 290 miles through North Mississippi, Alabama and various parts of our own beloved State, I seize my quill to inform you that the cause of Reformation is beginning to excite interest, awake attention, produce a spirit of inquisitive investigation, and arouse the fiery opposition of sectaries swarm to their errors and to their parties. I preached 13 discourses in Holly Springs, where there is more blind, determined and defamatory opponents of the pure, primitive, regenerating and sanctifying Gospel of the grace of God's own Son, than I ever before witnessed. We have to contend against the trinity of sin—1 sectarianism, 2 worldlyism, and popularism. I succeeded in removing much prejudice, and in disabusing the public mind of false impressions—immersed 3 ladies—1 the wife of a Roman Catholic—1 the grand-daughter of a Methodist preacher—1 a young lady at "the same hour of the night." I intend to locate permanently in Holy Springs; and by the blessing of the God of truth, I shall aid the Disciples in planting the standard of the Bible in that land of intelligence, wealth and fashion. It ought to be done; it can be done; it must be done—it shall be done. Nothing is wanting but a devotion that prefers the interest of the Dear Redeemer's Kingdom to our chief good, and an energy, zeal and activity worthy a soldier of the Captain of our salvation. O for the zeal of a Paul, the eloquence of an Apollos, the strength of a Samson and the skill of a David, with the smooth pebble of almighty truth to break the orthodox skulls of our party Goliaths! In Tuscumbia, the cause has been deserted and now is waning. Brethren, go to Tuscumbia and preach the life-giving word, and set things in order among the few remaining disciples there. Go—God will reward you. Dan. 12: 3.

Before I close this note, already too long, permit me to speak a word in reference to Bro. John M. Barnes. He is engaged in a flourishing school in Maury Co., and from the manner his patrons universally express their approbation of his labors, I can say that Middle Tennessee ought to encourage his school liberally. He is a skillful instructor, is possessed of brilliant talents—is assisted by his highly accomplished Lady, and does business with an energy and activity worthy of this best of employments. Brethren, send him your sons, and he will make them ornaments to the State, the church and the world. He educates *for both worlds.*

Your Bro. in the Hope,
Nashville, Dec. 28, 1843.　　　　　　　　　　　　　　　　　W. S. SPEER.

ESSAY ON CREEDS—BY JACOB CREATH.

ARGUMENT FIRST—We shall use the word creed, in its usual and popular acceptation. Judge Blackstone, says it is the usual or common signification of a word that determines its meaning. Words are the stipulated signs of ideas. Ideas are clothed with words, as our bodies are with garments. Webster defines the word creed to be a brief summary of the articles of Christian faith. The popish Manual, contains a brief summary of the Catholic faith: The Episcopal Prayer Book, contains a brief summary of the faith of the Church of England: The Westminster Confession of Faith, contains a brief summary of the Presbyterian faith—it is styled "the Constitution of the Presbyterian church in the United States:" The London and Philadelphia Confessions of Faith contain a brief summary of the Baptist's faith: And the Discipline contains a brief summary of the faith of the Methodist Episcopal church—according to the above great names of Blackstone and Webster. A creed, according to them, and the above illustrations, is a *visible—tangible—written and printed book*—set forth to the world by each of the above named and highly respectable and numerous denominations, as a brief summary of their respective faiths.

The English word *Creed,* is derived from the Latin verb *Credo,* I believe— and from the Saxon word *Creda,* I believe. According to the above popular use of the word *Creed,* a man's writings are not his creed—his sermon is not his creed—his views are not a creed. Calvin's institutes are not the Creed of the Presbyterian church—but the longer and shorter catechisms. Wesley's sermons and writings, are not the Creed of the Methodists—but a book called the Discipline. Gill's and Fuller's writings are not the Creed of the Baptists —but the London and Philadelphia Confessions of Faith. We do not call the sermons, nor the discourses, nor the writings of one man, the creed of a denomination—but a brief summary put forth by the whole fraternity. According to Webster, these denominations have not their creeds in their heads, nor in their pockets—but in a printed book. This is a fair and common sense meaning of the word *Creed.* There was no Hume's History of England, nor Gibbon's History of the fall of Rome, before they were written, printed, and circulated. They were not called *Histories,* while they were in their author's *heads*—but when they became *visible* and *tangible.* A man cannot carry Hume's History in his head. The word Creed, is a definite and clearly defined word, as much so as the word history, chair, table, or house. A person cannot carry a Creed, nor any of the above-named things, in his head. A creed must be written, printed, visible and tangible; so that it may be examined and appealed to by the denomination who set it forth, and by the public. So much, therefore, for the popular meaning of the word creed. And, according to this broad and popular meaning of the word creed, the denomination to which the author of this Essay belongs, has no creed—if it has, he has not seen it, nor heard of it. And if our denomination had a written and printed creed, that would not prove that it was right to have creeds —two wrongs cannot make one right—two blacks cannot make one white.

The next question is—Are the above creeds authorized by the word of God —the Bible—or are they made by human authority? We say they were made by poor fallible man. Let him that says they are authorized by the sacred writings, point us to thus saith the Lord—you shall have a brief summary of faith. This the advocates of creeds are bound to do. Protestants, in their discussions with Catholics, about the utility of the Mass, the Cross, and the Pope's supremacy, say "give us Apostolic precept or example for these things, and we will have them too." James, the Apostle, says there is one lawgiver, who is able to save the obedient, and to destroy the disobedient. Reader, how many do you say there are—one or four—one or fifty? Is the Pope the one lawgiver? or is it Luther, or Calvin, or Wesley? We say it is Jesus Christ, the son of God.

To all persons who believe that uninspired men have power to make laws to bind the consciences of men, we submit the following interrogatories: 1st. Has the Pope and his Cardinals, a right to make a Creed for the Protestants? 2d. Has the Pope a right to make a Creed for all the world? 3d. Who gave him such authority? 4th. Has one Protestant denomination, a right to make a Creed for all the other Protestant denominations? 5th. And will all of them agree to be bound by the Creed of one? 6th. Can any one sect in Christendom, renounce their Creed and submit to that of any other, and maintain its own separate existence afterwards? 7th. For example, can the Baptists adopt the Creed of the Methodists, and remain Baptists afterwards? 8th. Can the Catholics adopt the creed of any one of the Protestant sects, and maintain the separate identity of the Catholic Institution afterwards? 9th. Can America adopt the British Constitution and maintain her Republican institutions afterwards? 10th. Can the European States adopt the American Constitution, and maintain their Kingly governments afterwards?—11th. Can two Constitutions be obligatory upon one people or nation at the same time? 12th. Can America be bound by the British Constitution and the Bill of Rights, at once? 13th. Can any denomination of Christians be bound by a Creed and the Bible at the same time? 14th. Can all the European governments be *grouped* under the American Constitution, and support their separate identity? 15th. Can the Catholics and Protestants be grouped under the New Testament, and still remain Catholics and Protestants? 16th. Can all the Protestant sects *be couched* under the New Testament, and remain as they now are?

We subscribe, most heartily, to the following quotation from the 20th page of the Presbyterian Confession of Faith:

"The Supreme Judge, by whom all controversies of religion are to be determined, and all decrees of councils, opinions of ancient writings, doctrines of men and private spirits, are to be examined, and in whose sentence we are to rest, can be no other but the Holy Spirit, speaking in the Scripture." And on page 150: "The Scriptures of the Old and New Testament are the word of God—the only rule of faith and obedience."

They are not simply a rule of faith, or the rule of faith and obedience—but the *only* rule of faith and obedience. Therefore, it is wrong to have any other rule than the *only* rule of faith and obedience.

Thus we have demonstrated, fully demonstrated, I trust, to the entire satisfaction of the reader, our first proposition, to wit:—That human Creeds are unauthorized of God—that they are human productions—that they were made by fallible men, that they are human opinions, inferences and deductions of the human mind from the Scriptures—that they are traditions of men, that they are not binding upon the human conscience—that they are unscriptural and unnecessary.

EXTRACT FROM THE OPENING SPEECH, DELIVERED IN
LEXINGTON, AT THE COMMENCEMENT OF THE LATE DEBATE,
NOVEMBER, 15, 1843.

Gentlemen Moderators:—*Mr. President,* I feel myself peculiarly happy in being specially called, in the good providence of God, to appear before you. Sir, and your honorable associates, in the midst of this great community, to act an humble part in that long-protracted controversy, commenced more than three centuries ago, when the genius of Protestantism first propounded to Europe, and the world, the momentous and prolific questions:—Is the Bible an intelligent document? Is it a book to be read by all the people? Does it fully contain, and clearly reveal, the whole duty and happiness of man? The bold and intrepid Luther promptly responded in the affirmative; and immediately a numerous and powerful host gave in their adhesion,—seconded his efforts,— erected their standard,—unfurled their banner, and rallied under the sublime motto—the Bible, the whole Bible, and nothing but the Bible, is the religion of Protestants.

The Pope, his cardinals, and his lordly prelates heard with a scornful and indignant smile this bold and comprehensive declaration of independence. Little did his Roman Holiness, Leo X., and the lions around him, imagine what mighty revolutions of empire, civil and ecclesiastical, were concealed under those symbols.—No one, indeed, then living comprehended that motto in all its amplitude. No one saw that the regeneration of a world was in it. No one anticipated the mighty impetus which it was about to impart to the human mind, to the cause of human improvement, to the advancement of civilization, and to the eternal redemption of the world from ignorance, error, and crime.

It was not merely a renunciation of popery—of all sorts of popery, ecclesiastic and political. It was not merely a renunciation of despotism, of tyranny, of anarchy, of misrule, of every species of cruelty and oppression on account of opinions, on account of human traditions or political interests. It asserted the rights of man—liberty of thought, liberty of speech, and liberty of action. It asserted that God had no vicegerent on earth; no representative amongst men; that he alone is Lord of the conscience.

From that moment to the present, the march of mind has been onward and upward. The mighty spell that had for ages held all Christendom in abject slavery to kings and priests, those demigods of human admiration and worship, began to be broken. Opinions held sacred from times immemorial, began to be discussed; learning awoke from the slumber of centuries; science assumed her proper rank; the arts, both useful and ornamental, began to be cultivated with new vigor; and, Protestant society at least, laid aside the austere sanctimoniousness of a religious grimace—put off the cowl of superstition, and appeared in the more pleasing costume, of an open countenance, a smiling face, a generous heart, and a more spiritual devotion.

Still, however, all error was not detected, discussed, and repudiated. The human mind, like the human body, takes but one short step at a time, and that step rather indicates the decrepitude and feebleness of age than the vigor and energy of youth. Unfortunately, Protestantism soon obtained favor at court, and immediately mounted the throne of the greatest empire in the world. In doing this, she had, indeed, to retain so many of the traditions and doctrines of the fathers as secured the favor of kings and princes, and flattered the pretensions of bishops, arch-bishops, and their dependents, who, in affection, were wedded to Rome, while abjuring her power, merely because it eclipsed and diminished their own.

The leaven of popery, Sir, still works in both church and state. The hierarchies of England, Scotland, and Protestant Germany, alas! too fully substantiate the allegation:—Oxford is not the only university, nor her tracts the only documents, which show a profound sympathy with some of the bolder attributes and views of the papal power. That sympathy is clearly evinced on the continents of Europe and America; and what strange involutions and evolutions may yet farther characterize its movements, the pages of the future alone can disclose.

The power of Protestantism, in some important points of view, is comparatively feeble, greatly feeble. Its strength lies in the great leading truths of the system. Its feebleness is wholly owing to errors long cherished, and still sought to be retained as fundamental truths, by many of its warmest friends and admirers. These errors make parties; for, while truth is essentially attractive and conservative, error is necessarily repellant and divisive:—numerous as the sects that have impaired the protestant influence and power, are the errors that have generated them. Every party has its truth, and probably its error too; for, even when truth makes a party, error not only occasions it, but generally infuses itself into the system. Good and wise men of all parties are turning their attention more and more to the causes and occasions of schism; and that, too, from an ardent wish to fathom the occult causes of so much discord amongst brethren; in the hope, too, of discovering some grand scheme of union and fraternal co-operation in the cause of our common Christianity.

The last century terminated with the downfall of consolidated atheism in France: after a reign of terror—the darkest and most desolating written on the roll of time. All Europe stood aghast at the awful spectacle, and saw in its developments of the tendencies of sectarian discords that suggested to the reflecting and intelligent the necessity of some very important changes in the social system. One of the results was, that the present century was ushered in with the formation of one grand Bible Society, composed of various denominations, cherishing the truly magnanimous and splendid scheme of giving the Bible, without note or comment, to the whole family of man; so that every man might read in his own language the wonderful works of God.

This truly benignant scheme has in various ways already greatly contributed to the introduction of a brighter and a better era. The project of divesting the margin of the Sacred Writings of Prophets and Apostles of the cumbrous inscriptions of sectarian tenets and traditions, the dogmata of all schism, under the insidious pretense and title of notes and comments on the sacred text, has given a new impulse to the mind, because it has proposed the Bible to mankind in harmony with the great Protestant motto. A new and improved system of hermeneutics is another happy effect of the attempt to make every man more or less his own interpreter of the testimony of God. The improvements in sacred criticism, and in biblical philology in general, have already elevated the present century as much above the last as the sixteenth excelled the fifteenth, in the grand developments of truth and of the elementary principles of a new order of things.

No living man can fully estimate the exact momentum of the principles at work in his own time. The objects that obtrude upon his consideration are too near him to be seen in all their just proportions. Time, that great revealer of secrets and infallible exponent of the wisdom of all human schemes, must pass its solemn verdict upon every human enterprise before its proper character can be fully and justly appreciated.

The points of debate on the present occasion may, to some minds not conversant with such matters, appear to embrace points extremely frivolous and unimportant. The question, for example, of baptism, as respects its actions, whether it shall be understood to mean sprinkling or immersing, is frequently made to assume no higher importance than that of a mere scuffle about the difference between a large and a small basin of water. It is, indeed, an *elementary* question; yet it may possibly have much of the fortunes of Christendom in its bosom. It stands to the whole Christian profession as circumcision to a Jew—as hereditary descent to a British lord, or the elective franchise to an American citizen.

Let no one undervalue the paints at issue in the present controversy. Let no one be startled when I affirm the conviction, that in the questions to be discussed on the present occasion, the fortunes of America, of Europe, and the world are greatly involved. Can that be regarded by the mere political (to say nothing of the philanthropist or the Christian,) as a minor matter, that gives to the Pope of Rome one hundred millions of subjects every three-and- thirty years, and that, too, without a single thought, volition, or action of their own? Can anyone regard that as a very unimportant ceremony which binds for ever to the papal throne so many of our race by five drops of water and the sign of a cross imposed upon them with their "Christian name!"

The omission of an *h* in pronouncing a word, became, providentially, the occasion of the slaughter of forty-two thousand Ephraimites in one day. The conversion of an *o* into an *i,* divided the ecclesiastic Roman empire into two great parties, which disturbed its peace, fostered internal wars, and exhausted its blood and treasure for a succession of several imperial reigns. And the eating of an apple brought sin and death into our world, and has already swept the earth clean of all its inhabitants more than one hundred times. Let no one, therefore, regard any thing in religion or morals as excessively minute, or unworthy of the highest conscientious regard. There is sometimes more in a monosyllable than in a folio; − a *yes,* or a *no,* has slain millions, while a thousand volumes have been written and read without   and   visible

disaster to any human being.

The greatest debate in the annals of time, so far as consequences were involved, was upon the proper interpretation of a positive precept. The fortunes, not of a single nation, of an empire, or an age, but of a world, were staked upon its decision. The parties consisted of two persons; the word in debate was *die,* and because of the misinterpretation if it one of the parties lost Paradise, and gained labor, and sorrow, and death.

In this world, we have great *little* matters, as well as little *great* matters. To the former class belong the affairs of kingdoms, empires, and of all time: to the latter, individual purity, holiness, happiness. To infinite space, an atom and a mountain bear the same proportions. In the presence of endless duration, a moment and an age are equal. If then, by a drop of water and the sign of the cross, Gregory XVI. sits on yonder gorgeous throne in the midst of the Vatican, worshipped by more than one hundred millions of human beings; and if the Protestant Paedobaptist Churches in America annually increase more by the touch of a moistened finger than by all the eloquence of their seven thousand ministers, then, I ask, is not so much of the present discussion as pertains to that single rite, of transcendent importance to this nation and people, whether contemplated in their ecclesiastical or political character!

In justice to my respondent, and his church, I must distinctly state, that this community are not at all indebted to me for the present discussion. It originated with our zealous and indefatigable Presbyterian brethren, who have ever been forward in the great and good work of religious controversy; and, as an Apostle commands us to render honor to whom honor is due, we must award to them the honor of the present debate and all its happy influences on this community.

The present interview, when solicited by Mr. Brown, was indeed acceded to on my part with an expressed and covenanted understanding, that it was to be a frank, candid, full, and amicable discussion of the great points of difference between us,—that each party was to affirm and maintain what is taught, and thus give to our respective communities authentic views of our peculiar tenets, so far as they may materially conflict with each other; and thus furnish the public with a book containing the numerous and various arguments by which our respective tenets may be assailed and defended.

That the discussion should have all authority with the people, it was stipulated that, in case of a single combat, one person should be chosen as the oracle of the party, with whom I would enter into a formal debate on all these questions, and that other ministers should be present as helps and counselors. I am happy in having the assurance that my friend, Mr. Rice, appears here in consequence of that agreement, as the elect debatant, chosen by his brethren while assembled at Synod, and he is not only one of the five persons chosen at the meeting of the Synod, but he is the one chosen by the other/our, and commended to my acceptance by Mr. Brown, one of his electors, in the words following:—"We have selected the man to whose hands we think proper to commit the defense of our case.—His standing is well-known in Kentucky and out of it. We will not select another." To add to my satisfaction, he is also aided and sustained by a learned cohort of divines of high standing in the Presbyterian church, and not by these only, but doubtless by many others, present and absent. Such an array of talent, learning and piety, would seem to authorize the confident expectation that, if those tenets of his party from which we dissent, can be convincingly maintained and made acceptable to this community, it will now be done.

In addition to all this, I am assured that my friend, Mr. Rice, is not compelled into this discussion by the mere authority and importunity of his brethren; but that he enters into the business as one that has long and ardently panted to render some distinguished service to the church of his ancestors and *of* his adoption, and to deliver himself fully on the great questions before us. It is our singular good fortune to meet on this arena a gentleman exceedingly zealous for the doctrines and traditions of his church, and who, for one year at least, if not for several years past, has been in habitual preparation for such an occasion as the present.

So desirous of merited applause, and so untiring in his zeal and devotion to ancient orthodoxy, he has been in one continued series of conflicts,—wrestling with tongue and pen,—entering the lists with all sorts of disputants, Baptists and Reformers, old and young, experienced and inexperienced; and, in amicable discussion, breaking numerous lances upon the brazen shields and steel caps of such members of the church militant as either foreordination or contingency threw in his way,—and on these very subjects now before us. Neither his devotion to the cause of truth, nor his labors of love, have been confined to Kentucky; but, in his pious opposition to heretics and heresies, like one of old, he has pursued them even unto foreign cities—Nashville yet resounds with the praises of his zeal and the fame of his achievements in the cause of Presbyterianism. If, then, flaw or weakness there be in that series of arguments and evidences that I am prepared to offer on the present occasion, or if my facts and documents are not true and veritable, I have every reason to expect a full detection and a thorough exposition of them. But should they pass the fiery ordeal of the intense genius and vigorous analysis to which they are now to be subjected, may I not, in common with those who espouse them, repose on them as arguments and proofs irrefragably strong and enduring!

The questions to be discussed on the present occasion are, it is conceded on all hands, not only elementary and fundamental, but of vital importance to every saint and sinner in the world. They alike enter into the peculiar essence and living form of the Christian religion. Accurate and comprehensive views of them, not only promote the purity and happiness of the individual, but also conduce to the union of Christians and the conversion of the world. So long as we have in the Christian profession two faiths, two baptisms, and two spirits, we shall have a plurality of bodies ecclesiastic, arrayed in open hostility to each other; and, by consequence, the whole train of evils and misfortunes incident to alienated affections and rival interests. I rejoice in the present discussion, because it strikes at the three main roots of modern partyism—the creeds, the baptisms, and the spirits of moral philosophy and human expediency. Before a holier and a happier era, we must resume the original basis of one Lord, one creed, one baptism, and one spirit—United on these, we stand: divided, we fall. These spurious creeds, baptisms, and spirits, must be repudiated; hence the necessity of discussion.

Either there must be a conviction of these errors and a repudiation of them; or else an agreement to regard them as matters of opinion, as matters of forbearance, and take no account of them: one of these results is essential to union. With these views and convictions, and with a supreme desire for holy union, harmony and love in the truth, and for the truth's sake, with all them that believe, love and obey it, I consent unto the present discussion. The two baptisms, the human and the divine, are first in order. In distributing the subject into its proper parts, four questions arise—*What is the action called baptism? who is* the *subject? what its design?* and, *who may administer it?* Without farther introduction, I proceed to the first proposition; and. may the spirit of all wisdom and revelation direct our deliberations, subdue all pride of opinion, restrain every illicit desire of human approbation, inspire our souls with the love of truth rather than of victory, lead our investigations to the happiest issue, and give to this discussion an extensive and long enduring influence in healing divisions, in promoting peace, and in extending the empire of truth over myriads of minds enthralled by error, and oppressed with the doctrines and commandments of men!—*Millennial Harbinger.*

From the Christian Journal.

THE DEBATE.

We have no space for remarks of our own upon the conclusion of the Debate. Suffice it to say, that Mr. Rice sustained to the last—HIMSELF, after his own peculiar *manner;* and Bro. Campbell sustained the TRUTH triumphantly. We had supposed that the Presbyterian committee on the manufacture of public sentiment in relation to the Debate, had performed its duty so satisfactorily to itself, and to those by whom it was employed, as to leave no room for such demonstrations as the following;

A GOOD JOKE!—The manufacturers of public sentiment about Lexington yesterday (Lord's day) after sermon, took a vote on the merits of the recent discussion. The vote was nearly unanimous, that Rice had gained a splendid victory! But the fun of the thing is—not more than half the voters had heard the discussion! They voted, however, *negroes* and all! *"Gloomy* times for 'this glorious Reformation"!! We obtained this information from a Presbyterian gentleman of high standing in this city, who expressed his strong disapprobation of the whole procedure. All who live in Rome do not worship the Pope. There were two votes cast in the Church of Christ—that is to say— two persons of intelligence and high standing, confessed the blessed Savior and were this day *'buried with him in baptism.'*   E. S.

Several more have obeyed since—ED.

MEETING OF THE BRETHREN.

DEAR BRO. FERGUSON:—You are aware that the great Debate ended on Saturday. Immediately after its close the brethren present were requested to meet in the basement story of the house, in which it had been held. The meeting was organized by Elder William Morton, who took the Chair, when the following was introduced by Elder P. S. Fall, of Frankfort:

"Resolved, That the discussion which has just terminated between Alexander Campbell and N. L Rice, demands the serious and anxious attention of the community;—that the publication of said debate, will promote, in the most efficient manner, the great cause we plead;—that the circulation thereof should be earnestly desired and encouraged; and that Alexander Campbell deserves the sincere thanks of his Brethren, and of the world, for his manly, able, successful and Christian-like defense of the truth."

It is needless to say, that the above was unanimously voted. The number of preachers present was large, although some had already left to attend their appointments. Such requested others to express their sentiments in relation to the above.

The Brethren who attended this protracted discussion, carry with them into their several communities the conviction that the cause they urge upon human acceptance is one against which the 'gates of hell shall not prevail.' *The* WORST *that can be said of it, they have heard;* and may they profit thereby I 'It is lawful to learn, even from an enemy.' With care, prudence, zeal and intelligence on the part of its advocates, this mighty cause, which has given religious society so much uneasiness, *must prevail.* It is the cause of God, and of humanity.

Alexander Campbell, (his name needs no prefix) will leave for his onerous duties at home in a day or two. He will carry with him the affections of his Brethren of the Church of Christ, and the respect and admiration of the intelligent amongst his opponents. He will go no richer in the goods of this world than when he came. But what a man of God values, namely, the *approbation of his conscience,* after having defended, in all sincerity and without guile, the only system in which the happiness—not of a party, but of mankind is involved, he richly enjoys. He looks not here for golden thousands. To offer money to such a man, were to depreciate him. He awaits that great day, when the Judge—not of an *ex parte* crowd, but of MAN, shall say to him; 'Well done, good and faithful servant.' When Luther's friends bestowed upon him any temporal mark of their approbation, he was accustomed to say, 'I fear the Lord will permit me to have all my rewards in this life.'

I say not this, because the advocates of the present attempt to return to original Christianity, would not gladly give a substantial demonstration of their gratitude; but because I, for one of many thousands, would not deprive Alexander Campbell of that enjoyment which he may lawfully feel, in having respect unto that recompense of reward, which the Lord, the righteous Judge, will give him. I would not, were I he, exchange conditions, at this moment, with the most puissant monarch on earth. Faithfully, yours,

December 4th, 1843.

The Discussion will be published immediately, as will be seen by the Prospectus below. Bro. D. S. Burnet has become one of the Publishers. It will have an immense circulation among our Brethren.

PROSPECTUS,

For publishing the Debate, held in Lexington, Ky., between ELD. A. CAMPBELL, of Bethany, Virginia, and REV. N. L. RICE, of Paris, Kentucky, on the following propositions, viz:

1. The immersion in water of a proper subject, into the name of the Father, the Son and the Holy Spirit, is the only Apostolic or Christian Baptism. Mr. Campbell *affirms.* Mr. Rice *denies.*

2. The infant of a believing parent is a Scriptural subject of Baptism. Mr. Rice *affirms.* Mr. Campbell *denies.*

3. Christian Baptism is for the remission of past sins. Mr. Campbell *affirms.* Mr. Rice *denies.*

4. Baptism is to be administered only by a Bishop or Ordained Presbyter. Mr. Rice *affirms.* Mr. Campbell *denies.*

5. In Conversion and Sanctification, the Spirit of God operates on persons only through the Word of Truth. Mr. Campbell *affirms.* Mr. Rice *denies.*

6. Human Creeds as bonds of Union and Communion, are necessarily heretical and schismatical. Mr. Campbell *affirms.* Mr. Rice *denies.*

Reported by competent Stenographers, and to be approved and authenticated by the Debatants. Published in one 8vo. containing from *seven to eight hundred pages,* neatly executed on good paper, and well bound in cloth or muslin. The above work will be published as early as practicable, at $2, per copy. To large purchasers are proposed the following discounts, viz: To those who pay for ten copies and upwards 10 per cent; for fifty copies and upwards, 15 per cent; for one hundred copies and upwards, 20 per cent.

RECOMMENDATIONS: We cheerfully recommend the above work.—H. Clay, J. Sneed Smith, Geo. Robertson, *Moderators.*

We (Ministers of the same Church with Mr. Campbell,) cheerfully recommend the work. James Fishback, James Shannon, John Smith, A. Raines, L. L. Pinkerton, J. T. Johnson, B. F. Hall, Wm. Morton, D. S. Burnet, A. Kendrick, S. E. Shepard.*

We (Ministers of the same Church with Mr. Rice,) cheerfully recommend the work. Jas. K. Burch, Jacob F. Price, Jno. H. Brown, N. H. Hall, J. D. Matthews, Jno. F. Coons, J. G. Simrall, J. J. Bullock, J. Montgomery, Wm. D. Jones, R. C. Grundy, D. S. Todd, W. Y. Allen, John Watt.

We (Ministers of the Methodist Epis. Church,) cheerfully recommend the above work. H. B. Bascom, B. H. M'Cown, W. H. Anderson, R. T. P. Allen, *J.* L. Kemp, Thos. Lynch.

All orders should be forwarded by the 1st of February, 1844, to D. S. Burnet, one of the publishers, *Louisville, Ky.*

December 4,1843.

*To this column 60 names could have been added had there been space to spare.

THE DEBATE.

MR. EDITOR:—Presuming that many of your readers will be anxious to hear of the progress of the Discussion, I take advantage of a passing opportunity to give them a few observations. The first proposition (the *action* of Baptism,) has been disposed of; and I am constrained to say, that in the annals of controversy there has never been a more triumphant victory for the truth. Two days were almost entirely devoted to Greek and Latin criticism, which was necessarily, to a considerable extent, uninteresting to a greater part of the audience. Mr. R. made a good use of that part of the time; and by a repetition of the many witty sayings at his command, induced some of his friends to believe that he was gaining a signal victory. But, as the matter progressed, the tables were turned against him, and by arguments better adapted to an English audience, the proposition was unanswerably sustained. Mr. Campbell produced some *thirteen* sources of evidence upon which he relied for the support of his proposition, not one of which was shown to be irrelevant; and either of which would have been sufficient to settle the matter at once; and together they present a fortress as strong as the everlasting hills.

To give you some idea of Mr. R.'s method of meeting the proof submitted, I will present your readers with his course upon the first class of evidence. This was derived from the natural, proper and primary meaning of the Greek words *bap, bapto,* and especially *baptiso,* which was shown to mean 'to dip,' 'immerse,' and only metonymically to have any other signification. An appeal was made to the lexicons and classics. Mr. R. immediately took up those lexicons, and showed that they gave other meanings than dip, and argued boastingly and at length that Mr. C. was wrong. He paid no regard to the distinction between a primary and an accommodated meaning—a *literal* and a figurative. Dipping, in reply, was shown to be a means of washing, and that, in that sense, it could mean wash without affecting the point at issue; but that in no case could it be said that they meant to *sprinkle* or *pour.* Mr. R. still paid no attention to the distinction and true issue, and continued most fearlessly to reiterate, that Mr. C.'s own witnesses had given other meanings. Mr. C. still gave him cord, paying but little attention to his bold assertions, so that upon the fourth day, Mr. R. became sufficiently emboldened to declare, that he had not only shown Mr. C.'s witnesses to testify against him; but that there was not a dictionary *upon earth* that had said that *wash* was a figurative meaning of *baptiso.* Mr. C. then took him unasked him if he had ever seen a lexicon that he had in his hand—*Stokius*—Mr. R. said he had not. Mr. C. turned to the definition and found it to sustain him *throughout*—even asserting what was the name of the figure of speech used when wash was given as a signification. He also referred to Schleusner and several others, who amply sustained him. Never, in all my life, have I seen a professedly learned man so discomfited. He denied that it was so—Mr. C. proposed to refer it to the learned men present—Mr. R. refused; and such was his overwhelming confusion that one moment he would deny, the next admit, and attempt to show, by a reference to *Ernesti,* that the figurative sometimes became the *proper* meaning; and being confounded in his use of Ernesti, he would again deny. But he was never at a loss; no matter how contradictory or unlearned his statements were, he persisted in declaring and re-declaring all he had said before. In short, when Mr. C. would prove that dip was the primary meaning of all the words of the family of *baptiso,* Mr. R. would show that the figurative meaning was used and thus yield the first point When Mr. C. would prove that the figurative meaning had always the idea of dip retained, Mr. R. would assert that the primary was not to dip. But he was driven from every position and the proposition most learnedly, fully and triumphantly sustained.

There seems to be every difference in their manner of conducting the controversy. Mr. C. goes regularly and systematically to work, not allowing even the gross mistakes, or witticisms of his opponent to disturb the even tenor of his way. Mr. R. makes his appeals to the risible faculties of his audience—argues without reference to system, and by every turn and maneuver, attempts to divert the mind of the audience present from the point before his opponent. The one has given us a most concentrated and logical argument; and when printed will be found to be one exhibiting the most research and conclusive argumentation that has ever been offered to the public—the other a most disconnected, heterogeneous mass of attempts at wit, with many undigested assertions, based upon numerous references to passages in the Classics and Scriptures, having little or no bearing upon the point at issue. Mr. C.'s argument was evidently intended to be a standing refutation of all the important difficulties that have ever been presented on the opposite side of this subject—showing conclusively that neither pouring or sprinkling can be sustained by any thing that has been spoken or written upon the subject for the four past centuries. These are the impressions of all his friends, so far as I have learned, and especially of your correspondent, who is here merely as a   LOOKER ON.

Lexington, Ky., Nov. 22, 1843.   ______________________

DEBATE—No. II.

Mr. Editor:—In my last I gave you a general view of the character of the discussion upon the *first* proposition, which occupied four days. The second proposition has been taken up and disposed of. This proposition (*Infant Baptism*) having but little to do with Greek criticism, has, if possible, engrossed more attention than the first. There has been immense interest manifested upon both—the capacious house of our Brethren upon Main street has been filled with perhaps *two-thousand* persons every day—

some

some 200 of whom are preachers, from almost all parts of the Union.

Mr. R's first effort upon this subject was a reiteration of almost every argument that has ever been advanced upon it. He spread himself out upon the whole surface of the question, delivering decidedly the most desultory and disconnected discourse I have never heard. His object was, evidently, to offer so many topics and to present so many views of the subject, as to prevent Mr. C. from presenting a connected examination of infant baptism. Mr. C. had, during the discussion of the first proposition, said that he was not speaking for present effect when he was delivering his Greek criticisms. Mr. R. concluded that it would be the case upon the second, and accordingly so proceeded; but never was man so sadly mistaken. Mr. C. came to the work with a power such as I have ever before seen used. Every hold of his opponent was taken—every position was shown to be untenable, and many of them absurd and preposterous. Mr. R. professes to mark out a new course on this subject. He says he cares not a straw for the argument based upon the assumption that baptism has come in the room of circumcision. He abandons this fortress; and pretends to believe that his cause is not made dependent upon it. He knew he could not sustain it; that Mr. C.'s published arguments upon this subject were unanswerable. He was, therefore, driven to new ground, or rather to abandon a part of the old argument. He said that the church of Christ was organized in the days of Abraham, with children introduced into it. He says that there has been no positive enactment to east them out; and that, therefore, they are in it to this day. This position has called forth one of the most able dissertations upon the Covenants from Mr. C., in which he has shown unanswerably, that there are *two covenants*—based upon too distinct promises made to Abraham, entirely dissimilar in their nature, character, and design. The one concerning one nation—the Jews— alone; the *other* ALL NATIONS—the one fleshly—the other spiritual. He also proved, that it was a baseless figment of the imagination to suppose that there was a *Christian* church before *Christ* was born, &c. &c.

Mr. C. proposed to risk the whole controversy upon any one, two or more points that Mr. R. had made upon the subject, and although he had made these points of paramount importance, and had used them as involving the fortunes of the whole controversy, he would not accept the proposal; but has continued to the end, to make the most reckless assertions without allowing his opponent to close in upon him upon any *point!* Yesterday Mr. Rice denied, and labored the whole day to prove that there was but one covenant, although he said it had been spoken of at different times, and had different specifications. He represented it as a bond, with two or three specifications, some of which were fulfilled in the coming of Messiah. To day he was driven from that point, and Mr. Campbell proposed to rest the whole controversy upon it. He was made to acknowledge indirectly, for he had not the magnanimity to do it openly, that there were two covenants, Mr. C. having shown that the Scriptures had not only frequently so called them, but that they were different transactions, mentioned at different times, ratified differently, and under different circumstances, and each of these transactions called by the great name—covenant. His triumph was most signal, memorable and complete.

But I have not room to give you the particular method of Mr. Campbell in meeting his opponent. Let it be sufficient to say, that Mr. Rice was driven from the Covenants to the Commission—from the commission to household baptisms—and from these to the fables and visions of the so called Fathers of the first and second centuries, and from these two attempts, vain and frivolous, to show that Mr. C. was now teaching what he had repudiated in former years. This was his *dernier resort,* such was the desperation of his cause. I do not believe that there was a single disinterested man present, who did not see that every point and position he took was untenable and vain.

Mr. Rice, when baffled by the strong and powerful reasoning of his opponent, invariably makes false issues and forces them upon the incidental remarks of his opponent. He thus tries to impose upon his audience the belief that he is replying to his opponent; when, perhaps, he is noticing a verbal criticism, or that which Mr. C. had not at all connected with his argument. On the contrary Mr. C. never notices the mistakes or inconsistencies of his opponent, but replies simply to his argument—
seeming   to   respect

the cause more than the man—the subject more than the advocate. Indeed there is every difference in the manner of the two men. The one is the moot reckless in his assertions—the other is modest in assertion, but most powerful in proof. The one seems to pay no attention, either to the gravity or dignity, that becomes such an occasion—the other manifests the utmost calmness, the most solemn and dignified deportment, acting, to use his own language, as if he was standing in the immediate presence of God and those high and holy Spirits that belong to the vast assembly above. Mr. C. treats his opponent as though he was an impersonation of all the talent, moral worth and acquired ability or the Presbyterian church; intending, doubtless, that his arguments upon these subjects shall stand as his honest, calm, and conscientious convictions for thirty years of the most patient, dispassionate, and religious investigation. So far Mr. Rice's opposition has been but little more than the expense of so much idle breath.

I long to see the masterly arguments of the past three days' labor of Mr. C. in print. They will do immense good with all the thinking; and will exert a happy influence upon the fortunes of hundreds and thousands of Paidobaptists, so called. In the opinion of many of the most able and distinguished men present, they are considered the most conclusive that have ever been delivered. But more anon.

LOOKER ON.

Lexington, Nov. 23, 1843.

TO THE FRIENDS OF THE REVIEW.

The Editors and Publishers of the REVIEW, wish it distinctly understood that Unless the subscribers make remittances on the reception of the first No.,' the second will not be sent, for we cannot employ a Travelling Agent to collect so small an amount. We will endeavor to make the paper as interesting as we well can, and we wish to see every subscriber punctual. Many friends and congregations ought to subscribe for ten, twenty and fifty copies, for the purpose of circulating the truth far and wide. What say you brethren? We give you a handsome, well executed work—be punctual and we will make our appearance before you the first week in each month. Price, $1 in advance.

TO ENQUIRERS AFTER TRUTH.

Nothing is so well calculated to inspire confidence, or afford real enjoyment, as a knowledge of God's word. Believing so devoutly this proposition, and wishing sincerely to afford the whole world, as far as in our power, the means of learning or teaching the truth, we are induced, from the highest motives, to make the following broad and pointed proposition.

We seek and invite investigation on every topic connected with man's salvation; and therefore, we say to Jews, Catholics, Protestants, and the world, our pages will always be open for discussion; provided however, that all articles be written in a respectful manner, are short, and bear the author's real name. We are for fair sailing.   EDITORS.

TO CORRESPONDENTS.

We wish to give general intelligence of the progress of the Gospel, but this will be out of our power, unless our brethren will aid us by their communications. It is desirable to know where every church is situated, and its progress in spiritual improvement, and we present the following interrogatories to correspondents:

1. In what State and county does the church meet of which you are a member, and what is your Post Office?

2. How many members are in the congregation, males and females?

3. How often do you meet, and what are the purposes of your meeting?

4. What is the state of your organization; that is, do you have Evangelists, Bishops and Deacons, and do they perform their duty, and does the church perform its duty towards them.

5. What are your additions, and how many have departed from the faith? Will the brethren look to these subjects with the interest they deserve?

CHRISTIAN REVIEW.

VOL. I.   NASHVILLE, FEBRUARY, 1844.   NO. II.

TO THE FRIENDS OF THE REVIEW.

We take this opportunity of publicly tendering our thanks to the friends of the CHRISTIAN REVIEW, for the interest they have taken in its circulation. Some have sent five, some ten, some twenty, and one congregation proposes taking one hundred and thirty volumes, for the purpose of tendering to our friends an opportunity of investigating and examining the views and sentiments of the Christian Church, free of cost to themselves, if they should be so kind as to receive them into their families, peruse them, and preserve them carefully. How many will follow this noble example? One friend writes from Louisiana, that he will send near one hundred, and indeed, we have the assurance from friends, that the work is destined to do great good wherever it goes. We wish every individual subscriber to feel himself interested, and go to their friends and neighbors, solicit their names, and should it be justifiable, the next year it can be enlarged, or issued the more often. What say you friends and brethren! Will the brethren speak out upon these matters, as we wish to know what are the views of our friends. The REVIEW has been highly spoken of, for its neatness of execution, and its contents have been cordially received, and to continue its publication, we ask each friend to use his influence in sending on subscriptions as soon as practicable.

MESSRS. CAMPBELL AND RICE'S DEBATE.

I regret much to learn there is some difficulty in reference to the publication of the "Debate" between Messrs. Campbell & Rice, though I am not the least astonished. From a private letter of a young gentleman of Nashville, now in Virginia, to a friend in this city, I learn the following particulars: "Mr. Rice denies that the Stenographers have the right to give the four hour speeches which Mr. Campbell read, in opening the discussion, on the propositions in which he was in the affirmative, because they were not taken down." The Stenographers consider it their privilege to write out this part of the debate from Mr. Campbell's manuscript, but Mr. Rice, contends if these speeches go into the book, he should be permitted to write out four hour speeches in reply though they were not delivered at the time as Mr. C.'s were. The Stenographers have given Mr. Rice to understand that they will have their own way about it, and give what was read as well as what was spoken; but Mr. R. "refuses to sign it," and threatens a law suit. Well, suppose he does not sign it—what then?' if the Stenographers give their certificate it is the genuine debate, who should care for Mr. Rice's name? I would not give a bauble for it, the work will have full credit and authority. Mr. Rice's friends, I opine, have had their reward, in the loud boasting and puffs, which have been heralded through the country, and the book, is what I have never imagined they are willing the public should see. Though I am no prophet, I will venture one short prediction, viz: when the book is published, the friends of Mr. Rice, will be slowest to purchase and read it. It is scarcely probable the work will be out before March or April, but I hope the public will be patient, it will be amongst us before a great while.   T. F.

FIRST PRINCIPLES.

By far the greater portion of the teachers of the Christian religion in this age, take too much for granted. Preachers presume, generally, that the great facts on which the Christian fabric is built, are fully understood by the multitude; and that all know what it is to become a Christian; but in fact, these are the matters not known, and therefore, it is "beating the air" to exhort the mass to confess the Lord. If I am not egregiously mistaken, all men pursue that course, which they think will most conduce to their happiness, and usually, the reason mankind are not moral, temperate, and religious, is, they have not seen and weighed the superior advantages of a virtuous life. Men will not till poor land, for a scanty subsistence, when they have certain knowledge of gaining bushels of gold daily by another occupation; neither will human beings revel in wickedness, when they know assuredly by another course of conduct, their happiness will be augmented a hundred- fold. The Lord said of old, "my people perish for want of knowledge," and if this solemn declaration were ever true, it must be in this age. Of the seventeen millions of human beings in the United States, it is extremely doubtful if more than five hundred thousand, or one thirty-fourth part of our population, could tell when Christ's church was established in the world, the Gospel manner of becoming a member, or are at all familiar with the unspeakable blessings which accrue to the faithful. In this, there is no imagination; neither am I disposed to look on the dark side of the picture.

With these views, what could a reflecting man say to his contemporaries? In the fear of my Maker, I answer, *the pure, old fashioned Gospel of the kingdom, has yet to be preached, before man can possibly be converted.* The public mind must be disabused;—fables, airy visions, and all human religions must be swept from the earth before men can see, understand, or believe the truth, which alone can make us free.

If the Apostles were now on earth, it is extremely doubtful, if they would associate with one in a hundred of those who profess to be Gospel preachers at this day. If Peter or Paul, were to bear one of our modern sermons, on "total depravity," "inability of men to obey God," "the dogma of Trinity, or satisfaction," "or the fanciful speculation of abstract and unintelligible operations of Spirit to give men common sense, faith, religion, and good feelings," evidently, they would be greatly astonished, at the wondrous changes since their earthly toils ended. Were they to commence preaching again, no one can doubt, but Peter would announce the same Gospel he did on Pentecost, and Paul would boldly reprove men for worshipping "Unknown" Gods, and make known the character of the true God.

They would tell the world, the God who made all things "dwelleth not in temples made with hands, neither is worshipped with hands;" that he gave his son to die, "the just for the unjust," that he was buried, rose the third day, and ascended to heaven, where he ever lives to make intercession for his saints.

They would not only give the facts connected with Christ's life, death, burial, resurrection, and ascension, but present the proofs, to beget conviction. Were the same Gospel preached, there is little room to doubt, hundreds and thousands would daily submit to the truth, as persons did anciently.

Christ should how be preached, and him crucified; "the kingdom and name of Jesus Christ" should be preached, and enforced.

Do the brethren have more confidence in the simple Gospel, than in popular sermons? If so, my brethren, rely on the facts in God's word, to convert the nations, and marvelous will be the triumphs of the cause of truth in 1844.

T. F.

—

CHURCH ORGANIZATION.

Having called attention to the subject of Church Organization in the first No. of the Review, and thinking it should be a theme of abiding interest to the disciples generally, I will proceed with the discussion a little more in detail. I know of no error more fatal to the cause of truth or the honor of God, than the vague notion with all parties, that the Scriptures afford only "the great principles of government," but the wisdom of man—poor fallible man! is to extract the forms and systems for the people of God. What a monstrous idea, that a perfect, or suitable government for the saints of the Almighty, is not in existence. At this day, nine tenths of the religious world have no idea God's government is complete. Hence, we hear our sectarian friends, with much gravity, declaring, "no church can do without government;" plainly intimating that God has given none, and that they have a right to make them. Often have I heard of wickedness so gross as to "make angels weep;" but never have I witnessed greater insolence before high Heaven, than in the conduct of those who contend God's laws are not adapted to all the exigencies of man. I am aware all partisans wish to conceal their position; for, all the creeds say, "The Scriptures of the Old and New Testaments, are the only infallible rule of faith and practice;" but this is the sheerest mockery. To tell us the Bible is "the only infallible rule," and contend in the next breath, those who have not a human creed, are without government, is a palpable contradiction. The sects cannot believe the declaration that the Bible is a "rule," or they would be satisfied with it. They cannot avoid the dilemma by saying their "governments and organizations are authorized by the Bible," for if their governments be like the Bible, it is worse than folly, to make another book just like the Bible, and cat! it by another name. But why pursue this subject farther? It is becoming more and more glaring every day, and the hypocrisy of those who thus contend, will ere long be apparent to all good men. The Question is, does the Bible contain a full and complete government for the Lord's household?

No question is more clearly defined than this, and yet few believe it; expedients are the resort of the multitude, and very few study the Bible with full confidence man's ingenuity has nothing to do in church organization and discipline. "All inspired writing is profitable, for teaching, for reproof, for correction, that the man of God may be perfect, thoroughly furnished to all good works." "His divine power, hath given us all things that pertain to life and godliness." Hence, if any thing is essential to perfection, to life and godliness, it is full in the sacred scriptures.

The subject may be presented fully in the following positions:

1. There is a perfect form by which to become Christians. Paul says, "Although you were sinners, you have obeyed from the heart that form of doctrine, by which you were made free from sin, and became the servants of righteousness." Do men desire to become servants of God, the full form is given. An understanding and belief of the facts of the Gospel, change the heart; repentance changes the life, and obedience from the heart frees from sin, and constitutes servants of righteousness. The process and form which will make one Christian, will convert the world, and short of this, no man can be made free from sins, and be constituted an heir of God, and joint heir with the Lord Jesus Christ.

2. The Apostle tells of some who "have a form of godliness, but deny the authority of it," plainly indicating that God has furnished his people with a form of godliness or religion. This proposition is abundantly taught in so many ways that no Christian who wishes to know the truth can scarcely miss it.

3. We read also, of the "form of sound words" to be observed by all saints. There is no subject necessary for man's conversion, religious order, or conversation, which is not given in full in the New Testament,

Next, we should enquire if the churches in the days of hale and pristine Christianity, were organized, perfect and independent bodies, capable of worshipping acceptably, and performing all the will of God independently? This is the great matter, and the theme to which special attention is invited. The subject will be pursued, with perfect confidence the results will be most beneficial.

T. F.

THE STUDY OF THE BIBLE.

On no subject has the world ever been more mistaken than that of the utility of searching the Sacred Scriptures. Many are the causes which have produced apathy and criminal indifference in regard to this first, and most important obligation of man. A few of these might be appropriately mentioned.

Long has the fatal error prevailed that God's revelation to man is a sealed book; and not to be comprehended by any except the few inspired to understand and reveal the truth to the great mass. While this idea abounds, hopes of improvement cannot be anticipated. If a teacher were to induce a pupil to believe Webster's Speller, or Pike's Arithmetic, was an incomprehensible book, for all but instructors, ten chances to one if he would ever make an effort to investigate any subject discussed in one of these books. No individual can act with energy in any undertaking, unless he is first satisfied of its practicability. We not only live as Christians by faith, but the whole physical and intellectual enjoyments of man are suspended on faith. The child Who does not believe the parent's declaration, that fire will burn, will be sure to suffer, and he who is not previously induced to believe much can be achieved in the pursuit of science, will not have courage for vigorous effort. Papists and Protestants have both done much to deter the world from studying the Bible. It has been by the impression all men cannot comprehend God's message of salvation to man.

If it were true, the Bible is a revelation but to the few, there might be some plausibility in this practice; but when it is remembered under the new economy, "they should all know the Lord from the least to the greatest," and that the Bible is the Almighty's revealed will to the whole race of man, there is great motive to study and come to conclusions for ourselves.

The frailest and feeblest, who are responsible; thought *"fools,"* may read, understand and obey the Gospel with as much certainty as the wisest philosopher that ever lived. Another difficulty is the idea, that religious knowledge and Christian feeling come in some other way than through the word of God. When persons are looking, dreaming and praying for signs from heaven,—call it revealed religion, or by another name, they are totally disqualified: to study, understand or believe the Scriptures. No one can appreciate the Bible, who does not believe the Scriptures God's whole revelation to man.

The next prominent difficulty in the diffusion of light, is the common plan of text reading and preaching. One who reads for texts to support a system, which of course, he presumes is independent of the Bible, can never comprehend the import of its sacred truths. The Scriptures should be read by connexions, and always the author's intention should be before the mind of the reader. But the most important item in the study of God's word, is to be able in our investigations, to know the objects of the different books of the Bible. One who would read Genesis, or Job, to learn how to become a Christian, would find these unmeaning books, and he that does not know, the difference between the Gospel, and the Epistles, will remain ignorant of the truth.

We must know whether saints or sinners are addressed, and for what special purpose, before we can read the Bible profitably.   T. F.

PURIFICATION OF THE HEART BY THE SPIRIT.

In conversation with a learned friend, for whom I entertain the greatest respect, recently, he remarked that "Water Baptism signified a *purification,* and was emblematical of the purification of the heart by the Holy Spirit." This doctrine I have seen in books and papers, and heard from the pulpit and in public discussions, since I have been capable of noticing any thing in reference to religious instruction. Knowing this is the sentiment of all Paedobaptist denominations, I have a plain and friendly proposition to submit, viz: Will some kind friend in the Paedobaptist ranks be so friendly as to give us an article for the CHRISTIAN REVIEW, showing the Scriptures which teach water baptism is emblematical of the purification of the heart by the Spirit. My wish is that all such matters be discussed decorously, and assuredly no one can object to this course. If this point can be established by the word of God, many errors will be corrected, and if it be not true, the controversies in reference to the purification of the heart and baptism will take a new direction in most denominations. What competent man will enter the arena?   T. F.

REPENTANCE.

All learned men admit the Greek language the most comprehensive, full and accurate that has ever been in use. For this reason, it was wisely ordered by the Deity that the New Testament should mainly be written in this language. This fact being granted, it is perhaps, a universal rule, that all New Testament subjects are most correctly defined; by the meaning of the words in which they are given. The word *Pistis* gave the full idea and character of faith; *Baptizo,* taught the Greeks the complete idea of what we denominate baptism; and *Metanoia* gives the critic, the whole subject of repentance. Repent, is from the verb Metanoeoo, which is from Meta—after,   and

Noeoo, to perceive, understand, or consider. The word *Noos*, mind, is in the same verb, and when we place the parts together we have Metanoeoo, to perceive or change the mind afterwards. Repentance always has direct reference to the change of the mind of man. There are, indeed, two words in the Greek testament from which the word repent is translated. Metamolomai, is frequently used for mere regret or change of mind. It may be either for the better or worse; but *Metanoeoo* is never used in this sense. The noun *Metanoia* always gives the idea of a change of mind for the better. Or as the mind influences the conduct, the repentance required of the ancients comprehended such a change of mind or heart, as was productive of a reformation of life. Hence the subject of repentance is often expressed by a circumlocution in the Bible. Jesus says, the Ninevites "repented at the preaching of Jonah," and it is said in the book of Jonah, of the same transaction, "They turned from their evil ways." Hence repentance and turning from evil are used synonymously. "Cease to do evil, and learn to do well," is language which expresses the idea of repentance. Mere sorrow for sin is never used, in the Bible, to express the idea of repentance. Esau and Judas both had sorrow, or repentance, but there "was no place" for the amendment of either. The three thousand on Pentecost, had deep compunction, before they made the enquiry "what shall we do?" still they were commanded to repent, or turn from the wicked ways.

The Gospel repentance then begins in the heart of man, but it is never finished till the life is changed. So it is not difficult to perceive, genuine repentance comprehends the whole change of mind and life, which is so indispensable to conversion to God. He that repents, deeply regrets before Heaven his sins, and hates and turns from them. Hence the Apostle says, "Godly sorrow worketh repentance unto salvation not be repented of." As no man repents of the injury done his neighbor till he has repaired the breach, so no one has repented of drunkenness till he has quit it, and no one has repented "towards God" till he has felt that sorrow of heart which has led him to abandon all his sins.   T. F.

GOD'S FORE-KNOWLEDGE.

BRO. G. W. CONE, of Elm Hill, wishes to know "if there is any difference between the *fore-knowledge* of God and his *pre-determined will."* He says, "there is a difficulty in this matter to me and many others; for instance, when God placed Adam and Eve in the garden, commanding them not to eat the forbidden fruit, knowing at the same time they would transgress, did he not seem contradictory in commanding them not to eat, knowing at the same time they would eat. The Universalists contend the *will* of the Lord and his fore-knowledge are equivalent."

No question, perhaps, has been more perplexing in the religious world, than the one suggested by Bro. Cone. Not a few have been driven to madness and despair, and yet all the difficulties grow out of incorrect views of God's character, and the plain teachings of the Bible. To examine the subject fully, would require great space, therefore, in the present No. I will only attempt to remove some of the obstructions, and so direct the reader's attention to the Scriptures, that he may examine the matter for himself.

The first difficulty to be noticed, is the fact, that too many present to their mind's eye an imaginary God, and endeavor to reconcile their false notions of Deity with the Scriptures and the responsibility of man; which is impossibly, The false ideas of the words infinite, omnipotent, omniscient, and omnipresent, throw many into a labyrinth of the grossest errors. The question is not whether these terms can be appropriately applied to the Maker of the Universe, but whether or not scriptural terms in reference to God's character are not preferable. The Jews were required to believe "as *the Scriptures taught,"* and this is the only safe guide on all questions. The fruitful imaginations of men, have made many "unknown gods" in this age, and hence it is a common occurrence to speak of a "mysterious," "incomprehensible God," of which the Bible says not a word, and I cannot see how any one can believe in the God of the Bible, or worship him, whose ideas of his matchless character are not through, and expressed in the words of inspiration. Suppose we say God fore-knew, and therefore, willed and decreed every thing that comes to pass, as the *"Confession"* says, what must be the conclusion. First, God wills, and is the author of all evil as well as all good, therefore, there is no such thing as virtuous or vice in the world. All men's actions are decreed, and man is a mere machine, or irresponsible agent of the Deity. Secondly, if we say, he foreknew the virtues, in the common sense of fore-knowledge, and therefore, decreed that a Certain part should be saved, and the other damned; then no man could "make his election," as the Scriptures teach. Again, if this be true, those eternally elected, could never have been lost, without the decrees being broken; and consequently, Christ did not die for the elect, but for the "lost." This doctrine runs us into so many absurdities, and contradictions, that no man can believe it, and be consistent with himself or the Bible.

May I enquire next, what is meant in the Scriptures by the words *fore-know* and *fore-knowledge?* To have a clear view of the subject, I will examine first the meaning of the word *know* in reference to the Almighty. It is written that he will say to some "in that day, depart from me ye workers of iniquity, I never knew you." Can the word *know,* here, be understood indiscriminately? If so, then there are some persons God does not know. But the plain idea is, "I never acknowledged or approved of you." Let us see if this is the meaning of the word *fore-know* in Scripture. Paul says, Romans 8, 29: "For whom he did fore-know, he did predestinate." Not only so, but whom he predestinated, he "called" and "glorified." Mind this, he has already done, and it is not yet to take place. The word fore-know, is translated from the two Greek words *pro*— before or formerly, and *Ginooskoo,* to acknowledge. The plain idea of the passage then is, "whom he formerly approved (that is, of some of the ancient worthies) he predestinated or determined should be conformed to the image of his Son. Moreover, whom he did predestinate, them he also called, (when the Savior rose, God called some of the saints from their graves) and whom he celled, them he also justified; and who he justified, them he also glorified." That is, he took them to heaven. Thus, it is apparent, the passage which is supposed moot difficult, related exclusively to God's dealings with faithful men of ancient days, and can have no reference to a human being now on earth; only by way of encouragement. The word fore-knowledge is not found in the Old Testament. What can be the reason of this? If the idea had been there would not the word have been used? After considerable examination, I conclude the correct idea is, that *fore-knowledge* can be used only in *reference* to dispensations. Whatever was said in the Old Testament by way of approving men, or of the Son, and was recorded in the New Testament, is called fore-knowledge. This is obvious from the passage already quoted, Ro. 8, 28 and 9. Hence, I would read the verse, Acts 2, 23: "Him being delivered by the determinate counsel and former approval or approbation of God, ye have taken, and by wicked hands have crucified and slain."

Will the brethren investigate this point critically?   T. F.

TO YOUNG PREACHERS.

DEAR BRETHREN:—Having had some experience in preaching the Gospel, and knowing most of the difficulties with which young ministers have to contend, I take the liberty of addressing you on your very responsible vocation. The man who gives his life and energies to the work of the ministry, occupies the most honorable station before God and angels, and his office is most important of all others to mankind. The qualifications of a Christian teacher are various, extensive, and should be profound. The farmer, physician, lawyer, mechanic, or trader, may succeed well with a knowledge of his peculiar calling; not so with the preacher. His knowledge should be universal. He has to deal with this world in reference to the next, and he must be conversant with both worlds. To tell all that is indispensable to a teacher, in one short essay, would be impossible; but for the present, I must content myself with a few of the prerequisites of the preacher.

1. First of all, a young man should examine well the motives which influence him to become a preacher. If his idea be, that it is an easy life, which will save him from the toils of manual labor, his object is a corrupt one, and sooner or later he must bring reproach on the noble profession. If he be of the opinion, he can thereby gain the admiration of the multitude, his intentions and ambition are fleshly—carnal—devilish, and his "words will eat as doth a canker," and his converts will more than likely be of the same character with himself. If he supposes he can, by becoming a preacher, marry advantageously, his pursuits will be carnal, and destruction will follow his way.

No one should gain his own consent to be a preacher, till he is satisfied his sole object is to benefit the world, and in so doing save himself. It is the bounden duty of all Christians to exert themselves to the utmost of their ability to promote the cause of Christ, and he who can make known the glad tidings and will not, shall be beaten with many stripes.

2. There is a fault in young men attempting that which they are not capable of accomplishing with credit to themselves, or honor to the cause of Christ. The most detestable object in creation, evidently, is an ignorant, impudent preacher. All sects are cursed with such beings, and it should not be wonderful to see such in Christian ranks. On this subject the churches are too often at fault, and greater is the shame. Timothy and Titus are models for young teachers. If they be not grave, dignified in deportment, and intelligent, they should not assume to themselves the high honor of Christian teachers. No man dare go on his own accord. Their qualifications should be known and acknowledged by the church. Not only so, but they should be chosen and ordained, before they take the responsibility of evangelizing.

3. To be amply qualified, a young man to teach with success amongst all classes, should be a thorough scholar. The day is past for ignorance to be tolerated. If possible, a preacher should be a classical scholar; but in the absence of this, there are many eminent and useful men. English scholarship is indispensable. No one can speak, acceptably who does not understand his mother tongue, and to be able to speak pure English is a rare accomplishment. Many indeed who profess a knowledge of the classics are egregiously ignorant of their own vernacular. Not one in a hundred scarcely is capable of reading English, much less of speaking it. It is a small matter to put words and fractions of sentences together, and vociferate through an hour's sermon; but to read and speak to cultivated ears, requires much study and attention. The pronunciation, enunciation of the language and cadence of voice, are not to be overlooked.

But the most important qualification of a teacher of the Christian religion, is an accurate acquaintance with the Bible. The preacher should be familiar with every part. This blessed volume should be his study by day and by night, and he should treasure up its life-giving words in his heart, and he should reverence all its heavenly instructions.

As to the manner of preaching, volumes might be written. At present, however, I will only point out a few of the grossest errors and bad habits of young speakers. The young are generally ardent in their feelings, and thinking they see a point clearly, they wonder that the people are so ignorant as not to see it. Too often in this frame of mind, their expressions become too strong, and dogmatical. Hence, we so frequently hear of insults being given to pious persons, and through the misdirected zeal of the preacher, serious injury is done. Preachers, therefore, should be modest men, and always remember, strong arguments are greatly preferable to hard words and bitter sarcasms. Men will not be sneered out of errors though they are ever so gross. Brilliant preachers often in looking at the mistakes of men, put on ostentatious aim, become witty, deal in innuendoes, ridicule, and contemptuous sayings, and offend whole communities. Such a course is beneath the dignity of the Gospel minister. If we see motes in our fellow creature's eyes, we should feel pity, and endeavor with all kindness to take them out. This is a very tender and delicate operation. A sledge hammer or crowbar is not the proper instrument. We must not only entertain love for our erring fellow mortals, but manifest it, before we can benefit them.

Another malpractice of preachers is, that of diffuseness. Instead of being content with the discussion of one point, a great effort must be made, and the whole book from Genesis to Revelation is ransacked, without order or connection, and when the preacher lands at Revelations, he is exhausted, and the congregation fatigued and sick of such bombast. System and order are most essential to profitable teaching, I do not refer to "text preaching;" but it is a fact no one will deny, that there are hundreds of subjects in the Bible, on which the profoundest may discourse for months. No one can interest the intelligent, without being able to make points, and sustain them by strong arguments. Not unfrequently, young preachers are too anxious to make "big sermons." They are not satisfied with plain, sincere and sensible discourses, but eager to "tickle the ears" of the giddy and untaught, they try to become eloquent and flowery, and nine times out of ten, "make failures," and have to drink the bitter cup of disappointment and chagrin. The best preachers in the world are those who aim to speak the truth of God in a plain,   humble   and   connected   manner.

Such men never "fail"—never have a guilty conscience—always say what is good, and the people never fail to be benefited. Again, preachers are often so light minded and frivolous in their conversation, that their acquaintances neither respect them, nor their preaching, and if they *happen* to deliver a popular sermon, a little flattery fills them with such inordinate levity and vanity, that they soon destroy every good impression they have made. Not to be further tedious, the Gospel preacher should be solemn in all his deportment, modest, courteous, intelligent, gentlemanly and Christian in his behaviour. These qualifications will insure success in the best communities; but he that lacks one of them, in common parlance, "will last" no where.

With all affection,   T. F.

CHARITY.

In all the catalogue of graces, charity stands pre-eminent. Charity indeed, covers a multitude of faults, and when faith and hope shall have ceased and been forgotten, charity will still live in the hearts of Christians. From those considerations, we should by all means know what is meant in the New Testament by the word charity. Few, in this age, use the term in the Scriptural acceptation. Generally, the word is made to denote any thing, and every thing but the charity of the Bible. It is a good plan to present every topic negatively, particularly in a time when there are so few points accurately understood as at the present. Most usually, preachers tell us it is charity to visit the poor and needy. But if the idea of visiting, means merely *going to see* the fatherless and widow, I can see little utility in it. Anciently visits were for the purpose of carrying to the poor, food, raiment, and any and every thing calculated to give them comfort and relieve their wants The Apostle Paul, however, says, "though I give my body to be burned, and bestow all my goods to feed the poor, and have not charity, I am nothing." From this, it seems contributions to the poor, do not constitute the charity of the Christian institution.

Again, the overwhelming mass tell us, it is charity, to say, "every thing men THINK to be right in religion, is right to them." Thus, if one will say, Catholicism, Protestantism, and Mahometanism, are all from God, the advocates of the different isms, will pronounce him a charitable Christian. Does not every intelligent individual see, that be who contends, all the conflicting parties and contradictions are right, makes God the Author of confusion, discord, persecution, and bloodshed? With such a view, I do not see how an honest sensible man can believe in, and reverence the Almighty.

The idea is preposterous in the extreme. Do not all parties contend it is uncharitable to teach there is but one right way in the Bible, and that none can be saved who do not walk in it? Yet, I have never found the intelligent man or woman, who would not admit, in cool and reflecting moments, there was but one "strait and narrow way" in the Bible, and that it was salvation to walk in it, but death to miss it. Nothing is plainer in the divine volume, than the teaching of "one God and Father of all, one Lord, one faith, one baptism, one body, and one spirit," even as all have one hope? It is extreme folly to talk of a half dozen, much less, six hundred three score and six roads to heaven. The charity of the mass is, there is but one way to be an honest man, or prosecute,   any profession or calling correctly, but as to the matter of going to heaven, the ways are so many—all leading to the same port, that no one can miss the desired haven, it matters not which way he starts, or in what direction he travel. It is now charity, to bring religion to the taste of all persons—so it is religion, though more than half of it be of the devil, it is just the subject of "time and place," as Professor Stewart says of a part of it. This strain I cannot pursue further, and but one more error will I attempt to correct. Many confound brotherly love and charity; but Peter says, "add to your faith —brotherly love, and to brotherly love, charity." All parties love their own. Even robbers have attachments as strong as life itself, and it should not be at all extraordinary, that all religious sects love their own. Indeed, they could not act differently. Having shown the general false views of charity, it will require but few words to give the idea of Christian charity.

The word in the Greek, Testament is the same translated in various places LOVE. It is not the love of one's self, or party, as I have abundantly shown; but it is universal, philanthropy, Charity, is that love which thinketh no evil; speaketh not ill of mankind, but induces its possessor to exert all his energies to promote the happiness of his fellow mortals.T. F.

EDUCATION.

Perhaps no subject which has been discussed in the nineteenth century, has created more interest in the world than the different modes of educating youth. Time was, when few entertained the most distant hope of giving their sons a liberal education, but not so now; instruction is becoming more and more general every day, and I trust, the day is not far distant when it will become universal. It should be so. I am fully aware of the many difficulties, in attempting to carry into operation a new and untried system of training the young; yet reforms, real and important, have been affected in religion, and government, and there is evidently much room for reform in education. The truth of this proposition no one disputes; but the old adage that "parents will say worse things of their children, than they will suffer others to say" holds true on every subject. We are all free to confess sins, which, we will not suffer others to charge upon us. I am not unkind to the systems of instruction now in use, for I know they have been of infinite importance to millions of the best men on earth. Indeed, I wish success to attend every enterprise; which has the improvement of man for its object. And from my heart, I can say, I wish no angry controversy, with my many learned and pious brother preceptors; but believing more can yet be done; I beg leave to state a few palpable objections to the present plan of educating young men.

Education is, at "this day, partial. That is to say, but few out of the great mass can become learned men. The consequence is, the overwhelming majority must, and do consider themselves degraded. The poorer classes, hate themselves too often when in company with the more enlightened. Why is it so? Does property make the difference? By no means. A well-educated gentleman, is highly respected throughout the world, though he may not have a shilling in his pocket. To be plain, the present system requires so great an amount of money, that not one youth in fifty can be well educated. The farmer who has four sons must have an income of at least two thousand dollars per annum to be able to educate these sons, and support his family,   and then he cannot calculate on adding to his capital. It does not require an Arithmetician to see, a farmer with half a dozen children, must be favorable situated and own a capital of at least fifty thousand dollars to give these children the advantages essential to the best walks of society.

2. Another evil, of no small moment, attending our present system, is the practice of educating the brain, or intellect rather, and sacrificing the physical man. By this plan man becomes, in too many instances, a burden to himself, is of little use to society, and terminates his life prematurely. I have in my mind's eye, at this moment, several individuals, who have passed through college, and who are dragging out a miserable existence, for want of constitution and health. Not long since, a young gentleman tarried with me a few days, who had finished his course of collegiate studies, and whose head is pretty well   stored with knowledge, and although his family are stout, healthy and happy persons, his emaciated features, and delicate frame tell too plainly of his fate. On interrogating him as to the cause, the answer was, "long and close confinement while at school," had done the whole. There is no fiction in this, all sensible men can bear witness to the truth of the doctrine.

3. Next in order, I present an evil connected with our present course of education, that the whole world should lament. It is the practice of locating our best institution in towns and cities, where every species of vice is inviting our most favored youths to partake of the forbidden fruit, "whose mortal taste" never fails to bring moral death. In cities, the best preceptors can have students under their control but a short part of the twenty-four hours; the consequence is, many are led into vicious habits, and become wrecks to their own lusts and outrages. I fear not to declare, if a youth can be corrupted, every door is open in our city institutions. From my own observation, I have no idea half the young men trained up in our cities, are much honor to their parents, or use to themselves or the world. The best citizens of our towns feel and deplore this truth. Though I would not be misunderstood. Cities are indispensable to commerce, and are useful in many respects; but they are not the best places, in my humble opinion, for Literary institutions, or for training children.

4. Again, who has not seen the pernicious influence of dress, fashion, extravagance and frolicking, in our system of popular education. I do not mean to say, our high-minded preceptors inculcate these evils, but it is a fact no one will deny, that schools connected with the show and empty pageantry of cities, offer more facilities for these practices than are safe for the young. Fine dressing, spending money without judgment, attending giddy parties, shows, &c., occupy not a small portion of the precious time of youth. Neatness is a virtue, but dress, show and extravagance are no evidence of this cardinal accomplishment. I have often seen the filthiest and most slovenly youths, put on the finest exterior. A young man can be as neat, and acquire as valuable accomplishments in *homespun*, as the finest equipage, and will be as highly esteemed.

5. The last error which I am disposed to suggest in this essay, generally, never occupies the thoughts of parents or teachers. From the several unfitting practices which I have already designated, it is too obvious, much of the time of youths is spent in idleness and acquiring pernicious habits. Perhaps, not more than half the time is spent in gaining valuable information, which might be by a different course. By a change for the better, either the course of instru-

ction could be much fuller, or the same could be accomplished in less time. As pointing out objections is not a pleasant employment, I will let the foregoing suffice for the present, and promise to offer remedies for Some of the evils, when more at leisure.   T. F.

PURE SPEECH.

When the Jews who had been at Babylon in captivity, returned to their own land, they found themselves in possession of such an impure speech, that it required learned scribes, to give them "the meaning" of their own language. All admit there have been "dark ages," and some profess to have escaped the darkness of other times, but evidently, our speech has not yet become pure. The confused language of spiritual Ashdod, is one of the greatest barriers to the spread of truth in this age, and it is by for the ablest supporter of parties in modern times. Men become wedded to names, and a set of phrases, which they hold as dear as life. And what is most astonishing, many of these "orthodox" words convey no distinct idea to those who most love them. "Orthodoxy," "Trinity," Total Depravity," "abstract influences," convey no distinct idea to the world, and they are not received with the same acceptation by any two parties in Christendom.

But my object in this short essay is not to wage war with parties, but to forewarn my brethren of the rocks and shoals which, I fear, are before us. We have so far, avoided party names, and this our honest enemies will not dispute, but there are several words in use amongst us, which are unauthorized by divine sanction, and which may at some future day, be productive of mischief. For instance, the term "Proclaimer of the Gospel," is neither scriptural nor classical, and when we can find better words in the Bible to express our ideas, I can see no use in adopting it. As another instance of the language of Ashdod, I must be permitted to mention the very common sayings, "The Reformation," and "This Reformation," which we so often see in print, and hear from the preachers. Do the brethren use these phrases to denote something that began in this century? If so, I want nothing to do with such "New Reformations." But I am told "reformation" is a Bible term. Be it so. But I affirm it was not used by Paul to designate what my brethren generally employ it to express. Paul's time of "reformation" was that of the ushering in the Gospel dispensation; but he had no allusion to the Lutheran, Wesleyan, or any other modem reformation. My brethren, let us be cautious, and remember, "current reformation," or "this reformation," is expressive of no idea in the Bible. "This reformation" is no more expressive of the Church of Christ, than the names of the current sects. "What I say unto one, I say unto all, watch."   T. F.

BELIEF OF THE HEART.

The great Apostle to the Gentiles, said, "with the heart man believeth unto righteousness, and with the mouth confession is made unto salvation." The question might be emphatically asked, what is it to believe with the heart? The Saviour connected the understanding of the heart with seeing with the eye, and hearing with the ear, and if understanding the truth, is associated with the understanding, the truth must be perceived before any one can believe it.

When a man hears, and comprehends the truth, as a consequence, he believes and loves it, and makes confession unto salvation. No speculation in reference to God or his Son, is belief, but reliance on the facts of the Gospel leads to conversion, remission of sins, and all the blessings of the new institution. A man can be assured he believes, when he doubts not the promises of God, but on them alone he unwaveringly trusts for the salvation of his soul.

THE GREEK LANGUAGE.

This is an age of controversy, and it behooves every one who aspires to a critical knowledge of the Scriptures, to avail himself of all the possible facilities of acquiring information. It is generally admitted most, if not all the New Testament, was written in rite Greek language, and that translations are all more or less defective. These propositions being conceded, I know of ho aid, more essential in gaining a correct knowledge of the word of God, than acquaintance with that language. It does not require a great while, for any English Scholar to get sufficient information of the Greek to satisfy himself, as to the construction of most passages of Scripture. I am aware there is a good deal of truth in the old age "a little learning is a dangerous thing;" but the Christian should study the Greek language, for his own satisfaction, and to be the better able to teach the whole truth, with more confidence, to the world, and not for vain show. No young man should be content, without the means of reading the word of life in the original tongue, and it is in the power of most industrious persons.   T. F.

PROGRESS OF CHRISTIANITY.

In reflecting on the rapid progress of the Christian religion in the times of the Apostles, and the first century after them, and contrasting it with its progress at the present time, I cannot but be forcibly struck with the vast difference in its advancement, during the two periods; and in speculating on the causes of the difference, almost the only reason I can assign, is, the conduct of the professors of religion, is not in accordance with the precepts of their holy religion. I refer not now, to those moral duties towards our God, and our fellow mortals, which alas, are so often violated, that the mouths of zealous proclaimers of the "glad tidings," are almost silenced by the reproaches from the watchful men of the world, but to the fact, that the great majority of professors have lifted the burden of teaching the disobedient, from their own shoulders, and imposed it on a few, who proclaim the gospel.

It seems now almost to be considered an axiom that it is the duty of the preacher to convert the world, and of the members of a congregation to attend faithfully to their worldly affairs, but if I may be allowed to raise my voice, no not I, "if any man speak let him speak as the oracles of God," if the apostles may be heard, how strongly will they condemn such a sentiment. "Be ye ready always to give an answer to every one that asketh you, a reason of the hope that is in you, with meekness and fear." (1 Peter, iii, 15.) Any person who reads the first nine verses of that chapter, can come to no other conclusion, than that it was addressed to the brethren, and not to any preacher; hence, it is plain that quotation has not been misapplied, and it is the duty of all to obey the law, and always be needy. The above receives what it scarcely needs, confirmation from Paul, (Heb. v, 12) "For when for the time ye ought to be *teachers,* ye have need that one teach you again, what are the first principles of the oracles of God." What stronger evidence could we desire, of the duty of the common soldiers to share in the conflict, and not leave their leaders to fight alone? Let us examine how the primitive Christians acted? in Acts xi, 19, we learn that those who were scattered abroad, travelled as far as Phoenice, and Cyprus, and Antioch, preaching the word;" the 8 ch. and 1 v., informs us positively, who were scattered abroad; "at that time, there was a great persecution against the church which was at Jerusalem, and they were all scattered abroad, * * * except *the apostles;"* here we see the leaders left behind, and the common soldiers ardently engaged in the cause.

Contrast those times with the present; now, a man joins the church, attends service once a week or month, as the case may be, perhaps reads his Bible a little, on Lord's day morning; attends most faithfully to his worldly affairs during the week, scarcely thinking of his sinful fellow mortals, and at last drops into the grave, over which an epitaph is inscribed, stating that he was, for many years, an exemplary member of such a church, and died rejoicing in the hope of immortality. Is such a course consistent with the divine command, "as ye would that others should do unto you, do ye so unto them;" would we not desire our friends to tell us of our danger, if they saw us going directly over a precipice, how then can we be excused for not telling our brethren of their danger? Does a man love God, who seizes no opportunity of advancing his cause, but lets his sinful brethren run on in their wicked course, without one word of expostulation; does a man love his brethren, who never, never, says one word to persuade him from the path of ruin; can such a man meet with approbation from the Great Judge?

If disobedience to *one* command, will bring strong condemnation, how much stranger will our condemnation be, when by a course of conduct, we disobey two commands, "Be ye ready, &c.," and "as ye would that others should do unto you, do ye so unto them;" how much stronger will it be, when by our course, we disobey those two commands, and a third also, "Love thy neighbor as thy self?" And why may we not act as did the primitive Christians; are the souls of fellow beings less valuable now, than they were then; are the promises of the gospel less cheering now, that our hearts are not so strongly influenced; is that salvation, which the God of love has placed in our power not worthy of equal attention now, that we are not filled with the same zeal?

Let us arouse from our lethargy, and girding on our armor, go forth to the combat, with the sword of the Spirit in our hands, and subdue, the enemies of the cross, that they may enjoy eternal life.

Above all, let us act as the apostle commands, "with meekness;" let us with hearts glowing with gratitude and love to our heavenly Father, endeavour to adorn our characters with all the Christian virtues, and so to act that others seeing our good works may glorify our Father in heaven; then, indeed, to every one who asked of us, a reason of the hope that was in us, our replies would have a hundred-fold the effect they would otherwise have.

We should endeavor to advance the cause of God, though he had not commanded us to do so; how much more readily ought we to act, when he has commanded us, and obedience to that command will bring reward. A most glorious aspect, truly, would the followers of Christ present to the world, could they be seen walking in love to God and man, visiting the fatherless and widows in their afflictions, the sick and the imprisoned, comforting them and relieving their wants; carefully avoiding every appearance of evil in their conversation and behaviour; endeavoring to teach and persuade men to forget their animosity, and obey the Saviour; instead of permitting them to drop unadmonished into the grave; soon, indeed, would every morning's sun beam on countless thousands of thankful hearts, rendering up ascriptions of praise and thanksgiving to the glorious Majesty of Heaven.   B.

ESSAY ON CREEDS—BY JACOB CREATH.

Our reason for discussing the subject of human creeds at present, is, that much has been said and written on this topic recently, by the Baptist denomination, and by the community generally. And as the Baptists differ upon this subject, as well as upon others, and as it is presumed that a majority of them are opposed to human creeds, it would seem to be due from us to the community, to set forth our reasons respectfully for so doing. This we do the more cheerfully, because several years have elapsed since the discussion commenced, and because you have seen the strongest arguments in favor of the utility and importance of human creeds, set forth by Dr. Miller of Princeton, condensed, revised, and extensively circulated by the Franklin Association. As the difficulties on the side of the opposers of human creeds are represented to be appalling and almost insurmountable, we shall state some of our principal objections to them, that you may be convinced that the difficulties on the side of their advocates are equally as great, if not more insurmountable than those on our side. We shall offer no other apology for this communication than its importance. We shall use the phrase *confession of faith,* in its generally received and popular acceptation. We understand by it, such a one as the Popish manual, the prayer book, the Westminster, and the Philadelphia confession of faith.

We lay down, and shall endeavor to establish, the subsequent propositions, viz: 1st. That human creeds are unauthorized by Heaven; 2d. That they are only necessary to human establishments; 3d. That they occupy the same relation to these establishments that the Old Testament does to Judaism, the New Testament to Christianity, the Koran to Mahometanism, and that Oracles do to Paganism; they are the life-blood of the systems, without which they cannot exist.

After the Jews were called out of Egypt they had no king for the space of 450 years, except God himself, who promised to reign over, and protect them as long as they would obey him. In the days of Samuel the prophet, they became dissatisfied with the government of God, and petitioned the prophet to give them a King; he remonstrated against it, but a King they would have, who was of their choosing, but not of God's appointing. Their choice of him was a virtual renunciation of God, hence, he says to Samuel, "they have rejected me, that I should not reign over them." This fashionable King proved to be a curse to them, as our creeds have to us. Their kings, their idols, their rebellion and idolatry, ultimately ruined them. The first idol god that the Jews ever had, the golden calf, a most beautiful creature, proved a curse to them, and was an imitation   of   the   first idol that ever was made, the Egyptian Apis, which was an ox with a bushel turned over his head; representing Joseph and the seven plentiful years in Egypt. But this calf was prohibited by their law, and therefore Moses would destroy it, notwithstanding it grieved them much.

Paul says, "these things are examples or types to us, to the intent, that we should not lust after evil things as they did, and there fell twenty-three thousand in one day. And whatsoever things were written aforetime, were written for our admonition, upon whom the gospel age or dispensation has come." We most put away these kings, these calves, these golden wedges and Babylonish garments, or we shall never be able to stand before our enemies; we shall not be able "to stand fast in the liberty wherewith Christ has made us free." From these examples then, we see that both the kings and calves of the Jews, were unauthorized by heaven; and so are human creeds, by the Christian law, the New Testament; because, they must either be lawful or unlawful, authorized or unauthorized; they cannot occupy a middle ground. The correctness of the following maxim, adopted by protestants when combating the Catholics, (and the baptists have often been necessitated to use it against their Paedo-baptist brethren,) has never been questioned, viz: That whatever the Scriptures do not authorize, they forbid; if they do not authorize, or support the infallibility of the pope, the mass, the images, the baptism of infants, they forbid them; *for this plainest of all reasons,* that whatever is not in the book, must be out of it, it is human, and is nothing in religion,

We shall here draw an important distinction between faith, knowledge, opinion and tradition.

"The words, *faith, knowledge,* and *opinion,* should never be confounded. I *believe* what is testified to me, I *know* what I have observed and experienced, and I am of *opinion* in all matters merely speculative. I believe that Jesus Christ died for our sins—because it is testified to me; I know that the sun shines, the wind blows, the rain falls: and I am of opinion that all infants dying are saved. Faith is bounded by testimony, knowledge by observation and experience, and opinions commence where both these terminate, and may be as boundless as God's creation, or as man's imagination. There is one faith, says the Apostle, but no where in the volume is it said that there is one opinion." Honest men have always differed in their opinions, and will differ till the end of time.

Doctor George Campbell defines tradition thus: (Dissertation, page 266) "Here let it be observed, by the way, that the word *paradoseis*, as used by ancient writers, and sometimes by the sacred penmen, does not entirely coincide in meaning with our word *tradition.* The word tradition, with us, imports, as the English lexicographer rightly explains it, any thing delivered orally from age to age: whereas *paradoseis* properly implies, any thing handed down from former ages, in whatever way it has been transmitted, whether by oral or written testimony; or even by instruction conveyed to others, either by word or writing. In this last acceptation we find it used in Scripture: 2 These, ii, 15, "hold the traditions, *tos paredosas,* which you have been taught, whether by word or our Epistle:" 2 Thess., iii, 6, "now we command you, brethren, by the name of our Lord Jesus Christ, that you withdraw yourselves from every brother who walketh   disorderly,   and   not according to the tradition which he received, from us." It is only when the epithet *agrapha,* unwritten, is added to *paradoseis,* that it answers exactly to the English word; whereas, all historical evidence comes under the denomination *paradoseis,* tradition. In this acceptation of the term, therefore, to say we have such a tradition, is the same as to say, in English, we have this account transmitted from former ages." According to this definition and criticism, creeds are written traditions, which are every where condemned by Christ and the apostles. The great contest among the Jews at the birth of our Saviour, was, whether the written law alone was of divine authority, or whether that with their glosses and traditions, added to Moses and the Prophets, whose praises they celebrated in the loftiest strains, while they were entirely ignorant of their true import, and were living in the daily violation of their plainest and most important precepts. They have been followed by vast multitudes in every age since. They had two laws, one was given to Moses and was recorded in his writings, the other was delivered to Aaron upon Mount Sinai, he delivered it verbally to the next high priest, and he to the next, and soon until these traditions were finally collected into a book called the Mishna, by Rabbi Jehuda.

Our creeds answer to these traditions.

All the arguments employed by protestants in favor of the antiquity, utility and importance of human creeds can be successfully employed by the Catholics in favor of the whole system of anti-christ. If human creeds may be lawfully and innocently used without either apostolic precept or example, so may the cross, the infallibility of the pope, and the baptism of babes— there is as much scriptural authority for one as the other—they stand or fall together. The *onus probandi,* burden of proof, in this case, rests *upon the advocates of human creeds, they affirm their utility, and they are bound to prove it by the Scriptures—or the cause it gained by us.* Thus, we have endeavored to prove that human creeds are unauthorized by Heaven, and in *facto* prohibited—that they are written traditions, and are nothing more than the doctrines and commandments of men, which are every where condemned by Christ and his apostles, and that they stand on the same footing with the whole system of popery or anti-christ.

We shall now attend to our second proposition, which is, *that human creeds or opinions are only necessary to human establishments;*—or as it is expressed by the author of the "Reign of Grace," Abraham Booth, who stands pre-eminent among the English and American baptists, —"they are only necessary to human establishments, since the days of Constantine the great," since which time the spouse of Christ has been disrobed of her native majesty, beauty, simplicity, and purity, and has been adorned with the meretricious attire of human institutions and inventions. During the three first centuries of Christianity, when it was purer than it has ever been since, there were no human creeds— nor until the year three hundred and twenty-five— when Constantine the great, called a council of three hundred and eighteen luxurious and ambitious clergymen, over whom he presided in person, and which was after Christianity had weathered all the storms of pagan persecution, which is described in the sixth chapter of the Revelation of John.

Now, in establishing our second proposition, that human creeds are only necessary to human establishments, or, which is the same thing, they are unnecessary to Christianity, we have only to prove that it existed before them, and even exists in opposition to them. The congregations

planted by the Apostles were numerous, united and happy without them, and as his kingdom did not need them in its infancy, when it had two popular religions of antiquity to contend with, most certainly it does not need them now. If any creed *other than the New Testament,* had been needful, he would have told us, or given it to us.

If human creeds are necessary to the existence of Christianity, it follows, consequently, that Christianity *cannot* exist without them. But Christianity *did* exist more than the three first centuries without them. Therefore, they are not necessary to the existence of Christianity. But, again, if they are necessary to the existence of Christianity, then the New Testament is defective; for, if the New Testament is sufficient to the existence of christianity, then human creeds are not necessary. If any man, therefore, contends that human creeds are necessary to the existence of Christianity, he, at the same time, and by *all* the *same arguments,* contends that the Scriptures of the Holy Spirit are insufficient—that is, imperfect or defective. Every human creed is predicated upon the inadequacy, that is, imperfection of the Holy Scriptures to the existence of Christianity. If then, Christianity did stand, and walk, and run, and contend with all opposition, Jewish and Pagan, without the aid of human creeds, during the three first centuries of its existence, when it was in its infancy, most certainly it can do it now, when it is eighteen hundred years old, unless we intend to apply the common proverb to it, "once a man and twice a child."

The unavoidable inference to be drawn from the above reasoning is, that human creeds are not necessary to the existence of Christianity—but are necessary to the existence of self-created bodies, or human establishments. —"The Apostles and primitive Christians never thought of collecting into a regular system the principal passages in the Holy Scriptures, or of demonstrating them in a scientific or geometrical manner. They studied to express its influence in their dispositions and actions. Their method of teaching was as simple as the Gospel itself—they used no subtleties, no art, no philosophy." The congregation or kingdom of Christ, was cemented together by no other ties than those of faith, hope, and love. Dr. Mosheim, the ecclesiastical historian, says, vol. 1, p. 5, "As long as the Scriptures were the *only* rule of faith, religion was preserved in its native purity; and in proportion as its decisions were either altered or postponed to the inventions of men, it degenerated from its primitive and divine simplicity."

This is worthy of being memorized by every Christian, and reader of this Essay. "I find (says Cecil,) a grand peculiarly in the Bible, which seems to say to all who attempt to systemize it, I am not of your kind, I am untractable in your hands—*I stand alone.* The great and wise shall never exhaust my treasures, by figures and parables—I will come down to the feelings and understandings of the ignorant—*leave me as I am, but study me incessantly.* Martin Luther said, "I had the whole body of the papists to oppose, I preached, I wrote, I pressed upon men's consciences the declarations of the word of God, but I used not a particle of force. It is not I, I repeat it, but the *Divine Word,* [not creeds, nor dogmas, nor speculations,] which has done every thing." In this controversy, we occupy the Apostolic, the Puritan, the Protestant, and reformation ground, which is the Bible; the *Bible* is the religion of Christians. We have the right to ask for

Apostolic precept or example, for a scriptural commission, for a divine warrant, and the advocates of human creeds are bound to produce it, or cease to speak of their utility in preserving the unity of the church. Are they from Heaven, or are they of men? If they are from Heaven, we will tamely submit our necks to them—if they are of men, we must firmly and resolutely resist them. If they are from Heaven, it is wicked and blasphemous in us to resist them; if they are of men, it is wicked and blasphemous to wreath them about men's necks. Neither our fathers nor we are able to bear them. Are they obligatory? how far are they binding? and who made them authoritative? The Bible contains the laws and institutions of Heaven—the creeds contain the opinions, the commandments and traditions of men, and are *human* BIBLES. The Bible is an infallible rule—the creed is a fallible rule— the Bible is binding upon men—the creed is not binding—the Bible is something—creeds are nothing but the invention of men. The Bible came from Heaven, and human creeds came from London, Westminster and Philadelphia. The Bible is necessary to the existence and unity of Christ's Kingdom—human bibles are necessary to the existence and perpetuity of councils, of the dominion of the clergy over the laity, and to the existence of religious politics.

BAPTISM—BY JAMES FISHBACK.

From the fact that *rumor* has sounded through this country that Dr. FISH- BACK said, on divers occasions and in the hearing of different gentlemen, that he was convinced by the arguments of Mr. Rice, in the late debate with A. Campbell, that infant sprinkling was authorized by the Bible, and infants should be members of the church, we think it an act of justice to him, to let him speak for himself. If Doctor Fishback is a hypocrite, and said things with which he is charged, the public should know it; but if not, the world should know his position. The Doctor says to a friend in this city, who addressed him with reference to this report:

"DEAR SIR:—I heard nothing at all in the debate that I thought in any degree supported Infant Baptism or Sprinkling. Since I investigated the subject of baptism, I have had but one opinion about it, and that is, that in the Apostolic age, immersion was the only baptism. I never said, nor do I think that *Sprinkling is a valid divine baptism.* I say that sprinkling is a total misapprehension of the ordinance of the New Testament, and I have no doubt that many are immersed with wrong views of the ordinance. So that no view of baptism is itself an infallible test of the Gospel truth, or Christian character in the subject or administrator. I believe that *Baptizo,* and it was proven in the debate, is a word of a specific meaning in regard to the ordinance of the Gospel, and means to *immerse* as truly as the burial and resurrection of Jesus Christ in the christian faith and religion are specific. Upon the part of his resurrection, the religion and kingdom are based, as are the faith and hope and triumph of his true disciples. Sprinkling has no meaning here. Baptism is an *action,* not a mode. Our Pedobaptist friends say that purification is what is meant by baptism, and any mode of applying water will do. This is wholly gratuitous. In the Apostolic age, and for a longer period than the first century, baptism, was so well understood by all without any explanations about it, than what were connected with and explained by the preaching itself, that there was but one sentiment concerning it. When Jews, Samaritans and Gentiles, were preached to, as soon as they believed, they were baptized at once into the name of Jesus Christ. The Apostles never

preached a sermon in which they did not exhibit Jesus Christ crucified for our sins, buried and risen as the essential and prominent objects of discourse. Those who believed were baptized, or immersed into this very truth, and put him on as Prince and Saviour.

I am yours, &c.   JAMES FISHBACK.

ORDER OF THE CHURCH AT ROCK SPRING, RUTHERFORD CO., T.

To the Editors of the Christian Review:—

GENTLEMEN:—In the January No. on the 24th page, I see five interrogatories which I consider of vital importance to the improvement in knowledge of Christian duties. In what State and County does the church meet of which you are a member) and what is your Post Office? Mount View, Davidson Co., is my Post Office; Rock Spring Church, in Rutherford County, about 15 miles south of Nashville, is the place of my membership. This church has 90 white members and 30 coloured brethren; 43 white males and 47 females. We meet the first and third Lord's day in each month. The Baptist brethren having the right to half the time. (Bad plan.—ED.)

You ask for what purpose we meet? I answer, to express gratitude for the many blessings that we have received from our Heavenly Father through his Son and our Redeemer Christ. To break bread and drink wine in commemoration of the broken body and shed blood until he comes. After this we sing and each member contributes what he or she thinks fit. You ask whether we have Evangelists, Bishops and Deacons, and whether the church performs its duties towards them? This is a question I do not feel competent to answer. Brother Randolph Hall is our Evangelist; he meets us punctually once a month and preaches to us, and we compensate him sparingly; but probably as much as we ought until he teaches us our duty and declares the whole duty to the Disciples as their Evangelist. We have Bishops 2, and Deacons 2, nominally. Of the latter I am one, and knowing my want of knowledge, I am induced to respond to these interrogatories, hoping the brethren that are better informed, will take the matter under consideration, and teach and be taught until we can learn what is right and then do it. This is my earnest desire.

Your last inquiry is, how many additions the last year? I think eighteen. How many departed from the faith? I know of none, but one. Brother Holt has joined the Mormons, as I am informed. Though, on this subject, I am sorry to inform you that out of the ninety white members, there is much the largest portion do not attend our first day meetings. This does not indicate they are true disciples. I wish you to receive this from a brother, and take it for just what it is worth.

BEVERLY NELSON.

Will the brethren do likewise?—T. F.   ED.

EARLY TRAINING MOST IMPORTANT.

"If a child is neglected till six years of age," says Brougham, "no subsequent attention can recover it. If to this age he is in ignorance and dissipation, in baseness and brutality, in that vacuity of mind which habit creates, it is vain to try to reclaim it by reading and writing. You may teach it what you choose *afterwards,* but if you have not prevented the *formation of bad habits,* you will teach in vain. With children under the age of six years—school learning, should not be the chief consideration, but the formation of moral principle.”

LUTHER'S CATECHISM.

To the Editors of the Christian Review:

The following is an extract from Luther's Catechism; and contains the whole article on baptism. It was translated several years ago, by Charles Artz, of Pittsburgh. It shows how Protestants have degenerated, since the days of the great Reformer.

"1st. What is Baptism?

"A. Baptism is not common water all alone, but it is a water of God's institution, and combined with the word of God.

"Q. Which is that Word?

"A. It is the testimony of Matthew, last chapter, where our Lord Jesus says: Go ye out into the world, and teach all nations, and baptize them into the name of the Father, and the Son, and the Holy Spirit.

"2d. What gift is bestowed or what advantage obtained by baptism?

"A. By its effects our sins are forgiven, our souls are delivered from the power of death and Satan, and eternal happiness is bestowed to all who believe that God means to do all that he has said and promised.

"Q. Which are these sayings and promises of God?

"A. Our Lord Jesus Christ says, according to Mark's record in the last chapter—he who believes and is baptized, shall be saved; but he who believes not shall be condemned.

"3d. How can water do such great things?

"A. Sure enough, it is not the water that does it, but the word of God which is with and by the water, and the faith which believeth that such word of God in the water is true: for without the word of God, the water is simply water and no baptism; but with the word of God it is become a baptism; that is a most gracious water of life and bath of regeneration by the Holy Spirit, as Paul says in the Epistle to Titus, chapter iii, "God saves us through the bath of regeneration, and renewing of the Holy Spirit, which he poured out on us richly through Jesus Christ our Saviour. That being justified by his favour, we might be made heirs according to the hope of eternal life. This doctrine is true.

"4th. Such water immersion, then, what does it mean?

"A. It means that the old Adam within us, through daily repentance and reform, must be drowned, and die with all the sins and bad affections; and that daily there must come out and rise up a new man, to live in righteousness and purity before God to all eternity.

"Q. Where is this writing in Scripture?

"A. Paul in the Epistle to the Romans, chapter vi, says: We have been buried together with him by immersion into his death, that like as Christ was raised up from the dead, by the glory of the Father, even so we also shall walk in a new life."   R.

The foregoing signed "R," was sent to me from the State of New York, showing what Luther taught on the subject of Baptism; suffice it to say that all the learned of all ages, since the coming of the Messiah, have taught the same thing in substance, but they have not practiced what they preached, for the last twelve hundred years. It was the revival of the practice that raised the hue and cry against the current "Reformation." In 1823, Bro. A. Campbell in a debate with W. L.

McCalla, openly vindicated the doctrine of "baptism for remission of sins," and might have continued to preach it until now without opposition, had it never been reduced to practice, but in a few years afterwards it was reduced to practice by Bro. Walter Scott and others here in Ohio, since which time it has been every where spoken against, as though it were something new and unheard of before; whereas every prominent reformer from Luther down to the present day, have taught the same thing.

In haste,

Jamestown, *Ohio, February* 1844.   M. WINANS.

TO OUR READERS.

Having no object in view but the real benefit of the world, and believing the CHRISTIAN REVIEW will be well calculated to lead its readers to investigate the truth, we ask the friends of the Christian religion, to exert themselves to give the work a wide circulation. There is no subscriber who has not a friend that can be induced to subscribe for the Review, and if all subscribers would take this matter into consideration, the list of readers would be very considerable in a very short time.

☞IDLENESS in Christian communities, is the mother of sloth, lukewarmness, and moral death. He that gains a rich reward in any pursuit, must be punctual, diligent, and zealous.

NEWS FROM THE CHURCHES.

As it is our intention to give our readers all the information possible in reference to the progress of truth, we respectfully invite brethren, throughout the country, to send us monthly reports. Tell us, Brethren, where you labor, your success, and your reverses.

Bro. D. G. LIGON, of Moulton Ala., who was immersed in June, 1843, has zealously advocated the cause of his Master, at all convenient seasons, ever since, and writes, that "on a visit to Triana, Ala., seven most intelligent persons became obedient to the faith." Prospects are also good for many other additions.

On a visit of the writer, to Clarksville, in the month of December, '43, four were immersed, all of whom, I believe, had been or were members of the Methodist church. One mother in Israel, was added from the Baptist. I also visited Gallatin, Castalian Springs, Hartsville, Rome and Lebanon, at all of which, many intelligent persons were disposed to hear the truth. Dr. John McCall was obedient at Rome. We need humble, intelligent and faithful teachers, to "push forward the conquests of the Redeemer's kingdom." How many young men will enlist as heralds of the cross in 1844?   T. F.

☞BRO. C. CURLEE, of Cannon County, Tenn., writes, "I have had the good company of Bro. L. N. MURPHREE some two weeks. We visited the brethren at Philadelphia, Warren County; immersed seven, and one was added from the Baptist. I am going to ride this year as an Evangelist, in Bedford, Franklin and Warren counties.

PROPOSALS
FOR PUBLISHING IN THE CITY OF NASHVILLE,
A MONTHLY PERIODICAL, ENTITLED THE
CHRISTIAN REVIEW.

A work devoted to Primitive Christianity, affording facilities for investigation, and reports of the general progress of truth, is believed to be much needed in the South-West. Individual enterprise has already done much to remove erroneous views and unfounded prejudices, but the plan proposed in the CHRISTIAN REVIEW contemplates a larger sphere of action, and more extended means of advancing the cause of the Bible.

In pursuance of this object, at a meeting of the disciples of Christ, from various parts of Tennessee, at Rock Springs, Rutherford county, Tennessee, September 18th, 1843, it was unanimously resolved, a journal, advocating the interests of the Church of Christ, should be established in Nashville, commencing January, 1844.

W. H. WHARTON, J. C. ANDERSON, and T. FANNING, were requested to procure the aid of competent brethren in several of the States, as Corresponding and Reporting Editors; to make the necessary arrangements for publishing such a paper as they might think the times demand; to act as a Reviewing and Revising Committee, and take general superintendence of the work. JNO. M- BARNES, of Middle Tennessee, W. D. CARNES, of East Tennessee, and JNO. R. HOWARD, of West Tennessee, were requested to represent their respective divisions of the State in the Editorial, department. The CHRISTIAN REVIEW will be devoted to the cause of the Bible, embracing first principles, organization of Churches, order of worship, perfection of Christian character, the union of saints, the study of prophecy, religious education, and every other topic which will contribute to render Christians more intelligent and spiritual.

The work will consist of 24 pages, neatly stitched, with a colored envelope and title page, and will be issued monthly, at ONE DOLLAR, *and no paper will be sent to any one until the money is received.*

Any one who will obtain ten subscribers, and remit the money, free of postage, shall be entitled to one copy for his trouble. Ministers of the Gospel are expected to act as agents, and the publishers would be pleased for any others to do so, who feel sufficient interest in the publication.

Letters addressed to "Christian Review, Nashville," post-paid, will receive Strict attention. It is desired that returns be made as soon as possible.

CORRESPONDING EDITORS.—W. D. Carnes, Knoxville, Ten.; Jno. M. Barnes, Columbia, Tenn.; John R. Howard, Paris, Tenn.; W. W. Stevenson, Little Rock, Arkansas; M. Winans. Jamestown, Ohio; Jacob Creath, Jr., Palmyra, Mo. A. GRAHAM, Marion, Ala.; JAMES E. MATHEWS, Jackson, Miss.

PUBLISHING AND SUPERINTENDING COMMITTEE.—Wm. H. Wharton, J. C. Anderson and T. Fanning, Nashville, Tenn.

Mackville, Tenn., October, 1843.   ________________________

AGENTS FOR THE REVIEW.

JAMES C. ANDERSON, Travelling Agent. G. W. ELLEY, and G. HILL, Columbus, Miss. G. B. LONG, Hopkinsville, Ky. T. M. ALLEN, Palmyra, Mo. S. E. JONES, Tennessee. Post Master, Russellville, Ala. Post Master; Moulton, Ala.   ________________________

☛Any person wishing to subscribe for the REVIEW, will be kind enough to call upon their nearest Post Master; he being authorized to remit for third persons. Back numbers always ready to send to new subscribers.   ________________________

☛We owe Bros. GRAHAM and MATHEWS, an apology for not adding their names to the list of Corresponding Editors long since, but owing to the neglect of one of the Publishers, they were left out. We were told to do so by one of our Editors here, but being so pressed with work, we entirely forgot it. We hope the brethren will write often, and be so kind as to accept our apology for this neglect.

CHRISTIAN REVIEW.

VOL. I.   NASHVILLE, MARCH, 1844.   NO. III.

CHURCH ORGANIZATION—NO. 3.

In the previous Nos. of the REVIEW, I have attempted to call attention to the subject of church organization; but yet, I am not assured the brethren desire this matter discussed. I have been satisfied for years, accurate and full instruction on this subject is of absolute importance to the prosperity of the churches. No nation has ever existed long without good government and strict organization. Rome was once powerful, but her citizens gave themselves to luxury and idleness, and lost the form and authority of government; the consequence was annihilation to the proud mistress of the broad earth. While the discipline of Greece was strict, she was the light and admiration of the world, but when the reins of government were slacked, she fell, and had lived only in faint memory since. When Napoleon embarked for Russia, his army was numberless and his soldiers stout and brave, but any one who will examine the history of that event, will soon learn, his fall and miserable fate were the result of partial organization and want of good government, more than the opposition of the enemy. Communities and nations fall to atoms more frequently, from their own magnitude and want of discipline, than all other causes. The Jews were once God's host, and the terror of all nations—they forgot government, lost their organization, and the consequence is, they are now a "hiss" and "proverb" to the ends of the earth.

The meanest causes are upheld, and strengthened by rigid laws and submission in the subjects. See the prosperity of the present Roman hierarchy— how has this scarlet mistress of abomination lived fifteen hundred years? The story is soon told. Government and submission have accomplished all. Look, my brethren, at the prosperity of what you denominate corrupt religious establishments around you. How do they live and flourish in this enlightened age, while better causes are still obscure? They have laws, and live and in their defense. It is preposterous in the extreme to think of a good government sustaining itself, while the subjects are ignorant of its principles and neglect its ordinances. While the Jews knew their institutions and taught their children its precepts, the world could not withstand them, but when these cardinal matters were neglected, they were as feeble as the ill-fated Sampson shorn of his locks.

We have espoused the best cause in the universe, and by putting on the whole amour, the ends of the earth will soon be electrified; but if we fail in our duty, God will evidently visit us with fearful judgments, and we may yet become the reproach of nations.

With these reflections, I will proceed another step with the subject under discussion. I do not wish to go too fast, and I humbly trust the brethren will bestir themselves in their researches till we are fully equipped for the battles of the God of Jacob.

VOL. I.—NO. 3.

In the present essay, I wish to present barely two points for the next month's reflection.

1st, The primitive churches were fully organized with government, officers and obedient subjects. That the Apostolic teaching, which we now have in the New Testament, constituted a complete government, I have abundantly shown in previous Nos. That *officers* were necessary for perfect organization may be learned from the Acts of Apostles and letters of Paul and Peter.

When the Saviour ascended on high, he not only led captivity captive, but bestowed gifts on men. He gave apostles, prophets, evangelists, pastors and teachers, "for the perfecting of the saints, for the work of the ministry, for the edifying of the body of Christ." This was to enable the saints "to be no more children, tossed to and fro, and carried about with every wind of doctrine by the sleight of men, and cunning craftiness, whereby they wait to deceive. "But by "speaking the truth in love," they were "to grow up into him in all things, who is the head, even Christ: from whom the whole body, fitly joined together and compacted by that which every, joint supplieth, according to the effectual working, in the measure of every part, maketh increase of the body unto, the edifying itself in love."

If the Saviour of man employed such means to accomplish such results, who would presumptuously contend such agencies were not necessary for the same joyous state of affairs in the nineteenth century?

2dly. Was the primitive organization intended as a model to churches through all time? An objector may say, "these offices were *divinely* gifted, and of course the organization was miraculous, and inasmuch as we see no miracles now. such organization is not practicable." True, men could not preach at first without being "sent" and specially and miraculously inspired; but not so now. The institutions of heaven were then locked up in the secret chambers of God—not so in this age. The miraculous displays were only intended to *give* and *attest* the simplest instructions, and these instructions had the sovereign effect to perfect the body of Christ. We have the same, without personal inspiration, and yet they are as miraculous and are fraught with as much authority, as they were |n the Apostolic age. These tongues, signs and wonders were only in part—or were parcels of one great whole we now have. Hence the conclusion, that we are more wonderfully favored with revelations, than the individual Apostles.

In the incipient states of society, government and organization commence by means different from those which perpetuate them. For the sake of distinction and the greater perspicuity, I will for the present style the first officers, their work and the organizations all *extraordinary;* but having shown the purposes as well as necessity of these measures, I ask the candid reader, if he is to suppose there was any meaning or permanent benefit in these things, if they were not intended to exhibit a model for all future organizations?

Before dismissing this subject, I will state it as a fact hereafter to be proved that a church of God was never formed, and cannot be at this day, without cither extraordinary or ordinary officers, and divine organization.

Brethren, think of these matters, and think seriously and fast.   T. F.

To the Editors of the Christian Review:

GENTLEMEN:—No. l, vol. 1, of your periodical was laid upon my table by a friend. On the last page I perceived a dignified, fair and unequivocal manifesto of the course proposed to be adopted by you as "conductors of the Christian Review." I was struck with the coincidence of your opinion and my own views of propriety in the premises. When I had the honor of editing a religious journal, my motto was *"both sides—fair play."* You have been pleased to say, p. 24, "We *seek* and *invite* investigation on every topic connected with man's salvation; and therefore, we say to Jews, Catholics, Protestants and all the world, our pages will *always* be open for fair discussion; provided, however, that all articles be written in a respectful manner, are short, and bear the author's real name: *We are for fair sailing."* And so am I. Permit me, therefore, to solicit most respectfully to be permitted to answer for myself touching certain things whereof I have been accused by a certain writer (one of your corps editorial, I opine,) over the initials "T. F." who has performed the *"irksome"* task of writing a "Review of a Treatise on Christian Baptism, collated from divers authors, with original notes and criticisms, being a review of Campbellism, by T. W. Haynes.' "The *"preface"* to "T. F.'s' review embraces three items. The first item amounts to absolutely nothing worthy of notice. The *second* item develops most palpably the gross ignorance of the writer in reference to the views of the Baptist denomination. He asks "Is it possible my Baptist friends teach that Baptism is an ordinance for Christians to perform?" To which it may be replied, that this principle distinguishes them emphatically from Jews, Catholics, Protestants, and the World as a "peculiar people." He quotes from Mr. Howell on Communion, p. 117, as teaching that "Christian Baptism is the only authorized mode of entrance into the visible church." "This was enough," says T. F., "I looked no further." Herein T. F. erred. Had he "looked further" he might have saved himself the misfortune of misunderstanding and consequently of misrepresenting Mr. Howell, and the whole Baptist denomination. Mr. Howell, in common with all Baptist writers of any conspicuity in every age of the church, from Luke to the nineteenth century, maintain that *Christians only are to be baptized* and *Christians only are to be received into the visible church.* T. F. seems to adopt the Roman Catholic doctrine that *"in the church visible,"* is a phrase equivalent to *"in Christ"—"christian."* The plain inference from which doctrine would be that other papal dogma, that *out of the church visible there can be no salvation.* T. F. is challenged to name the page of any standard Baptist author of eminence in which the doctrine is taught that any one not *"in Christ"* is entitled to baptism. The author of the Treatise reviewed by T. F. limits baptism to Christians only by the phrase "Christian Baptism," and feels himself fortunate in having been so understood by at least one reader. But "I saw the expression *Review of Campbellism,"* says T. F., "and the thought occurred to me that this is a time of extreme indulgence." Indeed, is it a time of great indulgence in the United States of America in the nineteenth century. In the year 1843-4 in Tennessee, there is no Pope, Inquisition, Council, Sanhedrim, Emperor, King, Queen, Potentate, Governor or Magistrate, or censor of the press, who may constitutionally, or lawfully, under the terrors of an *"auto de fe,"* forbid any man, even "a Baptist preacher," from writing and publishing "a REVIEW of Romanism, Protestantism or Campbellism." This is certainly a time of most   extreme   indulgence   and   if   this   article   shall   be

denied admission into the "Christian Review," I shall be reluctantly compelled to the conclusion that if T. F. had lived in another century and in another land, and had possessed his present spirit and identity, that such "a time of extreme indulgence" by his consent had never dawned upon the world. Why should this expression be so offensive? It was most assuredly not intended by the author of the "*Treatise, &c.*" to be understood in any unkind sense. Alexander Campbell himself shall be our apologist. In his CHRISTIAN SYSTEM," p. 102, he says: "So many items of the Apostles? doctrine and so many notions of Calvin combined produce the compound called Calvinism." In this quotation substitute the words *Campbell* for *Calvin* and *Campbellism* for *Calvinism,* and how apropos! He continues: "So many items of Luther's opinions compounded with the Apostles? teaching make Lutherism." Here read Campbell instead of Luther and Campbellism instead of Lutherism, and can it be opprobrious? But further: "And so many portions of Wesley's speculations compounded with certain portions of the New Testament, make the compound called Methodism." Thank you, Mr. Campbell, a thousand thanks to you for this definition. Instead of Wesley read Campbell, and for Methodism substitute Campbellism, and your position is unequivocally defined. And in an article prepared by Mr. Campbell himself, for the "Encyclopedia. of Religious Knowledge," he begins "Disciples of Christ, *sometimes called Campbellites."* Can you find such an uninspired substitute for BAPTIST? But in reference to *names* I desire to write a chapter for your periodical at some future period. The *third,* item is either not candid or intentionally unfair. You charge me with quoting from Mr. Campbell's works without any acknowledgment. On page 51 of my Treatise, I say in so many words "the treatise on the *"Covenants and Seals"* prefixed to the present volume is *copied* from the Appendix to the Debate of Messrs. Campbell and Walker." T. F. either reviewed a work which he had not read, or this fact probably escaped his notice. He will doubtless correct this error. He says of MR. C'S treatise on the Covenants, "the style was manly, spirited, classical, clear and scriptural." "What learned Baptist, said I, has done this? I could think of none who wrote on this wise." He could not have been very familiar with Mr. C.'s writings certainly. But it was a Baptist. The Debate between Mr. Walker and Mr. Campbell occurred in 1820, At which period Mr. Campbell was a Baptist. T. F. says was *Scriptural.* So, Baptists regard it. If the treatise or the Covenants in the Appendix to the Debate with Mr. Walker, 2d Ed., 1823, be *Scriptural,* then the later writings of Mr. Campbell are NOT SCRIPTURAL, and this essay in the main. Scriptural, was introduced entire and unmutilated by me as containing a refutation of Campbellism or Mr. C's *opinions, notions,* or *speculations* which he has compounded with the Gospel in those very items in which he has renounced the doctrine of the Baptists as exhibited by him in those 23 pages of my pamphlet as copied from him. It is competent to quote from any author, and besides his copyright of 20 years had expired and the laws of my country gave the right to quote Mr. C., or even to have re-published the whole of that Debate and Appendix. Mr. Howell was only recommending a Baptist work when he recommended cheerfully Mr. Campbell's general views on the Covenants and seals, entertained by him when a Baptist, but he has abandoned but never dared to answer. T. F. devoted his review chiefly to the title page, preface and copy-right of my work, as though a *Baptist preacher* as such forfeits his rights as a man in this Republic by becoming a Baptist. The

last paragraph of T. F.'s review is employed in an unsuccessful attempt, to reconcile two,
contradictory propositions

which have been affirmed by A. Campbell—a work of supererogation for which Mr. Campbell will scarcely indorse. Mr. C. while a Baptist, in his Debate with Mr. Walker, 2d. Ed. p. 210, says, "the commission to baptize believers or *disciples,* prohibits the baptism of others." But at a later period after becoming the founder of a new denomination he asserts, "Christian System," p. 188, that "immersion was essential to discipleship," and elsewhere, "immersion is the discipling act." He that can reconcile those propositions can confound light and darkness—truth and error. And yet T. F. attempts it by alleging that disciples were called disciples both *before,* and *after* their baptism. Does this make the discipling act or essential to discipleship? T. F. says "*Mathetueo* the Greek verb used in the commission and translated by the word *teach* means to *disciple* or *make disciples.* Mind, this is *before* baptism, and without *this* discipleship" (before baptism) "Baptism is worse than useless. It is said Jesus *made* and baptized more disciples than John. The idea is very clear that Christ discipled before he baptized." I ask then did He disciple *by* baptism? or was baptism essential to discipleship? Or rather was not discipleship essential to baptism? But T. F. finds in John viii. 30, 31, "as he spake many believed on him." ("Now," says T. F. "they are the taught, believers, disciples in word.") I ask are they disciples in *fact?* in *truth?* in *deed?* Is believing not an *act?* a *deed?* The quotation from John continues "continue ye in my word, shall ye be my disciples indeed." Indeed, here is an adverb; and differs in signification from the phrase "in deed" compounded of a preposition and noun. A disciple in *word only* is a hypocrite, Did Christ make hypocrites and baptize them to make real Christians? Did John? Is this the meaning of the commission make disciples *in word only*—make hypocrites and by baptizing them, *make them disciples* in *deed?* Miserable subterfuge. T. F. was compelled to affirm the first proposition of Mr. C. his *Scriptural and Baptist* proposition. A disciple before baptism is a disciple. after baptism and equally entitled to the appellation before, in, and after that act. But my object is not discussion but simply a correction of the errors of T. F. who says in conclusion "a more-lengthy review of the pamphlet, under consideration, would be irksome to T. F." Doubtless for one reason worth a thousand, its arguments are unanswerable. Respectfully, your ob't. servant,

Nashville, Jan. 24th, 1844.   T. W. HAYNES.

————

REMARKS.—From the pompous and bitter spirit manifested in the above article, I had thought on first reading it, I should not publish or notice it; but on "the second sober thought." I could see no great impropriety in letting Mr. Haynes be heard in his own style. However, I must assure my Baptist friends, that I do not presume Mr. H. is a fair representative of their sentiments; and to the public, I wish to state, that with Mr. H. I seek no controversy. I noticed the pamphlet under consideration solely in consequence of the *endorsement,* and "recommendation" of the Rev. R. B. C. Howell. Taking it then for granted that Mr. Howell endorses both the pamphlet and defense, my controversy is with his teaching, and not with Mr. Haynes as a man, or Baptist preacher. Before replying to the defenses I wish to state, that for many of the Baptists, I entertain the kindest feelings, believing that in the great South-west, they are   much   nearer   the   Gospel   than   any   other sect. Indeed, I know many of the Baptists, in West Tennessee, Mississippi and Alabama, who preach and practice, in the main, the Gospel; but I am sorry to say, this is not the case in the Middle part of the State. And I am not sure but the disciples have contributed to keep the Baptists in this section in the back ground. Most men are pleased to lead in reformations, and not infrequently when they cannot lead, they become open opposers. I can call to mind scores of this class. Where the Baptists have been free to learn and improve, they come very nearly teaching the whole truth; but I am sorry—heartily sorry, this has not been the case in Middle Tennessee. The leading Baptists, amongst whom Mr. Howell stands foremost in Tennessee, have so long and so strenuously opposed the saints under the odious stigma of Campbellism, till the great majority of the members are bitterly opposed to us. This is much to be regretted; but I trust it will not always be so. If the more intelligent Baptists would cultivate more reciprocity of feeling, and become better acquainted with us, doubtless a great reformation might be affected in this country. But whether they oppose or forbear, my determination is not to treat them as enemies. As to the defense of the essay my remarks shall be brief.

1. The defender of the pamphlet says in reference to the author of the "review," "the first item amounts absolutely to nothing worthy of notice." "The second develops palpably, the ignorance of the writer in reference to the Baptists." These quotations are given as specimens of Mr. H.'s courtesy, and style of debating. On the same subject, he charges "misrepresentation" upon me, for asking if the Baptists baptize Christians. He says that "Mr. Howell in common with all Baptist writers of any conspicuity, from Luke to the nineteenth century, maintain that, *Christians* only are to be baptized, and *Christians only are to be received into the visible church."* Again, he says, "T. F. is challenged to name the page of any standard Baptist author, in which the doctrine is taught, that any one *not in Christ* is entitled to baptism."

It is really laughable to hear Mr. H. speak of a "Baptist church from Luke to the nineteenth century." The Baptist church is as great a stranger to Luke, the Bible, and to history for fifteen hundred years, as the Mormon or Quaker churches. The author and his friends are mistaken, if they suppose, the community can be gulled into the belief of the antiquity of the Baptist sect without the shadow of proof. But to the question. Is it the sentiment of Mr. Howell "that Christians only are to be baptized?" If so he contradicts himself and joins Mr. Haynes in contradicting the highest Baptist authority.— I quote Mr. Howell again on Communion. He says, p. 117, "Baptism is the only authorized mode of entrance into the visible church;" Does Mr. Howell explain this away, as Mr. Haynes intimates. What is the "visible church?'4 Is it not the body of Christ? Those out of Christ are in the world—sinners, and as Baptism is the only mode of entrance, in the language of Mr. Howell, of course all others are in the world. But Mr. Howell has written a book of 300 pages to prove Paedobaptists, are not authorized to take the Lord's Supper, and his sole argument is, they have not been immersed. It is too childish for our Baptist brethren to call the Paedobaptists Christians—God's people, and yet say, they will not commune with them. Oh, for more consistency and sincerity!! I am gravely challenged to show one good Baptist authority that teaches "any but Christians," or such as are "in Christ," are entitled "to baptism." I will try. R. *Pengilly,* a standard Baptist author, on pa. 81, of his "Scripture Guide to Baptism" says, "Baptism is designed to form a line of separation between the world and the church." Mind, Baptism is the

"line," on one side are worldlings or sinners, according to Pengilly, and on the other Christians. Again in the "circular of the Northamptonshire (England) Baptist Association," published in the "Baptist Manual" as "an exposition of the distinguishing sentiments of the Baptists in the United States," page 2, the circular says, *"Baptism is a solemn and practical profession of the Christian religion."*—page 7, read. *"Its* (Baptism) *design is to draw a line of distinction between the kingdom of Christ and the kingdom of Satan."* But Mr. Howell and Mr. Haynes teach "christians only are entitled to baptism." Then Christians can be in the kingdom of Satan. He says same page, "it is the boundary of visible Christianity." But my friends in Nashville have so sharp optics as to discover Christians before they enter visible Christianity.

In the "circular letter of the Hudson River Association of 1824," published by authority, on page 4th it is said Baptism is called *"that grand line of distinction between the kingdom of darkness, and that kingdom which is not of this world."* The authors of this letter say on the 8th page, "we warn Paedobaptists *to arise and be baptized and wash away their sins* (*in a figure*) *calling upon the name of the Lord,* This is honest, and I must say my Baptist, brethren in Nashville are greatly in the rear of these *standard Baptist authors.*

My friends certainly cannot accuse me again with "ignorance" and "misrepresentation" of Baptist sentiments. My brethren have never used stronger language than these venerable and learned Baptists, and I entreat Messrs. Howell and Haynes, not to attempt to correct our supposed errors, till they put these Baptists right. And when they have performed this task, they can be the better prepared to correct the writings of the late John Taylor of Kentucky, who mid in his history of the ten churches "God has connected salvation with Baptism," and that "Saul's sins were not removed till he was baptized." They may then be the better prepared to correct Eld. Poindexter, of Va. and Elder Merideth of Carolina, whose language in reference to faith, repentance and baptism "in order" to become Christians, is as pointed as any A. Campbell or any other disciple of Christ ever used.—Enough. The author seems to think if I do not publish his strictures, it would show if I had "lived in another country, and another land", and had possessed the power, *the "extreme indulgence"* of writing an expose of "Campbellism" would not have been granted a, Baptist preacher. No man on earth could say what he would do under different circumstances; but I do not really think I could be induced to hurt a hair on the head of any of my Baptist friends. But were I disposed to retaliate, I would advert is the conduct of some of his brethren, in a "hue and cry" against me, last April. I forgive, but I can not forget these things. Again, he says I am "uncandid" or "unfair," because I stated he had published 23 pages from A. Campbell without a mark of quotation. This is true to the letter, as any one can see by examining the pamphlet. True, Mr. H. says just before closing the expose, the treatise is from A. Campbell; but this has nothing to do with quotation marks, and to my own knowledge, the 23 pages have been read, and the impression made, that they were the production of T. W. Haynes.

As the reader will see, the writer of this defense says much that is uncharitable about "Campbellites," which is entirely gratuitous, and therefore, I consider further reply unnecessary. Once more I wish to state if any of my worthy Baptist friends wish to discuss the differences between themselves and the disciples, the columns of the "Christian Review" are open, but for the *public good, I Would greatly prefer another champion in the arena to Mr. T. W. H.*

TOLBERT FANNING.

BAPTIST UNION.

Bro. W. H. Muse, a Baptist minister of Huntsville, Ala., and Editor of the "Baptist Evangelist," in the January number of his work says, "I hope our brethren of the 'CHRISTIAN REVIEW' may find it their duty and pleasure to advocate a union of all Christians who are willing to take the New Testament alone as their confession of faith."

It is to me a strange sentiment for a Baptist minister to ask my brethren to do what has been the chief business of their lives. Union on the Bible! Why, Bro. Muse, we have never thought of any thing else. We have never refilled union on the word of God—we cannot—dare not. Our motto is, a full, hearty and perfect union with all christians on the scriptures of truth. Bro. Muse suggests, that before the year 1860, all Baptists, (by which I presume he includes the Disciples, as they practice immersion,) will be united. This is sincerely to be desired, if all parties will give up their party distinctions, and in fact and truth be satisfied with the teaching, designations and worship of the New Testament. Again, Bro. M. hints that the older loaders, who have been instrumental in producing the divisions, may endeavor to perpetuate them. This is touching the right cord. Preachers, like other men, frequently have much pride to gratify. The Venerable Garner McConnico, an eminent Baptist minister of this State, stated just before his death, "Thereto a pride of youth, and a pride of old age." His explanation was, young men strive for distinction," but said he, "when you shall have grown old in a cause, and see young men rising up round you, and hear them attack your teaching, and attempt to correct errors which they suppose you have been propagating through life, then you will feel the pride of old age.'" The moral of this to, that men strengthen in prejudice the longer they live in them, and when once confirmed in a theory it is next to impossibility to correct it. It may be taken as a sweeping postulate, that the profession of a party religion, or the advocating of a party cause, is neither a real blessing in time or eternity. Try it who will, the less a man has to do with sects and sectarian prejudices, the happier and more useful will he be.

Although it is desirable to see union amongst all the sincere and pious of all sects, but When we see party leaders generally, endeavoring to kindle strife, produce and perpetuate prejudices, the prospect to somewhat gloomy. There are noble exceptions, however, and I am assured, the most intelligent, learned and energetic Baptist ministers in the South-West are more than willing to see all christians united on the one foundation. Well, brethren, the disciples are ready, and if you will show us wherein we lack improvement, we will attempt a reform, but pray do not fell us to come to the Bible, till you go to it yourselves. When you shall have done to the teaching, profession and practices of the New Testament, inform us, if we shall not have advanced far enough, we will continue our journey till we meet you.

As this is a subject of deep interest, it is my purpose to discuss, it fully. Will our Baptist brethren interchange views with us?   T. F.

THE FAITH WHICH CHRIST APPROVED.

When Jesus entered Capernaum, a centurion applied to him to heal his servant. Jesus offered to accompany him home in person. This the officer modesty declined, saying "speak the word only and my servant shall be healed." —Mat. viii. 3. The reason of this confidence in the word of Christ—the officer illustrated by a reference to his own authority over his soldiers and subjects. Whatsoever in my limited authority I command, is done, therefore whatsoever you wish to effect within your extensive authority, can be accomplished by your word only, without your personal presence.—To this, Jesus replied ' "verily, I have not found so great faith, no not in Israel."

The faith then which Jesus approves, is confidence in the power of his word. His personal presence is no more necessary now, than it was then to affect any purpose in his boundless dominion. All authority in heaven and in earth belongs to him. Whether it is to cure the centurion's servant, to raise Lazarus from the grave, or to save a soul from sin, his word is adequate. He that doubts it falls below the great faith which Jesus, commends. "The gospel is the power of God unto salvation to every one that believes."   A. G.

―――――――――

THE CRUCIFIXION.

In whatever point of view, we place before the mind's eye for contemplation this greatest of all the events in the annals of time; whether we regard it in connexion with the causes that occasioned, or the consequences that followed it; whether we trace it upward to its source in the love of God, or downward as it terminates in the immortality and happiness of man—it stands forth broadly and permanently, the master-element, the very essence of the Gospel. All the other marvelous accompaniments of this grand central-fact—the wondrous birth, the mighty miracles, the various prophecies, the divine goodness, even the triumphant resurrection of Jesus the Messiah—are but as proofs and evidences of supernatural wisdom and power, operating upon us only in the production of faith. But the death of God's acknowledged Son to expiate the guilt of a perishing world, is the matchless Wonder of creation, the miracle of uncles! There we behold Omnipotent Love working out a new creation, bringing forth again order out of chaos, light out of darkness, purity but of corruption, life out of death. This is the peculiar glory that distinguishes the revelation of God's mercy to man, and places it at an immeasurable distance from all the schemes and plans which have ever been devised by the wisdom or the folly of human beings.

However pleasing the inviting theme may be—to trace the varied and momentous consequences of the sacrifice of the divine Saviour, as they stand related to time and to eternity —yet we would confine our thoughts for the present to the scene of his sufferings. But who can describe the horrors of that scene, when the hour of his utmost extremity had come? With trembling awe, let us draw nigh to that middle cross, and beheld him, stripped, and nailed and lifted high upon it. Read the superscription over his head—"Jesus of Nazareth, the King of the Jews." The women who followed him from Galilee, and wept so bitterly as, oppressed with his heavy cross, he marched before the unsympathising crowd up the gentle activity, have withdrawn, and stand afar off: in their cases, see the iron-featured soldiers of the Roman Legion, with   the instruments of cruelty and death in their hands. Hear them mocking and deriding the meek and innocent sufferer; behold them mingling the gall and wormwood to insult him in his last hour. And now his agony has reached its height his heart feels the bitterness of death; still, patience sits enthroned upon his thorn crowned brow, and the prayer of mercy is heard breathing from his parched lips,—"Father, forgive them; they know not what they do." Surrounded by his insulting foes, betrayed, derided, deserted by his earthly friends, he turns one last appealing look to Heaven, when—oh! last of all, and worst of all his woes—his God forsakes him!

All nature to its very centre feels the shock: the veil of the Temple is rent asunder, and the astonished earth trembles as he cries—"Eloi, Eloi, lama sabacthani?" Chaotic midnight spreads across the wide arch of the azure heavens its broad and shadowy curtains, and covers with disastrous darkness all the land. The accumulated weight of grief, and sorrow, and shame dissolves his soul, and he, who had not where in Heaven to look for succor, nor where on earth to lay his head, bowed that head, and died.   W.

CONTRADICTIONS BY DR. J. FISHBACK AND J. F. PRICE.

The reader will recollect, that a letter was published in the February No. of the CHRISTIAN REVIEW, in reference to Mr. "Rumor," who has reported in Tennessee, that Dr. Fishback had stated in the presence of several gentlemen in Lexington, that he "was convinced by the arguments of Mr. Rice, in the late debate with A. Campbell, that infant sprinkling was Scriptural Baptism, and that infants should be members of the church." The Doctor says in a letter to J. S. Fall, "I *never said, nor do I think, that sprinkling is a valid Baptism. I heard nothing in the debate that I thought, in any degree, supported Infant Baptism, or Sprinkling.*"

Mr. Jacob F. Price, of Ky., in a letter to Dr. John Kelly of Nashville, published in the S. W. C. Advocate, in reference to the same matter, says, *"Dr. Fishback told me, that this discussion upon the mode of Baptism was so able and sustained by Mr. Rice with so much argument, that all, or both sides ought to recognize each other's baptism as valid, and each other's church membership as true and good."* Mr. Price continues, *"The Doctor said more, that if he was a young man and about to start a church, he would receive members who were baptized by sprinkling or pouring, from other churches, as validly baptized, although he would only baptize himself by immersion."*

We have thus given the evidence of both parties, and we regret that party papers are not generally disposed to publish both sides of any question, when a disciple of Christ is one of the parties. This is one of the *signs of the times.* Now the question is, who is to be believed? If Dr. Fishback stated what is affirmed, he is not to be believed on any subject. We have little to do with the controversy, and care not to have any controversy about it, and we doubt not the public will learn before a great while who has told the truth, and who has spoken falsely. One suggestion, however, will not be amiss. Dr. Fishback is reputed to be a man of at least common sense, and has not heretofore been the subject of reproach. Is it possible a man of sound mind will say, sprinkling and pouring are scriptural baptism, as well as immersion, and yet he will practice none but immersion? This would be affirming there are two scriptural ways of performing an ordinance, neither of which would he perform; and for such a man to say he believes and loves the Bible, is outrageous. Can a sensible, honest man believe such absurdities? "As your faith is, so be it unto you." We affirm nothing. There is no necessity for it.

T. F.

____

EDUCATION.

The Subject of training the young, for this world as well as the next, is a theme of increasing interest in every section of the country. The instruction of youth is becoming a Science which, in point of importance, has no rival. In the February No. of the REVIEW, I glanced at some of the evils connected with the present system of education, for which I promised, at another time, to offer correctives.

1st. To make education *general*, it must be self-supporting; or in other words, a system must be established to enable young men to become educated without a large amount of money. How shall this be accomplished? There is but one remedy. Governments will do but little, and our popularity is so fast on the increase, that government would fail of means to educate the poor. It must be remembered, at the outset, that gold is not the only effective capital to improve the mental or physical condition of man. Labor is the best capital of a nation and the surest means of great achievements in individuals. It may be demonstrated with the clearness of a sun beam, that manual labor is indispensable to a healthy state of both soul and body; and that it may become effectual in the acquisition of the greatest Literary attainments. To be brief, before education can be general—universal, the community must be convinced that it is better for the young to gain instruction by their own industry, than by the dollars of parents. The first question to be determined is, can youths, in any system, procure the means of educating themselves by their own exertions? If the theory be correct, that six or eight hours only in the 24 can be profitably employed at books, at least six hours may be devoted to labor; and assuredly a young man would pay boarding, tuition, and clothe himself, by his own industry. The greatest difficulty is to make labor honorable. On this subject the taste of society is much corrupted. This corrupt taste should be corrected. But the manner of accomplishing it is the secret. With Christian people, it would seem this obstruction could be easily removed. The first argument to be adduced for its removal is the fact that the Creator of all things made man to "till the ground," and declared he Should "eat broad by the sweat of his face?" Both in the Patriarchal and Jewish ages, the most distinguished and best men, cultivated the earth, or minded their flocks for support. Abraham, Lot and David were shepherds; Noah was a "husbandman," and Jacob was a herdsman; and in the first days of the Christian religion, the founders and supporters of this sublime system were men addicted to industrious habits; The Saviour of the world was a carpenter; the Apostle to the Gentiles was a tent-maker; and it was a maxim of inspiration, that they who would not work should not eat. How has this system been changed!! At this day, speculation, and all kinds of speculation, are supplied for honest industry. We must return to primitive purity before man can honor his Maker.

2d. Labor is essential to physical, intellectual and moral health. This great truth must be written indelibly upon the hearts of the young. When the physical man alone is developed, a near alliance to the brute is made; when the intellect alone is regarded, a feeble coxcomb is formed; and *if the moral powers   alone are educated, the individual is an unenergetic and useless being. But let the body, intellect, and moral, powers all have proper attention at the same time, and the man is a blessing to himself and the world. The means of accomplishing these ends naturally suggest themselves.*

3d. Labor, to become sufficiently interesting to be pursued with pleasure, must be considered an important part of the education of youth. Connect Chemistry, Geology, Natural and Moral Philosophy, Botany, &c. with labor, and it will, in fact, be the most important part of instruction.

4th. To guard the manners and morals of youths, the *country* is the location for institutions of learning. I pretend not, at present, to describe the sources of corruption in most of our city schools and colleges, for these things are open to the eyes of all the world. My object is to show the necessity of separating youths from corrupt influences. A good man has said "evil communications corrupt good manners" and so sure as Solomon said, as man could "not take fire into the bosom without burning him," if youths are surrounded by corrupt associations, the large majority will catch the infection. The two surest safeguards of the morals of youth are, first, a separation, as for as possible, from contaminating influences; and secondly, the constant company and daily advice of preceptors. If parents would kindly council their children, and impress upon their young minds the melancholy evils of crime, and place before them constantly the incentives to virtue, the next generation would be much purer than the present. But as children, with the present organization of society, are generally under the necessity of leaving the protection of parents for the advice of preceptors, it is important that teachers should devote their *time* and *attention* to the interests of the students. On the usual plan of sending young men to cities to be educated, where they are under the direction of teachers only during a few hours in the day, for the purpose of reciting lessons, every door is open to acquire vicious habits. This evil can be corrected in no other way than by preventing corrupt associations as far as possible, and letting students be all the time under the direction of instructors.

5th. To prevent extravagance in dress, students should not only be separated from the vain and fascinating shows of cities, but should be taught that plainness and neatness are unequalled virtues. The whole error might be removed, if no youth would be suffered to purchase any thing of a showy or extravagant character, till he earns its value by his own industry. This would put a stop to many of the evils of the land.

6th; The last item of improvement which I am disposed at present to suggest is, the absolute importance of *employment all the time* of the young. It is a fact no one will deny, that with most young persons, while they are not profitably engaged, they are employed income amusement, or vicious practice, which has an injurious tendency. An objector may say, boys and young men, require time for play and recreation. True, all human beings should have recreation, but let our recreations be free from vicious indulgences. Let our books, our garden and farm exercises, and our devotion to mechanical and other improvements, be our delight, and we shall not fail to improve ourselves and those around us.   T. F.

BAPTIST POLICY IN ALABAMA.

BRETHREN EDITORS:—We have two Baptist papers in this State. The "Alabama Baptist" of this place and the "Baptist Evangelist" of Huntsville. It seems that the editor of the latter periodical is becoming a little heterodox, and our Southern editor is castigating him for it. In the last number of the Alabama Baptist, Mr. Muse of Huntsville is declared to be a "Campbellite" and unworthy of the fellowship of all old "Regular Bible Baptists." I have never seen the Baptist Evangelist and cannot pronounce upon its merits, but judge it worthy of attention, from the fact that our Southern Baptist organ has sounded the tocsin.

The character of the heresy may be guessed at from the following items given in the strictures of our orthodox paper:

"ITEM 3, I have taught, that faith is a sentiment originated in the mind by the force of testimony, and that this sentiment partakes of the nature of the testimony, whether it be human or divine, true or false."

"ITEM 6, I have taught, that the Holy Spirit operates upon the minds of men, alone through the words of truth."

"ITEM 7. I have taught, that the notion of an abstract spiritual operation is the sole inlet to all the fanaticism and superstition that how afflicts humanity."

Upon this last item it is remarked, "Here is a flat denial of what has always been a most prominent item of Baptist belief. The notion of an abstract spiritual operation is held to, by the Baptists, as an important point, and that its rejection leads to a rejection of Christianity itself. Take away this and you take away the only hope which the Baptists have that another sinner will ever be converted to God."

"ITEM 8. I have taught, that the doctrine of the total depravity of human nature, is a libel upon the noblest works of God."

For these and similar sentiments, our Southern Alabama Baptists denounce Mr. Muse and say they only mean to strip off the sheepskin and show the wolf. But controversy on the merits of the points involved is positively declined. To show that he is "not *a Baptist*" is the avowed object; but the question whether he is right or wrong is not to be discussed. This will give you some idea of Baptist policy in South Alabama.   A. G

FAVORITISM AND PROBATION.

MESSRS. EDITORS:—You have commenced your Editorial career, and before you go too far, I wish to hint, that nothing is like a good START. That is *starting right.* Your object may be, popularity and profit for it may be, for the *Truth's* sake alone. If for the first, you may miss it; for only a few made by *periodicals;* and if to give Religious Truth to the world, you may likewise fail, if you have it not to *give!* I know such a supposition is not courteous: But the times require all that frankness consistent with due respect: and so many are now teaching *Error* for Truth, you must own, I have a good apology at hand.

Do you mean to go on the system of *Favoritism;* or that of *trial* and *probation?* For no man of good sense, who has thought on the subject, ever doubted, but that one of them was the true Gospel System, and the other false, in *toto;* as well as all those numerous systems, formed by blending together, parts of those antipodal systems; for they are as opposite, as the two banks of a river: one must be true, and the *other false;* granting Christianity is true. And Creeds, or Systems, formed of *Truth* and *Error,* are erroneous. Hence, I wish you to ponder well which you will sustain. On your choice, depends your only chance for teaching the Truths and nothing but truths of the Gospel: for if you adopt any mongrel system, formed out of both, it is impossible.

There are difficulties on both sides. The world does not like either. Hence the numerous sects;—each attempting to make a palatable Creed out of the more pleasing parts of both. Those that go for the system of favoritism, have to hold, that God saves and takes to Heaven no man for his good works; but only for his love to them, on account of Christ's *holy* life and *expiatory* death. Most sects seem to go this far; but many of them with very inconsistent draw-backs! As that the belief of these truths must make us holy, or we cannot enter Heaven! Or, as the *Papists,* that this righteousness and blood of Christ must be applied by the Church, or it is of no avail! While others, which includes you perhaps (if not some of the leading Brethren.) think that Christ's expiatory sacrifice is the procuring cause of our pardon; but that, being thus once set free from death, by the virtue of Christ's blood, we must thenceforth work out our own salvation, with fear and trembling," or be lost! Pretty good patch-work!—but very inconsistent. For then none can obtain Heaven, but by its good works. His salvation depends on his *working it out;* and not on the love of God, irrespective of his works.

But the Universalians say, that as God's love to us, for what Christ has done and suffered, and not what we *have* done or *may* do, is the cause of any man's salvation, they can see no good reason why all should not be saved. Good works saves no man—but all are saved through the blood of Christ; and that has merits enough to save thousands of words. Why then should not a God of impartial love save all the human family? And echo answers why? These men hold the doctrine or system of Favoritism, without mixture; and are at least within *one* of being right! If the system of Probation is not true, they *are* right. Whereas those who take a little from both systems, and boast of inking a middle ground, have no *possibility of* being found in the truth. That is the *whole* truth.

The Calvinists hold this system of favoritism, as far as they go; for they say man is not saved for good works done of foreseen; but only by the electing love of God; and why they do not hold with universal salvation is hard to say. Every one of them, as it respects himself, is a Universalist; for he believes he will he saved, not for any good he has done; and that all the sins he *has* committed *or may* commit cannot prevent it. Hence, if all the world Were *Calvinists,* the whole world would be *Universalists!* But perhaps they are not willing all should be equally favored with themselves; or think that the courts above could not contain the number that should in that case be saved!

In neither of the above forms, do I suppose you can advocate the system of Favoritism. If not, you must go to the old system of *Patch* work; or come out boldly for the system of Probation! And what is that? Why, it is *do well* and *have well'. Obey* under any dispensation, and have the annexed reward—*Disobey,* and meet the threatened punishment. As I said before, this opposite system has its difficulties; no body likes it, nor is there a sect on earth that holds it in its purity. They must have some way of getting round the Cross (of) Christ, viz: *perfect obedience*—a plain proof that the system is attended with many weighty not valid, objections. I will mention one. It implies, that when God commands man to do either a *physical or mental* act, God will not do that act for him, or compel him, or help him to do it! And that when God acts, either on mind or matter, he cannot be either *assisted* or *resisted!* Should these consequences, or any others which you or your readers may suppose attends the system of Probation, appall you, let them be stated in the *Christian Review,* and I will try to remove them. For I believe that God never has placed man in any other state than that of trial and probation, from the time he formed him of dust, down to the present day, So says the Bible, as a *whole,* and any *texts* that seem to militate against it, can be explained so as to agree therewith.   H. H

EDITORIAL.—The writer of the foregoing is informed, that the conductors of the CHRISTIAN REVIEW teach the only system of Christianity taught in the Bible, and the object is to benefit the world. When we err, we shall thank any one to correct us.

CHURCH GOVERNMENT—No. 1.

To *the Editors of the Christian Review:*

BRETHREN:—In glancing casually over the so called Christian world, at the present age, and beholding the clashing sentiments and strife of those usually styled the ministers of the Cross, in reference to the legality and validity both of their churches as the true churches of God, as also of the authority of their officers to officiate in their respective stations, the reflecting mind is led to the conclusion, that there must be something necessarily defective at the basis of most of the present organizations in Christendom. While his holiness of the Vatican, with all his almost numberless dependents, contend most strenuously the for exclusive authority of the pretended apostolic successors, to convey official power by the imposition of their hands, the bishops of the English hierarchy just as strenuously contend, that the same power resides with them, although compelled to acknowledge the reception of it through the same corrupt and corrupting channel. Various and diverse are the schemes which have been devised by the different Protestant sects, which, while they apparently, at least, render them independent of the Roman church, secure to their respective clergy the right of ordination. But in view of such Confusion upon the subject before us, let the following facts be observed by all, that from the pages of history no testimony can be adduced proving that there has been a regular line of church officers ordained by the imposition of hands, except through the Roman church. Therefore, if it be necessary to the existence of the true church of Christ that she has such officers, no church can claim that title, except she be dependent upon, or has taken refuge in the bosom of, the mother of harlots?

These things promised, I proceed to the consideration of the subject in the view in which the Scriptures present it. So far as I am aware, it is the universally received sentiment with the brethren, that the church of God or kingdom of heaven, in fulfillment of the Jewish prophesies, was established upon the first day of Pentecost, subsequent to the ascension of our Lord. This I know is a disputed point in the religious community; but as I am now writing for the special benefit of my brethren, I shall take this position for granted, at least until put to the proof.

Notwithstanding I have assumed this attitude, it must be apparent, that we have many of the principles of the government and order of the kingdom presented to us in the Savior's teaching to his apostles preparatory to their official stations in that kingdom; yet many of those principles were not fully exemplified and carried out, until after the resurrection of the Savior, at which time all authority in such matters was committed, by the great Lawgiver, into their hands. "Go teach (disciple), all nations, teaching them to observe all things, whatsoever I have commanded you. Inasmuch then, as the apostles are thus authorized, as a matter of course, all testimony, either by precept or example, in reference to the manner in which the principles laid down by the inspiration of the Spirit, are to be carried out in the government of the church, must be drawn from the subsequent acts and writings of; those apostles. With these sources of testimony at hand, I am prepared to enter upon the subject;— and I therefore submit the following proposition:

1. It is not necessary to the existence of the church of Christ that she have a line of officers in regular succession from the apostles down to the present time—for the following reasons:

Because, upon the premises here laid down, no church can claim to be the church of Christ, but Papal Rome and her dependents.

On the principles upon which the Roman hierarchy bases its pretentions to apostolicity, it matters not as to the moral and Christian qualities of her votaries, so long as a lineal descent of officers is present with her, she justly claims the exclusive right to be called the church of Christ. Hence, she and the church of England, when charged upon with this error, openly avow, that the immoral character of their bishops, detracts not in the least from the validity of their ordinations. That such a principle is unfounded in the Scriptures, as well as the reason, must be apparent to any individual who will peruse with any degree of attention the apostolical writings. How often does the apostle John warn the seven churches of Asia, in reference to their moral conduct, lest their candlesticks be taken out of their places and where is the fitness of the language, if moral character has no part in pre serving the right to the title

There is none; and therefore, I discard the doctrine as false.

Gallatin, Tenn.   M. C. TIERS.

REMARKS ON BRO. M. C. TIERS' LETTER ON "CHURCH GOVERNMENT."

We are more than gratified that our zealous brethren are disposed to investigate the subject of church government. Indeed, it is scarcely possible a fall, free, and thorough discussion of this all-absorbing subject can fail doing good. At present, we are not disposed to put Bro. T's position to the test, for we want the whole ground occupied, but in order that Bro. T. and others may think closely and not venture too far, we will respectfully suggest a few interrogatories. Bro. T.'s position, and if we are not mistaken it is the position of most of the brotherhood, is, "That it is not necessary to the existence of the church of Christ, that she have a line of officers in regular succession from the Apostles to the present time." The reason assigned is "on the premises, no church can claim to be the church of Christ, but Papal Rome, and her dependents."

1. "Is not this saying that Papal Rome can prove the succession," and is this true? Where is the authority for the Roman Church, or her "dependents" back to the Apostles?

2. Were church officers, and regular organization necessary to the existence of the church of Christ primitively?

3. Was there ever a church of Christ planted on earth without officers, each as Gospel preachers at least?

4. Has the kingdom of Christ ever been destroyed, or have the "gates of hell prevailed against it," and if so, has not the word of the Savior failed?

5. If there has been a true church of Christ, from the Apostles, can the Bible be true? and, if there has been, was it not organized and ruled by officers; and if so, has there not been a regular succession of churches and officers from the Apostles to this day? Be careful, brethren.　T. F.

IMMORTALITY.

To the Editors of the Christian Review:

GENTLEMEN.—Looking at the letter to Timothy, I found the expression "brought light and immortality to light through the gospel." How could this be, when immortality was a common idea among the Greeks and Romans? Immortality being common among them, the Apostle could not say with truth that Christ had brought it to light. The word *aphtharsia,* should have been rendered incorruptibility. This was a thought unknown to mankind before the resurrection of Jesus. Immortality is as distinct from incorruptibility, as mortality is from corruptibility. Paul says this mortal shall put on immortality; the corruptible shall put on incorruption. The two Greek words *aphtharsis* and *athanasia* are entirely distinct; so are their significations. In the letter to the Romans the same word occurs ii. 8 v. rendered immortality. It is *aphtharam* incorruptibility. The incorruptibility of the body was an idea to be derived from revelation alone. The same remark I might apply to the immortality. of the soul. For, had it not been written that God breathed into man the *breath of life* and did we not find other scriptures to the same point, man would have been left in as much darkness on the one subject as the other. The immortality of the soul is not a matter known by the senses of man independent of revelation. The old philosophers doubtless-stole it from the Bible. The correct translation of these words takes from the materialist some portion of his trust. I sometimes hear persons quote from the Romans and argue that immortality is something to be sought for, it is not possessed by man in any sense whatever. Nothing is more-clear than this, *the soul cannot be killed.* The body is subject to death; hence Paul to Corinthians, this mortal *"phtkarton touto"* (*soma* supplied,) must put on *athanasian* immortality, *"phtharton touto" soma,* again supplied, must put on *aphthartian* incorruptibility. It is the incorruptibility and immortality of the body of which the apostle treats.

As I have said thus much I will *go* a little farther and notice some other portions that appear to give support to the materialist, observing first that the two Greek words *Pneuma* and *Psuchee* are used oftentimes interchangeably, the one for the other. But when a distinction is made, *Pneuma* represents the spirit of man which lives after the death of the body, and *Psuchee* the soul or seat of the passions common to man and brutes. The word of God divides the soul from the spirit, says Paul. In this we have an example, of the two words property distinguished. The word of God separates the spirit of man from the influence of the animal passions. The word *Psuchee* signifying the passions or senses, forms the adjective *Psuchikos,* sensual or animal. This we find used by the Apostle Jude, 19 verse, rendered sensual, or subject to the passions. It is used by Paul, Cor. 15, rendered natural, better translated animal or sensual. There is, says Paul, a *"soma Psuchikon,"* a natural or sensual body, and a *"soma pneumatiokon,"* a spiritual body. That is, there is a body in which dwell the passions or senses, which is the present corruptible body, possessed of such senses or passions as are needful for the present state, and there will be a body *Pneumatikon,* spiritual, in which the spirit will dwell, and which will be free from all the present passions or senses. Paul in another place says, "the belly for meats, and meats for the belly, but God will destroy both it and them." The Saviour says, that those who attain to the resurrection neither marry nor are given in marriage, but are like the angels of God. Hence there appears a very necessary distinction between *Psuchee* and *Pneuma* in some instances. Our present bodies possessed of those senses or passions necessary for multiplying our species, of hunger, thirst, &c., are called natural, animal or sensual bodies. Those men who are not governed by the word of God, are called sensual men, because they permit their passions to control them. The *Pneuma* or spirit of each man is oppressed and buried under the weight of the senses, and consequently remains in a state of alienation from God, never being raised by the power of truth from the dominion of passion. They are dead while they Live; they have no communion with God in the present state, and consequently must suffer an overthrow in the world to come, an everlasting destruction from the presence of the Lord and the glory of his power. This last expression is sometimes quoted to prove the annihilation of the wicked. Let us try this. Oh Israel, said one or the prophets, thou hast destroyed thyself; that is, thou hast annihilated thyself. Yet Israel existed and lived in destruction. Now if Israel lived and had a real existence in destruction, I may safely deduce this from that fact; *the wicked shall exist and suffer in everlasting destruction.* The spirit of man not being subject to corruption in that sense in which corruption is applied to the body, lives in this state apart from God, in a state of death; that is, having no union with God it cannot enjoy God or that which God's saints enjoy. Leaving this world it must remain separated from God and all those enjoyments belonging to his saints; at the resurrection, being condemned and driven away from its creator it suffers a second death—an everlasting deprivation of all connection, or the means of connexion, with God and his people. This is that destruction of soul and body of which Jesus and Paul have spoken. As Israel by not attending to God's law, had drawn on himself a separation from God or a destruction-from his presence, so the sinner by not attending to the gospel brings upon himself the sentence of condemnation, and in the world to come an eternal deprivation of, and destruction from the presence of the Lord and the glory of his power.

But the disciple in this state possessing a body with passions or senses necessary for present purposes, loses this body and possesses in the future state the body called *Pneumatikon,* wherein the spirit dwells, without any of the senses common to this state, because marrying and giving in marriage, hunger, thirst, &c., will not be known in that state. The sinner on the other hand making this world with its delights his Chief object, having lost this state with all its accompaniments, is everlastingly destroyed or deprived of all enjoyment. Hence the everlasting destruction in Hell of both soul and body, because both soul and body are eternally deprived of all enjoyment. The wicked never possess the soma Pneumatikon, because it would be of no avail, their spirits not having been rendered fit for such a habitation. It is the lot of the righteous to obtain the body spiritual, because having purified their souls or spirits in this state by obeying the Truth, they are qualified for such a habitation as the body Pneumatikon. This soma Pneumatikon, spiritual body, is incorruptible. It is this incorruptibility of body for which we seek. The spirit taking possession of this in the day of the resurrection, lives eternally in it possessed of glory, honor and eternal life. The incorruptibility of that body is contrasted with the corruptibility of this. Its immortality is contrasted with the mortality of this. Its eternal life is contrasted with the transitory and uncertain life of this. It is to this incorruptible, immortal, and eternally living body, that we look as the hope which is placed before us. How precious in the sight of God are the remains of all his saints. In hope of the Redemption of our body, I remain

    Yours,   H. T. ANDERSON.

REMISSION OF SINS—BY J. B. FERGUSON.

A pamphlet containing three discourses, by Bro. J. B. Ferguson, of Ky. published by Cameron & Fall, I have read with much interest, and take the liberty of giving an extract in the March No. of the Review, on Remission of Sins. Will the reader give the arguments of Bro. F. a careful reading?

THE EXTRAORDINARY CIRCUMSTANCES THAT SURROUNDED THE MESSIAH WHEN HE GAVE THE COMMISSION.

We have already been called to contemplate the Messiah pouring forth his soul unto death—.we have seen him numbered among the transgressors—Stricken and smitten of God and afflicted—bruised, buffeted, mocked and crucified for the sins of the world. The mighty Counsellor, the father of the Everlasting Age—he who was possessed in "the beginning of the ways of the Lord God Almighty— before the hills were or the mountains were brought forth— who is from everlasting to everlasting, was crucified, and in his crucified body is now conversing with a few timid, terrified, and grief-worn disciples. For he arose from the dead. Yes, he arose, as he declared he would. For three days the enemies of the cross had been triumphing, and the faith of the disciples, pressed down with grief was ready to fall. Surrounded by this little band, immediately after he had revealed himself to them thus bowed down —persons who had hoped "that he would have redeemed Israel," he shows to them his hands, his feet, his side, and by appeals to their senses, (the only means, by the way, of communicating information,) removes their doubts, and confirms their faith in his person and mission.

Having thus proved to them the unreasonableness of their incredulity, and shown them a just and full accordance in these circumstances with the declarations previously made them, "while he was yet with them" before his death, he proceeded to exhibit the perfect consistency of these events with the predictions concerning him in Moses, the Prophets, and Psalms. "He opened their understandings that they might understand the scriptures." He thus convinced them that every thing that had befallen him, was necessary to the development of his salvation—"That thus it behooved him to suffer, and rise from the dead the third day, *that repentance and remission of sins should be preached in his name among all nations beginning at Jerusalem."*

But there is still another circumstance that is inferred in the preceding, and which is given by Matthew in his history of the same occasion. In the conversation as recorded by this apostle, he says "*All authority is given me in Heaven and in Earth.* What a peculiar expression! Surrounded by all authority overall the creation of God. All power in Heaven! There is his royal seat— there the throne of his kingdom—and he reigns before his ancients gloriously, whilst they cast down their crowns before him, and worship the Lamb that was slain. "Angels, authorities and powers are made subject to him."

And all power in *earth.* His kingdom is not of this world—yet the heathen are his inheritance, and the uttermost part of the earth his possession—"all people, language, tongues, shall serve him"—all power

over all flesh is given to him; for he is the "Judge of the living and the dead?" How immense! how unlimited! It extends over Heaven, Earth, and Hell; angels, men and devils. He had just achieved a victory over the terrific horrors of the grave, and removed all the obstructions that the in the way of happiness—Having consecrated the grave the quiet resting place of the bodies of his sleeping saints, and having prepared it for a future bursting of its barriers, from which they may now expect a resurrection to immortal glories and honors in his everlasting age, be claims all power in Heaven and Earth; for he did not claim the power, nor the glory, honor or dignity connected with it till after his death and resurrection from the dead. When he thus declares his power, when he is just ready to give them his last parting benediction—and ascend to the throne prepared for him—surrounded by these extraordinary circumstances he proceeded to give them the commission—*"Go ye therefore."*

This power he makes the ground and reason of his commission; if he should say: If I have all power in heaven and earth; if all dominion is committed to me that all men should "honor the Son even as they honor the Father;" if I, who but lately as your redeemer, have undergone a baptism of sufferings, and sunk in death on the cross, am about to be "crowned with glory and honor at the right hand of God," and to be vested with effective might to subdue all things to myself,—I command you to go forth panoplied with this power, and make my salvation known to "all nations?" My respected hearers, here is an important point; and I would have you particularly to observe it. Here is the place where, and time when, we are to look for the laws that are to govern his people, and the persons who are to execute them for their benefit. Here we are to learn how we obtain remission of sins, and all the concomitant blessings, resulting from initiation into the favor of God. This being the case, let us now candidly inquire, *by what meant we may receive the remission of sins and be assured of that great blessing?*

But that this subject may be still more clearly before you—and that when we shall here find an answer to this important question, we may be assured the answer embraces us, let us first call to mind one other fact, viz: *That up to this* time, *in all the eventful and extraordinary life of the Messiah, he had not laid down the conditions upon which you and I could be saved from our sins!* True, to some two or three persons he imparted this gracious blessing. He had said to a paralytic, "Thy sins be forgiven thee— and to a woman that touched the border of his garment thy faith hath cured thee—and to a malefactor expiring at his side, "This day shaft thou be with me in Paradise."† But these were individual cases, intended to show his power to the conviction of his disciples. They were performed too during his *personal* ministry—and the persons blessed received the blessings from his *own lips* delivered in *propria persona.* They form exceptions to a general rule, as the translation of Enoch and Elijah does to the universal misfortune of death, only these cases happened before the rule was laid down. As well then, might we expect to be translated to heaven, as were Enoch and Elijah, as be saved as was the thief on the cross, the paralytic, or the woman who touched the garment of Messiah.

How vain, how worse than vanity, is that reasoning that would make these cases the rule by which we are to be cleansed from sin—cases as we will see *that occurred before the reign of Heaven was set up!*

But we have approached the last act in Messiah's life—in which life we *now repeat with emphasis he never instituted a plan of salvation* unless he did it here. Did he here institute it? If he did not then was he not the Messiah, for it bad been said of him that he would "save his people *from their sins;*" a distinguishing characteristic of his institution was to be "their sins and iniquities I will remember no more."‡ The question then recurs with double force, Did Jesus here, before his ascension into heaven, establish an institution "for the remission of sins?"We say he did. Here the text, "Thus it is written, and thus it behooved the Messiah to suffer and to rise from the dead the third day; *and that repentance and remission of sins should be preached in his name among all nations beginning at Jerusalem."*

---

*Matt. ix. 2 and 22. †Luke xxii. 43. ‡Matt. i, 21: Heb. viii. 12.

How free! how full! how boundless! All nations! the whole creation! We are made to exclaim with the poet,

> "How free and boundless is the grace
> Of our redeeming God,
> Published to Greek and Jew
> And men of every blood."

The question is here answered—and the difficulty here solved; and remission of Sins is proclaimed "in *the name of Jesus Christ.*"

IN THE NAME OF JESUS CHRIST! A very peculiar expression in our text— and a very prominent one in all the living Oracles. For says one in a certain place "To Him give all the prophets witness that *through his name* whosoever believeth in Him shall receive the remission of sins;" and again, "there is no other name given under heaven whereby you can be saved."*

But the enquiry still continues, *how do I enter that name?* Matthew relating the same conversation explains the whole: "Go teach all nations, *baptizing into the name,*" &c. Then it is by baptism the taught or believer, enters the name of Christ. Yes; for says Mark, who also gives an account of the same transaction, "Go preach the gospel (the death, burial and resurrection of Messiah, 1 Cor. xv. 1-5) to every creature, he that believeth and is baptized shall he saved."

Then it is clear that according to the arrangement here made—an arrangement too, made for "*all nations,*" under all the extraordinary sanctions of the extraordinary circumstances, that surrounded the Lord when he established the order—that in order to "obtain the remission of sins," we must enter his name; and in order to enter his name we must "be baptized into it." Yes, says an Apostle, "we are all the children of God by faith in Christ Jesus; for as many of us as have been *baptized into Jesus Christ* have put on Christ." * * And if we be Christ's (by this faith and baptism) then are we Abraham's seed and heirs according to the promise."† And from the very words of the promise it is clear that we must be *in* the promised seed; "for *in thee* and IN THY SEED, shall all the families of the earth be blessed."‡ And herein is exhibited the beauty and force of such addresses as the following, directed to the baptized into Christ: "All the saints who are in Christ Jesus, who are at Philippi;" to the saints and faithful brethren *in* Christ who are at Colosse;" "the church of the Thessalonians which is *in* God our Father, and *in* the Lord Jesus Christ."§ This peculiar relationship in Christ Jesus, was not a matter of uncertainty or doubt, but of the most explicit knowledge. Hence that forcible address of Paul to the Romans, sixth chapter— "*Know ye not* that so many of you as were baptized *into Jesus Christ* were baptized *into his death.*" Thus were they buried and raised with him in baptism—planted in the likeness of his death, that they might also be in the likeness of his resurrection: and though they had been the servants of sin, (v. 18) yet by obedience from the heart to the form of doctrine delivered to them they had become free from sin.

But I am anticipating my subject. For the purpose then of satisfying you on this and other important matters connected with this "last charge," I shall answer the following important queries, in the solution of which we will be made to see plainly the means ordained by heaven for the remission of sins.

I. Who were the persons appointed to proclaim salvation to "*all nations?*"

II. At what place were they to commence the proclamation?

III. At what time?

IV. How did they discharge their duty in its proclamation?

But a superficial glance will show that if we can, by the unerring aid of inspiration, ascertain the place where, and the time when the system of salvation was to be exhibited and the persons authorized to exhibit it, we Will be at no loss to find the means which heaven in his benignity has conferred for the remission of the past sins of every individual of our race. To the inquiry then:

I. *Who were the persons?* This is answered emphatically in the text—"*Ye are witnesses of these things.*" *Ye, my apostles,* to whom now I delegate all authority or power in Heaven and in Earth. Again, John xx. 21, "As my Father (says Messiah on the same illustrious occasion)—has sent *me* even *so send*

*Acts x. 43, and iv. 12. †Gal. iii. 26-29. ‡Gen. xxii. 18. §Phil. i. 1; Col. i. 1: Thes. i. 1.

I you;. . . . . . whosoever sins ye remit, they are remitted unto them; whosoever sins ye retain, they are retained." Again, Mark represents the Messiah as thus addressing these men—"Go ye into all the world . . . . .and these signs shall follow them that believe, in my name shall they cast out devils; they shall speak with new tongues; they shaill take up serpents; and if they drink any deadly thing, it shall not hurt them; they snail lay hands on the sick and they shall recover." Now take these declarations in connection with that of Matthew, where the Lord is represented as sending them forth by virtue of "all power in Heaven and in Earth," and we not only see who were me persons that were appointed to set up his kingdom, and from whom we must learn the terms of salvation; but we are also assured, from the immense and almost unlimited power vested in them as *the sent* or *apostles* of Messiah, that the master intended that no one should or could fill their place.

Such was the delegated authority possessed by these illustrious ones, that we find them performing even "greater works" than were performed by the *Messiah*. They healed the sick—cleansed the unclean—rebuked demons— raised the dead—and the very shadow of them in passing by relieved the afflicted of their sufferings. They acted in the stead of Christ—were his vicegerents and ambassadors—spoke as they were allowed of God being put in trust with the gospel, so much so, that it is only by this means that we can determine the spirit of truth from the spirit of error.*

Such were the men ordained by God to publish the gospel to all nations; through whom, he set up his kingdom; whom he appointed the stewards of all the laws and regulations that should govern it till the end of time; persons in every way qualified for the responsible station they occupied, having been with him from the time he was baptized till his reception into glory.

CORRESPONDENCE BETWEEN A. KENDRICK AND B. W. STONE.
From the Christian Journal.

ELD. B. W. STONE :

Dear Bro.—In the late discussion between N. L. Rice, (the Presbyterian champion,) and Alex. Campbell, Mr. Rice argued or said. that his opponent held in fellowship in his church, Unitarians who made our Savior a mere man, a created being;—and who openly denied the divinity of Christ. He seemed willing to drive Bro. Campbell from the fellowship of Christians, and of course from Heaven, because he would not drive you from the church on earth, and, of course, to hell—as he always gave your name in proof. Now, my dear brother, it is a fact of great solemnity, that the Presbyterians held you in their bosoms when your faith and piety were no better than they are now—and that now they are willing to denounce you, refuse the cup of blessing to you and even consign you to endless torment, in order to asperse bro. Campbell, and destroy the influence of our pious teaching. But it seems to me they are not satisfied with this, but willing to resort to willful falsehood and slander. I therefore hope you will state once more, before you leave the stage of action, though it be the thousandth time, that you never taught any such sentiments; and call on Mr. Rice to take back the slander. I hope you will publish your statement in the Christian Messenger, and send it to Mr. Rice at Paris, Ky.— Then we shall know that he willfully falsifies when he thus represents you, as he has been doing through this State. I do think it is due to yourself and to the cause you have so nobly and so successfully plead.

May the Lord preserve you and your posthumous influence from the aspersions of wicked and unreasonable men. A. KENDRICK.

REPLY—*Dear Bro. Kendrick:*—Bro. Campbell has to suffer on my account, what I have had long to suffer for him. He is malevolently assailed for holding me in fellow ship, for the reasons you have stated; and I nave been with equal malevolence assailed for holding him in fellowship, because of his supposed

---

*Acts ix. 32-42; 2 Cor. v. 18-21; Gal. i. 1; 1 Thess.; 2—passim. 1 John iv. 6.

errors. I have feared the real object of our opponents is, to divide and conquer, and not because they love the truth, as it is in Jesus. The most zealous against us I generally find to be those who possess the least of the spirit of Christianity. Would our opposers love brother Campbell more and willingly hold him in fellowship, were be to repudiate me! No such thing. They care, as little for him as they do for me. Though they fear him more, they do not love him better.

I am now on the eve of time, busily arranging my affairs for eternity. The vessel which is to bear me to my eternal destination across the dark ocean, is now in view. Soon I shall bid farewell to earth and be borne to another world. What I shall say may be considered as the words of a dying man, for which a speedy account must be rendered.

Mr. Rice is now in the acme of life; and in the confidence of his learning and natural endowments, feels his importance, and vaunts aloud in the presence of men. He takes the liberty to detract from others what he never gave, and to build for himself an indestructible monument of fame. Should he live to my age it is hoped his mind will be mellowed by years, that he will remember with sorrow his present course. But to the point:—

You inform me, that Mr. Rice publicly charged me with being a Unitarian, who made our Savior a mere man—a created being, and who openly denied the divinity of Christ.

Now I reply, for the last time (so now I think,) that at no time of my long life did I ever believe these doctrines—I never taught them either publicly or privately, from the pulpit or press. I am bold to say, no man ever heard them from me, or read them in any of the essays I have written and published on the doctrine of Christ. How Mr. Rice obtained his information, I can only conjecture. He must have been very confident of its correctness, or as a christian, or gentleman, he would have not dared thus to charge me before so numerous a crowd of people, and I not present. It looks like slander and backbiting, of which, one would suppose, Mr. Rice—the high-minded Mr. Rice was incapable.

His evidence for believing and publishing these things of me may be *fama clamosa;* (but what man of brains will admit her testimony, as often false as true?) or he may have believed them by detaching an expression from my essays written and published. For example, he may have seen in my writings this quotation, "There is one Mediator between God and man, the man Christ Jesus." Ah! excitingly he may have said, I have now caught him: he is verily a Unitarian, for he calls the Son of God a man, the man Christ Jesus— he must then believe him to be a created being. If Mr. Rice knows no better, we inform him that these are the words of the inspired Paul. If by them I am condemned a heretic, so is Paul; but Paul never believed that Christ was a mere man—a created being; and by him have I been taught to believe the same.

It is well known by all who know me that I differed from the Presbyterians on their speculations in their confession of faith on the Trinity, when I was a Presbyterian; Yet was I unanimously ordained by the Presbytery, and held in communion by them. I was never charged with these things until I withdrew from them.

A person by reading the Scriptures may, by detached texts and inferences, come to the conclusion, that Unitarianism and all its doctrines are taught in that book. This thousands of very intelligent men have done. It cannot be strange, if Mr. Rice with his ingenuity and prejudice against a humble uninspired man, should by the same means come to, the conclusions he has publicly stated against me. I should not wonder if he, by the same means, should prove any Trinitarian writer (those who wrote the confession of faith not excepted,) to be Unitarian. Even Professor Stewart can see but a light shade of difference between the notion of a derived being, (as the orthodox view the Son of God to be,) and of a created being, as the Arians assert he is. To quibbling there, is no end. I have long since viewed the practice as useless, and dangerous, and leave it to those who are fond of trifles.

I do not expect to change the mind of Mr. Rice by anything I have said or can say; for he boasted, I am informed, that he was dyed in the wool and therefore unchangeable. He will still affirm what he has said against me, manure all evidence. A noted physician of Spain had introduced a system of physic, upon which he had practiced and taught through life. When he became old, one of his former students advised him before he died to make a recantation of the system, as it was now found to be wrong, and injurious to the community. Sir, said the old doctor, let all Spain perish first; for I have written and published it. So may Mr. Rice say, let Stone's name be for ever blasted, and infamy be for ever attached to his character, before I retract, for I have said and published it to the world.

For the sake of others I will briefly state my belief on those doctrines with which I am charged.

1. "With us there is but One God, the Father, of Whom ate all things, and we in him, (*eis outon,* for him). 1st. Cor. viii., 6.

2. 'And (there is) one Lord, Jesus Christ, by whom are all things, and we by him, (*di'autou*) 1st. Cor., viii., 7.

From these texts I have concluded that the Father is the *but one God*— called by Jesus himself 'the only true God.' John, xvii., 5. This one God the Father it distinguished from all other beings in the universe by this attribute, 'of him are all things.' In the Greek it is *exhou,* of, or out of whom are all things. This is conceded by all to mean that he was the efficient or prime cause of all things in the universe, In the following verse Jesus Christ is called the one Lord, besides Whom there is not another in the universe possessing the same attributes here ascribed to him, as 'by whom are all things, and we by him? In the Greek it reads *di'hou,* by whom. This attribute *dia,* with the genitive, is no where ascribed to the Father, the one God; for it means the instrumental cause, as every Grecian will admit, and therefore cannot apply to the Father, the prime and efficient cause of all things.

3. According to this common sense exegesis, I believe that 'God created all things by (*dia*) Jesus Christ? Heb. i., 2. 'That he created the worlds and heavens, with all the inhabitants of heaven, whether they be angels, principalities, or powers, all were made by him,' (*di'autou,*) the instrumental cause, not *up' autou* the prime cause; this ('*upo*) can only apply to the Father in this *case*; and all things were made for him, (*eis autou,*) as being the heir of all things. By the Son the Father rules the universe; for the Apostle adds, By him (*di'autou*) all things consists i. e., are kept in being and order, by him, the Lord and maker of all.

By the Son, or Word, the Father spake to the world all the words of salvation, for 'God in these last days has spoken unto us by (*dia*) his Son,' by whom (*di'outou*) he saves, and will at last 'judge the world in righteousness:' and (*dia*) by whom he Wrought miracles, wonders and signs, for the confirmation of truth.

These undisputed truths, so clearly revealed naturally were linked with another important truth; seeing all things were made by him, therefore he "was before all things."—He that descended is the same also that ascended up where he was before, above all angels, principalities, and powers, into heaven itself. Just before he ascended, the Son prayed to the Father to glorify him with himself, with the glory he had with him before the world was. This, with many other texts, proves that the Son, or Logos, existed in glory with the Father before the world was—before all created things in the universe; without him was not one thing made that is made.

This glorious being is the Son of God, the only begotten Son of God, and therefore divine—the children of men are human, because begotten and born of human parents—so is the Son of God divine, because begotten of the Divine Father.

I have rejected the speculations respecting Jews by many, which rejection is the sum, or foundation of the heresy attached to me by the self-styled orthodox. The Jews concluded that Christ had made himself God and equal to God. because he said I am the Son of God. Though our Lord refuted the inference of duality of Gods in very plain language, yet the Jews would not open their ears to conviction: but accused him of blasphemy, for saying he was the Son of God; for which he was put to death. Christians have adopted their speculation, that he is the one God, equal to the Father, because he called himself the son of God.

Some say that he is the eternal son of God—this unscriptural and contradictory phrase I have also rejected as a mere speculation, and so have many of the orthodox, and evangelicals. Why are not they charged with unitarianism too? These latter say, he was never the Son of God, until born of Mary; the holy thing which is born of thee shall be called the Son of God. From this text they argue that he was never Son before, but that holy thing, when born, shall be called, in future, the Son of God, and was therefore, never Son before. This reasoning will prove fatal to the whole system. Isaiah ix, 6, 'For unto us a child is born, unto us a son is given—and his name shall be called Wonderful, Counsellor, the Mighty God, the Everlasting Father.' From the argument above it follows that he never was such till born—was never mighty God till he was born; for then, in. future he shall be called such. Would it not be better to omit these speculations, and confine ourselves to the language of scripture on this doctrine? I think; and have but little interest in them.

4. I believe the Father sent the Son to be the Savior of the world, that whosoever believeth on him might not perish but have everlasting life—I believe that all power and authority in heaven and earth are given unto him, and that he is able to save to the uttermost all that come to God by him—That in him are all the treasures of wisdom and knowledge, that it pleased the Father that in him should all fullness well —the fullness of the Godhead—the fullness of the Spirit—the fullness of grace and salvation—When we see him, we see the Father —his image, his character, his glory and perfection.—Let me lose life before I would detract from my Lord one ray of his glory. To him that sitteth on the throne, and to the Lamb be everlasting praise. Amen.—*Christian Mess.*

STATE OF THE CHURCH AT SYCAMORE.

DEAR BRETHREN:—The state of the church here is prosperous—our number the past year was thirty-five, fourteen additions during the year. Six removed and given letters of recommendation—one excluded, which reduced our number to twenty-eight: thirteen males, six whites and seven colored; fifteen, females, eleven whites and four colored.

We have two Elders and one Deacon, no Evangelist, nor are we in the bounds of any that I know of.

We meet every first day of the week for preaching and breaking the loaf; most of the members are very punctual in attending, not deterred from doing their duty by any inclemency or the weather, or any other circumstance, when practicable for them to meet. We continue to grow in grace and in the knowledge of our Lord and Saviour Jesus Christ—looking for the day when our Lord shall come and find us doing his will. If we know our duty, happy are we if we do it.   Yours in hope of eternal glory,

JOSEPH D. DARROW

Davidson County, Tenn., January 31st, 1844.

STATE OF THE CHURCH AT HOLLY SPRINGS.

HONORED BRO. FANNING:—Last Lord's day and Monday following, I attended a meeting near Tulahoma—where, chiefly through the instrumentality of our beloved Bro. Davenport, a church has just been constituted after the Apostolic model—its constitution and laws, that plainest of books, the dear Blessed Bible. Nearly all the members, some 36 in number, are from the Baptists. I delivered a discourse on Union on Lord's day—at evening addressed, aliens on the rewards, punishments, honors, blessings, and the laws of the New Covenant— showed that salvation was based upon conditions within the power of every go and daughter of humanity to comply with—that God has done his part, and now the standing invitation is to all, "Come—draw near—and the reward is obtained." Next day addressed the church on the duties of Christians as members of the body and as individuals. The Baptist preacher is bandying the word "*heresy*" around there very adroitly—but he never once made his appearance while we were present. The two-edged sword cuts both ways with its edges and pierces with the point—5 more nave confessed since my return to Holly Springs. The work still goes on. Farewell.   W. S. SPEER.

Holly Springs, Miss. February 7, 1844.

CHRISTIAN REVIEW.

VOL. I.   NASHVILLE, APRIL, 1844.   NO. IV.

CHURCH ORGANIZATION.

In the March No. of the Review, I stated, as a proposition to be subsequently proved that a church of God never had been formed, and could not be, without official acts and divine organization.

In the present No., I wish to present for reflection the importance of officers in all Christian communities. The history of the church and the world, fails to give any account of a church of Christ having been established or put in order without officers regularly appointed for that purpose. The simple and all-powerful Gospel never did constitute a church without the aid of an officer denominated a preacher. It is a truth not to be forgotten, that no one has become a Christian by merely reading, praying, or singing, or without the assistance of one of God's servants. It is a wise arrangement in the Divine economy, to suspend the conversion of the world both upon the influence of the church, and the efforts of the rebellious. The Savior said, "Go and disciple all nations," or "Preach the Gospel" for the salvation of mankind. All the conversions, from Pentecost to this day, have been made by the word of God in the hands of poor frail man.

The officer whose particular province is to convert others, is denominated, in the New Testament, Evangelist, Minister of the word, or, in the common style of the age. Preacher of the Gospel. A minister of the word is the first and most important officer in the church of God. To comprehend the subject fully and clearly, I will first ATTEMPT TO SHOW HOW PREACHERS ARE MADE, and Sadly, THEIR WORK OR OFFICE.

There is no truth more palpable in the word of God, than the position that every servant of Christ is divinely *called* to fill his station in the church. The Holy Spirit "made overseers" anciently, and no doubt deacons and deaconesses; and there is as little doubt with me, that the spirit makes officers at this day, just as he did primitively. I would respectfully ask, if the spirit, in the days of the Apostles, made officers by speaking to men? or was it by some deep impression, without words or ideas? or was it by his directions? When a man hearkens to the voice of the spirit, and follows his dictates, is he not called by the spirit, and led by the spirit? If the spirit calls and commissions independent of the word of God, then indeed it may be true, that the spirit of Almighty God has called Joe Smith and his brother apostles, and the thousands of ignorant, pert quacks of preachers who profess to have calls above revelation at this day.

Primitively, no one could preach the Gospel unless he had been specially called, qualified, and sent of Heaven. The reason is very obvious: the Gospel had not been given, and, per consequence, there was no written word. No man, therefore, could preach the gospel, who was not inspired with the very words to be delivered. For this purpose the Savior chose twelve, who were called Apostles and Ambassadors of Christ, and were the "'earthen vessels" containing the treasure of God's word. Through these men he made all his revelations known to the world; and since their death, there have been no men on earth to stand in their shoes. Notwithstanding the boasted pretentions of thousands, no one of the number has been able to speak a word of truth by direct inspiration, or exhibit the least "sign of an apostle." Even Timothy and Titus were not inspired, had no direct commission from above, and were compelled to study and "give themselves to reading" to gain information. Not so with the particularly called of God; they were "not to premeditate" or think what they were to say; for the "word was given them in the self-same hour."— Now the world is filled with professed ambassadors of Christ, many of whom cannot speak their own vernacular tongue with propriety; and not one of these latter-day apostles in fifty can tell how many books there are in the Bible, or the objects of any one of them.

The church of Christ is a school, in which all the pupils are required to exert themselves to their utmost in advancing the cause of the Saviour. All are required to perform service in proportion to natural and acquired ability. Some are able to exhort, others to wait as servants, and others to preach the word— God has ordained that each shall act the part he is most capable of performing. The next and most important question is, to ascertain who shall decide upon the qualifications of each. All who profess direct calls and inspiration, (and they constitute the overwhelming majority,) pretend they FEEL an *inward, silent* call, and none have a right to dispute the divinity of their mission. Others, with more reason, and I think much more Scripture on their side, profess to believe God has appointed the church to decide on qualifications. Hence, the qualifications of each officer are clearly laid down, and the saints have the divine right to "try apostles," and "prove them liars," when they have not the signs. Paul said to Timothy, "The things you have heard and learned of me, the same commit to faithful men, who shall be able to teach others also."— When one *proves* himself qualified as an Evangelist, he is appointed or set apart to the office by *prayer, fasting,* and *imposition* of the hands of the Presbytery. This was the ancient order, and I have found no example of any one being appointed a minister of the Gospel without this process. Mind, there is no instance on record of Evangelists appointing others, but the authority is of and from the church.

2d. Next, the office of the Gospel minister demands serious attention— His employments are various. It is his province, first, to preach the word; secondly, he sets in order churches; and, thirdly, he ordains bishops and deacons, and takes the general superintendence of the churches. Paul traveled much, and planted many churches after being sent from the church at Antioch, and on his revisiting his friends, he ordained Elders in every city, and felt, indeed, that the "care of all these churches" was upon him.

The work of the Evangelist fully suggests his qualifications, but at a future time I may give this subject some attention. I have stated, that Evangelists are the appointed messengers of Heaven, to set in order the things wanted in churches, and ordain Elders and Deacons; and, as I am aware this is disputed ground, I will submit an interrogatory or two, which I hope will find a place in the minds of the brethren.

1. Is there any example in the New Testament, of a church's setting itself in order independent of an Evangelist?

2. Is there any authority for a church's appointing its own Bishops and Deacons, without the assistance of a preacher? Write, my beloved brethren, now, or forever after hold your peace.   T. F.

THE STUDY OF THE BIBLE.

That the Bible is a good book, none will deny; and that it is a light to guide the wayfarer from this to a better World, all Christians rejoice to believe. But notwithstanding the momentous importance of a knowledge of God's book, there are few who have studied it, or know how to study it profitably. I have never yet seen the country, that I did not find anxious enquirers after truth, who knew not where nor what to read in order to attain the knowledge of salvation.

Christians contend the Bible is a revelation from the Maker of all things, but the objects of the different portions differ exceedingly, and unless the student first gain information on the objects of each portion, all his reading will be to little purpose. For a better solution of this point, permit me to say, it is as important to study the different portions of the Scriptures, with different objects in view, as it is, to use treatises on English Grammar, Arithmetic, Botany, Philosophy and Chemistry, to gain information on each of these sciences. It is not usual for teachers to adopt a system of Botany or Chemistry, to give a knowledge of Arithmetic or Surveying, and it is equally as unsuitable to appropriate Scriptures addressed to Christians, to Sinners; or those to Jews, to the disciples of the Lord Jesus Christ.

The whole Bible is recognized as the book of God; but it is composed of various revelations, made at different times, to different individuals, and for various purposes. The two grand divisions of the Bible are the Old and New Testaments. In the Old Testament there are thirty-nine books, and these books constitute three grand chapters. The first is a "CHAPTER OF HISTORY," composed of eighteen books; the second chapter is made up of the Psalms of David, Proverbs, Song of Solomon, Ecclesiastes, and Lamentations of Jeremiah; and the third chapter is composed of sixteen books of Prophesy. The first chapter is to be read as a plain history of the world, detailing events for about 300 years, in relation to which period, there is no other authentic history. The second chapter is composed of the Songs of David, and other poetical effusions of great value to all Christians; and the third chapter, of course, is to be read as predictions of God's Spirit with regard to the Jewish nation, and the rise and progress of the Christian institution. If these divisions are always before the mind of the reader, it will be an easy matter to comprehend much of the Old Testament. The New Testament is rightly divided into four distinct chapters. The first chapter is composed of the books of Matthew, Mark, Luke and John, and they constitute the Gospel of *Christ.* If the reader should wish to know the facts upon which the Christian fabric rests, he will gain all the information in this chapter, necessary to beget faith, change the heart, and produce supreme love to God. Too often speculators, and wild theorists have supposed foreign, collateral and extraneous evidence was important to produce faith, when in fact the Gospel recorded by these four faithful and inspired men, contains all the testimony in the world to produce faith. But as faith alone, never did, and never was intended to save the soul, a chapter was written by the finger of God, which may emphatically be called, the CHAPTER OF CONVERSIONS. If the enquirer wish to know how to become a Christian, he will find the Acts of Apostles, the only book of conversions, by the authority of Christ, on earth; and though he may read every other book in the Bible, and neglect this, he will utterly fail learning how persons anciently become the adopted sons and daughters of the Most-high. The fact is, no man can become a citizen of Christ's kingdom, who does not understand the conversions recorded in the Acts of Apostles.

The third chapter of the New Testament, is composed of twenty-one Epistles, all addressed to Christians, and may be appropriately styled the "CHAPTER OF THE CHRISTIAN GRACES AND MANNERS." To apply these writings to any but saints is doing great injustice to the order of God's teaching. But by carefully studying them, the disciples of Christ may have the means of "growing in grace and the knowledge of the truth."

The fourth and last chapter of the New Testament and the Bible, is the "CHAPTER OF REVOLUTIONS." There is but one book in this chapter, viz: the "Revelations of John" the beloved disciple. In this chapter, the revolutions of church, and the world are described in a marvelous manner. To be sure, in this book, there are some things hard to be understood, and it may be, for aught that I know to the contrary, these grand revolutions will be themes for profound study and deep meditation in the world to come.

Students of the Bible who will adopt this arrangement of divine things, can scarcely fail of learning the truths, which are able to save the soul. T. F.

"PURE SPEECH."

DEAR BROTHER:—In No. 2d, vol. 1st of the CHRISTIAN REVIEW, under the head of "Pure Speech," I notice Bro. T. F. give a caution to his brethren in good time and place. With regard to certain words in use, viz: Orthodoxy, Trinity, Total Depravity, &c., I have no doubt brother F. is correct in condemning them. But the word REFORMATION I have used, and still use it, intending to convey the idea of amendment; though I am not so wedded as to hold it as sacred as life. I know Bible words will convey Bible ideas. Will brother Fanning say a little more on the subject, and tell us his objection to it? for I am really at a loss, from his suggestions, to know what the word Reformation does mean.   C. CURLEE.

Cannon County, Tennessee.

REMARKS—I am truly glad the brethren are disposed to seek the old land marks, and study a pure speech. I am not at all astonished, that my worthy Bro. Curlee, should be somewhat startled at my remarks on the term Reformation. I use it, as well as brother C.; but I endeavor to use it in no other sense than that which is indicated by Paul, Heb. ix, 10. The word in the original language, is not the common one for Reformation. It is *Diorthosis,* which is from *orthos,* pure, correct, straight; and this is also the root of the word *orthodoxy.* Hence the words Reformation, Orthodoxy, (not modern) and pure Christianity, are terms of similar import. Either of these may be applied to the religion established by Jesus Christ; but it would not be correct to denominate the improvements on Popery made by Luther, Calvin, or Wesley,   "THE

Reformation.''   It   might answer to say, A reformation by Luther, or A reformation of "Father Matthew," the apostle of temperance, or any other man; but, to speak of something which had its origin since the days of the Apostles, as THE reformation, is true in no sense. To speak of the "current reformation," as something which is but 20 or 30 years old, and endeavor to designate the Christian institution by it, manifests either woeful deficiency in knowledge, or a disregard for the ideas of God's spirit.

I intend to be understood assaying, if we are the disciples of the Saviour, we should profess the old religion, which began eighteen hundred years since; but Heaven forbid we should profess a modem religion, and cloak it with old and honorable names! If we use the term Reformation, as denoting something new, we should follow the example of our sectarian neighbors, and say, "OUR reformation," "our church," "our Zion," "our cause."

The reader will observe, that, notwithstanding the term Reformation is scriptural, it may be used in a sense differing from its original import; and then, so for from being correct, it is opposed to the truth of God.

Will the brethren take these small matters into consideration?   T. F.

―――――――――――

"MESSENGER OF GLAD TIDINGS."

What think you, reader, is the meaning of this "Messenger" of pretended "glad tidings?" Anciently, the message of glad tidings, consisted in the good news of a Saviour's birth; and the appearance of one who would reward believers with everlasting happiness; but not so with this "Message of Glad Tidings." This latter day message sends the wicked rejoicing to heaven. Perhaps, the discrepancy originates from the birth place of the two Messengers; one originated at Jerusalem, in Judea, and the other at Wetumpka, Ala. The "Messenger of Glad Tidings," boldly advocates the restoration of men from hell, the destruction of hell, and the universal salvation of every rebel in creation.

Amongst all the doctrines taught in the nineteenth century, that of offering eternal happiness to those not at all qualified for heaven, is most preposterous and God-dishonoring. Where, indeed, is the importance of the Bible, the use of virtue, or truth, if thieves and robbers are to be companions with Abraham, Isaac and Jacob. Are men in earnest who advocate such absurdities? Tell us, Mr. Shehane, if you are not jesting, when you talk about the heavenly happiness of the finally impenitent? Pause sir, I beg you, and let no undue influences drive you to such a desperate conclusion.   T. F.

―――――――――――

HOW TO WRITE CLEARLY AND FORCIBLY.

A noble Lord once said, "A man fully possessed of his subject, and confident of his cause, may always write with vigor and effect, if he can get over the temptation of writing finely, and really confine himself to the strong and dear exposition of the matter he has to bring forward. Half of the affection and offensive pretensions we meet with in authors arises from a want of matter, and the other half from a paltry ambition of being eloquent, and ingenious out of place." These remarks hold equally true in reference to speakers. If men have subjects, arguments and facts, on which they are willing to rely, and can be satisfied with a plain style, success will be certain. The earnest conviction of the truth of any proposition discussed, is very important either with a speaker or writer.

LETTER FROM J. CREATH, JR.

To the Editors of the Christian Review:—

BRETHREN EDITORS:—I have received the two first numbers of the CHRISTIAN REVIEW. I was not at home when they came to hand. I have been preaching in the territory of Iowa for the last five weeks, and have just returned home. Our cause is springing into existence in that great territory, which lies north state of Missouri. We received twenty-five persons. That territory presents a great and an extensive field for evangelical operations. It is three hundred miles in length, and two hundred and fifty in width; extending from the Mississippi river to the Missouri river on the west. Great efforts are making to plant the bitter and poisonous sectarian trees in that fertile land. I have only glanced at the first number of the REVIEW.

We will for the present offer a few thoughts on the words simple and simplicity, and then apply them to Christianity and to her handmaids or daughters, the sciences. First, the English word *simple,* is derived from the Latin *simplex.* This Latin word is compounded of two words—*sine,* without, and *pliea.,* a fold; and properly signifies, plain, honest, uncompounded, unmixed with any thing else—like clear, transparent honey comb or ice held up to the sun, you can see through it—it is unmixed with any other substance. It is what it appears to be. Simplex stands in opposition to complex, derived from *complied,* to fold together, to make or twist one rope or strand out of many ropes. This is the radical or etymological meaning of the word simple. Every word, like every honest person, has but one name. It is as improper for one word to have forty meanings, as for one man to have forty names, or forty wives. Some persons are nick-named, and some words are used secondarily, figuratively, or by way of accommodation. Words, like names, are used to distinguish one idea from another; and names, to distinguish one man, tree, horse, or thing, from another. The word simple, when applied to men, or used figuratively, means innocent, harmless, without disguise—one who has no by ends in view, has no folds nor convolutions like a snake's coil. He is as clear and as unmixed in his course, as light is unmixed with darkness. God rejoices to meet with and bless every such person, although such persons are very unfashionable in this world of twistification.

Downright honesty and plain dealing have almost *bid farewell* to this world of folds and dishonesty. Hence, the word simple now means, homely, homespun, mean, silly, foolish. This reasoning will apply to many other words, as all words originally conveyed one idea, covered one act, and only one. The word sit covers the act of sitting down, and cannot cover the act of standing or walking; nor can the words stand and walk cover the act of sitting. The Greek words bapto and baptizo, in the days of Paul, were as well understood as the words simplex and complex were in the days of Cicero, the Roman orator. These words, in the New Testament times, as definitely, as logically, and as infallibly meant, to dip, to cover, to plunge or immerse a person or thing in water or some other liquid, as simplex meant clear, unmixed; or as complex meant to compound or to mix many things together in the days of Cicero; or as the words sit, stand, definitely cover these acts and no other acts. But, in these compound days of mixed religions, *bapto* and *baptizo* mean, to sprinkle, to pour, to apply water in any way that our conscience calls for. We have the mode of baptism by immersion, pouring, sprinkling; which is as good logic as to say, we have the mode of sitting by walking and the mode of walking by sitting. We have the mode of sprinkling by pouring, and the mode of immersion by sprinkling, &c. This is worse than the coils of a Boa Constrictor, or than the three days of darkness that came upon the Jews in Egypt. Is this simplicity, honesty, clearness? Or is it complexity, confusion, darkness? In the days of the Apostles, and for the two or three first centuries, *bapto* and *baptize* were as certainly understood to mean immerse or to plunge head and ears in water, as the English words, sit and walk are now understood to cover these acts and no others. Why are these words now mysterious and dark? Because the existence of the Roman Catholic institution, and of all paido-baptist churches, depends upon sprinkling a few drops of water on the face of a sleeping babe. Sprinkling babes is the ground and pillar of Popery. The salaries, the power, and authority, and pride of its advocates, are all at stake. Can a person be obligated to do what has not been clearly revealed to him? If God has not clearly revealed to man, that he must be sprinkled, then he is not bound to do it, and so of the other two actions. Is there any positive injunction, in either the Old or New Testament, left in darkness, and at our discretion, besides baptism? No. Then baptism is an anomaly, a riddle. If God had not told Adam plainly what tree he should not touch, he could not have been punished for disobeying him. He spake plainly to Noah, to Abraham, to Moses, to the Jews, to the Prophets, to the Apostles and Christians, in every case, except baptism. And why not in every case? For the reasons above given. By leaving out omega, the last letter in the Greek alphabet, (which answers to the English letter O,) from baptizo, and substituting a Roman *c* in its place, we have baptize, (instead of immerse,) which is neither Greek, Latin, nor English, but is a word as pliant as a nose of wax; it will turn three ways without breaking. How many sermons have we in the gospels and Acts, on the "three modes of baptism"? How many sermons did Christ and the Apostles deliver on the five points of Dort, to wit: particular election, particular redemption, special operations before faith, in order to produce faith in the elect, total depravity, and final perseverance of the saints? Not one. How many on the Trinity? Not one. If any one wishes to understand what Moshiem calls the beautiful simplicity of Christianity, let him study the New Testament, especially the Acts of the Apostles. All institutions and sciences are simple in their origin. There are a few great fundamental principles running through the system, and are to it what the Mississippi is to this country, and swallows all the rest. The Mosaic institution, as expressed in the five books of Moses, is a simple institution. It is built upon love to God and man. Medicine was simple in its origin; so was jurisprudence, or law. But how complex now are these systems. Christianity is a simple institution. The first great article of all revelation and religion is, that there is one living, true, and everlasting God, the creator of all things. Secondly, that Jesus Christ is his son, and the Savior of the world; that he died for our sins, was buried, and arose from the dead the third day, according to the scriptures. Then, to believe these great facts, repent, and turn from our sins, and be immersed for the remission of our past sins; then celebrate the Lord's day and supper as did the primitive Christians; then walk blamelessly in all the commandments of the Gospel till death, seeking for glory, honor, immortality, and eternal blessedness: this is the beautiful simplicity of Apostolic Christianity. They heard the Apostolic testimony concerning Jesus; they believed it to be true; they repented;

they were immersed: they then enjoyed its promises and blessings. It was as clear and as unmixed as the light of heaven—no darkness in it, no folds of error, no coils of sin; no creeds, no sects, no opinions, were then mixed with it. There was then one God and Father of all Christians, one Savior, one Holy Spirit, one faith in Jesus Christ, one church, one immersion for the remission of sins, one salvation for Jews, Pagans, and Samaritans; one constitution, the New Testament; one commonwealth of Christians, one kingdom of righteousness, peace, and joy. They loved one another, and the gospel ran and was glorified in the salvation of thousands. O regina epes nostra.

Palmyra, Mo,, March, 1844.   J. CREATH, JR.

REMISSION OF SINS—BY J. B. FERGUSON.
(Concluded.)

II. *The place and the time.* We will consider these propositions together; since both are proven from the same testimony.

It pleased the author of the destiny of nations to reveal, in a vision to a despot of ancient Babylon, the rise and decline of all the kingdoms of universal prevalence that ever should grace the earth. In this vision (which none of the wise, none of the mighty men of his realm could unfold) he exhibited in general terms the time in which he would establish the kingdom of his son; which existing at first as *"imperium in imperio"*—a kingdom in a kingdom, was destined to break in pieces and destroy all other kingdoms. As a stone cut from the mountains without hands, it was determined to roll onward and onward with increased velocity and accumulations until it should fill the whole earth. The *time* of this marvelous event was the days of "these kings,"—kings in the Iron Kingdom—or the kings César. But more definitely, both as respects time and place, did Isaiah and Micah, filled with the prophetic spirit, looking down the stream of time to the birth of the King of Kings, point out the mountain from which this stone should be cut, or the place where the kingdom should be set up. For say they, "It shall come to pass *in the last days* the mountain of the Lord's house shall be established in the top of the mountains, and shall be exalted above the hills; and *all nations* shall flow unto it: and many people shall go and say, come ye and let us go up to the mountain of the Lord, to the house of the God of Jacob; and *he shall teach us of his ways, and we will walk in his paths,* for *out of Zion shall go forth the law, and the word of the Lord from Jerusalem.* And thou, O tower of the flock, the strong bold of the daughter of Zion, unto thee shall it come even the first dominion; *the kingdom shall come to the daughter of Jerusalem."**

Such are the declarations of prophets, made hundreds of years before the appearance of Messiah. But the question now is, when commenced the *"last days?"* Having established the authority of the apostles, we will call on them for testimony. Peter expressly declares, that on the day of Pentecost was fulfilled a prediction of Joel intended to come to pass in the "last days."! This makes it evident, that the kingdom came to Jerusalem in the "last days"†—the day of Pentecost commencing the reign.

Messiah had, during his lifetime, also declared that to Peter would be given the keys of the

*Isaiah ii. 2, 4; Micah iv. 8. † Acts ii.

*Isaiah ii. 2, 4; Micah iv. 8. † Acts ii.

kingdom, at the time he would build his church. Keys are but a figurative name for authority; and Peter never exercised any authority in reference to the kingdom until after the ascension of Messiah. He had also declared immediately prior to his crucifixion that his Apostles, who had followed him as his disciples in his temptations and sufferings, should receive from him a kingdom and be seated upon thrones. This he declares was not fulfilled when he ate the last supper. The Lord, after he had taken his seat upon the throne of his Father, sent down gifts upon his church for the first time upon the day of Pentecost. The curious can examine Matt. xvi. 13-20; xviii. 27-30; Luke xxii. 28,29; John vii. 38. If, then, the persons who were to administer the government of the kingdom of heaven, were not capacitated for their duties until the day of Pentecost—If never until that day was Jesus Christ presented to all nations as the Messiah—If never until that day was remission of sins preached as embracing all nations, we are certainly warranted by the highest authority in saying, that the day of Pentecost, spoken of in the second of Acts, is the time appointed by God for disclosing the terms upon which he will pardon those who will receive Jesus as the Saviour of men. I am confident that no one will doubt these positions who respects the authority of the divine volume.

But we have, if possible, still more conclusive testimony that the kingdom was set up in that city on the memorable Pentecost. Our text positively so declares—*"beginning at Jerusalem—and ye* are my witnesses of these things; and behold I send the promise of my Father, but tarry ye *in Jerusalem until you are endowed with power from on high."* On the day of Pentecost—the last Pentecost, this promise was fulfilled—they were "endowed with power from on high."

We have found Jerusalem to be *the place* and Pentecost *the time* in which this last charge given to the apostles was appointed to be executed. Let us now accompany these men to Jerusalem, and wait with them till the glorious Pentecost, and inquire thereat,

III. *How did they discharge their duty?* Here is truly an important point in the investigation. We have now approached the end of all our enquiries. We have found the place where the Lord will teach us of his ways. We have found the time in which he will show us the means by which our sins can be blotted out. And we have found persons clothed with all authority in Heaven and in earth, commissioned to make proclamation of these means. We conceive it will be admitted by all that the apostles, after they were fully capacitated by the gifts of the Spirit, both understood and executed their Lord's commission in the manner appointed by heaven; and this admitted we have nothing to do but to examine their practice, as the best comment ever written upon it.

When the day of Pentecost was fully come, the Spirit was poured forth upon them in all its baptismal power, from their once crucified but now risen and highly glorified Lord according as he had promised—"Ye shall be baptized with the Holy Spirit not many days hence." The effect was wonderful! Illiterate Galileans, scarcely skilled in their own barbarous vernacular, have here assembled to publish the grand facts of the Kingdom of Heaven, to all the nations of the earth! They convene together; they lift their prayers and supplications, when suddenly as a mighty rushing wind a sound is heard, and all eyes and all ears are turned towards it. The populace run and in an instant tongues of lambent flame are seen encircling the apostles; and immediately devout men out of all nations assembled to celebrate this great festival, hear these Galileans pronouncing all the languages of the world. They inquire the meaning. Peter explains. He declares that a notable prediction of Joel is this day fulfilled; that Messiah had been received into the Heavens; that he was now fulfilling his promise of supernatural aid. He recurs to the wonderful tragedy just enacted in the streets of their city—speaks of the death, burial and ascension of Jesus the Nazarene—appeals to their own authorities, their own prophets—refers to the miracles, wonders, and signs that God did by him ; and concludes the whole of this wonderful discourse by saying, "Let the house of Israel know assuredly, that God hath made this same Jesus whom ye have crucified both Lord and Christ."

Multitudes are convinced of all they saw and heard—are pungently made to feel their guilt and danger, and in all the agony of their souls cry out, *Men and brethren what shall we do?* Seeing their deep contrition, and piercing penitence, Peter filled and surrounded by the fullness of God, fulfills his commission, by answering them in the following clear and forcible language, "Repent, and be immersed (or as it is in Greek *be baptized*) every one of you in *the name of Jesus Christ FOR* THE REMISSION OF SINS; and you shall receive the gift of the Holy Spirit. They rejoiced that remission could be so easily obtained under the blissful reign of the Messiah, and repenting, or changing their course, were forthwith baptized *for remission of sins.* With gladness they received the blessings of the Christian Kingdom; and such were the mighty wonders of that ever- memorable day, that three thousand were added to the Lord.

This only commences their proclamation. The many barred doors of the Kingdom of Heaven being now unbolted, we find two of them soon after preaching in the temple to a numerous audience, and *five thousand* are the trophies of the cross. Next, they are apprehended and brought before the rulers of the Jews. It is alleged against them that they preached and taught through Jesus the resurrection of the dead. They are ordered to desist. But they go on in the work even in the presence of the council, and in opposition to all the threatenings of priests and governors. Again are they apprehended and imprisoned; but an angel of Heaven releases them, and commands them to speak in the temple all the words of life. Again, brought before the Sanhedrim, they are charged with filling Jerusalem with their doctrine, but instead of being intimidated, they boldly disclaim the authority of the Judges, and openly avow their steady resolution "to obey God rather than man." Though beaten they rejoiced; though strictly forbidden to speak any more in the name of Jesus, they ceased not "in the temple and in every house to teach and preach Jesus Christ?" The council unable to resist the Spirit with which they spoke, became so exasperated, that they caused many to seal their testimony with their blood. Persecutions broke out every where—and the disciples were "scattered abroad, preaching the word," so that from Jerusalem the blissful blessings of the gospel were poured through all the Gentile lands. Of these teachers some travelled as far as Cyprus and Antioch, preaching to Jews only, for as yet they did not fully understand the extent of the commission. But God instructed Peter to preach the gospel to Cornelius and his house, and testified their acceptance into his kingdom, upon like conditions with the Jews, by giving them the same extraordinary gifts of the

Spirit. This convinced the apostles and Jewish

converts that God had "also to the Gentiles granted repentance unto life"— and from thence forward they "published to every creature the unsearchable riches of Christ." Meanwhile another apostle is especially chosen as a fellow laborer in the teaching of all nations. Paul first preaches in Damascus, then in Arabia, Jerusalem, Syria, Cilicia, and in short, became more industrious in this part of their duty than they all. The last labors of this noted apostle were spent in Rome, then the mistress of the world, where doubtless he sealed his testimony with his blood.

The Master had predicted that the gospel of the kingdom should be preached to all the world as a witness to all nations, before the end should come—the destruction of Jerusalem. This happened about forty years after the commission was given, sending his apostles to all nations. Nine years previous to this awful event, Paul informed the church at Colosse that this had been accomplished. *"Every creature* under Heaven" had heard it—"the grace (or gospel) of God had appeared to *all* men"—and such was its rapid and universal spread that what is said of the heavenly luminaries is applied to its proclaimers. "Their sound went out into all the earth, and their words to the end of the world." Thus, briefly have we seen how the apostles executed their commission.

There is yet one fact to which we must refer before we close our subject, viz: That the apostles, and those acting immediately under their authority, preached the same facts, enforced the same commands, and promised the same blessings, to all people under all circumstances. Indeed, had they failed to do this they would not have fulfilled their commission to *"all nations."*

Peter preached the death, burial, and resurrection of Jesus as the facts to be believed. His audience believing, he commanded them to repent and be baptized, to secure the blessings of the Christian kingdom—the remission of sins among the rest. This preaching had all the sanctions of God—"all power in Heaven and in Earth." As a consequence, three thousand were instantly immersed. Philip in Samaria, and to the Ethiopean Eunuch, preached the things "concerning the kingdom of God and *the name of Jesus Christ* (in which "all nations" received the remission of sins) and they were baptized both men and women." Paul when he heard the same facts "arose and was baptized and washed away his sins calling on the name of the Lord." Cornelius, when he heard that to Jesus "gave all the prophets witness that *through his name* whosoever believeth on him shall receive the remission of sins," was commanded to "be baptized in the name of the Lord," through which he and his house received "remission of sins," God again sealing the truth of the Apostolic proclamation by pouring out the miraculous gifts of the Spirit upon the Gentiles as he did upon the first fruits of the Jewish nation at the beginning. Lydia when "she attended to the things spoken by Paul, was baptized, she and all hers." The Philippian Jailor when he believed in order to his salvation was baptized the "same hour of the night." The Corinthians, though made up of the most abominable characters, were *washed,* were sanctified, were justified, *in the name of the Lord Jesus,* and by the Spirit of our God"—"hearing they believed, and were baptized." The Romans, when they had "obeyed from the heart the form of doctrine delivered them, were made free from sin," by being buried with Christ in baptism, and thus entering his death. And so, with the

Colossians. The Galatians became the "children of God by faith in Christ Jesus, for as many of them as were baptized into him are represented as having "put him on." The Ephesians by the "one baptism" or nuptial washing, were declared to be the saved and purified bride of Christ—-even "the washing with water by the word." The Thessalonians were *'"in God the Father* and his *Son Jesus Christ,"* the same as the churches which "were *in Christ Jesus* in Judea," who was reformant believers as we have already seen, entered by a baptism. The Hebrews were made to approach God through a *new and living* way (unlike the ways of their former dispensation) consecrated to God by the deaths of his son, "having their hearts sprinkled from an evil conscience, and their bodies washed in the water of purification." In fine, every where, to every creature, God by his holy Apostles has re-declared that "He *that believeth and is baptized shall be saved."* This is a statute of his kingdom, and thus reader through his abundant mercy, and not by works of righteousness that you have done, he will "save you through the washing of regeneration and the renewing of the Holy Spirit," for "except a man be born of water and Spirit he cannot enter the kingdom of Heaven." And if you have never yet entered the kingdom of his favor, permit me to conclude with a word in relation to your case.

Have you traveled with us through the leading events in the incarnate life of the Son of God? Have you witnessed his acts of mercy, condescension and love while he wandered away-laid, houseless, homeless pilgrim upon this the ungrateful footstool of his own creation? Have you seen him betrayed, by those considered his friends, into treacherous hands? Have you witnessed his death, under the accumulated guilt, not of himself but of the creatures of his care? Do you look upon it as the "bearing of your own sins in his body on the tree?" And have you thus by faith died with him to sin? Have you attended his burial? And have you witnessed his glorious resurrection? Have you heard his last farewell to his apostles (whom he makes ministers for your salvation) breaking forth in the same accents of love and tender compassion towards you—towards all nations? Have you heard him say that "*in his name* you shall receive the remission of sins?" Have you followed these apostles to the starting point of their ministry, and thence to the ends of the earth? Have you heard them command you to believe and repent, and by a baptism enter into the name of Jesus Christ? Have you seen thousands hearkening to their timely admonitions, and swearing allegiance to Prince Immanuel? If you have, I beseech you no longer delay, "Arise and be baptized and wash away your sins, calling on the name of the Lord!" Motives high as Heaven, deep as Hell, and as expansive as the love of your Heavenly Father impel you to this course.

"All on Earth and all in Heaven
Join to bid you welcome here"

UNITY AND CHURCH GOVERNMENT.

To the Editors of the Christian Review:—

The difficulties existing in the minds of many respecting the government of the church, are to be traced to the want of a proper knowledge of the Christian institution. I am persuaded that the church of Christ would need but little of that exercise of power which is so much dreaded, if the system of instruction was such as it should be. The foundation of the whole superstructure is this: that Jesus Christ is Lord. This idea has not been sufficiently felt. I say it has not been felt, because

I see that many are not under the influence of it. This was a truth which took possession of the heart and soul in primitive times. The acknowledgment of Jesus as Lord, was a matter which was not to the tongue alone, but it Ailed the soul with the idea of obedience to all his injunctions. The whole man, body, soul, and spirit, came into subjection. "You are not your own," said Paul. This thought, that Jesus is Lord, is ever present to the mind of the faithful follower and disciple, reminding him that he is not his own, but another's. All thought of independence, all individual welfare, interest, and good, is emerged in that grand idea, that cardinal truth, that Jesus is Lord. Men by this confession glorify God, says Paul.— By setting themselves up as independent, and capable of governing themselves, they glorify, or give glory to, themselves. It was the declaration, that Jesus is Lord, that, on the day of Pentecost, so pierced the hearts of the three thousand, and caused them to cry, What shall we do? The exaltation of Jesus as Prince, his being constituted Lord, was the prime idea in all the proclamation of truth. Peter failed not to make it known; both to Jews and Gentiles, he makes the same declaration. To Cornelius he says, "He is Lord of all." It was this that caused an immediate submission of every one convinced of its truth. Peter reminds the Elders to feed the flock of God, and not to be *lords* over God's heritage, knowing that there is but one Lord. I feel persuaded that this thought, properly urged, so as to be felt, would have the happy effect of bringing each end every one who has made, or who may hereafter make, the good confession, to an entire obedience of all the commands of Jesus. The usurpation of that authority which belongs to Jesus alone, has tended to the overthrow of confidence in man. Men have gained the confidence of their fellow men, and have abused it. The Pope and the clergy have assumed to themselves the power which belongs to Jesus, and have become the lords of the flock, instead of their feeders and instructors. The Catholic acknowledges the Pope as Lord, and therefore cannot reverence the authority of Jesus. The authority of the Pope, the council, the convention, the conference, the synod, the church, has taken the place of the authority of Christ. I sometimes have some fear of the authority of the co-operation meeting. It may terminate in an advisory council; and then, the next step will be resolutions, and the third enactments, and the fourth; —but the authority of Jesus is above all authority, as Paul says.

I must be permitted here to say, that I think that the three things, as they are sometimes called, faith, repentance, and baptism, have been preached to the exclusion of this truth, so important in its bearings on those who are enlisted. Permit me to ask the question, Should a man be convinced that Jesus is the Lord, could he for one moment call in question any appointment of his? If this is the all-absorbing truth of the Gospel, which takes possession of the heart and soul, and brings into captivity to it every thought, reason would say, Let it be impressed on all occasions, till it is thoroughly comprehended, and its force and power felt. Have we any thing like disunion existing in any congregation? What shall be done? Remind them of their confession, of the supremacy and power of Jesus; that they are not their own; that their thoughts, wishes, desires, words, and deeds, are not their own, but Christ's. When my Lord gives an order, what have I to do but obey? When he speaks, what right have I to think otherwise than as he thinks. When he decides, what power have I to sit in judgment? This right to think, to act, to judge, for ourselves, is a usurpation, an act of rebellion, a proud defiance of the authority of Jesus. What can I think, judge, or do, apart from Christ? Is he my head, and I a member of his body? then, his thoughts, his will, his judgment, his mind, are mine. Is he my Lord, and I, his servant? then, his law, his command, his appointments, I must obey, I therefore lay down this truth as the cardinal idea in the new institution. It is first and foremost both in bringing men to submit to Christ in baptism, and in producing that obedience requisite to good order in the church. It takes from man his respect for his own opinion and judgment; in truth, that man who confesses Jesus to be his Lord, yields himself as a captive, in body, soul, and spirit.

This thought gives a perfect equality to the whole church. The bishop only speaks the words of Christ, having no authority of himself. Jesus is the Alpha and Omega, the life, the light, the way of the church. Does he speak? he must be heard and obeyed. Does any man speak? let him speak as the oracles of God *require,* as it is frequently quoted. The teacher of the church, must use the words of Christ; and those who hear must hear as though Jesus himself spoke to them, Much indeed has been effected by the glorious gospel of Christ. Many are the souls that have been made glad by the freedom which it gives. The church has not all learned yet the length, breadth, depth, and height of those truths which they have received. There is power and virtue in them yet unknown. Can we think of any insubordination in a body of men and women fully under the influence of those powerful truths which the at the foundation of the new institution? Can any one who recognizes Jesus as Lord, ever do any thing without his authority? But the misfortune is, that some forget who and what they are, and act as if they were under a democracy, and not a lordship; in a republic and not a kingdom. Let such remember, that they are accountable to Christ, as to a master, who will judge each one according to his work. In the new covenant, it is written, that God will put his laws in the minds and hearts of the people. "Let that mind be in you which was in Christ," says Paul. "Be all of the same mind," says Peter. "Fulfill ye my joy, that you be like minded," says Paul, in another place. "I beseech you that you all speak the same thing." "I pray for them that shall believe on me, through their (the apostles') word, that they all may be one, as thou. Father, art in me and I in thee, that they may be one in us; that the world may believe that thou hast sent me," are the words of Christ. How it can happen that divisions ever exist in a church of Christ, is something inexplicable to me, save on one supposition, which is, that they are ignorant of the truth.

When considering the unity of the church of Jesus, for which he prayed, and which was taught and enjoined by his apostles, I am led into this enquiry, How can the church become united, so as to be one, as Christ and the Father are one? The prayer proceeds thus: "Sanctify them, through thy truth: thy word is truth." The word of God is the means of sanctification, purification, and salvation. By this word of God, we are begotten again, as Peter teaches. It is the incorruptible seed. He tells us, that this is the word which as good news has been preached to us. The Gospel of Christ is, then, the word of God, which begets, purifies, sanctifies, and saves. This gospel, Paul tells us, consists of the death, burial, and resurrection of Jesus from the dead. This is that word which was concealed as a mystery from the ages and generations going before. The word of God, the gospel, remains and abides forever, and is always the same, throughout all ages and generations, in all times and places.— Like the author, it is immutable. Without it, there is no salvation, sanctification, purification, or regeneration. The gospel, being always the same, must, when properly and faithfully preached, produce the same effects on all minds. The knowledge of God is conveyed to men through the gospel. The gospel, remaining the same, must convey to all minds the same knowledge. Men who look at and contemplate the character of God through the same gospel, should see that character in the same light. The character of God is one. Then, we should conclude that God, seen through the same medium by all men, would appear the same to all. The gospel may be compared to a seal, which would make a like impression on any object to which it might be applied. The human mind can receive but one impression from the gospel, if it receives any. The gospel, being but one, and always the same, cannot possibly produce two impressions of a different character. Therefore, all who believe on the Messiah through the Apostle's word, are one, and undivided, as the Father and the Son are one.

Division is caused by additions to and subtractions from the gospel.

Further, the gospel is but one, and the spirit of God is but one. The testimony is but one, The testimony, being but one and the same, must, like the gospel, have but one effect. The mind of man, placed under the influence of divine testimony, receives from it conviction of the truth. I repeat again, that, whenever divine truth has any effect, that effect is always the same; and, therefore, though millions of minds should be impressed with this truth, the impression being the same on each, renders the whole but one, united and undivided. It is truth, then, that unites. Jesus, who is Lord of all, abides in each mind and heart, by his truth and spirit, and produces that oneness which the apostles enjoined. We see the necessity of the most perspicuous teaching, that truth may be presented apart from all human appendages, and produce that impression which can alone bring the infinitely diversified minds of mankind to oneness and unity,

I delight to contemplate the unity of the church of Jesus. Under whatever similitude it is presented to us, the same unity exists. Christ is the chief corner stone, his disciples the lively stones constituting the temple or spiritual house. Christ is the head of the body; his disciples are the body or church.— Whatever is said of the church, leads to the same idea of oneness. I feel constrained to say, that I feel confident of the result, if the means are faithfully used. Let the gospel be preached in original plainness, and let the teachers unfold the bearings of the facts constituting the gospel, and urge them on the people, so that they may see, understand, and feel, and we shall have a perfect body, growing up into Christ the Head in all things, and, by joints and ligaments having nourishment ministered, making increase with the increase of God.

The church is called on to exhibit the perfections of Christ to the world. In order that these may be exhibited, they must dwell in the church. "Of his fullness have we all received, and grace for grace." Each virtue which shone in the character of Jesus while here on earth, must be possessed and exhibited by each faithful follower of his. In order that these perfections may be possessed by the church, Jesus himself must become the object of contemplation, love, adoration, and the subject of our thoughts, wishes and desires. His love must dwell most richly in us, in all wisdom;

we must be filled with the knowledge of his will, in all wisdom and spiritual understanding. He must dwell in our hearts by faith; then shall we forget ourselves, when all our thoughts, our minds, our hearts, are emerged in him. A church, under the hallowing influence of God's word, is a spectacle worthy the admiration of men and angels, an object of God's peculiar care, and his especial and faithful love and regard.

The word of God is not sufficiently read and studied. I have laid up thy law in my heart, said David, that I may not sin against thee. Oh, how I love thy law! it is my meditation all the day. Thou, through thy commandments, hast made me wiser than my enemies; for they are ever with me. I have more understanding than all my teachers; for thy testimonies are my meditation. I understand more than the ancients, because I keep thy precepts.— Psalm cxix. This should be the case with all the church. Each must be girded with the whole armor of God. But how shall this glorious consummation be attained? There must be a different order in the churches, a more thorough examination of the living oracles, a deeper teaching. The influence of the word is not sufficiently great, because there is not enough of it in the minds and hearts of the disciples. What are our bishops doing? Are they feeding the flock of God? Do they visit the members of the church, and advise them, and see that they take their advice? Is the conversation and conduct of the bishops such as to command the respect of the whole body? Is Jesus Christ the substance of his conversation, and does his example lead the flock to greater diligence in the divine life? Does he reprove, rebuke, exhort, with all long suffering? If not, the flock must become lean and helpless.— The evangelists, do they preach the word so that sinners may understand? Do they take heed how they build on that foundation which God has laid in Zion? Do they know that, if they build upon that foundation wood, hay, or stubble, their work will be burnt, and they suffer loss?

We must labour for that perfection of which Paul speaks, for that unity for which Christ prayed. While some are enlisting and bringing into the church men and women, some must be busily employed in teaching them the rule of life, that they may exhibit to the world the perfections of him who has called them from darkness into his marvelous light. The church is entrusted with the gospel, and this she must hold forth to men, that by it they may be saved. But let it be remembered, that she must not only preach the word, but live the life of her Redeemer, that men, seeing her good works, may glorify the Father who is in heaven. High is the responsibility of the church, great are her powers, glorious is her condition, mighty must be her efforts. Honor, glory, immortality, await her, if she fills the character drawn by the inspired penmen.

More hereafter.   HENRY T. ANDERSON.

CHURCH DUTIES.

To the Editors of the Christian Review:—

Beloved Bro. Fanning:—I have just returned home from Tippah County, where, in discharge of that part of the Evangelical office enjoining the setting the congregations in order, the old fashioned gospel order, I preached fifteen discourses, in four congregations, on a most laborious and exciting tour of 12 days. The burthen of my labors was the Christian Organization.

I

showed that Christianity was divided into two chapters:

1. The duties and privileges of the saints as individuals;

2. The duties and privileges of the saints as a body.

The discussion of the following questions, occupied much of my time.

1. What elements are essential to the existence of a church of God?

2. What acts are absolutely essential to acceptable worship by the church of God?

3. Is that a church of God, which embodies not these specific acts in her worship?

In answering the first question, I descanted at large on the elements:—

1. Oracles—her constitution and laws.

2. Her members.

3. Her worship.

4. Her officers.

5. Discipline.

Answer to query 2d, is as follow:

1. Time of meeting—every first day.

2. The Apostles teaching, without note or comment.

3. The breaking of bread.

4. The Contribution.

5. The prayers.

6. The singing.

The answer to query 3d, is one loud NO.

The officers of a church: 1. Bishops, 2. Deacons, 3. Deaconesses—ministers, teachers, exhorters, distributors, showers of mercy.

Query 1. May a man be ordained to the Bishopric of a congregation, who has not every qualification?

Ans. No, never, never.

Query 2. Who shall take care of a church having no Bishops?

Ans. The Elders, (seniors or older members.)

Query 3. What are a Bishop's qualifications?

Ans. 1. He must desire the office—not for the sake of gain. 2. He must be blameless; 3, have a wife; 4, Christian children; 5, not a riotous liver; 6, not unruly; 7, not self-willed; 8, not easily angered; 9, not given to wine; 10, not a striker; 11, not a gainer by base methods—(not a cheater;) 12, an entertainer of strangers; 13, a lover of good men; 14, prudent; 15, just; 16, holy; 17, temperate; 18, a holder of the true doctrine in the form of sound words; 19, watchful; 20, of comely behaviour; 21, fit to teach; 22, equitable; 23, not a brawler; 24, not covetous; 25, ruling well his own house; 26, not a new convert; 27, well reported of from without; 28, must not be a backslider; 29, an elder; 30, a member of the congregation; 31, selected by the brethren; 32, ordained by the Evangelist.

Query 4. For what length of time is a Bishop to be ordained?

Ans. 1, for life; or 2, during good behaviour; or 3, as long as he is a member of the church.

Query 5. How many Bishops to one church?

Ans. In all cases more than one.

Query 6. What are the duties of this office?

Ans. I. To preside in the congregation. 2; To teach, exhort, and confute the gainsayers. 3. To train the members. 4. To attend to all cases of discipline.

Query 7. Why is it necessary to be so very nice as to the character filling the Bishop's see?

Ans. Because from this office spring, and have sprung, many of the corruptions that disgrace the body.

Query 8. What is to be done with a young man, or a man lacking a qualification of a Bishop, who has been ignorantly put into that most responsible office?

Ans. Let him resign upon the spot, lest fire from God consume him, as Nadab and Abihu.

Query 9. A Bishop from Ohio moves to a congregation in Mississippi, is he Bishop in Mississippi, until ordained there?

Ans. Such a thought is too absurd to notice.

Query 10. To whom are Bishops responsible?

Ans. To the body from whom he derived his office, and to the regular Evangelist.

Query 11. How are churches liable to be ruined?

Ans. 1. By an itching for preaching. 2. By too many desiring to rule.

☞Preaching in the church on Lord's day, if it interferes with congregational worship, as above, is sin.

Query 12. What is to be done with a brother who attends meeting only once a month?

Ans. We have no use for such in our ranks.

Query 13. What shall we do with brethren who go on any occasions into groceries and drink?

Ans. Cut such off. We will have no such among us.

Query 14. May a member who is accused be allowed to partake of the public worship until his case is dispensed with?

Ans. By no means; suspend him until his trial is over.

But I grow tedious. There are four small congregations in Tippah county; of these, two assured me they would immediately go into the ancient order, and speedy arrangements are being made to the same effect at the other two. These churches are some 15 miles apart, and number in all some 150 members —generally poor and obscure. Several promising young preachers among them, as brethren Milus W. Moody, Miles Wells, R. Blythe Montgomery.— These would soon become able ministers of the word, if the churches would properly encourage and foster them. We need men who can and will lead.— Two men, and but two, in Tippah County, have Bishop's qualifications. These, Elders Northcross and Smith, will be ordained, as is expected, on my return.— I daily and hourly see more the necessity—the long, and strong, and imperative call for energetic and efficient rulers in the congregations. We must have men to train and take care of the disciples; until this be, vain are our proselyting labors.

I immersed four ladies at Piney Grove, one a daughter of a Baptist Deacon. She forsook all for the Savior, though I sent her again to her father. She is 13 years old, and will make a real Priscilla. [It is dangerous to flatter *children* too much.—Ed. Bro. Smith told me, that in his neighborhood Methodists generally immersed. People will learn, in spite of their ears and orthodoxy. I preached after a Methodist on my route. He believed in new revelations, mystic operations, &c. I hewed Agag to pieces! Prospects are beginning to brighten in the sunny south. Farewell.

Holly Springs, Hits., March, 1844.   W. S. SPEER.

A NEW POEM.

PARADISE RESTORED, *an anonymous Poem, published by* R. P. DONOUGH, *Cincinnati, Ohio; price* 30 *cents.*

MESSRS. EDITORS.—Will you allow me a page in your valuable paper to call attention to a new publication, just sent forth from the Western press. It appears without introduction, dedication or advertisement claiming a hearing from the public ear—now bedizened by ten thousand discordant strains from the many venturous ones who seek

"To wander round the verge of the steep Parnassus,"

—simply upon its own merits. And a hearing it most certainly deserves, if others are capable of receiving the same entertainment from the perusal of a good poem that I have received from the perusal of this small work.

I recognize in its easy flowing strains the voice of an old acquaintance whose arduous exertions in the Editorial and Ministerial duties of a public advocate for the Restoration of Primitive Christianity are known to all the brotherhood of the great valley of the Mississippi. These duties have been, I judge, sufficiently relieved to allow him to court the "muses" and to sing in a beautiful Poem,

—"The end of present things, and find

A blissful age propinquant to mankind."

It is not the intention of this notice to assume the task of a Review—it simply wishes to call attention to a Poem, the reading of which would richly repay the small sum at which the publisher proposes to furnish it. It is written in the style of Pope and Dryden, and is not unworthy of the flowing numbers of those distinguished masters of the Lyric Art.

The Poem is well worthy the genius of its author. His characters are nervously and strikingly expressed, and show the author's profound acquaintance, not only with neatness of expression and accuracy of style, but also with the true and scriptural views of the deep and interesting subjects whereof he treats. If his Poem has a fault, it is that one which has been legalized and practiced by almost all who take the poetic license. Some rhymester has expressed that to which I refer very favorably thus:

"Those who write in rhyme still make,

The one verse for the other's sake,

For one for sense and one for rhyme,

I think's sufficient for a time."

But as I dare not enter a complaint against all poets, I will not be allowed to file one against this. I will say, however, that in it the reader is not so much interested in the narrative of the events which led to the Restoration of Paradise as he is with the frequent and well-timed digressions of the Poet. As was said by a writer of the past century, in reference to a work of that day of another character, it may be said of this—his digressions are incontestably his sunshine— they are the soul of his work—take them out of his book, for instance, and you might as well take the book along with them—one cold eternal winter would reign in every page of it—restore them to the writer and he steps like a bridegroom and bids all hail! Brings in variety and forbids the   appetite   to fail.— This is the peculiar license of poets; and with few is it used with more *effect* than by our anonymous Bard.

We make a quotation below, not so much to furnish a specimen of the style as to show the author's supreme devotion to the truth of the sacred history of the scenes he so forcibly describes. It is the scene of Pentecost—dear and honored name to the heart of every intelligent Christian.

> "JERUSALEM ! within thy walls.
> Within thy heaven-built Temple's echoing halls,
> When fires of Pentecost reveal'd their flames
> To men of various tongues and various names,
> The fact evangel, wing'd on pealing cheers,
> Sonorous thundered in their opening ears.
> Jesus *is Christ,* the flaming Peter cried;
> *Jesus is Christ,* his bold compeers replied;
> The fiery voice their bloody guilt pursues—
> *What shalt we do?* inquired the trembling Jews.
> The voice divine in dulcet numbers then
> Prescrib'd allegiance to repentant men;
> Which having vow'd, admiring thousands rise
> As from the tomb to new celestial joys.
> Pardon and peace, and love and innocence,
> And spirit-anchoring hope, arose from thence.
>   Around the city then the tidings flew,
> And other thousands paid th' allegiance due;
> Ev'n priests at last, (forever slow to learn,)
> Confess their sin and to the Lord return.
> Through all Judea flies the o'erbounding word,
> In all her tow'rs the shout of joy is heard;
> SAMARIA glows from Jordan to the sea,
>   And heav'nly glories flash o'er GALILEE.
>   Then went the heralds of salvation forth,
> From east to western lands, from south to north.
> On ZION'S summit the great cistern stood.
> With life's pure water filled, (celestial flood!)
> Thence down the Mount in living streams it ran
> And slak'd the mortal thirst of mortal man:
> And thence again in smaller streams it flow'd,
> Unspent, unspending, streaming all abroad!
> O'er plain, o'er desert, irrigating still,
> Roll'd the pure lake, or shot the bounding rill;
> While happy millions their Deliv'rer own'd
> High in the palace of his glory thron'd;
> Obey'd his Law in all they did and said,
> And made confession by the lives they led.
>   Then Bishops, Presbyters, assumed their charge,
> Nor knew a Metropolitan at large.
> Each taught his flock and rul'd it too, for each
> Was humble, vigilant and "apt to teach;"
> Each walk'd before and led in wisdom's ways,
> Unlike the Presbyters of later days.
> Then love fraternal in each bosom glow'd;
> Their love of men evinc'd their love of God.
> The world admiring saw, and seeing, own'd
> The power of love o'er human hearts enthron'd;
> Admiring saw—and this great lesson learn'd—
> Turn'd to the Lord, in countless thousands turn'd."

I have not room for further quotations. Let all lovers of the Lyre obtain a copy.

Merriville, 1st 1844.   J. B. F.

TO YOUNG LADIES.

Having formerly addressed young ladies on gardening, &c., I take the liberty of presenting them another subject in which I feel a deeper interest, and which is to them of far more importance. The Christian Religion is my theme now; and I am particularly anxious to engage the young in the study of this noble science. I call it a science, because it can be learned only by study.

It is not something we can pick up in this place or that—it will not come in a still small voice, or run over us like a shock of electricity, paralyzing the faculties and rendering us incapable of sensible thought or action. No, as I said "before, it is a noble and beautiful science, to attain a correct knowledge of which requires the exercise of the best powers of the soul—the most earnest desires of the heart. I speak to the young, because it is in the morning of life we should commence the acquisition of this knowledge, should lay up the rich stores which will make Us wide unto salvation.

I know the lightness, the gaiety peculiar to youth causes the Christian Religion to be regarded as something dull and gloomy—something that is calculated to lessen its happiness: but let me tell you that it forbids nothing that is not ultimately injurious. Does it forbid the amusements in which the thoughtless votaries of pleasure engage with so much eagerness, and which often cause their ruin, temporal and eternal?—if it does, it is because they are hurtful.— They may give a transient glow of pleasure for the present, but leave a sting behind. I have seen the young, the gay, and the beautiful the, without hope and without God in the world, and have heard them lament with their last breath that their parents had not restrained them in their gay career, had not taught them to live for *Eternity* as well as for time.

Had they in early life been taught to regulate their lives and conduct by the Christian Religion, how much anguish would have been spared them in that last sad hour when death feels about the heart with his icy fingers, blasting the bright hopes and stopping the warm pulse of life.

The Religion of Christ is the preservative principle. It is the salt of the earth. Without it, the character of woman, old or young, is defective. When well understood and practiced, it gives a dignity and propriety of conduct, a softness and gentleness of disposition, that renders youth most engaging, most lovely. A woman who is uninfluenced by the pure principles of the Gospel, is a branch from which emanates no verdure, for the principle of life is wanting. I have seen some who would even sneer at the sacred volume—at the world's best friend, the only hope of man. If you have ever spoken lightly of, or treated with scorn, the Gospel of the Saviour, let me persuade you, for your own sake, from the consideration that the Christian Religion has done so much for woman, to refrain from what appears so odious. Willis, speaking on this subject, makes some beautiful and suitable remarks:

> "Oh what is woman, what her smile,
> Her lip of love, her eye of light—
> What is she, if she still revile
> The lovely Jesus? Love may write
> Her name upon her marble brow,
> And linger in her curls of jet;
> The young spring flowers may scarcely bow
> Beneath her step, and yet, and yet,
> She is, she is, and still must be,

A lighter thing than vanity.

I have to leave off at present, but, nothing preventing, I wish to speak to you on the importance of becoming Christians early, that you may be educated, that you may be trained for the society of Heaven. You know that here we have to be trained for good society before we can enjoy it. So it is with regard to the future life. Were we placed among the pure spirits of the Holy Land, we would be miserable, unless previously prepared to participate in their enjoyments. At some future time, I will speak to you of this important preparation.   LUCY.

CHRISTIAN SALUTATIONS.

To the Editors of the Christian Review:—

While the law of the king and the prevailing sentiment of the age, guarantee to us the right of expressing our thoughts, on all subjects, in such language and style as we may choose to adopt, it often becomes necessary and proper to note, and if practicable correct, improprieties in the style of brethren, whose *general* good sense and discretion are highly commendable.

In the 3d No. of the Review, we find two cases in point. I allude to the communications of Brethren H. T. Anderson and W. S. Speer. The former addresses the Editors of the Review as *"Gentlemen,"* while the latter, addressing but one of said Editors, styles him *"Honored* Bro. Fanning"!! Now, while we are ready to concede, that the Editors of the Review are *"Honored Gentlemen,"* and indeed faithful and efficient co-workers in the patience and kingdom of Jesus Christ, we are by no means inclined to regard the introductory style of said communications as being in harmony with that of Paul, Peter, John, and all other apostles and primitive Christians, whose writings have come down to us. Every subject possesses its peculiar style—medicine, law, politics, religion, &c., &c. The style of the Christian religion, is essentially its own; nor is it varied in order to minister to a vitiated taste. It, at all times and in all orders of society, expresses the same holy relation to God, and to each other.

The boat is about to start, and I must leave; but let me request brethren, when they write to each other, to address each other as brethren, saints, &c., and not as *gentlemen* merely!! Your Brother,

Nashville, Tenn., 18th March, 1844.   J. H. JOHNSON.

INDEPENDENCE OF LUTHER.

Although the history of Martin Luther's doings and achievements, is old, yet it will never lose its power. When summoned to appear before the diet of Worms to answer on a charge of heresy, his friends pleaded with him, not to venture, but the Monk said, "Though they shall kindle a fire whose flame shall reach from Worms to Wittenberg, and rise up to Heaven, I would go through it in the name of the Lord, and stand before it in the names of cardinals, bishops and princes, and the emperor or all, I Would enter the jaws of the Behemoth, break his teeth, and confess the Lord Jesus Christ." He journeyed in an open wagon, and meeting with his old friend Spalatin, he said "abstain from entering Worms." Luther still undaunted, said, "Go tell your master, that should there be as many devils in Worms as there are tiles on its roofs, I would enter it."   T. F.

THE VANDOIS OR WALDENSES.

There is scarcely a vestige of history connected with these ancient and pious people, which is not of deep moment to the Christian world. In a late London Quarterly Review, the leading article is an able and concise argument to prove the duty and propriety of British Interference to protect the Vandois in the free enjoyment of their religious institutions.   T. F.

It appears that the two Protestant powers of Europe, in 1690, England and Holland, then united under one head, in a secret article of their treaty with the Duke of Savoy, provided for the security of the Vandois in the exercise of their religion and in the enjoyment of their property. By this treaty the Duke of Savoy GAVE THE RIGHT to England and Holland of distinct interference, in his territory, for the perfect security of the Vandois. This was the treaty of the Hague in 1690. It was renewed and confirmed in the treaty of Turin in 1804. In obedience to this treaty, and in spite of the remonstrance of the pope, an edict was issued by the Duke confirming the treaty, and giving a formal guarantee of immunity to his anti-papal subjects. The King of Sardinia now holds the territory in question under the stipulations of the treaty alluded to, and the reciprocal obligation of that treaty has never been denied. This obligation on the part of the King of Sardinia he has inherited with his dominions, and on the part of the British and Dutch government the duty is binding and clear.

The treaties referred to have been laid before the House of Commons, and a memorial has been presented by the Archbishop of Canterbury and others to Lord Aberdeen, calling his attention to these important and interesting facts. We will look with some anxiety for further steps to be taken in this matter.

THE BIBLE, THE FATHERS AND MAJORITIES—BY M. LUTHER.

Bro. B. F. HALL of Kentucky, who has been much devoted to the study of history some years past, has collected and published many valuable extracts in the Christian Journal, and from these I have selected a few which I think will be read with interest.T. F.

"One of the most successful arguments brought against Luther was, that he stood alone against the whole church; that he taught new doctrines. How did he answer these powerful arguments? Hear him. 'Who knows,' replied Luther, 'whether God has not called and chosen me for this very purpose, and whether they who despise me have not reason to fear lest they be found despisers of God himself? Moses was alone when the Israelites were led out of Egypt; Elijah was alone in the time of King Ahab; Ezekiel was alone at Babylon; God has never chosen for his prophet either high priest or any other person of exalted rank; he has generally Chosen men of mean and low condition, even in the instance of Amos, even a simple shepherd. The saints in every age have been called upon to rebuke the great of this world—kings and princes—priests, and scholars—and to fulfill their offices at the peril of their lives. Has it not been thus under the dispensation of the New Testament dispensation? Ambrose in his time stood alone; after him Jerome was alone; later still, Augustine was alone. I say not that I am a prophet; but I say that they have the more reason to fear, *because* I am alone and they are many. Of this I am sure, that the word of God is with me, and that it is not with them.'

'It is asserted also,' continues he, 'that I am bringing forward novelties, and that it is impossible to believe that all other teachers for so long a time have been in error.' 'No—these are not novelties that I preach!—But I affirm that the doctrines of Christianity have been lost sight of by those whose special duty it was to preserve them—by the learned—by the Bishops. I doubt not, indeed, that the truth has still found an abode in some few hearts, were it only with infants in the cradle. Poor husbandmen and simple children, in these more of *Jesus Christ* than the Pope, the bishops or the doctors.

Obituary—To the Friends of the Review.

'I am accused of rejecting the holy doctors of the church. I reject them not, but since these doctors all labor to prove what they have written by the holy scriptures, it follows that the scriptures must be clearer and more conclusive than their writings. Who would even think of proving what is in itself obscure by the help of something obscurer still? Necessity, therefore, obliges us to have recourse to the bible, as all the doctors have done; and to test their writings by it,—for the bible is our only rule and standard.'

'But it is further objected that men high in station pursue me with their censures. What then!—do not the scriptures clearly show that they who persecute are generally in the wrong, and they who suffer persecution in the right, —that the majority has always been on the side of falsehood, and the minority only on the side of truth? It is the fate of truth to occasion an outcry?"

OBITUARY.

Died, on 22d of March, 1844, Sister ELIZABETH WOODS, consort of Bro. James Woods of Nashville, aged 40 years, 4 months, and 15 days, leaving her husband and eight children to mourn her sudden death. It is with much regret we record the departure of this excellent disciple. For twelve years she was a member of the Christian Church, and it may be truly said she was one of its brightest ornaments. As a mother, wife, neighbor, friend, she was excelled by none. A friend of the poor and needy, she went about doing good, and many there are who will ever bless her name. Hers was a character of gentle loveliness, formed upon the precepts of the Gospel, and her love to God and her fellow men spoke not only in her words, but in all her actions. We have personally known the warmth of her friendship, and it is with feelings of grateful love that this small tribute is offered to her memory. When such friends, and sisters are taken from us, it is a duty and a privilege to remember their virtues. We love to think and speak of their goodness, and we deeply sorrow that the sweet ties which bound them to us are severed. We sorrow—but blessed be God, we sorrow not without hope. We know our Father will not forget his children, although they are laid in the lone grave; but we look forward with humble hope that we shall be raised together from the dust, and live on in happiness, where the sadness of earth shall no more pass over us. This hope is our comfort when we speak of the dear sister who is now sleeping in Jesus. We speak of her, that we who remain may lay it to heart, and take her example of *living* the life of the righteous, that we may be his. Her departure was sudden, so much so that she had not time to say farewell to her husband and children. Most truly do we sympathize with them in their great affliction, and hope they will take the admonition; "Be ye also ready, for at such an hour as ye think not the Son of Man cometh?'   A SISTER.

TO THE FRIENDS OF THE CHRISTIAN REVIEW.

The Publishers have taken the privilege of sending a goodly number of the REVIEW to friends that are not subscribers, and we hope an active part will be taken in its circulation. Since the publication of the second No. we have many additions to our list—one friend takes 100 volumes, and who will do likewise? Should any one wish to subscribe he can go to his nearest Poet Master, who is authorized to make remittances to third persons. We would ask each individual subscriber to feel himself interested in procuring additional names, as we are anxious, (if our friends say so) to place the REVIEW upon a solid footing. Who will take these matters into consideration, and each one exert himself as much as possible. All Preachers and Evangelists will be kind enough to act as Agents, in procuring subscribers and making remittances.

It is not a favorable indication of modesty for preachers to speak a great deal of their own performances.

CHRISTIAN REVIEW.

VOL. I.   NASHVILLE, MAY, 1844.   NO. V.

THE USE OF THE PRIVILEGES, &c. OF THE CHRISTIAN CHURCH.

Extract from an Address to the Disciples of Jesus Christ, now seeking a union of Christians upon the one foundation of the Apostles and Prophets, in opposition to all human traditions. By J. B. FERGUSON.

To the Editors of the Christian Review

BELOVED BRETHREN :—The position which you occupy before the world is truly an imposing one. Your as yet infantile efforts to gather together all the Israel of God, who have long been dispersed by human authority, and enslaved under the cramping influences of the Man of Sin, whose vice-godly hierarchy has extended over all the nations of the earth, have, under the good providence of your sovereign King, been crowned with greater, more extensive, and, we would fondly hope, more hallowed influences, than has ever attended, during the same length of time, the well-meant efforts of the many Reformers who have arisen since the great apostasy. From a small grain of mustard seed, cast but a few years since upon the world's broad field, has arisen a tree whose dimensions bid fair, like its ancient prototype, to spread above the produce of the earth, and extend its branches in every direction, inviting to its pleasing shade all the wearied sons of God who have anxiously sought to serve him under priestly domination. The leaven of the one truth—"The Bible and the Bible *alone,* is the religion of Protestants,"—long since accredited as true, but rarely acted upon, bids fair to leaven the whole lump of sectarian Christendom ; so that even now we find in almost every ecclesiastical body that surrounds us an energizing effort, noble and praiseworthy, to return to the primitive simplicity and the ancient order of things. Men have become, and are becoming, tired of human creeds; they are beginning to discover that there is a vast difference between the religion of Jesus Christ as it appears in the New Testament, and the religion of priest craft as *it* is exhibited in the formularies, traditions, and regulations of the sects that surround us; and the truth cannot be withholden from them, that there is a day of spiritual metamorphosis at hand—a day of purifying, of refining transformation —the ultimate consummation of which we may anticipate to be nothing short of the restoration of the true Israel of God from their Babylonian slavery, and the erection of a temple of loyal sons and daughters, to which the Desire of all nations shall come; and to which the people of the Lord shall return with songs of everlasting joy upon their heads. Creeds, formularies, dogmas, implicit reliance upon unexamined opinions, are losing their hold upon the world—the homage paid to man is being supplanted by the homage due only to God; and a flood of enthusiasm for Christianity as it is, is pouring into all the channels of the wellbeing of society, which is destined to be as resistless as the development of the dormant powers of mind. Investigation, controversy, are giving light, and freedom, and virtue, and happiness to many in all the denominations; and the providence of God is increasing human intercourse; intercourse and communication, which are   spreading   knowledge

and diffusing blessings beyond all former expectations. And, although evil is mixed with the good thus diffused, yet philanthropic enterprise and gradual reform and development, must as inevitably ensue as there is an intelligent design in the creation and preservation of man.

And, my brethren, I could now give the names of more than twenty of the most distinguished men in the republic of letters, whose attention is being directed to the very principles which have liberated you from sectarian thralldom and who are now broaching as *new* discoveries, the very truths for which you have suffered almost all things of a disheartening character. True, also, that many of the weak-hearted are sinking with fear in the midst of the great ocean of excited investigation. Some, as in England, in the person of the well-meant Puseyite, fear a total demolition of all religion in the fast receding deference paid to the priest and prebendary of their order; or in the High Kirkman of Scotland, in the prevalence of liberal principles: but the very existence of these fears serve only to exhibit the disturbed and distorted features of the human systems of the age, in such a deformity as to cause hundreds and thousands to examine more closely the placid features of Christianity as she dropped from the pencil of her divine Author. But even in the more secluded walks of philosophy, this same spirit is seen, and the grim visage of fear has taken up its abode in the face and heart of many who in the developments of the time see naught but peril and devastation. Wild and tremendous, violent and tumultuous, the sea of human investigation no doubt appears; and disastrous doubtless it will prove to many a slender baroque now out upon its agitated waters: but destruction will be beneficial—the tumult will produce good; for the power of Jesus is there, and when the proper period arrives, from the heavens above a voice will issue forth, saying, "Peace, be still," and far more glorious in its results than that which was witnessed

By the trembling Hebrew, when he trod

The roaring waves, and called upon his God,"

will immediately succeed.

But how have I wandered—I did not intend a congratulation of my brethren so much as a warning. And that warning must be given. For, in the midst of the progress and development of the great principles which distinguish us, we are in great danger of that most common and fatal of all errors— We are apt to attribute to ourselves what belongs only to the great Spirit who watches over the progress of human affairs. The religious advantages which we suppose, or which we really possess—the privileges which we enjoy over our friends, and to which, without acknowledging our advancement, they are now in their own bodies aspiring—the long lost badges we wear in contradistinction from the Methodist, Presbyterian, or Episcopalian sectarial designations—and our professed superior knowledge of the divine Chart of religious freedom and advancement—all these, and much more, are calculated to give us not only pride and satisfaction in possessing such advantages; but also a disposition carelessly to place our trust in these independently of the thing which we make of them. We are apt to suppose—it is a common frailty of human nature—that the simple possession of advantages and privileges, implies necessarily some superior benefit to the possessor.

That we have advantages, none can deny. That we have no creed but the New Testament—no denominational cast; but an open door to all the followers of Jesus Christ out of every denomination, who are willing to yield with us their opinions for the acknowledged facts of the gospel—that we have no names but those of divine appointment—that we have a rational method of examining the word of God, and a rational test of our motives, feelings and conduct in the divine life—that, to a great extent, we have been freed from the fanatical and deceptions teaching of the age—that We have primitive usages and institutions —that, in a word, we have attempted With great success, under the blessing of heaven, to practice upon the rule—to hold no sentiment or institution in religion binding upon ourselves or others, for which we cannot give inspired authority—that such are our advantages, no one of common observation will deny; and that hundreds and thousands of us have found an asylum from the cramping influences of human authority, under the teaching of the holy Apostles, where the Master has prayed for our union with each other, himself and the Father, we rejoice to know. But we are disposed to ask, Of what good is it that we should merely possess these advantages? Unless we properly use them, the mere possessing will prove in the end an abuse of them. It will be attended with the same fearful consequences as the burying of the talent in the earth; as the bearing of no fruit to the glory of God in the salvation of man.

But before I produce the effects of the matter I wish to contemplate, permit me to state a truism, in the form of a proposition, and proceed to its illustration —premising only, that the illustrations I give are not the only ones, they serve but to illustrate the truth of a great principle, which should be embraced by every individual, and should never be lost sight of; which should not in these cases alone, but practically, throughout the whole life of the Christian, lead him to abjure similar errors; and with an incessant vigilance, remember that the more secure we feel, perhaps the more danger there is of that spiritual pride "which goes before a fall."

That proposition we state thus:

That a disposition to contemplate the peculiar advantages and privileges placed in our possession by an all-bountiful Providence, and a failure to use them properly, tends to cherish one of the worst features of our frail nature, and will lead to inevitable destruction.

It has been said by Solomon, that "the thing which hath been, it is that which shall be; and that which is done, is that which shall be done;" we should, therefore, be disposed to learn in the misfortunes of the past history of our race, what may happen to us in the present, and carefully avoid them. With what barren wonder do we contemplate the lapses, abused privileges, and neglected advantages of the children of Israel; forgetting that their errors were the common errors of man, only varied by the peculiar circumstances of their time and legion; forgetting, also, that their history has been declared by inspired authority, to be ensamplary to Christians through all time. Throughout their history, it will be discovered that they prided themselves upon the possession of peculiar privileges. They were the chosen nation of God—they held, as in a depository, the oracles of Heaven, contradistinguished from all the human impositions of their heathen neighbors. Theirs, too, was the flesh of Abraham —theirs a nation of priests—theirs the Law, the Prophets, and the Psalms. No one doubts but that they were highly favored.

But they trusted in the simple possession of their advantages—they thought that having the presence, and word, and promises, and temple of the Most-High, that therefore they were secure. And the destruction of that people, and their consequent captivity in Babylon, did not undeceive them! They looked, in their desolation, for the coming of Messiah to "restore all things"—He came; but O the sad reverse of their expectations! He was despised and rejected by them; and he, in return for the abuse of their many privileges, rejected them; burnt up their city; withdrew his presence from the temple, and ploughed its foundations in the dost. We wonder, I say, at their conduct—we are astonished that they should thus abuse their Heaven-entrusted advantages; but what are we doing? We have greater privileges, superior oracles, and more heavenly visions: let us also fear, lest in the midst of our enjoyments and immunities, our Bible, like their temple, shall prove our destruction; our name, acknowledged the most sanctified, shall prove our disgrace; and our rejection of human authority be abused to the rejection or non-use of divine. Have we not seen of that exhortation which speaketh to us as to children, and says, "Be not high-minded, but fear"? Let us not, then, lust after evil things, as they also lusted and fell by thousands under the severe judgments of God. For although judgment seems now to be delayed; and although mercy and long-suffering are the characteristics of our dispensation; yet, for mercy abused, for long-suffering slighted, for privileges and blessings contemned, God will bring us to as much sorer punishment as the blessings of our dispensation are superior to theirs. "Think not." says the Reformer John, "to say unto yourselves, that Abraham is your father; for God is able of these stones to raise up children unto Abraham; and now the axe is laid at the root of every tree; every tree, therefore, that bringeth forth not good fruit, is hewn down and cast into the fire." *"Every tree that beareth not good fruit"* Let this principle be remembered; and let it not be forgotten, also, that, in the administration of the government of Heaven, "there is neither Greek nor Jew." "God is no respecter of persons;" and if you and I misuse our privileges, acknowledged great and admirable; if we cause the name of God, which we wear, to be evilly spoken of by our neighbors, "we cannot escape." "For if God spared not the natural branches, how will he spare you?"

Of all people upon earth, we have the least cloak for our sins. Then let us, by all that is holy in that name that was called over us in our adoption into the royal family of our King—all that is salutary to mankind in the principles and practices of primitive times, and saints in whose footsteps we are professing to tread—by the rich and unfading reward of the faithful in Christ Jesus—by all the misfortunes and abused immunities of the ancient Israel of God,—"let us make straight paths for our feet, lest that which is lame be taken out of the way." And to this end let us remember the exhortation of the Apostle, "to meditate upon these things, giving ourselves wholly to them; that our profiting may appear unto all; taking heed unto ourselves and unto the doctrine; for in doing this we shall both save ourselves and those who hear us."

O that we could appreciate the neglected truth, that the most alarming denunciations of the gospel are not less against negative than actual evil; and that the most affectionate exhortation, lively remonstrance, and pointed parable, are exhausted against the tree which bare no fruit; the lamps which had no oil; the unprofitable servant who bad made *no* use of his talent. The punishment following positive crimes seems logically and naturally obvious; and consequently the divine writers have not thought it so necessary to insist upon these; but as Christianity has been founded upon the principle of self-sacrifice, we are distinctly informed, that the most awful part of the decisions of the last day are reserved for neglected privileges and omitted duties. "You gave me *no* meat; you gave me no drink; ye took me *not* in; ye visited me *not;* you clothed me *not:* these are the grounds of rejection from the great and glorious honors of the everlasting kingdom, and against whom the most severe sentence is denounced.

Brethren, you have talents—you have life—you have time—you have money; and you have great advantages entrusted with you. I will not particularize how or in what way you should use them, lest in the few particulars I should give, you would sum up all your duty. But in the name of all that is reasonable in your faith, your practice, and your hopes, look well to your stewardship; for the reckoning will soon be at hand.

In the second place, we should remember, that that long night of apostasy and defection from the faith, was brought on by a pride in privileges possessed, and by a trust in those privileges more than in their proper use. This remark needs no illustration to the mind of the student of ecclesiastical history; for its every page affords a familiar one. That abominable commixture of Paganism, Judaism, and Christianity, which we all agree to execrate under the name of Roman Catholicism, is but a development of abused privileges. In order to be philosophically understood, its history should be read backwards; and by so doing it would be found that the extravagantly absurd theories of that church, had their origin not so much in a misinterpretation of the principles and revelations of the religion of Jesus Christ, as in a predisposition in man — not only *Roman* Catholic, but universal man—to accommodate every thing within his reach to the gratification of his own selfishness. If, e. g., we ask the genius of history, how the Romanist came so strangely to misinterpret and misapply the passages of scripture to which they refer in the support of the supremacy and universal authority of their church, we will find that it was the natural disposition of man implicitly to trust an infallible guide; and to find a defense for doubts and difficulties, in some unquestioned and unlimited authority, which existing really in Apostolic Inspiration, was gradually established and rested in the Roman see. Mankind submitted not because they believed this authority divine; but because they were disposed to submit, they acknowledged the assumption unquestioned. This, too, may be said of almost every error of that church.

Men are apt to find whatever they desire in their own hearts; and the people in the days of the rise of the Roman hierarchy, were seeking for authority for their own lusts of power and opulence; and priding themselves upon their superiority as Christians so called, over their Pagan neighbors, they struck forcibly upon a chord in the heart of man, whose vibrations all society was made to feel with a dreadful energy. It seems to be the nature of man, that whatever powerfully moves the public mind, agitates it to excess; and as the truths of Christianity were moving the mind of man, in the early history of its progress, it soon formed an alliance with popular passions; and soon a dignity, power, and influence were given to the officers of the congregation of saints, which professed to seal the eternal destiny of man. Thus "the pure gold became dim—the beloved city a harlot."

But I am not tracing a history. We all acknowledge the groundlessness of the claims of the Roman Catholic Hierarchy; the weakest of us believe we can expose her doctrinal errors and absurdities. But do not these very facts sometimes induce us to flatter ourselves that our universal repugnance to that church secures us entirely from the dangerous position in which she is placed? 'Tis true we have escaped many of her errors; but are we not, as human beings, in danger of similar ones? She trusts in false names; in false authority, ceremony, and observance: is there not great danger of our trusting in real names, ceremonies, and observances, as having in themselves intrinsic efficacy? Have not Protestants fallen into the same errors with the Romanists, though they dignified them with other names? Have they not copied the papal authority, in the establishment of their authoritative councils, conferences, and associations? Is there any other difference save that instead of one they have many Popes? Are not their creeds human authority? What more is papacy? In what does a mourning-bench excitement differ from the penances of Catholics, save in the name? Wherein does purchasing salvation by the fasts, penances, and bodily chastisements of the papists, differ from the groans, vociferations, and repetitious prayers of a Protestant revival meeting? Do not both teach virtually, however they may deny it, that the Deity can be propitiated by other mediation than that of Jesus Christ, secured to every obedient disciple? And what else is the whole but paganism? And wherein does a Methodist class-meeting or a Baptist inquest differ from *auricular* confessionals? And. wherein does the priestly domination of Rome differ from that of England—Scotland? or in what does submission to Gregory differ from obedience to the human laws of Henry the Eighth, Calvin, Wesley, or the authors of any human creed? And in what does withholding the Scriptures from the laity differ from teaching them that they are a sealed book until opened by the superior wisdom of "the ambassador of the skies," which Protestant ministers impiously claim to be? Is not Protestantism a copy, in many respects, of Catholicism, as Catholicism is of Paganism? No one will deny it, who will honestly reflect upon the premises. And if Protestants have thus copied the errors of Papists, are we secure, surrounded as we are by the example of both.

We should never forget that the Church of Rome was built by Apostles of Jesus Christ upon the one foundation; she had the oracles of God, and a pure worship: she had all the wealth that was necessary to spread the great principles of her profession—richly endowed with all means temporal and spiritual; and she had learned to despise the superstitious idolatry of her neighbors; but all these invaluable privileges, while they caused her greatly to rejoice in the deliverance that had been wrought for her, did not save her from losing all in that great whirlpool of misused and abused privileges in which she is now placed. "She was seduced from humble vigilance into proud and careless reliance on the greatness of her advantages, till she lost the talent which she neglected to employ."

Let us also fear. We profess, and the world around us by their conduct is acknowledging, that we have greater principles and advantages than have been enjoyed for centuries. In these additional privileges we have additional responsibility. And if we would avoid the awful destruction that came upon the Jewish nation, or the still more fearful indignation that is threatened to Mystery Babylon the great and her harlots, we must shake off our lethargy—we must use the truth in our profession, for the formation and perfection of our own character and the salvation of others.

Where now are the churches of Jerusalem, of Antioch, of Philippi, of Corinth, and of Thessalonica, whose epistolary treasure you so much delight to review? They have gone. The page of history scarcely marks their exit.— The Moslem has erected his mosque and his minaret, where she whom we are wont to regard as the Mother of us all, was first established amid Pentecostal hallelujahs! As with the city so with the Church.

"The crown of her pride to the mocker is gone.

And the holy Shekinah is dark where it shone."

But they are gone not because they had not the truth, nor the means of perpetuating it; but because they misused it, or did not use it at all, the descendants of the primitive churches were thus scourged. But Christianity lives on— the gates of Hades have not prevailed against her, though they have prevailed and will prevail against many who were once its acknowledged depositories. And so Christianity will still live on; and though you and I may fail to be vessels of honor through which it may be conveyed to the succeeding generation, yet it will be conveyed, though we lose the reward. The reward of turning many to righteousness, will still exist, although our churches may loose it.— But let us remember, that all such, like the Jews of old; becoming vessels of dishonor fitted for destruction, will be rejected with all the prostituted and abominable, for whom the blackness of darkness is reserved forever. "May the God of peace, who brought back from the dead our Lord Jesus, the great Shepherd of the sheep, through the blood of the everlasting institution, make you fit for every good work, to do his will, producing in you what is acceptable in his right, through Jesus Christ, to whom be the glory forever and ever. Amen.

AN IMPORTANT DUTY NEGLECTED.

To the Editors of the Christian Review:—

The pernicious effects of tale-bearing—Evil speaking—Discipline of the Church, In our disposition to throw all important truths into general principles, and then apply them to the regulation of the conduct of our congregations, it is not unfrequently the case, that, we lose sight of some of the most important duties of the Christian government. Without entering' into an explanation of the origin of this deficiency, or attempting to establish a just medium between generalizing and particularizing, I propose to call the attention of the reader, if he be a disciple of the Lord, to a very important, though much neglected particular duty—a duty upon the observance of which depends greatly the character and happiness of almost every individual in the kingdom of heaven. That duty is couched in the following precept of the Royal Master: "Moreover, if thy brother shall trespass against thee, go and tell him his fault between thee and him alone; if he shall hear thee, thou hast gained thy brother; but if he will not hear, take with thee one or two more, that in the mouth of two or three witnesses every word may be established; and if he shall neglect to hear them, tell it to the church; and if he neglect to hear the church, let him be onto thee as a heathen man and as a publican." Matt, xviii: 15—18.

It is not my intention to enter into an examination of the question, whether this passage is applicable to the Christian dispensation in the government of the church as such; for, though inclined to the opinion that no man could be excluded from a Christian congregation by its

authority, as the last act to be taken with the individual offender, seems only to render him a heathen and a publican to the offended against; (Let him be to *thee;*) but I wish to call the attention to the wisdom of the precept in its application to the course to be pursued by every one who has sustained an injury at the hands of his brother. For all will admit, that the principles which the Lord intended should govern the conduct of his disciples as such in one period, should govern them in all.

First, then, permit me to say, that if we find ourselves the subjects of an offence or injury at the hands of a fellow-citizen of the kingdom, offered either against our person, character, or property, it is our imperative duty to go to such person *alone,* and admonish him of his wrong. This should be done before we ever mouth the matter to another individual. This is the force and spirit of the command, and its wisdom will be apparent to all who reflect for one moment. Suppose, for example, that A has offended B, and the offence is one affecting his reputation; and B, instead of going to A to seek redress, becomes the trumpeter of the failings of his brother to C, D, E, and F, some one of whom, as is frequently the case, is not upon the most friendly terms with A: and is it not most manifest, that when B, in a partial compliance with the precept under consideration, relates his grievances to A, that, although he may convince him of a wrong committed, yet, if the offender finds out that B has retailed his grievances to others, so far from making reparation, feeling himself disgraced, he will forget his own wrong in that of his brother. Irritation and resentment are immediately created, and the enemies of God have the malignant pleasure of seeing professed brethren at variance. The very design of the precept is thus destroyed; the offence from being a private becomes a public one, by its unfortunate notoriety; the Christian profession is disgraced; and, instead of reclaiming an erring brother, we have doomed a soul to death, and caused a multitude of sins. Thus, too, from a small beginning, I have seen a stream of discord and backbiting created large enough to deluge the influence and destroy the very existence of a congregation of the Lord. How true, in this case, that a very small spark will kindle a flame, where every thing is in readiness to catch it, to the consumption of all the zeal, devotion, and love of the brotherhood. And who does not know, that the veriest trifle will oftentimes become the proximate cause of quarrel, and a most silly jealousy be allowed to fret the minds of men, until every means within their reach will be put into requisition to avenge the petty indignity, and that too, when the least reflection would have discovered that the offence at first was but a harmless indulgence at our expense. And do we not know, that oftentimes the very circumstance of our offence, if it has not been invented by a supposed friend, has received the worst construction upon it at his hands, when, if a full explanation could be obtained, there would be an immediate exchange of forgiveness for asperity, and the progress of the disorder be checked. Well has an old English bard said,—

"Oh reputation—that's man's idol
Set up against God—the maker of all laws,
Who hath commanded us we must not kill.
And yet we say we must for reputation!
What honest man can either fear his own,

Or else will hurt another's reputation?

Fear to do base and unworthy things, is valor;—
If they be done to us, to suffer them
Is valor too!"

I have known the veriest rumor to influence a whole neighborhood. The first would lead to surmises; the next, to jealousy; the next, to feud and every species of foolish hatred. All this would be avoided, the cause of Christianity would not be disgraced, and fraternal regard would be greatly augmented, if the precept before us in all such cases were rigorously obeyed. But,

Secondly, the aptness of men to color a fault by its passage through their hands, is another reason why we should go to the individual alone. The author of the Jewish law, knowing that but few men ever relate all the circumstances of a case that comes under their observation, wisely appointed that there should be at least *two* witnesses in every trial. I have never yet heard a witness depose in a court of justice, notwithstanding he had sworn to "tell the whole truth," in whose testimony I could not see to which side he leaned. This is not owing so much to the perversity of man, as to the tenacity of our memory to remember all those circumstances that favor our friends, and to forget or not to observe those that would favor an enemy. The disposition of all men to paint in striking and lively colors all those circumstances we love to relate, is a sufficient reason why we should adjust a private offence alone with the offender. For, should he hear a report of the wrong he had committed, after it had passed through the hands of a second or a third person, and after it had received the coloring of a heavy or a light brush as the case may be, perhaps with some plausibility he would pronounce that a falsehood which he would have acknowledged as true if it had come from the mouth of the individual he had offended. Thus, again, by the error of the second, the first individual is made to perform a second wrong; and thus, a stream is poured forth from the mouth of the dragon, which destroys alike the reputation and the happiness of both parties, for whom Christ died. A ball of snow, composed of a few small flakes, by continued rolling, becomes a great mountain of icy coldness and death. But,

Thirdly, let us enquire, Why is it that a precept so wise, so self-evident in its appropriateness to all circumstances, is so much neglected? The only answer I can give is, that many have not a sufficiency of moral courage or moral principle to put it into practice. When the devout and pious of every congregation, shall refuse to hear the story of a brother's complaint, until that complaint has been made alone to the individual complained against, we will cease to be cursed with all the evil consequences that result from the disobedience to this divine precept. But how few, alas! have added to their faith courage! How many men possessed of the greatest amount of physical courage—men who can look stern death, arrayed in all the horrors of the "tented field," full in the face undismayed,—have not one spark of moral courage |— But when we shall have moral courage enough to regard the high obligations we are under to the King of Kings, and not until then, will we put this wise and prudent precept into practice, and refuse to hear the scandal of our brethren until the proper steps have been taken in their behalf by those from whom private offences come. And at this point, I will say, that it does seem to me, that every individual who permits himself to hear the private griefs of an offended brother, and becomes in turn the telegraph for their further publication, is far from the spirit of a Christian—is no better than a dealer in contraband wares. The Lord being judge, he is the receiver of property that does not belong to him—property that belongs to his brother. And the reason why such are always ready to communicate these wrongs to others, is perhaps the same that governs the receiver of stolen goods; he is afraid lest he be detected in their possession and charged with the theft. Every brother's private fault is a stolen article in the hands of any other person than the offender or the offended against. I know this is a heavy charge, but I dare not cancel it; for I am fully satisfied that a dealer in the faults of his brotherhood, is a dealer in scandal, and, in a moral point of view, is equally culpable with a receiver or retailer of stolen goods. And although such may outwardly appear to better advantage to men, the Lord of heaven has decided that inwardly they are full of hypocrisy, deceit, and iniquity.

I do not intend any remark in this article as applicable to public offences.— The Apostles have given laws in reference to these. I presume, too, that every reader can distinguish between public and private offences. Permit me, then, to conclude these hasty remarks in the forcible and argumentative language of the Apostle—Titus iii, 1-10: "Put them in mind—to be ready to every good work, to speak evil of no man, to be no brawlers, but gentle, showing all meekness to all men. For we ourselves were sometimes foolish, disobedient, deceived, serving divers lusts and pleasures, living in malice and envy; hateful, and hating one another. But after that the kindness and love of God our Savior toward man appeared. Not by works of righteousness that we had done, but according to his mercy, (Lord accept our gratitude for thy unparalleled mercy,) he saved us through the washing of regeneration and the renewing of the Holy Spirit; which he shed on us abundantly through Jesus Christ our Lord, that being justified freely by his grace we should be made heirs according to the hope of eternal life." Let us be careful to maintain good works.— All of which is respectfully submitted to the faithful, by their brother and fellow companion in the kingdom of the Lord Messiah,

J. B. FERGUSON.

DUTIES OF EDITORS, TEACHERS, &c.

To the Editors of the Christian Review:—

GENTLEMEN :—The times demand of editors of papers and proclaimers of the word a greater diligence than has been hitherto manifested, in endeavoring to teach the church the ways of the Lord. The disposition to proselyte, has produced an extraordinary effort on the part of the churches and proclaimers throughout the land. This has been met by the parties with an equal zeal, which has aroused the country for years past. Multitudes have been enlisted under the Captain of our Salvation, and the knowledge of the Bible truth has been greatly extended. The first principles of the doctrine of Christ have been sounded abroad, and the triumph of truth has been great. The light has penetrated the veil of sectarian mystery, notwithstanding the astonishing and continuous efforts of the priests to prevent it. The word of God is not bound, and cannot be. Thousands rejoice in the gospel of Jesus Christ, and the salvation which it brings. As it is not to be expected that children will become men in a day, and, as it is expected that children, in order to become strong men, should be fed with proper food, and that regularly, I would beg leave to say, that there is nothing of greater importance, at the present time, than a regular　　　　　　　and　　　　　　　well　　　　　　　conducted system of teaching, on all matters that pertain to the wellbeing and growth of those who are now members of the Christian community. As we do not approve of a man as a speaker, who would throw together, in his speeches, a heterogeneous mass of matter, without order or arrangement; so, we should not think that a paper should be conducted without an eye single to the profit and advantage of its readers. Whatever, therefore, is calculated to profit, and increase the knowledge, wisdom, and goodness of men, should be considered by the editors. The vast community to which we belong, presents a field for the labor of the writer and speaker, of no ordinary interest. The proper instruction and training of those within, is that which presses most urgently upon us. The duties of teachers, exhorters, readers; of bishops, deacons, evangelists; the responsibilities of office, and the obedience which all owe to Christ, are subjects high and holy, worthy of the attention of all, demanding all our diligence in their study and development, and calling for unwearied exertion and patience, in preparing for and filling them all. It requires no depth of thought to perceive, that without order, knowledge and wisdom cannot increase. If the teacher be sound and healthy in the doctrine of Christ, if his mind be clear, and his perception of all the duties of men to Christ be correct, then may we expect to see, in the church of which he is overseer, an abundant harvest of fruit to the honor of the Lord who bought us. It is, then, of the greatest importance, that editors and proclaimers look to the order of the churches, and principally to that point which is so important in the apostolic teaching, and which, if gained, will redound to the glory of God and the praise of our common Lord.

There is, at present, no church of my acquaintance, which has ever taken into consideration the duties which it owes to those who teach, who watch over them in the Lord; and there is no bishop of my acquaintance who considers himself responsible or answerable for the *souls* of the members of the church. It must be evident to any person who will bestow a moment's thought upon the subject, that the duties of an overseer are very great. He is answerable to the Lord for the manner in which he teaches and governs the church.— Paul, to the Hebrews, says, "Obey them that have the rule over you, and submit yourselves; for they watch for your *souls,* as they that must give an account." The bishops are accountable to the Lord for their behaviour, and for the leanness or loss of his sheep. The character of a church is formed after the character of its teachers. The most unfortunate mistake which has been made in this our attempt at reformation, has been the putting of men into office who were not such as the Holy Spirit requires. This has been done inadvertently, in our hurry to set up a church. Time, however, must remedy this evil. The remedy is often slow, however, and attended with some difficulty.

The bishop must be taught to feel his accountability to the Lord, and his duties to the church; and the church, if it would enable the bishop to do his duty, must remember that they give double honor *(pay)* to those who labor in the word and teaching. There is no bishop of my acquaintance who receives anything for his teaching. Indeed, it cannot be expected that a man shall be paid for doing nothing. I say for doing nothing, because I do not find it recorded in the book, that it is the duty of a bishop to read a chapter or two on Lord's day, attend to breaking bread, and call on some of the members of the church to pray or sing. If this is the duty of a bishop, then surely Paul has drawn a character for nothing; for any man can do this. But we read of ruling, teaching, feeding, presiding, watching; of the bishop's being an example to the flock. To fill these various duties, would require time, reading, reflection, visiting the members, a knowledge of all their ways and doings, of their associations and habits, of their manners and conversation. The bishop is likewise to comfort the feeble mind, convince the gainsayers by sound doctrine, to warn the unruly, and give comfort to the afflicted and distressed. It requires, then, a character just such as the Holy Spirit has been pleased to draw by the hand of Paul, that all their duties may be discharged with faithfulness and perfection. What can deserve attention better than the attainment of such a character. It is vain for the old men of the church to form excuses for themselves, and say, "We are not such; we have not the character." You must have it, my fathers in age. You must acquire knowledge and wisdom for the work. The salvation of the young depends on your teaching and example. Where shall veneration find an object, unless your gray hairs are a crown of glory to you, made so by your superior knowledge, wisdom, gravity, excellence in deportment and conversation? The younger must respect you. But let not, I beseech you as fathers, your old age become wanting in honor, from your backwardness in serving the Lord, your want of confidence in the truth, your lack of diligence in teaching the ways of the Lord.

The church, with its thousands of young men and maidens, needs the utmost vigilance and care. The forming of the youthful mind to the mould of the doctrine of Jesus, requires patience, skill, and no ordinary ratio of perseverance. Shall I say, then, that it is the duty of editors and proclaimers to call the attention of all to these subjects, that there may be growth in grace, and in the knowledge of the Lord Jesus? There is hope to him who sows his seed, especially when the soil is good. You have, gentlemen Editors, a goodly soil on which to cast your seed. Many prayers will ascend for your success; therefore, as Solomon saith, "In the morning sow thy seed, and in the evening withhold not thy hand: for thou knowest not whether shall prosper, either this or that, or whether both shall be alike good."

Pardon the boldness with which I have written, and may the good Lord give success to your work.

Yours,   HENRY T. ANDERSON.

THE CHURCH OF CHRIST.

To the Editors of the Christian Review:—

Jesus said to Peter, "On this rock I will build my church, and the gates of Hades shall not prevail against it." The church of Christ has never been overthrown, so as to be destroyed. This being admitted, it may be asked, What is the church of Christ? The word *ekklesia* signifies, a congregation or assembly of persons, called together for any purpose, civil or religious. This may be seen by the use of the word in the New Testament. But when applied to the church, it means an assembly gathered out of the world. No assembly can ever exist without a call of some kind. No call can be made without the agency of some person. A church, being an assembly called together out of the world, must have been called by some person. This person who calls, has the authority to teach, instruct, and put in order. It will follow, therefore, that, the church having existed from the beginning to the present, there has been a succession of teachers from the   first.   If   the succession of teachers be denied, then the existence of the church must be denied also; for we have shown that no church can exist without some one to call that church, or, in other words, to teach men the gospel of Christ. A church, being a number of persons believing in Jesus, must have heard, from a teacher, or preacher, or evangelist, the good news concerning Christ; for "how shall they believe in him of whom they have not heard?" Furthermore, faith comes by hearing.— There must have been, from the above facts, a continuous succession of teachers and taught from the days of the apostles to the present time. Why men should he ready to admit the existence of the taught, and deny the existence of the teacher, is a something, or rather a question, that I can solve only by supposing that the idea of Romish and Episcopal succession has taken hold of them in such a manner, that they think, if succession of any kind be admitted, that succession must be either Romish or Episcopal. It is this that frightens many away from the true and proper authority given by the apostles, to the officers of the church, and from the proper manner of setting them apart to those offices.

Since the establishment of Popery, there has been, we may say, a line of Popes, possessed of the authority granted them by the constitution of the Romish church. The same remark may be applied to the institution of Episcopacy. But what has the one or the other to do with the teachers of the Christian religion, and with the authority committed to the officers of Christ's Church? The Romish and Episcopal authority is a counterfeit authority; each establishment is a counterfeit. But the counterfeit proves the true coin. Therefore, there has been a true church, and a true authority possessed by its teachers. Why we should be afraid of the counterfeit, when we are possessed of every means of detecting it, in the inquiry for and examination of the truth, I know not. That we should reject the existence of a true authority because of the existence of a counterfeit, is strange. But perhaps there may be a fear on the part of some, that this false authority may be introduced into the church a second time; and therefore, they decree that there shall be no authority at all. One extreme begets another. If, however, the character, qualifications, and authority of the officer, be plainly marked and expressed, there can be no danger of the exercise of too great power or authority, in an intelligent and well taught community. The character, qualifications, authority of, and method of setting apart, the officers, are most clearly marked and expressed by the Apostles, so that there can be no want of unity of mind on these points, provided the mind be not possessed of some passion for or against some religious establishment, which may have incorporated some of the usages of the church with its own.

The imposition of hands is objected to; but why? Ah! why object to the only method by which officers were set apart in primitive times? Is it not because Rome and England have abused the institution? But Rome and England have made an improper use of baptism; then let us throw this away, that we may not be like them in any thing at all. I am told, however, that baptism is more clearly taught and positively enjoined than the laying on of hands. I had thought that one single example or precept was sufficient, when coming from God. Baptism is more important than the Lord's supper, because it is mentioned more frequently. Singular method of giving importance to an institution! Now, let it be understood, that frequency of mentioning any institution does not give it importance; but the position in which it stands, and its relationship to the order, well-being, and government of the church. Had there been no good reason for this institution, it would not have been noticed or used. But we find that officers were thus set apart; and, if such was the practice of those days, we, desiring to be apostolic, should act as they did.——Authority must be possessed by the officers of the church, and the laying on of hands being the method by which this authority is conferred, it will follow, that no man can be recognized as an officer until he has received authority.——The case of the seven deacons, of Paul and Barnabas sent forth from the church at Corinth, of Timothy, of the bishops, are all in point. It is an act of great solemnity, calculated to have a good effect on the officer and on the congregation over which he is to act as bishop.

But I did not intend to argue the subject of imposition of hands. I will say no more than this: Let any person show from the Scriptures, that any man was set apart to office in any other manner, and I will yield the point. I want no supposition, but a clear, unequivocal preceptor example for setting men apart to office in some other way. If it shall appear that no other method exists, then the church must be of one mind and one heart as to this matter. It must be evident that the possession of character and qualifications cannot be the appointment, but the appointment to office is a consequence of the possession of these. Election and appointment are not the same. There must be in the man to be set apart, knowledge of the office, wisdom, and experience.— On account of these he is chosen for the office, and having been chosen, he is appointed to the office. So speak the inspired men, and so let all the learners speak, and there will be no want of unity. Unity of thought, judgment, speech, and action, is the requirement of the Apostles. To this let us hasten.

Yours,   H. T. ANDERSON.

ORDINATION OF EVANGELISTS, &c.

DEAR BROTHER FANNING.—The REVIEW of the present month has been received, and brings an article from you which contains two question, the answers to which, if properly given, will prove of great advantage to the wellbeing of the Churches. So far as I am concerned, you are well acquainted with the answers that would be given. As you are engaged in that department of the subject of church order, I desire not to interfere. But with your permission, I will offer some remarks on these as well as some subjects connected with them, which I wish to serve a two-fold purpose, being an expression of what I consider the truth touching these matters for your readers, and a reply to sundry things written in the Christian Journal. In order that I may be clearly understood, I will put the substance of what I wish to say into the following form:

1. Whatsoever was the practice of the Apostles and primitive saints in setting men apart to office, should be the practice of all ages.

The apostles and primitive saints practiced the laying on of hands in setting men apart to office. Therefore, the laying on of hands should be the practice of all ages, when men are set apart to office.

2. Certain persons, possessed of a certain character, were authorized to put the Churches in order and appoint men to office by-laying on of hands.

Whatsoever was the character and whatsoever the name of such persons in primitive times, must be the character and the name in all ages.

We learn that such persons were named Evangelists or preachers of the Gospel, their character being that of faithful men, able to teach others, and possessed of the same spirit of faith. Therefore, the persons called Evangelists or preachers of the gospel, possessed of the character above, are authorized to put the churches in order and ordain men to office by the laying on of hands.

3. So far as I am informed, there is no diversity of sentiment among our writers on the subject of the character of bishops. Paul has drawn the character, and no writer that I know of has been bold enough to say that a man *may be* a bishop without that character which Paul says he *must have.* The introduction of a man into the bishop's office without the character, would be attended with consequences more fatal than those which attended the effort of Uzzah to support the Ark. The death of Uzzah was the consequence, of the one; the spiritual leanness and consumption of a church are the consequences of the other. The same remark applies to the usurpation or misapplication of authority in any case, whether by the church, bishop or evangelist. Each department is to be guarded with diligence. The church has its powers, the bishop his, and the evangelist his. The one must not take the place of the other, if harmony and good order are desired.

4. There would be no objection, I suppose, to the ordination of an evangelist by the Presbytery. The Church send forth the preacher, the Presbytery ordain, as in the case of Timothy.

It is affirmed that men preached in ancient times without the imposition of hands, and this is alleged as an objection to the practice. Strange!! Men are not made preachers by the laying on of hands; but hands are laid on to give them authority because they are preachers. Paul and Barnabas were preachers, and because they were qualified for the work, they were thus set apart to it. Hands were not laid on them to give them the gift of speaking, but because they were already qualified. Timothy had a good report in the Churches ere Paul took him, or the Presbyters ordained him, to the work. Many persons are frightened out of their wits by the idea of ordaining men because Rome and England have abused the practice.

The writers in the Christian Journal may have succeeded well in convincing themselves, but surely, they have come very far of the mark, so far as I am concerned, and some others, mine equals and superiors. I will notice one attempt which seemed to be a favorite with some two of them. It was a notice of the word Cheirotoneo, used in the participle form, in the 14th of the Acts. Dr. Doddridge is brought in to aid the difficulty, who renders the portion thus "And when they had, by the concurrent suffrages of the people, constituted Presbyters for them in every city." Now this is strange. Paul and Barnabas constituted elders for the people—how? by the concurrent suffrages of the people. What would have been the use of saying that Paul and Barnabas constituted elders, when the evident intention of him who used this rendering or paraphrase was to prove that it was done by the people? The argument is, that the people choose by voting. Now if the people choose by voting, then Paul and Barnabas did nothing. But the sentence says, Paul and Barnabas constituted elders. Then Paul and Barnabas did something. The paraphrase is a fraud; for while it pretends to represent Paul and Barnabas as doing some thing, it really takes every thing out of their hands and puts it into the hands of the people. It is the most deceptuous sentence ever penned. I do not blame the borrower, however, for he was hard pushed. Now, there are not less than ten participles in about 7 verses, all of which are used to inform us of the actions of Barnabas. I do not pretend to say that Cheirotoneo has not this signification of electing by lifting up the hand: but how many instances are there of words which have their meaning changed by use. The primary meaning of many words is lost and they receive another, related however to the primary. The word means, in this case, neither more nor less than to appoint, or ordain. Paul and Barnabas appointed or ordained by the imposition of hands. OF this there can be no doubt, because it was the established practice. That the people had some part in the selection, I never doubted; but this fact is not expressed by the participle in use, I may hereafter notice this custom of tracing a word back to its primary meaning and show the fallacy of such a course. For the sake of this I will propose a word which they may see has changed its use. Trace Sukophanteo to its primary meaning and translate it accordingly as it occurs in the New Testament. This will suffice for the present. Congregations, in conjunction with the proclaimers, choose men according to the law given. The proclaimer then ordains them by imposition of hands. I will add a remark or two and I am done. If the apostolic and primitive practice does not obtain, that the church will be under the necessity of making a law. Who will set the examples of legislating for Christ? If the practice obtains, the Scriptures have pointed out the persons who shall ordain; so that the church is left without excuse. She must adopt the law of her Lord, or sit silent making a law for herself, which may the Lord forbid. Yours,

    April 4th, 1844.   HENRY T. ANDERSON.

[The Christian Journal will be so good as to copy this.]

THE JESUITS.

To the Editors of the Christian Review:

Some two or three weeks past, I noticed an article on the revival of the Catholic order of Jesuits, which was contained in a Presbyterian paper published in Philadelphia, and which affirmed that the Bishop of Cincinnati had lately appeared as the defender of that notorious priesthood, denying the more heinous accusations Wherewith it has been charged almost "from time immemorial." It is well known to such as have read the discussion between Mr. Alexander Campbell and Mr. J. B. Purcell, that the latter presents therein palpable indications of a strong predilection in favor of the disciples of "St. (?) Ignatius." All declamation apart, a condensed, synoptical history of this fraternity may not, perhaps, be uninteresting.

"Ignatius (Inigo) of Loyola, a Spanish nobleman—born in 1491,—naturally inclined to fanaticism, who, in his youth, had done military service in the army of Ferdinand the Catholic, received a wound at the siege of Pampelona——1521,——and completely inflamed his fancy by reading legends during his illness"—a *religious Don Quixote!*—"laid, after a singular preparation and toilsome collection of brethren, the foundation to an order, which, after pope Paul II. had sanctioned it in 1540, his successor to the generalship, Lainez——1556,——and, one generation later, Aquaviva—from 1581 to 1615,—were enabled to give by their genius the most powerful influence upon church and state.

The 'Society of Jesus,' as the Loyolites called themselves, took, besides the three principal vows of monachism, a fourth upon itself, unconditional obedience to the pope in every thing that related to the service of the Church, especially against heretics and infidels; and elevated itself quickly, by the favor of the Roman chair, by the most extraordinary privileges, and still more by the wisdom" (cunning?) "of its internal organization, in splendor, wealth, and influence, above all the monastic orders of Christendom, The Jesuits strove to be *'all to all,'* in particular to stand influentially beside *princes,* as counsellors and confessors, by the instruction of youth to fill the rising generation with ideas that were advantageous to the policy of the order, and by extensive connexions with *all classes* to govern them all. Everything, even science and morality, was made by accommodation subservient to the same object. Thus it came to pass that this order exercised, for nearly two centuries, an influence constantly powerful and too often preponderant in the great affairs of the Church and of states, that it 'gave laws at the same time to savage, half-civilized, and very refined nations, with success propagated and established certain ideas, and made weak private men lords of the earth and their Kings?—The expression of admiration"—wonder not approbation?!—continues the humane and enlightened historian*—"the expression of admiration at the mighty effects produced by the Jesuits, is stifled by the exclamation of regret: 'What great, *glorious,* and *beneficent* services might they have rendered mankind, had they labored for the cause of *light and justice!'"*

But the star of Jesuitism, which had so long and so dazzlingly culminated, was destined to decline. It is but too true that whatever proud, aspiring schemes mortal man may concoct, all are certain, like their author, to experience the imbecility and inappropriateness of age, and Anally, extinction. The sudden, electric diffusion of inestimable knowledge, the magic resuscitation of intellect from the asphyxia of the Middle Ages, occasioned by the Reformation, had imparted more noble and elevated ideas to mankind, had discouraged bigotry, favored tolerance, and promoted, independence and true piety. Portugal, Austria, Germany, France, at length all Europe, began to question the haughty assumptions of the Loyolites, and discovered with indignation the atrocities that had been practiced upon them. "The danger of a society," says Rotteck, "which, in the choice of means, knew only the law of prudence, and in the selection of objects, but that of the most insatiable ambition and rapacity, was seen more and more." Policy at first, then religious hatred—indeed, purity, integrity, virtue—solicited the suppression of the obnoxious community. Clement XIV. yielded to the exigency of circumstances. He published on the 21st of July, 1773, the bull, *"Dominus ac redempter noster,"* by which the order of Jesuits was suppressed in all the states of Christendom.

"In 1801"—I extract from the "Debate" aforesaid, as quoting from the "Encyclopedia of

---

* Charles Von Rotteck, L. L. D., Professor in the University of Frieburg, Aulic Counsellor, Member of the Chamber of Deputies of the Grand Duchy of Baden, &c., &c. I quote from his "General History of the World" (vol. 3, p. 65)—in many respects a commendable work to such as wish to acquire sublime, liberal, expansive views of the past. The author is himself a Catholic, "but he would believe that he denied the character of the historian and the man, if for any consideration he ever hesitated to pronounce the truth or his convictions." v. p. 73—note, *in l.*

cit.

Religious Knowledge"—"the society was restored in Russia by the emperor Paul; and in 1804 by King Ferdinand, in Sardinia. In August, 1814, a bull was issued by pope Pius VIL, restoring the order to all their former privileges, and calling upon all Catholics to afford them protection and encouragement."

I purposely forbear to speculate upon the consequences which may attend—remotely-upon the restoration of this "trained band life-guard of papacy.? No one, of any sensibility, can peruse the history of the Jesuits without excessive excitement; with what sensations, then, does he contemplate their establishment in our midst? Our defense must be in God: He can preserve us, if such is His will, from all dangers and temptations!

Respectfully,   G.

EULOGIES ON THE DEAD.

It is customary to eulogize the dead. Let a man live in wickedness until he is hoary with age, let him rebel against the God of Heaven till his last sickness comes upon him, and then if he say a few prayers, talk about the Bible he has despised, regret he has been so wicked a sinner, and is willing to serve God, it is taken for granted his sins are forgiven; and a sermon is preached, or a notice written that he has gone to rest in Abraham's bosom. What a sin and a shame! that the youth of our country should be impressed with ideas so utterly at variance with the truth of the Gospel. Preach to them, that their wicked men, whom they have all their lives seen in the commission of crime, by a few moment's repentance have been washed from their sins, and made fit for the society of Heaven, and all motive for virtuous life is done away.

They will say, I can live as they have done, and can still the death of the righteous. It may seem uncharitable to mention, that the Christian Religion offers not much encouragement to those, who with the Bible in their hands and houses, have reviled their Maker even till death came upon them. Easier is it for the Leopard to change his spots, and the Ethiopian his skin, than for one who has spent a long life in wickedness, to turn from all the evils of his way, and serve the Lord with true purpose of heart.

God says he will have all men to be saved, and come to the knowledge of the truth, and we must attend to this when possessed of power to reflect—to consider. We seldom come to a correct knowledge of earthly affairs, when stupefied by disease, racked with pain, or scorched with fever.

So, it is with the Christian Religion, we must study its precepts in health, must mould our characters by it, must perform the duties therein enjoined, for it is not every one that *saith* Lord, Lord, shall enter the kingdom, but he that *doeth* the will of the Father in Heaven.

But while the lives and deaths of those who have been wicked, should be viewed in their proper light, those who have been devoted to God should be held up as patterns for the imitation of all. It is proper to mark the end of the upright, it is correct to tell of his virtues, of his holy life, his peaceful death. These things should be told that the living may be benefited, that the young may be early impressed with the importance of forming pure character, and not waiting till death comes to say, Lord be merciful unto me a sinner.   SARAH.

CAMPBELL AND RICE'S DEBATE.

No discussion of religious topics, in the nineteenth century, has created so much excitement, and none is destined to be so extensively read, as that of A. CAMPBELL and N. L. RICE, held in the city of Lexington, in the early part of the winter of '43. Many have been the reports in reference to the success of each disputant; but the genuine debate is now before the public, and it is the privilege of all to read and judge for themselves. I have done myself the pleasure of examining carefully the discussion, and feel fully prepared to report my views of the arguments. In future Nos., I expect to be able to give, at least a synopsis of the whole matter; but at present, a few reflections must suffice. It may be thought invidious in me, to speak of the ability of the disputants, and their peculiar styles in debates; yet, as all public men are public property, it cannot be wrong to stale some of my opinions of the men. It is scarcely probable any one has had a better opportunity of knowing the powers of these two individuals than myself. One, I have heard in frequent debates; and with the other, it has been my province, or perhaps misfortune, to hold a discussion. It is true my personal attachments to Bro. Campbell are very strong; still, I entertain no unkindness to Mr. Rice, and I flatter myself I can do him justice.— When I shall have expressed my opinions of the debaters, I design giving specimens of the arguments of each confirmatory of my views; and if I find leisure, I wish to review the whole debate.

Mr. Rice being the younger man, and less known to the readers of the Review, I will speak of him first. He is about thirty-eight years of age, a gentleman of pleasant address and good personal appearance. He has had the advantage of a classical education, and has attained considerable fame for his acquisitions in modern theology. As Phrenologists and Mesmerisers would say, he has a strong bilious temperament, (which is the best in the world;) has a most active intellect; excels in language and powers of declamation; is quicker than thought; can take advantage of every circumstance to create prejudice against an opponent; is unequalled in sarcasm; could "laugh to scorn" the Savior, if he were now on earth; can turn the gravest and most conclusive argument into ridicule; is one of the best special pleaders of the age; and as a party leader, has no superior. Upon the whole, I look upon Mr. N. L. Rice as a very considerable man, and more admirably adapted to the business of advocating sectarianism, with the great mass, than any one of my acquaintance.— Assuredly the Presbyterian Church was most fortunate in the selection of Mr. Rice. Yet I do not esteem Mr. R. as possessed of, by any means, strong logical powers, or a systematic debater; as powerful in scriptural argument; as at all frank and fair in debate: and I express my sincere opinion, when I give it as my firm and deliberate conviction, that I think Mr. Rice utterly reckless in arguments and assertions. At the same time, I doubt if out of all parties, a more successful opponent to primitive Christianity could be found in the West. The Presbyterian Church, however, has men of a higher order of intellect, profounder learning, stronger reasoning powers, of much more dignity, and of characters which will be admired by the good and great when N. L. Rice will have been forgotten.

Alexander Campbell is about sixty years old; has been blessed by nature with a fine constitution; has led a most active life, and consequently enjoys remarkably good health for one of his age, and his intellect is as vigorous as it was a twenty-five. In personal appearance, there is no man like him. His scholarship is admired by both friends and foes; and in logical powers, the world, in my humble opinion, has not his equal. As a disclaimer, he is not generally admired by the multitude; but men of the best order of mind are always delighted with his addresses. He is most chaste, pointed, and dignified, in all his public exhibitions; knows not how to take the advantage of an opponent, and will not condescend to little tricks for the sake of applause. His arguments are always well arranged, and are generally full and satisfactory on every point he touches. It is scarcely probable any man has ever become truly distinguished, who has not attained his pre-eminence for some one particular trait, and evidently A. Campbell owes his greatness to his powers of *concentration,* and his habit of presenting the greatest subjects in a few *pointed* and *palpable propositions,* His doctrine is, that the universe is ruled by a few general laws, and to illustrate the most important truths, a few leading points only need be discussed. For logic, scriptural knowledge, genuine criticisms, dignity of manner, fairness and Christian courtesy, it is barely probable A. C. has an equal living. Yet with many he has defects as a debater. He does not attempt to answer all the quibbles which too often weigh with the thoughtless multitude, and he will suffer opponents to assail him most violently, oftentimes, without a reply. From these facts, many take the insults and buffoonery of an opponent as unanswerable argument. It is a current remark, that "more men are governed by sound, than sense and reason;" and hence it is that men of the greatest pertness and strongest assertions, are often esteemed most talented, and are most generally supposed to advocate the truth. Still the thinking part of the community, at all times, are pleased with sober truth and a manly style, and while this truth remains, A. Campbell will, perhaps, in his department, have no superior. These are some of my sober convictions in reference to the powers of N. L. Rice and A. Campbell.

A gentleman of fine taste and a most chaste scholar, who attended the debate at Lexington, in a private letter to me, in answer to enquiries to him of the disputants, says: "You ask if Mr. Rice exceeded my expectations, and if Bro. C. came up to them fully? Let me say, in relation to the latter, that whatever ideas an acquaintance of twenty years with him had impressed on my mind as to his wonderful abilities and attainments, as well as his entire submission to the power of the Christian religion, were more than realized. I never before saw so fine a specimen of the grandeur and dignity of the Christian debater—never before was so fully aware of the impregnable strength of the cause we plead. And while I accord to Mr. Rice a perfect knowledge of all the *arts* of debating—a facility of seizing on all the minor matters of his opponent, and of producing an effect thereby upon the audience—an adroitness in shifting the issue—a ready, but low style of *wit*—and an ability to conceal the real question from his hearers, and to make them think he has the right of it, when he knows he is in the wrong. I must say, that in all that constitutes a fair, open, honest, manly, Christian, gentlemanly debater, I do consider him at the very lowest ebb. From all that I had heard of his powers, I had prepared myself to find a much more able and logical disputant than I did. Still in this opinion I know I am opposed by the great body of those who heard him, but not by any one who judged dispassionately of the course he pursued. The one reminded me of a great constitutional lawyer, arguing the great principles of national law, and defining the rights of *man.*

The other, of a county court pettifogger, who was determined to make the jury give him a verdict, right or wrong. The one fought for himself; the other, for the human race."

I expect to begin with the arguments in the next No. of the C. Review.

A FAIR OFFER.

Being fully aware our religious partisan friends differ from us in sentiment, and that all cannot be right, we propose a friendly investigation of the points in dispute between us, with any or all who may feel so disposed. Would it not be fair, to discuss both sides of any question which divides religionists, in the various journals of the country? Who of our sectarian friends will open their columns for investigation? Are they afraid to do so? Do they know their systems will not bear the test? Come neighbors, if you have any confidence in your systems, publish the arguments in opposition, as well as those in favor of them; if they bear the ordeal, your brethren will be stronger in the faith. That there may be subjects for investigation we propose the following:

1. Does the Bible contain all the revelations God has communicated to the world, or does he give special and direct communications to persons now, as is professed in *"religious revivals."*

2. Is faith reliance on the truth of God, or is it the result of the direct agency of the Spirit.

3. What is repentance?

4. What is Baptism. Is it sprinkling or pouring?

5. What are some of the objects of Baptism?

6. What are some of the evidences of pardon? Does any man on earth have a direct witness of the spirit, without, or in addition to the word of God, that he is a Christian?

We state plainly, if our sectarian neighbors who have presses will not open their pages for the discussion of these topics, we propose to them to open ours.— What say you, who are always denouncing the disciples as heretics, will you not show your strong reasons for your conclusions?

LETTER FROM ABNER HILL.

To the Editors of the Christian Review:

BROTHER FANNING:—I rejoice to believe that the truth is on the advance. I have had the reading of the CHRISTIAN REVIEW, and am well pleased with the spirit it breathes, and the ground it occupies.

My humble prayer to God is, that his blessing may be on the work, and that it may be the means of doing much good. I was engaged in the good cause of the Redeemer, before you came into the field, and with others borne the burden and the heat of the day, before you came on the arena. I am old and poor and have but little means of making money; though I am desirous of reading the Review, as well as of being heard through its pages. I am identified with the Disciples in name, though I differ from some of them, at least on some points. Many of your readers will be my old friends, to whom I used to preach, when I itinerated in this country. My old friends, I think, would be glad to hear from me occasionally. I am on my way to North Alabama, and from there on through the North part of Mississippi and on to Texas. I expect to see James E. Matthews, E. D. Moore, Manuel W. Matthews, and many other of the Christian friends. My object in this communication is to make to you this proposition. If you will bestow on me the reading of the Christian Review, I will do what I can in this tour to procure subscribers, as I shall travel through Arkansas, Texas, Missouri and Illinois, between now and midsummer. I think I can do something in this way. Now if you will do this, you will send me on the three first Nos. of the Christian Review to Russelville, Franklin County, Alabama, so soon as it can be done by mail. The first No., I think, has a prospectus which I can use, and the three first Nos., I will have to let the friends see a specimen of the work. The balance of the work I want sent to me at Canton, Fulton County, Illinois; which is my present place of residence. If you cannot bestow on me the Christian Review, I cannot take it, as I am not able any longer to bear the burden and heat of the day, as to silver and gold; but such as I have, give I thee. I want to read the Review and I want to be heard through its pages. In haste, your friend and brother in hope of immortality,   ABNER HILL.

BRO. HILL shall assuredly have the reading of the Review as long as he lives to read it, and it is published. I am greatly obliged to my highly esteemed old Brother for his kind letter, and I have taken the liberty of publishing the whole of it. Will Bro H. advise us of his whereabouts, and the general prospects of the cause of truth in his travels?   T. F.

TO YOUNG DISCIPLES.

Feeling much interest in the welfare of young persons, I address them a few lines on the importance of Walking worthy the Vocation wherewith they are called. It is of great moment that, as they have commenced the Christian course, they should *go* on in it, and grow in grace and the knowledge of the truth. To this end I would add my little mite, and should feel happy to think I could in the least benefit one. I wish to ask a question or two.

Do you attend places of amusement, such as balls, parties, theatres? If you do, you cannot, my young sisters, possess that purity and spirituality of feeling required by your religion. If you go often you are obliged to spend much time and money to appear fashionably dressed; and if it is true that we have to give account of time, money, and all the talents committed to our charge, can we go into the presence of God with the consciousness of having done our duty, of having used the blessings given to us, to the best advantage?

Did any of you ever devote several days in preparation, say for a party—did you attend, spend the time in frivolity, return at twelve or one o'clock at night? Did you return. I say, improved in health of mind or body? Before you retired could you kneel before God and ask his blessing on what you had done? Did you not rather feel guilty before him, and try to sleep without thinking you had to appear in his presence? Would you have been as willing to have died that night, as if you had devoted the preceding time to your God?

You will say, I am young and must have amusement; that is true, youth should have its pleasures, but then if you profess to be the disciples of the Lord, these pleasures should not be in opposition to his law. If you serve him, you are commanded to be sober-minded. What is the use of professing the Christian Religion, if you live in disobedience to its commands?

If we devote ourselves to the fashions and gaiety of the world, what do we more than others? I tell you, my sisters, it is not the most fashionable part of our lives we will remember with most pleasure when we come to leave the world. No, we will then look back to the time we sincerely devoted to the Lord, with most comfort, and will wish our whole lives had been spent in his service. It is only when we live with death in view that we are truly happy. We are then certain to act correctly; we ask is this right, or that wrong, and do not engage in things that injure us.

Suppose, by attending the gay resorts of the world, you learn the most approved manners of the time; you learn to sit, stand and move with that graceful ease you and your mothers desire— still there is one thing you neglect, and it is that discipline of heart and mind that will teach you with ease. While you are learning the things of the world, you are neglecting that holiness, without which no man shall see the Lord.

Not that I object to polished and graceful manners. I think them most desirable, but Christians can acquire these without going to the world for its tinsel. A woman can become more truly polished by studying and practicing the Religion of the Bible, than by any other means whatever. This teaches her every thing that is calculated to render her character pure and lovely—it inculcates modesty and discretion—teaches her to be kind and affectionate, to avoid all evil speaking, and in meekness and lowliness of heart to do her duty, and leave the rest to God. The Christian Religion gives more true refinement of feeling than all the rules of etiquette on earth. It may not teach a woman to smile, to flatter, and express herself delighted where she feels disgust, but it gives a serenity and truth of character that sooner or later will command respect.

Let me ask you, my young sisters, to study earnestly the precepts of the Saviour. Let the Bible be your companion part of every day. In the hurry and bustle of the world, let your hearts ascend to your Father who is in Heaven. Accustom yourselves to hours of secret prayer. Pray without ceasing; if you neglect this duty, your interest in the Christian Religion will be small, your enjoyment of it less; it will soon become irksome, you will go to the world for excitement, and will, in course of time, lose all relish for its sacred and holy principles. That you may be truly devoted to the Lord who died for you, is the prayer of your   SISTER LUCY.

NEWS FROM THE CHURCHES.

DEAR BROTHER WHARTON:—Believing it would be some gratification to you, and the Brethren, to know how the cause is progressing in this part of the country, I am happy to inform you that it is making a little progress. I held a meeting at the county-line meeting-house, in De Soto county, on the fifth Lord's day in December.—and constituted a church of eighteen members, one Baptist, one Presbyterian, and one from the world. On the second Saturday in January, I attended a Baptist meeting, thirty-five miles from the former place; the Preacher invited me to preach; I did so, after which, a Baptist preacher rose and applied for a letter of dismission from the Baptist church; his name is John Slaughter; he also stated that he did not want a letter binding him to the same faith and order. In justice to that church, I must say, they gave him a free letter. He has come out on the side of the reformation. I preached the same night at a brother's house; one made the noble confession and was immersed. I returned to the county-line church on the first Lord's day in this month, where I met Bro. Speer; there were fifteen added,   twelve

Baptists, one from the world, and two of the scattered sheep returned to the fold again, making thirty-three members at two meetings. May the light of the gospel continue to shine brighter and brighter, until all the mist of darkness and superstition shall be driven from the land, and the standard of King Jesus be planted in Mississippi, and the flag of Peace raised to the top, never to be taken down.   I remain your Brother, in hope of eternal life.

Holly Springs, Miss., Feb. 13, 1844.   L. DAVENPORT.

ABSURDITY OF CUSTOM.

The Chinese is esteemed a man of sense in his own country who feels himself able to prove the nine incarnations of the Wisthnow; and the worshipper of Moslem as a man of science, who can maintain that the earth is carried on the horns of a great bull. Does any person ask, why is this? The answer is obvious——it is because they maintain opinions generally received in their countries. And is it not true in our country that, in relation to religious truths, solid argument and reason lose all their force when expended against two almost universally received missionaries —Custom and Fear. Else how could such absurdities as are witnessed at what we call *revival meetings,* ever be fallen into by enlightened men? Is it not because reason has been driven from her office as master by the menial slave, Custom? Let the candid answer.

Merriville, April 1, 1844.   J. B. F.

IMPARTIALITY,

It is said of Philip of Macedon that when he presided in a court of Justice, he used to stop one ear, which he said he reserved for the defendant. This rule holds good in all cases of controversy and litigation—especially in religious matters. All parties, by suppressing some circumstances and artfully varnishing others, by producing false evidence or mis-stating acknowledged facts, cause falsehood to bear the resemblance of truth. We should, therefore, however clearly conviction offers itself to our minds, upon the first hearing of a disputed point, suspend our final judgment, till the other party exhibits his state of the case, or by his silence justifies our giving credit to the statement of his antagonist. By this course we would save ourselves from many awkward positions, many unfavorable impressions, many zealous but ignorant prejudices, and establish our character for that much honored but much neglected virtue, *impartiality.*   J. B. F.

SUPREMACY OF REVELATION.

That compromising adage, "No matter what a man believes so his heart is right," may be tolerated amongst the exercises of Christian charity, but it would be a fatal motto for a minister. He must receive and proclaim all the truths of God's holy oracles. There is no doctrine in Christian theology unimportant, or non-essential; what the world pretends to mean by the non-essentials of religion, I never knew. The Christian religion has no non-essentials in it. All God's truths are profitable, and there are none of which we should be ashamed. Then upon the immutable basis of God's eternal truth, let us build; for no admixture of human philosophy, or refined sentimentalism, can take the place of God's revealed truth.   FOUNTAIN E. PITTS.

VOL. I.   NASHVILLE, JUNE, 1844.   NO. VI.

A. CAMPBELL AND N. L. RICE'S DEBATE.

In the May No. of the Review, I intimated, that I would, at convenient seasons, report what I considered the pith of the arguments, in this most important discussion, on the subject of religion, that has occurred in our country. It may be thought a hazardous, if not a fruitless attempt, to give the arguments spread on nine hundred large pages, in a few short essays; but when it is remembered the arguments are not very numerous on either side, and that much which was said, and which is in the book, is repetition, the matter will not appear impossible. The points, manner of discussion, and sources of evidence, may be recorded on very few pages.

Brother C. opened the debate, on the proposition, *"Is Immersion the only Scriptural Baptism?"* His first effort was to show, the controversy was not to be decided by logical deductions and rhetorical flourishes, but from the meaning alone of the word *Baptism.* The whole dispute was concerning *a fact*— the meaning of a single word, in the Greek language.

The next position was to establish the point, that all words, in any and every language, were either *specific* or *generic* in meaning. He argued that *Baptize* was specific, and that all such words were expressive of the *manner* of performing an action. Sprinkle, pour, and dip, for instance, are specific, and the meaning of one can never be substituted for another.

The first argument of authority, was drawn from the Greek Lexicons, which had defined the word *Baptise,* and the only one in dispute. Bro. C. adduced Scapula, Hurilus, Stephanus, Thesaurus of Robertson, Schleusner, Pasor, Parkhurst, Donnegan, Dr. Jno. Jones, Greenfield, Rast, Bretschneider, Bass, and Stokiers, who all deposed that *Baptizo* signified, to *dip,* plunge, immerse, literally, and all admitted it was used to denote a *washing,* and some of the Lexicons, as Stokiers, gave as the effect of dipping. As washing a garment is not sprinkling, pouring, or bare immersion in water, but the effect of the latter, it is obvious *wash* is used, in the case of Paul for instance, as indicative of the cleansing which was the result of his burying, which he mentions Romans sixth chapter.

In reply, Mr. Rice adduced about the same number of Lexicons, all of which defined the word, to dip, immerse, and wash, and one of them, Grove, gave the meaning of *Baptize* to *sprinkle,* in conformity to the customs of the times. This is the manner of Noah Webster's defining it. So, both seeming to have testimony which was satisfactory, of course, claimed the victory. However, there is a vast difference in the weight of testimony. Bro. C. used Paedobaptist lexicographers, who all testified *immerse* was the primary meaning of Baptizo; and no man on earth, who has a knowledge of the Greek language, has ventured to give *sprinkle* and *pour* as the literal translation of the word.— Mr. Rice's position is, that the word does not indicate   the   *manner*   of   *performing,*

Vol. I.—No. 6

but the thing done. That is, baptize indicates a certain duty of the New Testament, which may be performed by immersing, sprinkling, or pouring.

In reply, Bro. C. showed, that sprinkle, pour, and a thousand other words, indicate nothing but the manner of performing an action, and that it is unreasonable to conclude God has commanded an ordinance, and yet the word is so vague, no one can tell definitely how to obey it.

Bro. C.'s third argument was from the use of the Classics. There is no instance of any Greek writer ever using the word *Baptizo* to denote sprinkle or pour, or *vice versa.*

4. He adduced ancient and modem translations, as testifying to the truth of immersion. His fifth class of witnesses were critics. But, not to be tedious, he adduced thirteen classes of witnesses to prove that baptism was immersion only.

To all of these, Mr. Rice seemed to reply most promptly, and evidently, he did it with much ingenuity. Yet we are not to suppose there was no means of deciding the question. Mr. Rice admitted that Martin Luther, Wall, Dr. Geo. Campbell, and many other most learned paedobaptists, gave *dip* or *immerse* as the meaning of *Baptize;* but he contended that they were decided immersionists, and therefore partial, and their authority was not to be received. To my mind nothing could be more erroneous than Mr. R.'s conclusion. These learned men, and indeed the wisest of all ages, have defined the word to dip, and these critics, such as Calvin and Stuart, have not and do not practice sprinkling and pouring because it can be proved from the word, or because of their antiquity, but solely on the ground that the ordinance HAS BEEN CHANGED. This was the manner in which Bro. C. answered the argument, and before I forget it. I wish to state, that after examining all the sources of evidence of the age in favor of sprinkling and pouring, I am satisfied the strongest argument for them is founded upon the right of changing from immersion. This is professor Stuart's strongest reliance for rejecting immersion, and it is easy to prove that the greatest men of the paedobaptist world, contend for the right of change; and, indeed, that sprinkling and pouring have no other plausible foundation in the estimation of Paedobaptists themselves. Who will dispute this point? It may be proved by the Bible, by history, and by living witnesses, that the right to "change ordinances" is the foundation of sprinkling and pouring for baptism.

In pursuing the discussion carefully, it was not very difficult to see the points upon which the whole matter turned. Both, for instance, agreed that *immerse* did not misrepresent Baptizo, and both admitted it had been translated to *wash.* But while Mr. R. supposed wash was its literal meaning, Bro. C. contended, was only indicative of what had already been done—that it was the result of the dipping. He certainly did prove, beyond a reasonable probability of a doubt, that wash was only the consequence of immersion. For instance, the putting of clothes into water was not washing, as I have before stated, but washing is the legitimate result of placing them in the water. This was an important point in the controversy, and upon the establishment of the fact that wash, when used to express baptism, was a metonymy, (the effect for the cause) the whole matter was decided. If it be true that wash is a literal meaning of *Baptizo,* our paedobaptist brethren may, with a little show of plausibility, contend that washing can be performed by sprinkling and pouring, but when this prop is taken away, the whole fabric falls. I could employ myself in writing out these arguments a week, but it is useless; I have given the most important features. In fact, all other arguments are inferior to those I have mentioned. I repeat, that Bro. C. established the points: 1st, That all the world agreed Baptizo was to immerse; 2d, That wash was not the literal meaning of the word, but the consequence of immersion; and 3dly, That Paedobaptism must forever rest upon the right of changing the ancient custom of immersing, to the modem plan of sprinkling and pouring.

T. F.

IS THE BAPTISM OF THE SPIRIT ESSENTIAL TO ENTER THE CHURCH?

Bro. C. CURLEE, of Cannon county, says, in a letter to the junior Editor— "Some of the brethren in these parts, would be pleased to have a clear view of the 13th verse of the 12th chapter of 1 Corinthians."

That some of the brethren should have difficulties in understanding fully the meaning of the Apostle in this verse, is not astonishing, when it is remembered, zealous partisans have distorted the passage in every possible shape, to sustain a darling theory. The views, however, of parties and party leaders, are not uniform. Perhaps the correct plan to present the Apostle's idea, will be, by contrasting it with some of the speculations of modern theology. In this country, there are at least three solutions given to the passage, each of which I will give in order.

1st. Doctor McKnight, who is, to say the least, very high authority, in the Presbyterian Church, makes this a "Baptism of the gifts of the Spirit," by which persons enter "the one body or church of Christ." But the Doctor did not reflect, (and his brethren of this day are equally unthoughtful,) that there never was a "Baptism of gifts;" and if indeed, "with the gifts of one spirit" the people in ancient times were baptized, there are no such things in these days; and therefore, the speculation is most foreign.

2d. Most denominations contend that all persons who become Christians, are baptized literally by the Spirit of God, to constitute them members of the body of Christ. This was Mr. Rice's position in the discussion at Nashville, and he, moreover, contended this was the "one baptism" of Paul; and his friends, both Presbyterians and Methodists, rejoiced much at the argument. Will this theory bear the test of criticism? We will see. Was the baptism of the Spirit appointed by the King for entering the church? Where is the passage? Did one ever become a Christian, or enter the body, by the baptism of the Spirit?" The baptism of the Spirit was first experienced by persons who were pardoned —by disciples of Christ. See Acts, 2 chapter. Cornelius and his friends were baptized by the Spirit before any of them were *pardoned, saved,* or had *entered* the church of Christ. Indeed, Peter had not spoken the words by which the angel testified Cornelius and his house should be saved, when the Spirit was poured out, or done what Peter was authorized of God to command him to perform. After the Baptism of the Spirit, Cornelius was commanded to be baptized "in the name of the Lord Jesus." Query: If the baptism of the Spirit made Cornelius a Christian, or saved him from his sins, did not the angel in saying, Peter should "tell him words by which he should be saved"? Were these words told him before he was commanded to be baptized? Do not all intelligent paedobaptists admit, the expression of Paul, Gal. v, 27, "As many of you as have been baptized into Christ, have put on Christ," alludes to water baptism? If this be

water baptism, by which we put on Christ, and yet there is a baptism of the spirit to enter the same body, are there not two ways of entering the church of Christ, or does not every one who becomes a Christian, enter the church once by the baptism of the Spirit, and again by the baptism in water? Are not these incongruities too gross for an enlightened public, and would not the admission of them destroy our confidence in the validity of the Scriptures?

Before proceeding further, it may be well to make a suggestion or two in regard to the baptism of the Spirit, or spiritual gifts in general. The position can be easily sustained, that no direct miraculous influence ever changed or directly bettered the moral condition of its subject. Baalam, and King Saul, and even Baalam's ass, had displays of God's spiritual power which enabled them to speak or prophesy the truth of Heaven; yet it bettered not the condition of either. The disciples, on Pentecost, who were the first to be baptized by the Spirit, were not made purer in heart, or freer from sin, by it. Cornelius was never benefited a whit by his personal baptism of the Spirit. The outpouring of the Spirit on him, was God's argument to convince the six Jewish brethren with Peter, and through them the Jewish world, that the Father of all was no respecter of persons. The Jews were *personally* benefited by the miracle on Cornelius, and Cornelius and the Gentile world have been greatly profited by the baptism of the Spirit upon Peter and the other Apostles. The baptism of the Spirit, as it will be obviously seen, was designed to "bring to the Apostles' memory all things the Lord had spoken to them, to guide them into all truth— in a word, to enable them to give a revelation to the whole world. All who were baptized by the Spirit, could "speak with tongues;" that is, languages which they had not learned. Can our friends who profess to be baptized with the "Holy Ghost sent down immediately from heaven," at this day, generally speak plain English? much less foreign tongues!

3d. Now to the passage itself. The first question to be determined is, does Paul, in I Cor. xii, 13, speak of a *baptism of the Spirit,* by which we enter the "one body"? To the affirmative of this, I have the following objections: 1st. The words do not indicate a baptism of the Spirit. 2d. If the baptism of the Spirit anciently constituted persons members of the church, there is no one now on earth a Christian; for there is no one who can give the slightest evidence, (unless an impudent profession is such,) that he is baptized by the Spirit. 3d. If the words, "By one Spirit are we all baptized into one body," indicate a spiritual baptism, it is received before persons "drink into the one Spirit," and the spiritual baptism and drinking of the Spirit, are different influences. 4th. If this teaches a baptism of the Spirit introduces us into the Church, it contradicts every other passage where baptism is alluded to as introducing us into a new relation in the Bible.

The words literally convey the following idea, viz: "By, (in Greek *en,*) in, or by the authority of, in obedience to, or as the one Spirit of Christ teaches, are we all immersed (in water) into the one body of Christ. This, I have no doubt, is the Apostle's teaching; but a greater than I has testified to the same effect. Dr. Clarke, the only truly learned authority in the Methodistic ranks, says, on this passage, "As the body of men, though composed of many members, is informed and influenced by one soul; so the church of Christ, which is his body, though composed of many members, is informed and influenced by one Spirit." The consequence of the investigation is this:

The one Spirit of God has taught, and still teaches, all the world, in the Scriptures, that those who enter Christ, or come into his kingdom, or under his government, must do so by a humble submission to him, in the action of immersion, as the children of Israel were "baptized into Moses" in order to enter Moses, or come fully under his government. T. F.

JUDGMENTS AND SPECIAL INFLUENCES.

A brother, and old friend, in Alabama, who has recently done himself the honor to leave a sect for the sake of truth, has propounded various interrogatories, to which appropriate answers would contribute much to the removal of error and prejudice; and divers of his remarks will be of service to enquirers after truth. His first question is

1. "Does God work now as in the days of Nadab and Abihu"?
2. "Has revelation ceased"?
3. "Is the Gospel, as addressed to the intellect of man, the power of God to Salvation"?
4. "Is the judgment to take place after death, or is it in progress while men are in the flesh"?

These questions, though containing subjects of vast moment, are not very difficult to be answered. While I am far from admitting our Heavenly Father is unmindful of his creatures in this age, I am as far from the conclusion, that he is performing miracles with men on this earth as in the days of Prophets and Apostles. Miracles are not, in the common acceptation of the term, revelations, but have always been performed to attest some great truth. They have been performed, only in the absence of perfect revelation. If it be admitted we have a perfect system of religion, it would be highly preposterous to look for "signs." Indeed, a sign now, would be indubitable evidence against the perfection of the Gospel. In as much as wonders were always exhibited to confirm truth, and if a miracle were to be exhibited in this age, it would be undeniable proof that our Bible does not contain all truths indispensable for the salvation of man. The consequence is, we must either argue the revelation is not perfect, or reject the miracles of this day, as impious pretensions of men of corrupt minds.

God has honored man above the brute by giving him an intellect, and he has graciously taught, it is to this intellect he has addressed his all-powerful Gospel, and it is through the mind the affections are changed and won to God. If the heart is moved or acted upon in any manner but through its faculties, I cannot see how any one can be accountable to his Maker. On the hypothesis of the abstract influences, all responsibility is annihilated.

The brother adds, "In reading the periodicals of the day, I am very often perplexed to understand the meaning of the writers." (Nothing strange, many writers profess to believe in mysteries, and of course, they cannot write intelligibly for others.—Ed.) "In one paper, I saw an account given of a man, who was described as being almost perfect, he tried very hard "To GET religion" (what an idea! we had as well talk of getting honesty, or a knowledge of Arithmetic, by the quart, lump or bundle—Ed.) but failed. He was determined not to be outdone, and commenced the performance of all the good deeds possible, and prayed night and morning and at length one night when he least expected it the Lord SPOKE PEACE TO HIS SOUL. On hearing this it struck me, the man was a little like Cornelius, except in the manner of his conversion. To one the Lord sent his servant Peter; but to the other he spoke himself. Would to God men would hear the words of Peter and the rest of the Apostles, as they did in days of old. The Lord appeared to Paul not to convert him (this was the work of Ananias—ED.) but to make him a *"witness;"* yet at this day, good and sensible men, on other subjects, have given out trying to become Christians, because they cannot persuade the Lord to appear personally to them as he did to Paul, or speak peace as in the case just named. Some do get their imaginations (that's all—ED.) to such a pitch, as to suppose the Lord has pardoned them. Such fanaticism and superstition stand more opposed to Christianity, than avowed unbelief itself. I read another piece not long since, in which the writer stated "the Lord has in mercy visited McMinnville with the powerful influences of the Holy Spirit (through the word of truth.") Now the word "VISIT" is what puzzles me. This reminds me of the anecdote related to me by an aged brother. When a boy, he was taken to meeting with instruction, to do just like other people did. When others kneeled and shut their eyes, he was ordered to do the same. On a certain occasion he attended at the water where baptism was to be performed. While here, the congregation, and of course the little boy, kneeled down; the good pastor prayed for the "angel of the Lord to move upon the water." He said "then it was" he would have given anything, to know if his parents were looking at him, for above all things he wished "to see the angel troubling the waters, and know for himself if the preacher's prayer was heard." So, it seems to me if the Lord is thus partially *visiting,* for the sake of party revivals, and moving upon the waters more at one time than another, he must be *absent* from one place while visiting another. This is a pretty fair statement of the practices of many religionists in this age, but to me the whole system seems a glaring perversion of truth, and utterly opposed to the character of God, and to his dealings with man. But the practices of this day, are too ridiculous for publication.			T. F.

A NEW REVELATION.

As it is the duty of all philanthropists to make known to the world, whatever light they possess above their contemporaries, and as it is possible that I have stronger evidence, of being in *someway* connected with a divine communication, than the great mass of my fellow creatures, I cannot withhold from the public what I have *seen* and *felt.* But before divulging the secret, a word on the credibility of heavenly witnesses will be in place. In olden times, two or three witnesses were necessary to establish facts, but in this *enlightened day,* of steam boats and rail roads, and when revelations are made to every man, women and child, black or white, learned or unlearned, who can get to a revival meeting, or into the atmosphere of a revival preacher, sent directly by the outpouring of the Holy Spirit, one witness, to any great fact *must* answer the purpose.

Many of my excellent acquaintances in Tennessee and other parts of the earth, I have known every *summer* to attend *"exciting and awakening meetings,"* and after going to the "altar," or *solemn bench for mourning,* and struggling with the devil a reasonable space of time, to rise

shouting, with the intelligence that the God of all grace had made an inward revelation to them
by

his Spirit, that their sins were all forgiven. To deny the truth of these direct communications, as evidence of pardon, would be contradicting the experience of four-fifths if not nine-tenths of the professors of religion in the United States. The man who dares utter opposition to, or doubt that at all the great revivals, the Spirit of Almighty God is not given to the "mourners and seekers after religion" is evidently unorthodox, and heretical, and richly deserves many opprobrious names.

Some three years since, I was attacked, in Dresden, W. Tennessee, by a very popular "Presiding Elder," who has satisfied thousands that he was a *chosen vessel* of the Lord; and, after various corrections of my supposed errors, he learned from me that I, and the disciples of Jesus Christ, profess to believe in no other revelation than that given in the Bible, "Oh," said he, "you see the gentleman denies *revealed religion.*" True, I had been so simple as to suppose *"revealed religion"* was that communicated and taught in the Bible; but from the best sources of human wisdom, judging by numbers, I perceive it is, with the mass, what is communicated to every one, immediately from above, and not that dull light which comes through the old "dead letter" called the Bible. To this effect, Mr. McMillon, an eminent *"divine"* of the Presbyterian order, testified, in Moulton, Ala., in June of 1843. So contended Mr. Rice, the champion of orthodoxy, and the boast of all the "orders," in a discussion with the writer, in the city of Nashville, in the month of July, 1843. Said the latter gentleman, while discussing the point whether God has always spoken and still speaks to the world, BY WORDS; "when a man has not this *inward peace,* or revelation, "which teaches him he is pardoned," even in the absence of Baptism, it is only evidence he is ignorant of this matter himself, but it is no evidence others have not this divine "unction which teaches them all things, in this day." In looking over the assembly, at the moment, I saw I was overwhelmed with the argument in the estimation of many of the zealous, who were much delighted at the idea that Mr. Rice had proved, that God had proved, that they had special revelations from above; that they were pardoned, whilst I and my brethren were scoffed at, for relying solely on the word of God for evidence of pardon, and being entirely content with the revelations given in the Bible.— This is not all; a few years since, in Columbus, Miss., a Doctor O., of considerable celebrity, proved conclusively, that my brethren were in gross error, and that revelations are made to men's consciences, in this age, by a direct appeal to his brethren. "How many," said he, "present, can testify that God has spoken peace to them by his Spirit?" and there was almost a simultaneous groan of triumph through the whole house. This was the most effectual mode of proving that point; and no wonder Mr. Rice confounded me, and has since triumphed over Bro. A. Campbell, on the same subject. "Ah!" he contends, "seeing and hearing are only believing, but *feeling* (a revelation,) is the naked truth."

But, not to be very prolix, I have borne the taunts and sneers of *clergymen,* men, women, boys and girls, black and white, and mixed, long enough, for not having special revelations as they have. Let it be noted, however, notwithstanding I have *seen end felt* something, as I first suggested, I do not say I have with these natural eyes seen Gabriel, or the Savior, as an influential man told me he had done not long since, or felt any thing for which I could not account: still, if the reader will be patient, I will tell what I have seen and felt —and it is my opinion, I have stronger evidence that an angel has sent a revelation to me than those who boast so much of their divine evidences from above. Be it known to all whom it may concern, that, as I sat in my room, at Elm Crag, on Friday evening, the 3d of May, 1844, a small figure passed into my room, which I took, at the time, to be a little negro boy, and deposited on my table, without saying a word, a very neatly bound Up little bundle, with many seals ; and upon the opening of the envelope, I found a book, and a letter, written in a fine hand, to the following effect:

"FRIEND TOLBERT FANNING:—In compliance with our duty, we address you. It is in relation to a book, the contents of which have been received through the medium of revelation, by a member of our body or church of New Lebanon, state of N. York; and by the same authority whence this book originated, we are requested to circulate the same among rulers, teachers, guides, and leaders of the people; and from your character, believing that you constitute a personage of this class, and in compliance to the revealed will of Heaven, we send unto you a copy of the book. We hope you will bear with us whilst we conscientiously fulfill this sacred injunction of the Almighty. As to our confidence in the divine origin of the book, we feel it our duty plainly to state, that we are unwavering, because of evidence we cannot, nor do we wish to resist. The evidence, we would say, is not that only which is outward, by the quickening of the mortal body, but by an indelible impression of the quickening spirit and power of God upon the immortal soul, by which we know this is from God, and proceeds from no other source. He who sent to the earth, stands pledged for the and fulfillment of what is therein contained, in his own good time. But from what is written you will see, that we as a branch of the church, or members of the body of Christ, have been visited with the same gifts and powers of God, in common with the leading branch or church of New Lebanon; so that, without doubt, hesitation, or wavering of spirit, we are enabled to bear testimony to the truth of the divine origin of this Sacred Roll, or Book, which we now send (by command, mind) unto you.

We earnestly desire that our friend will not cast the book off, as the offering of phrensy or fanaticism, but, as one who has confidence in God, and desires the well-being of his fellow-sojourners on earth, both in time and eternity, he will carefully read it through, and see if it does not bear the divine impression of the hand who gave it, and if much good would not result to the inhabitants of earth of what is therein written.

With all due respect, we remain sincerely your friends and well-wishers,

JOHN R. EADES.
CHARLES P. JOHNS.

NOTE—It is necessary to remark, that the words written on the first leaf of this book, were commanded thus to be written by the mighty Angel, who has directed this work from the beginning. We would also suggest, it would be agreeable to us to have this book circulated, particularly amongst the class of people described in this letter, so far as is consistent with your means, or at, least so far as your feelings may lead you so to do.   J. R. E.

C. P. J."

Now, reader, be assured, when I finished reading this letter, I found myself still in my right mind, and disposed to look with great commiseration on the errors of the age, and from my soul pity the weaknesses of my fellow-creatures.

Next, I anxiously opened the Book, and looking on the first leaf, I found the following words:

"A present unto you, by the command of Him who seeth not as man seeth. Let him that readeth understand.

J. R. EADES.
CHAS. P. JOHNS."

It must be remembered, here are two witnesses, who testify that this book was sent to me by the Almighty himself, or by his angel. Now, I ask the question, if these witnesses do not as conclusively prove the truth of this revelation, and that it was sent to me, by divine appointment, as the mere *unaccountable feelings* in religious excitements, prove their possessors have revelations by the Spirit that they are Christians. Thi*s feeling* we are told is the witness of the Spirit, and it is the witness for which all the popular sects of this country contend; and I maintain if we believe all the camp-meeting converts have revelations made to them, there is still greater evidence to believe this book is from God, and that the great angel sent it to me.

But am I told, these people who "get revealed religion," become pious, and thereby give evidence to the world, "the work is of God"? I answer, the people by whom this book has been presented, have more character for piety than any sect of the land.

To the Book, however, I must devote a few words. It is a very pretty little volume of 222 pages, neatly gotten up at Canterbury, New Hampshire, a few months since, and styled "A Holy, Sacred and Divine Roll and Book, sent forth by the Lord God of Heaven to the inhabitants of the Earth." The revelation purports to have been made May the 4th, 1842, to Philemon Stewart, of New Lebanon, N. Y., and to have been written out as the angel of the Lord read it to him. So much for the title—now for the contents. To my mind the whole work is an impious and ignorant tissue of unreasonable assertions, vulgar allusions and ridiculous prophecies.

Suffice it to say, it is a Quaker production, which places "Mother Ann Lee" as the "Daughter of Zion" and "Queen of the Christian Empire." There is a great deal said about fleshly lusts, which is only to be tolerated for purposes therein specified... Debauchery is certainly encouraged on p. 85, in these words, "Nothing of that nature (carnal indulgence) was ever tolerated by any of the Apostles, only in the line of permission, or an indulgence for the time being, because of their great weakness in those respects." This does not change my mind in the least in reference to these *"pious"* and *"inspired"* Quakers.

On page 148, "All preachers are commanded to obtain this new revelation, and to keep a copy in their pulpits, and they are commanded *"to often look thereon."*

There are awful predictions of mystical spiritual operations just ahead. On p. 169, the Lord is represented as saying, "I give you a little fore-knowledge of many strange operations and exercises which I shall cause on mortal bodies. *Violent shaking,* until thrown heavily upon the floor or ground; every limb of the body made stiff and unyielding; eyes set with deathly appearance; pulsations of life nearly extinct; gestures and exhibiting frightful attitudes "But enough. All these things are said to be at hand, and I would only add, they are not new, as any one may be assured who will attend some of the religious revivals of this favored land.

One reflection, and I shall close this by far too protracted notice of this affair. Should we wonder at the ignorance of the great mass of our countrymen in reference to the Bible, and at the sectarian zeal of this age, when we see such productions as this coming forth almost every year, and find at least four fifths of professedly pious persons the subjects of some strange delusion in the form of a dream, or supposed spiritual revelation without language; and almost nine-tenths of our beloved contemporaries love to have it so? The witnesses of this book say, they "feel from an inward consciousness," that the thing is a revelation from above; others more respected, say they "feel their sins pardoned, and know they are Christians by special communication of the Spirit, not through the word; and now I ask the world to state the difference?

This spell must be broken before Christianity can prevail. Brethren, let us have no unkindness towards the subjects and friends of these delusions, for they are legions, but let us pity the weakness of our deluded fellow-citizens, and exert ourselves to correct these popular, but vain and soul-blighting pretensions.   T. F.

FRANKLIN COLLEGE.

Perhaps it is not known to the readers of the Christian Review, that arrangements are in progress to establish by the beginning of another year, Franklin College, at Elm Crag, the residence of the writer. A charter was granted at the last session of the Legislature, and as the system proposed to be adopted has some new features, which must be a decided improvement on all the plans of the country, the Prospectus, giving the general outlines of the plan, we publish below. Education, in this establishment, will be divided into Physical, Intellectual, and Moral. Each department will receive a proper degree of attention. In the mean-time, it is hoped the disciples of Christ are ready to pay more regard to the great subject of training the youths of the country than formerly.   T. F.

The Trustees of "FRANKLIN COLLEGE," feeling deeply sensible, the importance of adopting a system of education, by which the youths of the country may be properly trained and fitted for usefulness, take this means of communicating to the public the distinguishing features of the plan which will be pursued in the first institution of the kind which has been attempted in America. This the community require at our hands, and we cheerfully submit the system we propose, hoping, if it has defects, they will be designated, that we may correct them, and if it be an improvement on the usual plan, the whole community will be benefited by its speedy adoption.

Perhaps no word has been used more vaguely than the term Education.— Frequently it is used to denote the exercise of memory, regardless of perception, reflection, physical or moral culture. Genuine education implies not the exercise of the mind alone, or any one of its powers, but it is the full development of the whole man—body, mind, and soul. It is not the mere acquisition of knowledge, but it is that system of training most essential for the *Physical, Intellectual,* and *Moral* perfection of the world. For the sake of perspicuity, the divisions will be presented separately.

1. PHYSICAL EDUCATION.

In conformity to the ancient maxim, that "in a sound body alone can a sound mind exist," we regard PHYSICAL EDUCATION as the firm basis of all useful training. As a broad, deep and solid foundation is essential to the stability and safety of an edifice, we esteem proper Physical culture as the ground work of the highest Intellectual and Moral attainments. Not that size and mere physical force are always sure criteria from which to infer the greatest strength of mind, but that the full development of the physical man is important to the greatest mental and moral energy.

Believing these are plain principles in nature, the truth of which no intelligent mind will

Believing these are plain principles in nature, the truth of which no intelligent mind will we proceed to detail the plan which we propose adopting for the accomplishment of this important improvement, in the system which we present for consideration.

Notwithstanding the strong prejudices against manual labor, as connected with the education of the young, we believe and trust they can all be removed, and that physical education will, at no very distant day, become one of the most agreeable parts of juvenile training. Experience and observation have and do demonstrate the great truth, that exercises in the way of sports are the engrossing employments of youth; and this clearly proves, that physical exercises are disagreeable only from association. Parents as well as youth must be convinced that physical labor is at least as important as mental, before it will be appreciated.

The objects of the Trustees may be more clearly seen by carefully studying the following propositions:

1st. Physical Education is essential to good health, a vigorous constitution, and a sound mind.

2d. It was designed by the Creator as a blessing to man. He was made to "till the earth," and was placed in the garden of Eden to "dress and keep it."

3d. Labor has been honored by the best of men in all ages, should be honored now, and the young should be taught to regard it as respectable and highly important to their well-being.

4th. While manual labor affords exercise of body, it offers recreation and variety to the mind.

5th. It will enable youths to acquire knowledge of Agriculture, Horticulture and the Mechanic arts, which will be very useful to them through life.

6th. Labor, in an institution of learning, will supply the place of idle and vicious sports, and will be the surest preventative of dissipation.

7. Students, by devoting a portion of their time to physical culture, can apply themselves more clearly to books, and can think more intensely on all subjects.

8th. Physical Education gives energy of character, and habits which will enable their possessor to succeed with more certainty in every avocation of life.

A full discussion of each of these propositions we deem unnecessary, for they are self-evident, and only require the intelligent to see them to be satisfied of their truth.

All learned and reflecting men admit there is a strong tendency to deterioration in the human family, and that idleness, from whatever cause produced, is productive of sloth, feeble muscular powers, defective intellects, and consequent depreciation of all the powers.

There are two extremes in society which we have but little hope of materially benefiting by the system we propose. The very degraded and the very opulent, too generally, view labor as a punishment, and therefore will be loath to adopt any industrious avocation. It is a lamentable truth, that not one young man in fifty, brought up in luxury and idleness, ever becomes educated, is successful in business, or is even capable of retaining the estate inherited. Hence the doctrine of one of our profoundest statesmen, that generally in three generations property, and often respectability, passed from families. Not one in a hundred who does not understand the means of accumulating wealth by industry, is competent to take charge of it.

But objections are strenuously urged against labor as connected with education. It is said "Manual Labor Schools have been attempted and failed."— This is true, and we add it was but just that they should have failed. When labor is performed as a degradation, it cannot but be objectionable.

The evils are two, but both can be corrected.

1st. The character of the employments were such as to forbid success. The hard labor of the cornfield, without science to direct, is truly uninteresting.— It is our object to have such improvements and operations in the farm, garden, nursery and workshops, as will in themselves be interesting to youth. The importance of every performance will be fully explained by those amply qualified, and we doubt not by the proper classification of students, and division of labor, commendable emulation may be excited, and students thereby will become as much interested in physical as mental labor.

2d. The character and qualifications of those who conducted the physical operations in the manual labor schools with which we have been conversant, were such as to forever preclude success. Men without education have been employed, as a kind of overseers, to drive boys to their labor as slaves. To remedy this glaring outrage, we contemplate having all the physical labor conducted by professors, tutors, and officers of the institution, or gentlemen eminently qualified, and no student will be asked to perform service in which the teachers shall not diligently employ their time.

On this plan the farm and garden will afford the best facilities for the study of Geology, Chemistry, Botany, Tillage, the care of crops, the propagation of fruits and ornamental shrubs; while the workshop will constitute an excellent laboratory for the study of Natural Philosophy. And it is not to be forgotten, that all men, whether lawyers, physicians, preachers, merchants, or others, will be much profited through life by a practical knowledge of Agriculture, Horticulture, and the Mechanic arts. As to the importance, however, of labor, more is needless—it only remains now to state briefly the employments and time to be spent in labor.

We do not expect to cultivate a large farm, but it is our object to employ enough land in Agriculture to enable students to learn the full management of the farm. Each student will be instructed in the breeding, rearing, diseases and general management of farm stock. Considerable attention will be given to Horticulture. All the students will be theoretically and practically instructed in the cultivation of vegetables and flowers. Orcharding, or the cultivation of fruits and shrubbery, will claim considerable attention.

Work-shops will be erected for the manufacture of Agricultural and Horticultural implements, and such other articles of mechanism as will be useful to the country.

An important feature of this system is to enable destitute young men, acquainted with and persevering in business, to defray their expenses by their industry. We presume from three to five hours in the day will be devoted to labor, and we have but little hesitation in saying that young gentlemen, acquainted with any department of labor, can pay expenses by the work of their hands, and accomplish a full course of study in almost, or quite as short a space of time, as if there were no employment but the study of books. Still, if a youth were to spend from six to ten years, in acquiring a thorough education, and pay for it by his labor, the system would offer inducements to the poor which have never been offered in our country.

2. LITERARY DEPARTMENT.

In the literary course of the Institution we propose but little that is new.— It is our object to receive pupils of the different ages, and for each division have a competent teacher to take charge of the students in the school room, physical exercises and all the recreations. A full course of English literature will be taught, the Ancient and Modern languages, a full course of Mathematics, and as full a course of science as at any other institution of the country.— Chemistry will be taught not only as a science, but as connected with Agriculture and its kindred branches. Geology, Botany and Entomology will receive special attention.

3. MORAL DEPARTMENT.

The morals and manners of the students will be watched with much vigilance. The Bible is the only book which will be recommended as authority in morals, but nothing of a party character will be suffered in the institution.— Teachers will be required to spend much of their time with the students, and by this means their conversation will be guarded and chastened and their manners much improved.

Full details of the system and the government of the College will be published before the opening of the Institution.

The farm belonging to T. Fanning and B. Embry has been leased for a series of years, the lease renewable at pleasure, as the site of the College. We consider the location most favorable. It is in the heart of one of the best countries of the earth, is considerably elevated, and is supplied with the very best spring water. The College will be sufficiently near the city for students to be supplied with all necessary articles at the cheapest rates, and yet, is at sufficient distance to prevent them from corrupt association. The society of both the country and town is the best. T. Fanning and B. Embry have been employed to erect a College edifice, with dining room and other buildings. The buildings are to be ready for the reception of students by January, 1845. They have also been employed to manage the farm, garden, nursery and workshops during the year 1845.

The property and money already vested, amount to about fifteen thousand dollars, and still there will be a deficit to finish the building, of about four thousand dollars. We have asked, and of course received, no aid from the State; but, in conformity with *universal* custom, we appeal to the public for aid. The amount needed is not very large, but if the institution is opened with a debt hanging over it, we shall be defeated at the threshold in our chief object.— Our intention is to afford boarding and tuition at low prices; but if we have to pay Professors and liquidate a pretty considerable debt from the profits of the establishment, we cannot do so. We suppose the boarding will not be more than sixty dollars per annum, and the tuition from twenty to forty or fifty dollars, and a portion of the students will doubtless be able to pay a part or all of the cost by their industry. We are fully aware that the times are not most favorable for raising funds, but the facts that quite a large amount has already been vested and the institution offers advantages heretofore unknown, encourage us to look with confidence to the friends of industry and education for help. The Trustees have appointed David G. Ligon, Esq., of Moulton, Ala., Dr. M. W. Philips, of Edward's Depot, and Gen. Patrick Henry, of Hinds co., Miss., Hon. J. A. Gardner, of Dresden, W. Tenn., Col. Sam. Martin, of Campbell's Station, E. Tenn., and Dr. Jno. Shelby, Dr. Jno. W. Richardson, W. G. Roulhac, J. J. Trott, Turner Vaughan, and T. Fanning, of Middle Tennessee, to explain the objects of the institution to the public and solicit donations. Books, apparatus, specimens of Natural History, and any property which could be made available, would be as thankfully received as the cash. Most of the contracts for the building have been made payable January, '45, and January, '46. Notes payable to the treasurer for the benefit of the institution would answer the purposes of the trustees, next to cash. However, we wish no one to advance or premise money who does not do so with the view of benefiting the country and with a determination of being punctual in meeting engagements. Believing there are many wealthy gentlemen who have sons or perhaps poor relatives or friends, whom they would like to educate, the Trustees propose to any one who will pay to the treasurer *five hundred dollars* in two or three annual installments, to grant to him the privilege for life of sending one student free of cost for tuition fees.

Arrangements have been made to elect a President and two Professors for the College, so soon as competent gentlemen can be employed, and J. H. Foster, W. H. Wharton, and F. McGavock, have been appointed a committee of correspondence, to ascertain the qualifications of candidates for these chairs, and receive propositions. T. Fanning, T. Vaughan, and Jno. W. Richardson, constitute a committee to employ other agents, if in their judgment more will be needed.

JAMES H. FOSTER, *President.*

B. EMBAY, *Secretary.*

Nashville, Tenn., April 1st, 1844.

WESTERN BAPTIST.

The above is the designation of a weekly Journal, published at Buchanan, Botetourt Co., Virginia, by Elder W. H. Hugart, of the Baptist denomination, which advocates the "pure religion" of the Bible. On our exchange list, there are two papers issued from the Baptist ranks, which pleads for primitive Christianity, and others which are making their way in that direction. This is as it should be, and it is truly gratifying to see it. Our Baptist brethren must, and will come to the Bible; except at least, those who the in great ignorance, or confirmed sectarianism. They are in pretty thick smoke in this country, and it seems the leaders love this darkness.   T. F.

REGENERATION OF THE CHURCHES.

To the Editors of the Christian Review:—

BELOVED BROTHER FANNING :—In the divine providence of our Heavenly Father, I have been recalled from the South—designing, God willing, to spend the summer with the disciples in Tennessee. I had the satisfaction of immersing *four* citizens of Holly Springs, the day before I left, in a stream of pure water adjacent to town—making in all about fifteen that I have immersed in N. Mississippi this year. My labors as an Evangelist have been chiefly aimed to introduce the Apostolic organization and the pure primitive worship among the congregations. And now permit me, for the opening of the brethren's eyes, to state a few facts that necessarily present themselves to an Evangelist's attention:—

1. I have grounds before me broad enough to state that only a lean minority of the churches in Tennessee, professedly reformed, meet together every First day!!

2. That the churches generally only meet monthly!!

3. That of the churches that meet weekly, or monthly, only a lean majority of the members of each attend constantly!!

4. That in a vast majority of our meetings, weekly, monthly, and semimonthly, not only the contribution but the "Lord's Supper" are either woefully neglected or hurried through with in such indecent haste as to sully the dignity and thwart the design and efficacy of this gracious institution! And further, that the reading of the Apostolic epistles is almost totally unheard of as an essential part of orderly worship!!

5, That the ostensible reason many congregations meet not weekly is, the absence of a preacher? Not a king nor a priest in all the churches!!!

6. That many public teachers among us consider themselves pastors of *four* churches!!!

7. Consequently, many of the churches are without Bishops—think that the Elders have no more voice in ruling and attending to the business of the church, as discipline, prayer, giving of thanks, officiating at the table, or baptizing, or reading the word, or directing the public worship, than the veriest stripling in the house!!

8. That many of those churches that meet not every First day, or when they do meet, neglect some one or more of the absolutely essential items of worship, yet claim to themselves the title "the churches of God"!!!

9. That in membership with churches above described, stand enrolled the names of some of the most eminent and veteran preachers among us!!!

10. That some of the churches in Tennessee are living in a state of schism and division—I think.

11. That we have some teachers among us, who, zealous above their knowledge, are seriously injuring the cause they would advance. The eye must not assume the function of the ear.

12. That the churches are criminally neglectful to send forth and sustain Evangelists, after they are orderly ordained.

13. That there are many Bishops (?) among us who have never been ordained by an Evangelist—and some Evangelists (?) who have never been called and sent by the brethren.

The conclusion from the whole premises is, the love of many, teachers and taught, is waxing cold; the cause once flourishing, and advancing, and conquering, is now at a stand—heaven mourns and hell is holding a jubilee.

Evangelists, Bishops, Elders, brethren—all, without exception, arouse you, arouse you from this horrid slumber! To the rescue! to the rescue! of the heritage of God. Tell me not we are before sectarians—what the' we be? We must oh, we must on to perfection. Christ calls us from our sloth—all heaven —the spirits of the just—good men on earth—the glory of God—the honor of the Reformation—our own hope of eternal life—the salvation of sinners—the interest of your children whom you are commanded to train up for God and for his church—the cause of the Bible—the conversion of a world—the union of Christians—the triumph of truth—the reign of Jesus—all, all ask us—Shall things always be so? From the Ohio river on the North to the Mexican gulf on the South, and from the Alleghany to the Ozark mountains, but one voice is heard—but one call is made—but one demand is uttered—but one echo is heard reverberating throughout the length and breadth of the Mississippi Valley, by all the judicious, reflecting, and pious in the Reformation—and that call is for the *Regeneration of the churches.* Now, brethren, now is the time and the hour of need. If no better a plan will do, cease proselyting and baptizing this year, and work solely for the purification of the house of God. It must be done. This is the year for making, and the awful crisis we have approached demands, the longest, strongest, most united effort we have ever yet made. Let us untiringly operate and co-operate in this noblest employ that ever won the affections or enlisted the energies of earth or heaven. Let us meet the tempest—fight with courage. Unless we toil—unless we deny ourselves the love of inglorious ease—we cannot reign or wear the crown—unless our light shine through our actions, and not merely by our words—things will always continue unchanged—the old dying without God and without hope, the young growing up into sin and impiety! In theory, we have taken a mountain stand, while sectarians are on mole-hills below us—our pretensions are many and great—in practice, wherein do we excel? I candidly think this is no time for idling. The distinction between the family of holiness and the children of unrighteousness is not clearly enough visible to satisfy the enthroned Twelve.   Farewell.   W. S. SPEER.

Three Springs, (near Columbia, Ten.,) *April* 16, 1844.

EDUCATION.

To *the Editors of the Christian Review*

BRO. T. FANNING—*Dear Sir:*—If you continue to conduct the Review with the same ability and spirit with which you have commenced it, it cannot fail to be highly useful to the South-Western country. As I am on the eve of leaving home, I will throw out a few hasty hints, in this letter, on education. Why do we meet with so few examples of eminent piety in the world, in these latter days? We are, most of us, corruptly educated, and then turned loose to take our course in a corrupt world; so that it would be marvelous if we were to find numerous examples of great piety in our days. A majority of mankind are undone from being born and bred in families that have no religion; by which means they are made vicious and irregular by being like those with whom they first associated. Thanks be to the God of all grace and mercy, who gave me   pious ancestors—a righteous father and mother who set before me good examples, life and death; who restrained me from vicious company and habits; who taught my feet to visit the house of God; who taught me to read the Holy Bible; and who taught my knees to bow morning and evening to the Giver of all good, and my tongue to pray, and my lips to sing his praise! Who knows how to estimate pious parents and religious tuition? What sort of an education do a majority of virtuous and sober parents, and learned tutors and governors, give to those children under their care? If we had continued perfect, as God at first created man, perhaps the perfection of our nature had been a sufficient self-instruction for every one. But, as sickness and diseases have created the necessity of medicines and physicians; so, the change and disorder of our rational nature have introduced the necessity of education and tutors. And as the only end the physician has in view is to restore nature to its state; so, the only end of education is to restore our rational nature to its proper state. Education, therefore, is to be considered as reason borrowed at second hand, which is, as far as it can, to supply the loss of original perfection. And as physic may justly be called the art of restoring health, so education should be considered in no other light than as the art of recovering man to the right use of his reason. Now, as the instruction of every art or science is founded upon the discoveries, the wisdom, the experience, and maxims of the several great men who have labored in it; so, that human wisdom, or the right use of our reason, which young people should be called to by their education, is nothing else but the best experience and finest reasonings of men who have devoted themselves to the study of wisdom and improvement of human nature. All, therefore, that the great saints in the Bible, and dying men, when fullest of light and conviction, and after the highest improvement of their reason—all that they have said of the necessity of piety, of the excellency of virtue, of their duty to God, of the emptiness and hollow heartedness of riches, of the vanity of the world,—are the sentences, judgments, reasonings, and maxims of the holiest, wisest men in the Bible, when in their highest state of wisdom; should constitute the morning and evening lessons of instruction for youthful minds in the family circle and prayers. Brethren—readers of the Review—how many of us are modeling our sons' minds and morals after the model and pattern which Moses, Abraham, Abel, Isaac, Jacob, Joseph, Job, David, Samuel, Joshua—the holy Prophets—a John the Immerser—the Apostles, Confessors, primitive Christians, and the great reformers and benefactors who have lived since, have left us. These are our exemplars, our moral warriors and heroes— our statesmen, judges, legislators, and models. Christian mothers! readers of the C. Review!—many of you I do not know—nor shall I ever see you in the flesh—how many of you are training your daughters for the skies, *to ape* after Sarah the mother of all good women—the openness, simplicity, kindness, and courtesy of Rebecca—the ardent devotion of Hannah, Huldah, Ruth, and all the other great and good women of the old and new Testaments and Christian history? These are your models. Your daughters are to be your representatives in a few years; it will be known what sort of training they had—what sort of mothers. How absurd for Christians to name their children after pagans, politicians, and wicked men and women! Adieu.

Palmyra, Mo., April 12, 1844.　　　　　　　　　　　　　　　J. CREATH, JR.

TO YOUNG LADIES.

I take my pen to night in continuance of the subject on which I last addressed you. The Christian Religion is necessary to the present, as well as future happiness of all reasonable beings. Without it, there is an aching void this earth cannot fill.

There are periods in which youth, as well as age, feels this most deeply. When your dearest friends are taken from you, and laid low in death, when you see them in the last struggle, how bitter—how dark and gloomy the prospect if there is no hope of a better world. You may until then, have thought lightly of these matters, but now you own with stricken hearts that an unshaken hope in the God of Heaven, is of more value than the wealth of worlds.

As you know that all must bow to the King of Terrors, why not now, while health and vigor are yours, apply your hearts to wisdom? Why not give to your Creator the strength and energy of the intellect with which he has so richly endowed you, instead of wasting it in the pursuit of that which perishes in the using.

The study and *practice* of the Christian Religion gives more happiness than all things earthly, robs death of his sting, and although its votary walk through the dark valley, he fears no evil. He can say thy rod and thy staff comfort and support me. Religion was not given for death alone, but it was made for the regulation of life. It is a principle that must control every action, and form good and pure character.

If you ask, how you are to acquire a knowledge of it? I answer alone by studying that book in which its history is given. It is there only you must look if you wish to be rational and intellectual when you think of preparing for Eternity.

You may neglect the Bible and feel about in the dark for something you can't tell what. You may seek and pray for Religion, but mind, the Lord never told you to do that, and has given you no promise that he will hear such prayers. You may say, I have read the Bible, but still know nothing about it. Did you ever take it up with a sincere desire to learn what it teaches, study it with the idea that it may be understood, and put in practice; or did you conclude it to be a dark and mysterious affair altogether?

In the latter case, it is not possible to understand any book. Give a child a grammar and teach him he cannot learn its contents; do you think he will make much progress?

In order to be benefited by reading the Bible, we must understand why the different parts are written and what was the aim of the writers. Now, you might study the books of Genesis, Exodus, Leviticus, all your lives, and find nothing concerning the Christian religion. You would see the history of Creation, the fall of man, the Deluge, all the events relative to the Jews, but nothing about being Christians. You may pass through the Old Testament, studying the books of History, the Psalms, the Proverbs, the Songs of Solomon, and still not know what to do to be saved. You may go on still farther, and hear the prophets in majestic strains telling of a mighty personage to come upon the earth. Enwrapped in vision, they look through the dark vista of future ages, and foretell of a Saviour's sufferings to redeem their sin-smitten world. They tell of his being a man of sorrows, acquainted with grief, a mourner all his days.

They tell too that his word was to go forth from Jerusalem, that there the laws of his kingdom should first be promulgated, still they give not these laws to the world, that being reserved for another book, for another age, for other men. It is in the New Testament we find these laws given for christianizing the earth; it is useless to look for them elsewhere. Nothing preventing we will in future call your attention to them, and bid you adieu for the present.

LUCY.

IDOLATRY.

To the Editors of the Christian Review:

BRETHREN EDITORS:—It is thought exceedingly strange in this enlightened age, that men should ever have been addicted to idolatry. What! bow down to sticks and stones! fancy the sun a deity and call the moon his companion and a goddess! and view the stars as so many objects of worship!

It is true, we think it a marvelous departure from the use of right reason that men should worship and honor the creature more than the creator. But the age of idolatry has not passed, though the age of miracles may be gone by. The law of Solomon suffered not a witch to live. Alas for our generation, if a like law prevailed in reference to the bewitched! For covetousness is idolatry, and fall many a slave to Mammon bows the knee. By strong enchantment fastened to his throne.

There has ever seemed to me to be some apology for the adoration of the Luminaries of Heaven. The sun after years of familiarity is still the sublimest of created objects, the brightest image of the Eternal, the father of day, the regulator of the seasons, and the dispenser of innumerable blessings to mankind. The moon has ever been the symbol of female majesty, and a queendom was assigned her at her creation. The stars are glorious appearances, fit likenesses of the sons of God "high and lifted up," and human nature "ever looketh up for succor" and scans the heavens for the residence of a deity. Far less honorable was that groveling spirit which led. the children of Israel to bow down before a golden calf, or that not less debased and idolatrous spirit which leads thousands in our day to the altar of Mammon.

That alter—upon it what sacrifice are offered. I have heard infidels object to the bloody altar at Jerusalem, and speak of the rivers of blood, of the evils and agonies of innocent beasts, but one thing can be said in its favor, it was never stained with human gore. Not so with the altar of Mammon. Life, limb, liberty, affection, philanthropy, patriotism, honesty, chastity, hospitality, benevolence, all the virtues that adorn human nature, are made a whole burnt offering to this God.

Of all the delusions of this age none is so strong as that under which the votaries of Mammon labor. Not long since one of the worshippers at his shrine, amidst the toil and fatigue occasioned by the unwieldy burden which his manifold cares and perplexities about lands, cotton, and currency imposed upon him, was heard to console himself with this most comfortable saying, that "through much tribulation we must enter the kingdom of Heaven."— Tribulation for the kingdom of Heaven's sake!!

A. GRAHAM.

CHURCH ORGANIZATION.

In previous Nos. of the Review, I have endeavored to urge upon the Disciples the *importance* of complete organization, and the appointment and work of Evangelists. Next, some of the qualifications of Evangelists, and the appointment of other officers will be considered. The twelve Apostles, Timothy, Philip and Titus Were Evangelists or Gospel ministers, and if their qualifications can be ascertained, it will not be very difficult who should be preachers in this age. When we reflect, Evangelists anciently were directed to "*set in order*" things needful; "*ordain Elders*" in the Churches; "preach the word;" to be instant in season, out of season; to reprove, rebuke, exhort, with all long suffering and doctrine," we are led. to the conclusion, they were men of peculiar qualifications. It is a very grievous error of the times to suppose almost any pert, loquacious youth, though destitute of Christian gravity, zeal and research, is prepared for Evangelical operations. Boys, striplings, and men without great seriousness, and a good stock of knowledge, should not be sent out as representatives and advocates of the Christian Religion. The churches should educate all their members in the school of Christ, and as fast as they become qualified—not before—for the different stations, they should be *installed* into office. The idea of men's travelling, almost from the rivers to the ends of the earth, as preachers, who are not specially commissioned by their respective churches, is ridiculous in the extreme; and such a practice must prove extremely deleterious. No man should be permitted to instruct the public on the subject of Christianity, who is not deeply pious, conversant with the word of God, and acquainted with his mother language, so as to speak at least intelligibly. If we wish the cause to be respected, we should have able and zealous advocates. I do not mean by this that an orator, a man of wealth, or great show, should be selected. Far from it. These are serious disadvantages. Next, I must bring to the notice of the reader Bishops in the Church of God. I state it as a fact, which may be proved by any one who will take the pains, that no church is fully organized and qualified to do all things in order, to have complete subordination amongst the members, or can be prepared to exhibit fully the beauty and transcendent excellency of the Christian institution, without Bishops and Deacons. I frankly confess however, I approach this subject with some degree of diffidence. I hesitate not because of lack of information, or decided convictions of what is right; but because I am well aware few of the churches are prepared to appreciate its importance. The appointment of those officers, indeed, seems to be a mere matter of chance and fancy. If the *notion* strike some preacher or member, and there are men sufficiently popular to get a majority of the votes, he is set apart to the work by holding up hands, acclamation, counting the ayes and noes, or in any other *expedient* manner, without much regard to Gospel qualifications, or to the special directions of the New Testament. Hence it is truth indisputable, there is but little dignity or responsibility with most bishops— less knowledge—no government at all of themselves, and less than no respect paid by the flocks. Hence, too, the complaint that "bishops do no good." The causes of these grievances may be briefly noted.

1st. The qualifications of Bishops and Deacons should be strictly regarded. 2d. The order of their appointment should not be forgotten.

3d. If they do not perform the work prescribed, they should be put out of their bishopric.

In reference to the qualifications, I am sorry to think any disciple of the Savior should advocate a kind of liberal construction of the Scriptures, which at once says the Apostles have made unnecessary requirements. Paul, in our holy confession, prescribes the following qualifications, which should be well studied before an appointment is made. If a single one be lacking, no man dare go into office:—1 He must desire the office; 2 He must be blameless; 3 The husband of one wife; 4 Vigilant; 5 Sober; 6 Of good behavior; 7 Given to hospitality; 8 Apt to teach; 9 Not given to wine; 10 No striker; 11 Not greedy of filthy lucre; 12 Patient; 13 Not a brawler; 14 Not covetous; 15 One that ruleth well his own house, having his children in subjection; 16 Not a novice; 17 He must have a good report of them without; 18 Not accused of riot or unruly; 19 Not self-willed; 20 Not soon angry; and 21, and lastly, he should be "proved." It will not answer for the brethren to treat these matters as the sectarian world treat the commands of God, by asserting some are "ess*ential*" and some "*non-essential.*" When we take the liberty of saying most of these are important, but we may dispense with the idea of a Bishop's having one wife, faithful, obedient children, being able to teach, exhort and convince the gainsayers, we may on the same parity, dispense with every requisition of the Bible. Remember it, brethren, this is a dangerous position. Tell me not, if you have not men who come precisely up to the qualifications, "you must select those who come nearest the standard." If every qualification is not obvious to all, let men be educated in the churches till there is no dispute, and I am happy in expressing the belief that there are men in most churches who might be qualified by devotion to this single object, in a year or two, to take upon them the sacred responsibility of taking care of the church of God. Not more than two or three years generally elapsed after the Apostles planted churches, before they returned and ordained Elders in every city, or appointed some one to attend to it, but not so now—churches grow old without Gospel Bishops. When the Evangelist or Evangelists of a congregation and the members all see, that certain brethren have proved themselves called to act in the capacity of an overseer, the church should signify satisfaction of qualifications and the Evangelist should proceed to *ordain* or set them apart to the work, by prayer, fasting and imposition of hands. In the examples of the New Testament there is no instance of a church ordaining its own bishops, and who ever does it, or recommends it, transcends the teachings of the holy spirit. I am aware the contrary of this has been often asserted, again and again, but it is all worse than nothing so long as there is no attempt at proof. For authority that Evangelists alone ordained Elders anciently, I refer the reader to Acts 14, 23; Titus 1, 5.

In the next No., all things concurring, I will call attention to the difference, if any, between Elders and Bishops, their employment, and the qualifications and work of Deacons. In the mean-time, I will be pleased to see the views of any of my beloved brethren. If I do not state what is true, brethren, show it; and if I do, adopt it in your practice.   T. F.

CHURCH GOVERNMENT.

As Church Government is now a most interesting subject of investigation, and you invite the attention of the brethren to a proper examination of it, I shall make a few remarks on the subject, in the hope that they may tend to excite more diligence in the search after truth. Before examining any subject, it is better to know precisely what it is we wish to investigate, and define the terms we use in expressing the subject under consideration.

Though we find the word church, frequently occurring in the epistles, almost all who have any knowledge of the original language, admit the word congregation would more properly express the meaning of the word in the original. As far as I can learn, the word church in its true scripture sense, is applicable to the whole community of Christians, and not to any particular portion, in any place: hence in the following remarks I shall use it in that sense. The first position assumed, will be one which all parties unanimously unite in condemning, but as they oppose us on many other points, we need not lose courage, and refuse, to investigate, for fear of their opposition.

The position is this, the Bible is the sole and sufficient, authority for us, in matters of church government. The reverse is believed and taught by the various parties, namely that the Mosaic law was an inflexible law, suited to *one* people and country, alone, while the Christian religion, being suited to *all* nations and climes, is of a plastic nature, molding itself to the different periods "and circumstances, of those who come under its government, and that no revelation whatever, is made in the Bible, in regard to any form of church government. All cheerfully admit the claims of our Saviour, to be the supreme ruler, and lawgiver; now either he has given us a law for the government of his church, or he has not, but has left us to provide for ourselves as circumstances may demand; if we say he has not, then no law, no transgression, being the rule, we must recognize all the conflicting claims to the governing power, the of

Catholic Popes, Cardinals and Councils; the Presbyterian lay Elders, Presbyters, Synods, and General Assembly; the Methodist Presiding Elders, Bishops and Conferences, and of all the numerous sects, as being right, and sanctioned by Christ himself. Hence the former position, that a law has been given us, is much the most reasonable. Another conclusion, our Saviour either could not give us a law of Church Government, or he would not; the first position, no one will assume; if the second is taken, then looking around on the innumerable conflicting, sects we must say, he has left us to grope our way in darkness, and thereby cast a stain upon his character for benevolence and love. Consequently, we must conclude that a law has been provided for us, and as we have no authentic revelation from above, since John wrote the final Amen to the Apocalypse, to the Bible alone must we go for the law. Let us consider it in another point of view, we must say Christ has given us a law for church government, or has not; if he has not given us one, but left it to the prudence of man to decide by whom, and in what manner, he shall be governed, then everything done by officers thus constituted, must be done, either with his sanction, and full approval, or the contrary; if by his approval, then all the rules and regulations of the Catholic Councils, Methodist Conferences, Presbyterian General Assembly, &c., are binding on the community, and ought to be religiously obeyed; in addition to this, if we assume the position, we at once declare, that our Saviour knew not the best mode of enlarging his kingdom, and impugn his character for reason, knowledge and prudence; for those conflicting claims have retarded his cause more than anything else. Few will take this position, On the other hand, if everything done by those officers, be done without his approval, we have men usurping his place, and legislating for us, who have not the shadow of a right to the place they have taken, and when we obey them, we disobey the Lord, and all who have ever obeyed such officers, have sinned; in addition to this, we must assert that our Lord has left us to wander without a guide, and do what he knew he would not and could not approve, thereby impugning his character for love and kindness. Hence, the position that he has given us a law, is the best, and we must again go to the Bible.

Again, if we assert that our Saviour has given no officers and form of government, then we must inevitably conclude a total change in man's nature has been wrought; in consequence of which, the laws execute themselves; for never before, from the time the angel was placed at the gate of Paradise, to see that the law of expulsion was executed, has it occurred, that executive officers were not necessary. But it is sometimes asserted, that church officers and government are not necessary now; that the officers mentioned in the New Testament, were given for a temporary purpose, and when that object was attained, the necessity for them passed away: well, the reason why those officers were given, was, that the saints might be perfected, consequently the saints are now perfect; rather absurd, I think. Again, if we assert that church officers and government are not necessary, we must conclude that Christ's promise has failed, and the powers of darkness have prevailed against his church, for we can find no authentic records of a church existing for any length of time, without officers and government. Having now shown that officers, and government, are necessary, I will add one more argument, to prove that those mentioned in the New Testament, are alone proper: if we are not to have the same, we must add to, or diminish from the number; if we say we may add thereto, we must either put these officers in, for the purpose of enacting new laws, or of executing those already given; no one will assert the former, and the moment we assume the latter, we pronounce his system imperfect, and impugn his wisdom and knowledge. If we say we may diminish from the number we again pronounce his system imperfect, and impugn his character for wisdom and knowledge. Now, as there are but three kinds of authority; legislative, judicial and executive, and the authority of those officers is not legislative, it must be judicial and executive. All I ask now is that some one better acquainted with the New Testament than I am, will show us what officers are necessary; their qualifications, the extent of their authority both judicial and executive; and finally, the powers of a properly organized congregation of the Lord.   W.

"ASSOCIATION OR FOURIERISM."

As a Journalist, and annotator, I esteem it a privilege, and duty to notice such of the passing events, as seem to have for their object the melioration of the human family. All religions, all societies, and enterprises, *profess* to have for their object, either the benefit of a few individuals; or, the great bulk of mankind; and yet, it is an undeniable fact, that many human establishments have conferred but little real advantage, and others have been a real disadvantage. It is rash to pronounce sentence in reference to any matter, without comprehending it, and it is safe, to receive every *untried* scheme at considerable discount. Theories sometimes look fair, but owing to lack of qualifications in agents, or some unseen, and unanticipated defect, the practical results, sadly disappoint all calculation.

To state briefly what is intended in this essay, let it be noted, that many individuals both in Europe and America, of a nigh order of talent, as well as men of more circumscribed acquirements, are at this time, deeply interested in the subject of *"Association"* This is another name for "Fourierism," and to understand both, suffice it to say, that *Charles Fourier,* a Frenchman who died at Paris in 1837, after forty years patient investigation, declared that he had discovered the true mode of *organizing* society, so as to avoid most of the *physical, intellectual, Moral, governmental, commercial, social,* and *religious* evils of the world. To give the details of his system has required the publication of many books, and it cannot be expected, in a work of the character of the Review, more than the skeleton can be presented. Fourier argues that the evils of man, originate not from imperfection in political governments, or natural depravity; but from the disorganized state of society. He contends, that the surrounding circumstances bring upon us, most of our miseries, and if our *"antagonist"* relations were changed, so as to harmonize with nature, and our own constitution and wants, the consequence would be perfect peace and happiness on earth.

The advocates say, "The relations instituted among men, by the present form of society, are those of *extreme* individual selfishness, and lead directly to *Indigence, Fraud, Oppression, War, Disease* and *False, Delusive Doctrines,*—effects which cannot be prevented short off through *Re-organization."*

"Association" is designed to abrogate the present corrupt system of trade, prevent circumvention, lying, and duplicity of every character, ignorance, laziness, party strifes, in politics and religion, and make the earth a perfect paradise. Now the only question is, will it do it? *Nous verrons.*

The means are simple. First, all men are required to give up exclusive interest in property. Or in other words, let societies or associations be formed which shall have one common interest; so, when one labours, or trades, self is not all he has in view; but the benefit of a community. Call this *common stock,* or *joint stock,* or a *partnership plan.* Every man who comes into the arrangement would be required to subscribe stock, to the amount of what he puts in, and although it would be active capital to the "Phalanx," yet he would own, and be entitled to profits, in proportion to capital vested, labour performed, or skill exercised.

Five-twelfths of the profits are allowed for capital, *four-twelfths* for labour, and *three-twelfths* for skill.

All men, women, and children, would be required to devote a portion of the time to labour, another portion to study, and another to moral culture.

"Industry" is said to be "every productive exertion of human faculties and forces, and may be distinguished for sake of precision, into, 1st Domestic services; 2d Agriculture; 3d Manufacture; 4th Commerce; 5th Education; 6th The study and application of the Sciences, and 7th The application of the Fine Arts.

The objects of such associations would be to produce unity of action in every thing, to bring the rich and the poor in contact, that each may pursue the same avocation and be entitled to credit in proportion to merit. Every one would occupy the station to which his qualifications would entitle him, and all would labor in "groups" and "series," in order to prevent confusion, promote the general weal, and enable each to exert himself in the capacity which nature has designated for him. The three main points are, 1st To make labor attractive by inuring all to it as a virtue, and placing the proper motives before the operatives; 2d To Educate all connected with the Association, and 3d To give a practical exemplification of thorough moral culture. No sectarianism is to be preferred; but the Bible recommended as supreme authority, though all sects and even unbelievers to be received as members of the phalanx.

This, I am aware, is but a faint view of the system, but enough has been said to cause reflection. If the cause be a good one, it will commend itself to all as fast as it becomes known; but if not of God, it must come to nought. I give no opinion as to the full details; but the leading principles are as true as God is true. That Unity of action is indispensable in any great achievement, and Physical, Intellectual and Moral education should be combined to perfect society, no one can doubt. At a future time, I may pursue the subject, but at present I close by propounding two questions.

1st. Are the people of this age generally prepared for such a state of things?

2d. Can all men be Christians, circumstanced as they now are?   T. F.

OBITUARY.

The following lines were written on hearing of the sudden and melancholy death of my amiable friend Mrs. A———, of C———, La., who was remarkable alike for intellectual worth and moral excellency. This noble lady, characterized by the Christian virtues, and graces—'beloved and praised in the churches—the illustrious ornament and model of her sex,—having enjoyed the pure delight of an affectionate meeting with the Lord's people around His table, was returning home and while yet the joyous accents of praise to God, had scarcely died away from her lips and His goodness filled her soul with heavenly love; her horses started; she was precipitated from her carriage violently and instantly expired. Her husband and two amiable little daughters saw her thus suddenly snatched away. May the Lord protect and guide them to the haven of eternal rest, whither the wife, the mother has followed the Lord of glory.

The solemn tale of death succeeding death,
>   With fearful haste again and yet again,
With heavy peal and grating sound to health.
>   The ear fills and the sad heart rends with pain!
Another saint is fall'n! In mid-life's bloom,
>   And joy, and hope, and vigor fall'n asleep!
Yet slumbers she in Christ; nor is her doom.
>   To sleep unending, though profound and deep!
Oh! lovely, kind and holy was her mind—
>   Pure as th' unsulli'd etner, or the light!—
Her love and goodness embrac'd all mankind.
>   While each her presence fill'd with pure delight!
Affectionate sister and faithful wife.
>   Kind friend, good mother, all in thee centred!
Thy many works of love ended alone with life,
>   When into rest by death thou hast enter'd!
The monster fell tore thee unwam'd away.
By one decisive blow! when just complete
>   Thy last action of love and faith's sweetsway!
As home thou' turn'd with grace of God replete!
>   Thou wast remov'd with but a moment's pain—
Nor suffered pangs of loath'd disease severe—
Nor didst the last and sad farewell remain
To speak to husband, friends, and daughters dear!
Be this thy epitaph: Here doth repose
>   She, whose pure life is hidden with Christ the Lord;
Of whom the worst of all that her worst foes
>   Could say, was that she taught and preach'd His word.

Newton Place.   P.

OBITUARY.

Death has again been amongst us, and another of our loved and cherished ones has suddenly departed from our midst. We speak of Sister MARGARET, consort of JOSIAH WILLIAMS, who died April 14th, leaving her husband and a large family in great sorrow. It is about nine years since she yielded obedience to the Saviour, and became a member of the Christian Church. Those who knew her best, can tell of her devotion to the cause—that she walked meekly and humbly before her God, fulfilling the duties of life as became a Christian. As a member of the same band, we mingle our sorrow with those most deeply afflicted, and although all our hearts are bowed down at the ravages death makes amongst us, yet we do not repine, we bless the hand that chastens, that teaches us we are but dust, and lifts our hearts from the perishing things of earth, to a brighter and better world. To her daughters we would say, walk worthy the vocation wherewith you are called. Let not the vanities of earth allure you from that path of piety, in which as disciples of the lowly Redeemer, we should all walk. To her sons, let the memory of her deep, her undying love come to your hearts as the voice of an angel whispering of purity and goodness. Let it incite you to form such character as in the intensity of her affection she often wept and prayed you might possess. Let her example and precepts cause you in early life, to bow down and worship at the holy shrine of your mother's God. If her friend and companion in the sorrows and sufferings of life, has never submitted to the Saviour, it is hoped, this heaviest of trials, may lead him to place his affections on things that perish not, that he may meet his lost and lone one, where the anguish of earth is not known, and where God shall wipe all tears from our eyes.   A SISTER.

NEWS FROM THE CHURCHES.

PORT-GIBSON, March 25th, 1844.

DEAR BRO. FANNING:—I have seen the third No. of the Christian Review; I have read the Review with interest and feel flattered that it will do much good in the cause of truth. I have procured you a few subscribers whose names you will find subjoined.

I see in the first No. of the Review a request to the Brethren to forward you the State of affairs among themselves as Churches or congregations. I am now preaching for a fragment of a church at Grand Gulf, Claiborne Co., Mississippi. I preach here once a month. At the Grand Gulf there are five denominations, (us inclusive) using one house as a place of worship; the progress of truth is much retarded by opinionism, I preach once a month in Port-Gibson, once at Willow Springs, and once per month for the Church at Utica, Hinds Co. I have been but a short time in this section of country, and have met with much opposition. I do not know the number of Brethren in the Church at Utica, but it is not over 25, Bro. Foster is their Deacon. At Willow Springs, we have no brethren at all; At Port-Gibson, we have not organized; we have no place to preach except in the Methodist meeting house, and that at night in the week, we cannot get it on the Lord's day. I have been enabled by the Spirit's arguments to remove a great deal of prejudice, and I do pray that ere the year closes the Lord may bless my labors for good in this section.

Yours in Christian Love,   C. O. FERGUSON.

FOREKNOWLEDGE AND DECREE,—BY J. C. ANDERSON, ED.

If God's foreknowing an event will take place is the same as his decreeing it, no man ever did or ever can please or obey God. For illustration, God says to Adam "Thou shalt not eat of a certain tree," this is a decree expressed, but he foreknew, and therefore decreed he should eat of it. Now if Adam abstains from eating, he violates the decree of God's foreknowledge, and if he eat, he violates the decree expressed in words. So, with all men, God says in his word thou shalt not do so and thus; this is his expressed decree, but he foreknows and of course decrees, men will perform what he has forbidden. If, then, men sin, they violate God's decree expressed; and if they sin not, they violate his foreknowledge; so do as they may, they are compelled to break a decree.

CHRISTIAN REVIEW.

VOL. L   NASHVILLE, JULY, 1844.   NO. VII.

FIRST PRINCIPLES.—NO. I.

In the world, there are but two classes—*saints* and *sinners;* and in the Bible, there are but two kinds of teaching; the first is designed to convert men to God, and the second is intended to perfect Christian character. While the overwhelming majority of the world are without God, and without hope, "FIRST PRINCIPLES" must engross the attention of the ministers of the Gospel. The Savior said, "Go teach all nations;" and, when we examine the doings or "Acts of the Apostles," we learn they spent much of their time in instructing both Jews and Greeks in the very first lessons of the Christian religion. In the world's history, no individual has succeeded in learning the details of any science, without comprehending the first principles. We have the alphabet of Geology, Chemistry, Philosophy, and Botany, as we do of Arithmetic, Algebra, Geometry, and Grammar: the same is true of Christian science; and it is utterly impossible to master any subject of deep interest, without an intimate acquaintance with the first lessons. For the sake of perspicuity, I will proceed to discuss, numerically, the "beginning of the doctrine of Christ."

1st. THE SUFFICIENCY AND AUTHORITY OF THE WORD OF LIFE.—No one can fully appreciate the salvation of the Gospel, unless he acknowledge both the *sufficiency* and *authority* of the Scriptures. All the creeds, in word, confess the sufficiency of the Bible; but in recommending another law, the authority thereof is denied. The power of a government is its authority; hence the Apostle denounced some as "having a form of godliness, but denying the power." All men, or churches, admitting the sufficiency of God's word to furnish in all good works and righteousness, and contending at the same time for creeds and human authority, thereby deny the power of God, and need instruction as to the first lessons of the Bible.

In admitting the sufficiency of the Scriptures, no one should presume to countenance the systems of the age; for in so doing, the word of the Lord loses its effect on the heart, and the mind becomes bewildered by the traditions of the fathers. All persons desirous to know the whole truth, should meekly receive the word of God, tremble at its admonitions, and seek daily to find the path of life. Connected with this, the Scriptures should be regarded as revelations of God, to his erring creatures indiscriminately, and not intended for a few favored persons. Individual responsibility is a great matter, in becoming wise unto salvation. The first reflection of every son and daughter of Adam should be, that each is accountable to God for knowledge and purity, and, if blind and slothful, he or she must "fall into the ditch." Indeed, unless human beings have confidence that they are addressed in God's proclamation, and that it is in their power to understand its sacred truths, they can have no courage to study it. Convince a child that Arithmetic and Grammar are so deep and recondite, that none but teachers can fathom them, and it would be unreasonable to

suppose they could comprehend them. When our contemporaries learn that the Bible is an intelligible book, addressed to all intelligent creatures, they will be far elevated above the present condition of the world, and a new era will commence.

Next, in point of importance, is the great truth, that the "Gospel is the power of God to the salvation of all who believe." So long as the precious word of truth is esteemed a *dead letter,* incapable of effecting any good, till the Spirit descends, applies it to the sinner's heart, and makes it effectual in the conversion of the soul, we cannot hope for the spread of Christianity. All parties, at this day. Catholics, Episcopalians, Presbyterians, Baptists, Methodists, and Quakers, contend for an application of the word to the heart by the Spirit, to produce any beneficial results; and until this spell is broken, and mankind are convinced the word is the good seed, which, sown in "good and honest hearts," produces thirty, sixty, and a hundred fold, we dare not anticipate much religious reform. This absurd dogma is at this day holding the civilized world in chains of bondage. That there may be no misunderstanding, I will introduce a few most pointed arguments in favor of the power of the word, from the Book itself. David says, "The law of the Lord is perfect, converting the soul." "The entrance of thy word giveth light; it giveth understanding to the simple." For the purpose of enlightening and converting mankind, the Messiah said, *"teach all nations."*—"Go *into all the world, and preach the Gospel to every creature,"*— But why direct to teach or preach, if the proclamation be not sufficient to accomplish that for which it was intended? In the second place, Christians are "furnished to all good works," by the inspired Scriptures. The belief of these heaven-born truths, will do more in reconciling man to his God, than all the plicate and clergy of the earth are now doing. It should be inscribed upon all our banners, that God's word is mighty, and will prevail.

2d. Rules for Interpreting the Bible.—Under this head, much might be said, of unparalleled interest; but my object, for the present, is to present to the student of the Bible a few plain rules, which will serve as landmarks in all his future investigations of sacred literature.

Rule 1st. In approaching the Bible, contemplate it as a revelation made to man in his lost state—fully adapted to all his exigencies, and able to make him wise unto salvation.

Rule 2d. Contemplate the Bible as proving a "savor of life unto life" to them that believe and obey it, but as "a savor of death unto death" to them, whom its sacred truths are revealed, and who prove incorrigible to the end.

Rule 3d. In opening a book, in either the Old or New Testament, the student of the Bible should enquire, Who is the author? Was he master of his subject? Did he intend to teach others? When did he write? Where did he reside? and lastly, What were his motives in writing?

Rule 4th. Title pages, though little things, should not be overlooked. For illustration, in opening the first book in the Bible, the reader notices the caption "Genesis;" and when, upon enquiry, he learns it denotes *generation,* or *the history of the creation,* he will examine the book with this impression fully imprinted upon his mind. If the *Book of Conversions,* in the New Testament, is read, as its title implies, the whole DOINGS of Apostles will have their wonted influence on the mind.

Rule 6th. The characters addressed must be known, to determine the objects of the writer. Let the student of the Scriptures ascertain whether saints, sinners, penitents, or impentients, are addressed. If, for instance, one who wishes to know what to do to be saved, should open at the Epistles, it is not probable he will find the least item of instruction.

Rule 6th. There are at least three styles of writing in the Scriptures, each having its own peculiarities, to be studied, viz: LITERAL, METAPHORICAL or SYMBOLICAL, and PROPHETIC. In the interpretation of literal language, the student will receive the words in their ordinary acceptation; or, if the words have different meanings, the circumstances and connection must decide which shall be preferred. The *kind* of metaphors should be known, and their fitness to illustrate the subjects. It is not to be presumed they are given to conceal the truth, but to *demonstrate* it. The greatest difficulty in understanding metaphors, consists in attempting to illustrate too many subjects and points. Each parable or metaphor is intended to illustrate one point; and when fitness is sought in a dozen features, the illustration is overstrained, and generally loses all its force. *Prophecies* are often of difficult interpretation; but, if the reader will keep in mind, they are drawings or histories of events in future, and aim only to learn the substance and soul of them, he may comprehend quite a sufficiency for all practical purposes.

Rule 7th. In commencing a book, let the reader inform himself whether it is a history, epistle, or a book of statutes; and, this decided, he should proceed as he does in a history on any other subject, as he would in reading a letter from a friend, or as in studying the laws of his country.

Rule 8. The places described, dates of books, and customs of the times, should have a bearing on all the investigations of the Scriptures.

Rule 9. No one should suffer himself to proceed, in reading, faster than he masters the subjects and makes them his own. If one word, sentence, or verse, is passed without understanding it, all future investigations become more and more doubtful. The meaning of that *word* or *verse,* might be a key to a whole book. Let each reader have a dictionary at hands and never pass any thing without a strong effort to understand it.

Rule 10. False rules of judging of truth, such as being influenced by majorities, the long standing of a doctrine or practice, or the learning, wealth, and friends in favor of it, must be banished from the mind.

Rule 11. A sincere desire to know the truth for oneself, and a determination to follow it, is of the first moment in the study of the Bible.

Rule 12. Confidence that the truth will make us free and happy in time, and secure us a seat on high, is of very great importance to all who seek the wisdom which comes from above.

CHURCH ORGANIZATION.

In the prosecution of this subject, I wish to show from the Bible who Elders, Bishops and Deacons are, and their duties.

1. ELDERS.

Too many have concluded that the term Elder is indicative of office, and hence the "Elder's office" is a very common expression. In classic usage, Elder is invariably used to denote seniority; the same is true in reference to its application in the Old Testament and New, and why intelligent Christians could have come to any other conclusion, I am at a loss to determine. Paul says, "rebuke not an Elder, but entreat him as a father;" and Peter says, "The Elders who are among you I exhort," and who will say that these were any but old members in the church, who were to be respected on account of age; and on the same account were commanded to take the "oversight" of the brethren. The term Elder is *adjective* or descriptive, and not substantive. What is more ridiculous than to set apart young men or striplings, and call them Elders or old men!! I do humbly trust my brethren will investigate this subject, and abandon their childishness. The term implies a certain qualification of an officer, but never denotes either office or officer. Knowing that the brethren have written and spoken differently, I challenge a discussion of this subject. Who will undertake to prove that Elder and Bishop are synonymous?

2. BISHOPS.

The term *Episcope* in the Greek Testament, is always indicative of an officer, and *Episcopee* of office.

Bishop and Bishopric are good translations. A Bishop then is a man of age, sobriety, intelligence and other qualifications, who is to rule, nourish, instruct, and admonish the churches. This is a most responsible office, and for it men should be as strictly educated as for law, medicine, or for preaching the Gospel. Bishops are always mentioned in the New Testament as connected with churches, in the plural number. The idea of one man arrogating to himself the Bishopric of a state or a territory is a strange perversion of the order of the Almighty. Bishops, in every church, are as essential to their well-being as civil officers are to society in its present organization. It is certainly remarkable, that few of the churches have given this matter the requisite attention. I do not know a church of qualified Bishops in the U. States, and the greater is the shame, when we reflect that almost any church might have such, were the members disposed to learn and teach as the Gospel requires. Evangelists should give lessons on this subject, and cause the churches to raise up men to teach, admonish, watch and govern the members. Were the congregations every where furnished with Gospel Bishops, the aspect of affairs would be greatly changed in a short time. Instead of ignorance and indifference, intelligence and zeal would be apparent—congregations would grow in grace—our countrymen would see the light, and myriads would be converted to God where there is one poor rebel taken now. Eloquent preaching in this age is the main implement to slay the enmity of sinners, but with proper organization, eloquence of Christian works would do much more.

3. DEACONS.

Deacons are described by Paul to Timothy and Titus, and their character should be carefully studied by the congregation. There is but one difficulty to be settled, and that is to determine if the Apostles taught all that was important on the subject, and nothing more. Both Deacons and Deaconesses should be in every church. What do we lack yet, my Brethren?   T. F.

CAMPBELL AND RICE'S DEBATE.

In the 6th No. of the Review, I endeavored to present, briefly, the main arguments of Messrs. C. and R., in reference to the action of baptism; and in this No. I wish to show the most important positions on the *Subjects of Baptism.*

Mr. Rice, having the affirmative, proceeded to show, that infants are proper subjects of baptism, from the following considerations:

1. He contended, a majority of religionists who believe the Bible, have always pleaded for infant membership; and that it is not probable so many wise men could be mistaken.

To which Bro. C. replied, in substance, that, from the days of Adam and Eve, in the garden, to the present time, the overwhelming mass have been in gross error, and under the dominion of sin. Indeed, that the majority were wrong in the days of Noah, Moses, Abraham, and all the prophets; that few were right in the days of the Savior and his Apostles; and, finally, if Mr. Rice had been in the place of Martin Luther, he would have admitted the force of the argument, that the great multitude of the learned were opposed to him; and therefore a reformation would not have been attempted. Bro. C. argued, that majorities and minorities were no tests of truth, and that it is a lamentable truth, that the greater part of mankind, at this day, are idolaters, barbarians, infidels, skeptics, revilers, and opposed to God and virtue.

2. In the second place, Mr. Rice proceeded to prove, that the Apostles were not commissioned to organize a *"new church"* but to "extend the privileges" of the Jewish congregation. Mr. Rice contended, that the Apostles were sent to "make *disciples,"* by baptizing, and afterwards teaching, and that in case of infants, of course, they discipled always by baptism; and under this head he undertook to prove the identity of the Jewish and Christian religions and churches; and upon the settling of this question, the whole controversy must terminate. In proof of the identity, he contended, 1st, That the same God reigned; 2d, The same moral code was binding; 3d, That (as he stated) the Gospel was preached in both churches, and that circumcision was the door, to mates, into the church, and that females entered by virtue of the circumcision of brothers and fathers, under Moses; and that baptism was the door under the new economy.

To all of which, brother C. replied, 1st, That the commission gave absolute authority for the nations (infants and others) to be *taught* before baptism, and that he who did not hear the Gospel and believe it, could not be baptized, according to ancient usage; 2d, That the same God, governing by the same moral principles, no more proved the identity of the Jewish and Christian churches, than it proved the identity of France and the U. States; because the omnipotent Being presides over both countries, and the same moral code is authority in each. As to the universally received dogma of Pedobaptists, that circumcision was *a* door, or *the* door, into the Jewish church, brother C. denied it as truth. Here it may not be amiss to remark, that, if it be shown that circumcision was not the door of entrance into the church, the whole Pedobaptist fabric must fall. I state it as a fact that should be understood from the "rivers to the ends of the earth," that circumcision was never a door into any church; and that if baptism came in the room of it, nothing is gained to the cause of Pedobaptists. Am I asked, how persons became members of the Jewish church? I answer, that by virtue of the blood of Abraham flowing in the veins of infants, they were members; and, although people of other nations, by circumcision and other rites, were permitted to take the passover and attend to other privileges, still, they were never considered BRETHREN amongst . . . the Jews, and were in fact not members of the church. Paul tells us (Gal, ii.,

15) of "*Jews by nature,*" or birth; but nowhere in the Bible is there a single intimation of men, women, or children becoming Jews by circumcision.

Before dismissing this part of the controversy, it should be remarked, that if Paedobaptists fail to prove the identity of the Jewish and Christian churches, and that circumcision was a door into the former, and baptism a door into the latter, the whole cause, in language of debate, "goes by the board." I wish here to state *the* argument on which Mr. Rice mainly relied, and, indeed, it is the chief argument of all Paedobaptists, to prove the identity of the churches. Mr. R. said there was but ONE COVENANT made with Abraham, and that upon this covenant both churches were built, and of course, must be the same. He says, p. 312, "in Scripture we never read of COVENANTS, but of one COVENANT with Abraham." In proof of this position, he quoted 1 Chron. 16, 15, 17. "Be ye mindful always of his covenant, with Abraham, Ac." Ex. 2,24. "And God heard their groaning, and God remembered his *covenant* with Abraham, Isaac and Jacob." To this Bro. C. replied, that Paul spoke of COVENANTS to Israel, Ro. 9 chap, and also of the "*two covenants*" in Gal. 4 chap. The first covenant to Abraham was that of the Saviour, recorded, Gen. 12,3. This was made 430 years before the law, Gal. 3, 15. Another covenant was made with Abraham ten or twelve years after this, mentioned Gen. 15,17—21. "In that day," says Moses, "the Lord made a *covenant* unto Abraham, saying, "unto thy seed have I given this land, from the river of unto the great river—the river Euphrates." This makes the 2d covenant with Abraham, and Stephen speaks. Acts 7, 8, of "*the covenant of circumcision,*" which makes the third covenant with the father of the faithful. On this point more from Campbell, would be unnecessary to prove Mr. Rice was mistaken, at least; but I must take this occasion to state, that Bro. Campbell often fails to expose the sophistry of his opponent, and therefore, mere deception is taken as argument. As an instance, that A. Campbell might have demonstrated that N. L. Rice was either grossly ignorant, or miserably wicked, I will state as a fact, that the passages on which Mr. Rice depends, to prove there was one *covenant* only, with Abraham, and that on this the church of Christ was built, neither of them has the most distant allusion to the foundation of any church. As proof read again. Ex. 2, 24. "And God heard their groaning, and God remembered his *covenant,* with Abraham, and with Isaac and with Jacob." Notice, this was a covenant remembered, in the time of the *groanings* of the children of Israel. Why so? See, Gen. 15, 13 and 14. "And he said unto Abraham, know of a surety, that thy seed shall be a stranger, in a land that is not theirs, and shall serve them and shall afflict them four hundred years. And also, that nation whom they shall serve, will I judge, and afterwards shall they, with great substance, come out." In reference to what was this covenant? God covenanted with Abraham to deliver his posterity from bondage, when he should be in his grave, and he "remembered" it when the children of Israel were in Egypt; and is it not strange that such a man as Mr. Rice, should quote these passages to prove a proposition to which the writer had no reference? Mr. Rice makes God's covenant with Abraham, that he would deliver his posterity from bondage, the covenant upon which the Jewish and Christian churches were both built!!! This is the kind of argument that triumphs over all that A. Campbell could say; at least in the eyes of Paedobaptists.

Bro. Campbell proceeded to show that God made a "new covenant" (Jer. 31, 31,) with the house of Israel, and with the house of Judea; not according to the "covenant" made with the Fathers, that is the covenant of the law church; but the new covenant was the Gospel church, which should constitute the abode of all the faithful. In reference to this church, John the Baptist said, "The kingdom of heaven is at hand," and the Saviour declared "on this rock, I WILL build my church." Mind, this was predicted of & church yet to be built, when the Jewish church was in existence.

As to the household baptisms, Mr. Rice had but little to say to establish infant membership; but as his great reliance was to establish his point by merely *asserting* that *Baptism* occupied the same place to families under the New Testament order that Circumcision did under the old, I will let Bro. Campbell speak for himself to prove the dissimilarity of Baptism and Circumcision.

1. Only males were subjects of circumcision. It belonged, then, to but half the Jewish church.

2. Infant males were circumcised the Eighth day.

3. Adult males circumcised themselves.

4. Infant males were circumcised by their own parents.

5. Infant and adult servants were circumcised neither on *flesh,* nor *faith,* but as *property.*

6. Circumcision was not the door into the Jewish church. It was four hundred years older than the Jewish church, and introduced neither Isaac, Ishmael, Jacob or Esau into any Jewish or patriarchal church. It never was to a Jew, its proper subject, an initiatory rite.

7. The qualifications for circumcision were *flesh* and *property* Faith was never propounded, in any case, to a Jew or his servants.

8. Circumcision was not a dedicatory rite. The rites of the dedication of a first-born son were different in all respects.

9. Circumcision requiring no moral qualification, neither could nor did communicate any spiritual blessing. No person ever put on Christ or professed faith in circumcision.

10. Idiots were circumcised; for neither intellect itself, nor any exercise of it, was necessary to a covenant *in the flesh,*

11. It was a visible, appreciable mark, as all signs are, and such was its main design.

12. It was binding on parents and not on children. *Circumcise your children.*

13. The right of a child to circumcision in no case depended upon the faith, the piety, or the morality of parents.

14. Circumcision was a guarantee of certain temporal benefits to a Jew.

15. It was not to be performed in the name of God, nor into the name of any being in heaven or on earth.

16. The subject of circumcision was a debtor to the whole law.

When the points of non-identity of the churches and the dissimilarity of circumcision and baptism, are established, the whole controversy is at an end, and therefore further arguments are unnecessary on either side.   T. F.

BAPTISM OF THE HOLY GHOST.

To the Editor of the Christian Review:—

DEAR BRETHREN If, after a perusal of this article, you shall think it worthy a place in the Review, I shall be pleased to see it there. I do not claim to have made any new discovery in investigating this subject; yet, if I so arrange and so present it as to create a spirit of examination in some of those persons who have heretofore remained satisfied with the popular views relative to it, I shall have effected all I anticipate.

There are those who say that the baptism of the Holy Spirit, in primitive times, was in order to, or for the purpose of, forgiving sins; and that it is now requisite to the pardon of individuals. My object is, to disprove this in a way plain and simple; and in doing this, I shall bring forward those passages in the New Testament that have a direct bearing upon the subject, and in the order they occur there. The first, then, I will notice, is John's declaration, "He shall baptize you with the Holy Ghost," &c. Now, if it be true that this baptism of the Spirit was to pardon those people's sins, it is evident that, during all the time of John's ministry, and up to the time the Savior (after his resurrection) breathed on his disciples, and said, "Receive ye the Holy Ghost," not one single person received the remission of sins, except those Jesus spoke the sins of, forgiven; and that all the faith in the promised Messiah, the most sincere repentance for past sins, and the baptism of John combined, was not sufficient to save a soul from destruction: and yet it is expressly declared by Mark, that he (John) "preached the baptism of repentance for the remission of sins." Again, it follows, if this be true, that the twelve disciples Jesus sent forth to preach, "The kingdom of heaven is at hand," and likewise the seventy sent out shortly after for the same purpose, were in their sins; and had any of them died while in this employment of the Savior, they must have been lost; for it does not appear that the Holy Ghost had come upon them, or that the Savior had pardoned them. As absurd and as preposterous as it may be to suppose that they were in their sins, I heard a Methodist preacher say, he believed it, and gave Judas as a proof of it. Strange indeed that he should take Judas's case to prove this, when the Methodists teach that *it is possible to fall from grace!* for, if his case proves that the balance of his brethren were in their sins, one apostasy in the Methodist Church would prove all the balance to be in their sins also.

I pass from this to the commission, "Go ye therefore and teach all nations, baptizing them in the name of the Father, and of the Son, and of the Holy Ghost." Now, if it be true that the baptism of the Holy Ghost is requisite to the pardon of sins, the commission should read thus: "Go ye therefore and teach all nations, baptizing them with the Holy Ghost;" or, according to Mark, "He that believeth and is baptized with the Holy Ghost, shall be saved.' But, instead of this, the Lord did not say a word about it in the commission. This brings me to the Acts, and I ask, did the Holy Spirit come upon the Apostles to pardon their sins, on the day of Pentecost? If so, then their sins were not forgiven when they were baptized of John, or when the Savior breathed on them and said, "Receive ye the Holy Ghost;" and he had empowered them to remit sins before their own were remitted. Now for Peter's sermon. "Ah!" says one, "that's the passage you stand upon, and without it you could not exist." Or, as the preacher above alluded to said to me, *"That's what we call your sugar stick."* Well, this is what I call deriding the immutable word of the Lord, and for

which an account will have to be rendered in the day of judgment. The teaching of Peter is precisely in accordance with the commission. First, "Teach all nations" or "preach the Gospel;" this he did faithfully, and proved most incontestably, by the Scriptures, which those people professed to believe in, that Jesus was the Christ. They were convinced that they had crucified the Lord of glory, and asked, "What shall we do?" Peter, true to instructions, tells them, "Repent and be baptized, every one of you, in the name of Jesus Christ, for the remission of sins, and ye shall receive the gift of the Holy Ghost." Now, according to the rendering of the popular teachers, Which is, "Repent and be baptized, every one of you, in the name of Jesus Christ, because of the remission of sins," water baptism stands directly between the pardon of their sins and the gift of the Holy Ghost. But this is not the only difficulty; they have those people repenting after their sins are pardoned. Really, if I took the liberty of uttering God's word at all, I would not make him the author of utter nonsense. In the 8th chapter, we have the same teaching, and the same things followed. The reception of the Holy Ghost was after water baptism, and I presume no intelligent man will make the apostles contradict each other, by saying that Peter preached water baptism for one purpose, and Philip for another. Then let it be "for the remission of sins," or "because of the remission of sins," it does not change the case; the Holy Ghost was given after their sins were remitted. As to Simon the Sorcerer, what I have said relative, to Judas, is applicable to him. Peter says nothing to him about the sins he may have committed before his baptism; he only accuses him of one sin; he tells him to repent of, and pray for, the forgiveness of one sin; and that was the wicked "thought, that the gift of God may be purchased with money." "Thou hast neither part nor lot in this matter: for thy heart is not right in the sight of God." What matter? The gift of the Holy Spirit. When did his heart get wrong? When he took it into his heart to buy "The gift." But let him have been a hypocrite, as some would have it, no one teaches that hypocrites received the remission of sins in the act of water baptism then, or at any other time. So, if his heart was wrong when he was baptized, baptism could not have benefited him, neither could the *Mourner's Benefit* have profited him any thing. But it is time to leave Simon. Will any one pretend to say that the Eunuch was not pardoned? If the baptism of the Holy Ghost was necessary to the forgiving of his sins, he was not, for it is not said that he received it. Philip preached the same things to him that he did to the Samaritans, he believed the same things, and he received water baptism at the hands of Philip just as they did. And here he was left, and there was no person sent to him from Jerusalem to pray that he might receive the Holy Ghost. Saul's conversion comes next in order. If he was baptized with the Holy Ghost, when he saw the "Heavenly vision," as some think, it surely could not have been to pardon his sins, else why did Ananias say to him three days after, "And now why tarriest thou? arise and be baptized, and wash away thy sins, calling on the name Of the Lord"? It would seem from this, that his sins were still hanging around him, and that it was necessary for him to conform to the appointment of Heaven to get rid of them. Well says one, the Holy Ghost fell upon Cornelius in order to the remission of sins, and you cannot say, Sir, that this was after water baptism. No, and I am happy that it was not, for notwithstanding the Holy Ghost fell upon him and his house before baptism, the passage affords the most conclusive proof that it was not for the purpose of pardoning sins. The angel told him "Now send men to Joppa and call for one Simon &c., he shall tell thee what thou oughtest to do." Or "who shall tell thee words whereby thou and all thy house shall be saved." Then it is palpable that he (Cornelius) was to do something, and he was to hear "words" &c. and if I can show what he was to do, and what these words are, then I shall have established my position. Did Peter tell him to pray for the gift of the Holy Ghost? He did not. Did he tell him that this gift was necessary to save him and all his house? He did not. Then Peter did not go for that purpose; and we are authorized to believe that so far from his being called to teach any such thing, he did not so much as expect such an occurrence, else why were "they of the circumcision which believed, astonished"? What then did he tell? "The word which God sent to the children of Israel"—"How God anointed Jesus of Nazareth with the Holy Ghost, and with power &c."—He told of his death, and his resurrection. He also told him "That whosoever believeth in him shall receive the remission of sins;" finally, "And he commanded them to be baptized in the name of the Lord." Then it is plain that this is what Peter was sent to tell; and it is also plain what Cornelius was to do. He was to believe in the Lord Jesus Christ, and be baptized in his name. This is what saved him and all his house, and not the Baptism of the Holy Ghost. I come now to speak of the second part of the subject, which I shall dispose of in few words. Is the baptism of the Holy Ghost requisite to the pardon of individuals now? The Bible no where tells me, that the baptism of the Holy Ghost is at any time to be attended by signs, and evidences differing from those that accompanied it in the apostolic time; and as we have no such evidences and signs now-a-days, of course we have no baptism of the Holy Spirit. But pardon is still offered; individuals are forgiven on the same conditions now, that they were in the apostolic days; and they have the same testimony of the fact now, that persons had then ; so the Baptism of the Holy Ghost is not requisite to the pardon of the sins of any person. I may be asked, what then was the Baptism of the Holy Ghost for? This I will perhaps answer at some future time.

Your brother in Christ,   R. A. ARMISTEAD.

CHURCHES AND EVANGELISTS.

To the Editors of the Christian Review:

How shall they believe in him of whom they have not heard, and how shall they hear without a preacher? and how shall he preach except he be sent? Rom., 10,14.

DEAR BRO. FANNING:—I have selected the above passage of scripture, not as text for exposition on the pages of the Review, but simply as a motto which shall give character to my suggestions upon a subject, which in my judgment, is of vast importance, but one which has been sadly neglected by our brethren generally; it has respect to churches and their evangelists, and the duties of each, and of both; The subject to which I allude, and of which this letter is designed to speak a little, is one which, when I shall have presented it in its true light, if indeed I am capable of so doing, I am very sure will merit your grave consideration, even should I fail to state myself in a very interesting manner. I shall speak the language of experience, and think I cannot be greatly mistaken; it has been near ten years since I settled myself in Alabama, and what do you think, my

dear brother, when I tell you I heard not the ancient gospel during all these ten years, after 1 heard you in. Nashville, until last September, when Bro. Butler came amongst us, and announced once more the old-fashioned Gospel. Bro. Butler is an able and valiant soldier of the cross. Bro. George W. Elley of Kentucky, and Bro. J. H. Curtis of Columbus, Mississippi, have been here, they preached one week in Gainesville, and neighbourhood; the future is big with interest; never were the people so much excited; never was there a greater prospect for the triumph of truth. The last- named brethren evince a zeal and devotion worthy of the great cause which they so ardently advocate. We are prepared from what has been done, and the presentiments of the times, to cherish the most sanguine hopes that truth will ultimately prevail gloriously, in this part of the State; so much for the present state of religious affairs, and future prospects with us. Let us not now, in ecstasy of heart which we feel at the present success of the good cause, forget entirely the past, with all the sore travail of soul of which it has been replete to your humble servant; for the history of this past period alluded to, is not my complaint alone, but that of many others, who have been placed in similar circumstances; and it is now the source of complaint to many who are just as I have been. Why is this the case? Why is it, that the brethren scattered through the country by the oppressive hand of necessity, are left entirely destitute of the Gospel, to live alone, or join a sectarian church? Why is it that so many fine fields for the proclamation of the Gospel are overlooked and neglected?— These are questions of grave import to every lover of the ancient Gospel of the blessed Lord. And is there not a remedy? Cannot something be done to remedy what must be regarded a great defect in our evangelizing system? I most sincerely believe, and devoutly hope, there can and will be something effectually done in this matter.

There are in many churches in Tennessee, Kentucky, Indiana, Missouri, Illinois, Ohio, Virginia, and other States, a superabundance of evangelists, while many of our churches in this State and others, are entirely destitute, and have preaching only once and a while. Now, my brother, we profess to have the Gospel in its purity, and should we not use every means in our power to disseminate among others what we enjoy so much ourselves? This seems to be but the dictate of benevolence. 1 wish to enquire, then, if these churches, so much blessed with gifted evangelists, are not able to pay them for their services, and send them out into the field white unto harvest? and if not individually able, are they not able by two or three, or more, combined, to do so good a work? You may say, this would be a hard burden upon the shoulders of the churches in which these evangelists are; and you may suggest that they who receive the service, should pay the worthy laborer his hire. This is all, perhaps, quite true; but there are two ways to obviate this apparent difficulty. 1st, The brethren receiving this benefaction from the other churches, should feel bound, when able, themselves to send out other evangelists. 2nd, The brethren who receive the labor of evangelists generally, when able, compensate them for services; this would enable the evangelists to refund to the church which sent him out whatever might be over and above what it was able to contribute to the cause. In this way brethren and churches would become co-workers with the Lord. Will the brethren think of this thing? and more, will they *act?*

Sumpter County, Ala., May 5, 1844.   THOMAS TERRY.

REFLECTIONS ON THE DESTINY OF HUMAN SOCIETY.

"Though dark and despairing my sight I may seal,
Yet man cannot cover what God would reveal;
'Tis the sunset of life gives me mystical lore,
And coming events cast their shadows before."

It is a remarkable fact, that preceding every great era or revolution in the world's history, either the prophetic indications of the Bible, or sear and venerable tradition, or the impulsive force of events themselves, have swept forward, and vaguely and marvelously, but certainly, divined the future. The Poet, in the sentiment quoted above, has but embodied what must have been observed by every student of the annals of time; for the general mind has always been greatly stirred and rendered preternaturally alive to "coming events," by the startling character of their preceding shadows. There has been an almost universal grasping after some expected blessing, or a fearful foreboding of some impending evil, preceding the rise of all the great transformations of human society. Such a shadow anticipated the reign of Augustus Caesar—the most remarkable era in the social relations of man—the coming of the Son of Man— the downfall of Jerusalem—the overthrow of the Roman Empire—the great Protestant Reformation of the sixteenth century—the dark days of the French Revolution—and even the declaration of the inalienable rights of man in our own American Revolutionary struggle. No one conversant with the writers of these periods, can have failed to mark this remarkable fact. To many, these shadows may have appeared but trifles, when viewed in the light of the events themselves; but to the eye that sees aright, such trifles have great significance. It has been said by some one, that great minds only can appreciate trifles—the solemn underrate, the trivial exaggerate them.

That mind must be grossly dull, that cannot see what every one calls a great event or a great action; but it requires some sagacity to view in the indication of events, the events themselves. And, from the prospect now afforded us, by the historians of this age, perhaps it may not be too much for us to expect, that certain laws will yet be deduced from the history of the past, by which, with the assistance of the prophetic indications of the Bible, we may arrive at some certainty even in anticipating the future. History may yet be a science; the vague and uncertain phantoms of past generations of ignorance, may yet be of use; and, in the great stride after the greatest and best discoveries, feeble and uncertain though our guide may be, wavering as he directs us, and therefore by many depreciated and abused, yet he will surely lead us aright, if we have faith in his indications. There is a spirit that presides over history, and when we shall become acquainted with its arts of direction, it will be to the social system what the soul is to the body. Like the union of faith and works in the high and noble object of making the finished Christian, though separately of little value, yet, when united, they effect what would have deterred the boldest adventurer and the most curious investigator in the religious powers of man. — So the spirit of history and the events themselves, should never be separated, and our researches will be of practical use; for, not only in Israelitish, but, among all nations, what has happened, has happened for ensamples of admonition to us, upon whom, in more senses than one, the ends of the ages have come. Guided by an impression of this kind, I have for twelve months been looking most steadily at the past; and the result of my observation is, that I am strongly persuaded that the present generation of men stand upon the very eve of the mightiest revolution that the annals of time record, I will not give the historical argumentation by which I have arrived at this conclusion; for, if it be true, it will require but the statement of a few facts and observations to awaken the attention of the discerning, whilst others will not believe or prepare though one rose from the dead.

Let it be observed, then, that preceding every great revolution, there has been a general expectation that something wonderful was about to take place. As already indicated, preceding the advent of our divine Redeemer, the public mind, though the world, was in a state of peace, was remarkable for a general ferment, occasioned by confidence in the appearance of a coming deliverer, which caused a vague and mysterious agitation among all orders. And is there not at this moment a vague consciousness of great changes coming upon society? Does it not pervade all orders? The statesman expects a political regeneration, the philosopher a mental one, and the religionist a moral one, after his own creed or party idiosyncrasy. Each individual looks for his own kind of change, yet he looks for *a change.* The various temperaments, characters, and desires of men, paint and color the picture according to the definiteness or indefiniteness of their expectations—some, like Mr. Miller, attempting not only to fix its character, but also its *date.* But this is to be expected; and if there is any astonishment, it is, that amidst all the diversity of sects, creeds, opinions, educations—the ignorant and the cultivated, the refined and the unrefined, the student and the idle observer, the politician, the sage, and the theologian—that, while all should agree in expecting the establishment of some change, great and unexampled in the history of the past, there should be so few contradictory speculations with reference to it. The visionary speculations of the devout Second Advent Man, only serve to show that expectation is on tip-toe; and, however absurd and self-fatal they may be, it should not have a tendency to make the reflecting sleep, as though all was a dream. When Messiah first appeared, many of the Jews expected that they would be the only favorites in the new reign—that their theocracy would be established in a new and more enduring form—their ancestors would arise from the dead—the solemn judgment would be held—the hostile nations would come bending before them, or be thrust down to hell; in a word, they expected a simultaneous regeneration of all things with his coining. *Their* expectations were disappointed; but HE came. Because they made him the Savior of their nation, he did not refuse to come as the Savior of the world! And, however erroneous their views of his character, they knew that he would come to Bethlehem, and were not greatly mistaken with regard to the *time.* The Romans expected a prince like Julius Caesar or Vespasian—the Persians a second Ormuzd or Æon. But their expectations, though regulated by the political or philosophical desires of those who entertained them, did not prevent the revolution that followed. It came—the history of ever since, has been its history.

May we not, therefore, hail, from whatever source it may be desired, or however it may be colored by the coloring imagination of man, the present almost universal expectation as the Harbinger of a coming era?

But look again. Even Mahomedans are expecting some great and to them appalling event. And what to me is a most astonishing fact, they expect a downfall of their religion and an overthrow of the political despotism connected with it? A gloomy foreboding seems to pervade the mind of the once invincible followers of the son of Abdallah, that the day of their glory is past —that the sun of their dominion is setting—and that their recent misfortunes and discomfitures are but the prelude of greater woes.

But this general preparation is producing a correspondent preparation for the event, whatever it may be. It is the method of God's dealings to arrange from a distance the forces with which he accomplishes his purposes. Invention after invention in the arts—discovery after discovery in the sciences—truth after truth connected with man's moral history from the Bible—has been unfolding— all having a formative influence upon society; preparatory and remodeling. They have already changed the whole force of society. Secretly and silently at times, and again with the voice of thunder, these improvements have claimed the attention of man. Remote, indeed, may be the connection of these events, but not more remote than the tyrannical government of Herod the great; the exploded superstitions of philosophy, falsely so called, and the peaceful character of the age, and the introduction of a suffering Savior into the world! Not more remote than the conduct of the gay and cowardly Erasmus; the keen, stern Calvin; the powerful and denunciating Luther; the zealous and indefatigable Zwingle; the Jupiter-and-Pan-like Henry VIII; the literary and voluptuous Leo X.—and the great and glorious Reformation of the 16th century! Yet the conduct of each was connected; and each-became an instrument in the mighty achievement subservient to the power of the Ruler above—the God of history. Catholic princes from jealousy checked each other till the Reformation was beyond their power of control. The savage Turk appeared in Europe and diverted the attention of the trembling council of Nuremberg from the rising heresy, until the deep foundations of Papacy trembled to their centre and the glory of the tiara with many passed away forever. What connection is there between these events, and a thousand others that might be enumerated? Is it not the connecting of seeming independent events that proves an overruling Providence?

I will not burden the reader with an attempt to show that there is now a convergence of great and small circumstances to a crisis. I will not attempt to prove to him that Italy, the seat of the last power that shall destroy the earth, is now placed upon the very verge of a smoldering political volcano; that all her Southern governments are in a fright; and that, as they subsist not by opinion, but by suppressing opinion—their tenure is short. The governments of the Papacy are old in corruption, and the success of their old and infernal plans has benumbed their faculties, so that they cannot discern coming results. Every nerve is straining to extend her superannuated and hysterical dominion; but her nerves will break, I fear—I hope—in the struggle. Nor will I speak of the present critical situation of all Europe. I only wish to awaken reflection, by a simple suggestion. To my mind, the materials accumulated within the last century, taken in connection with the present political and religious state of things, are more ominous of extraordinary events—of rapid and radical changes —than those of five hundred years preceding. I will not speak of the two French Revolutions of the past century—of Greek emancipation—the humiliation of the Ottoman empire—of the Political or great Religious Reformations of the same period—of the unparalleled advances of the physical sciences; but certainly, I may say, that a silent, rapid, and irresistible preparation has been making—making, perhaps,   for   a   sudden, subversive, and universal change.—What will it be? The battle of Armageddon? The Millennium? The new Heavens and Earth? Perhaps all of these, preceded by the coming of the Son of Man in the clouds of heaven. Nothing in the prophecies withholds his coming, that I have seen. The events we expect to precede that great event, may *follow* it. The character of the second, as was the first advent, may have been mistaken. Nothing withholds the revelation of this great period, but the long suffering of Messiah, if I have read Peter and Daniel and John aright.——I expect no reign of peace, till human passions and human interests shall once more have expended themselves in a grand convulsion—until the nations who have given their power to the Beast, shall have made a battle-field of the globe, and the earth be once more drenched in the blood of her presumptuous and haughty sons. The result will, nevertheless, be glorious. Messiah directs the storm, as it sweeps the land, not only as a destroyer, but also, as a renovator. The great sea of nations, upon which the power of the Apostate Mother has been seated, will be alike the scene of his majesty and her destruction; for by his almighty power, he Will penetrate to its very depths, and roll its abominations in thunder to the shore, changing its whole motion, its aspect, and its uses; giving it a grandeur in its convulsions, equaled only by the grandeur of its ultimate serenity—when every nation and kingdom under the whole heaven shall bow to his authority, and that of the saints. HE will drive the waves of human commotion, lashed into fury before the rolling mountain of his kingdom, to a calm like that which fell upon the dark sea of Galilee, when he said, "Peace, be still." My soul, be ready for the day; for he comes—

> The Godhead comes, behold I from far
> He comes, triumphant in his cloud-rapt car.
> Whilst twice ten thousand angels cope the sky—
> The harbingers of his dread majesty.
> The stars have dropt—the sun has sunk away—
> It is—alas! *'tis neither night nor day!*
> The burning basis of Messiah's throne
> Spontaneous splendor beams——a glory all its own.
> Look! look! my soul!
> The fatal covers part,
> The rock is open—melt, my heart!
> Ah! whither—whither shall I fly,
> In this my soul's extremity?
> Whither, but to thee, my God, my stay!
> O save me this all dreadful day,
> And let mankind and angels see.
> That blessed is the man that puts his trust in thee!

Merriville, May, 1844.   J. B. FERGUSON.

INTERPRETATION OF PROPHECY—DESULTORY THOUGHTS.

To the Editors of the Christian Review:

DEAR BRETHREN In the interesting study of the prophecies, it is not unfrequently the case, that we loose sight of a truth, well calculated to throw immense light upon what would otherwise, be almost entirely dark and obscure. That is, that many of the predictions of the Old Testament, and some of the New, contain what may be called a double *entendre*—look forward to two fulfillments; the first typical, and illustrative of the second. I know that scoffers have urged this *double sense* as an evidence of such an obscurity as would prove a lack of a solid foundation for the whole; but this has been done entirely without reason. So far from any reasonable objection lying against the divine inspiration of the predictions for this seeming ambiguity, it affords an additional proof of the infinite knowledge of that power, which has so constructed the predictions as to give them an application to events, apparently unconnected with, and distant from each other. He who made man, and sees the end from the beginning of his multifarious actions, has in the fore-knowledge of his omniscient mind, displayed in the divine volume, anticipated at the distance of hundreds of years, and with reference to individuals and nations entirely dissimilar in their habits, the same similar ends.

Thus what was promised to Abraham—concerning Isaac, was remarkably fulfilled in him, and his history became typically significant of the history of Jesus, the Christ. They were both *sons* of promise, and *fathers* of nations— the one the Son of the Father of the families of the faithful, and in turn the father of *one* of those families himself—the other the Son of the Father of Abel, and in turn the Father of the Everlasting age of whom the whole chosen family of Heaven and Earth, is named. No student of the sacred Oracles, can have failed to have noticed— that both were children of promise before they were born—that both were born miraculously— that they were the *only* offspring of their Mother—the only legitimate heirs of the promised inheritances—they were both doomed to the—and were both respited from the dead; the one figuratively, the other really. Many other particulars could be noticed, but these are sufficient. It will be seen that in every particular, the fulfillment is more remarkable in the second than in the first individual.

But we take another case. Moses declares† to the murmuring sons of Israel, that the Lord their God, would raise them up a Prophet like unto him. This prediction was fulfilled in Joshua, the heroic son of Nun; but more remarkably in the second Joshua, the Son of Mary. The history of the first, became the typical history of the second, so much so, that their very names are the same. The same may be said of the predictions of David concerning Solomon; which were partially fulfilled in him, and fully accomplished in David's Son and Lord—Jesus.

What is true of individuals, is true also of nations. For example, all those sublime predictions of Isaiah, Micah and Joel, relative to the introduction of the gospel age, had a partial and fulfillment upon the day of Pentecost; but they also look forward to a more notable day of the Lord—a day of which Pentecost was but a type—a day when the sword shall be beaten into a ploughshare, the spear into the pruning hook—when war and bloodshed shall be succeeded by interminable peace,

"And the tempest blast shall be heard no more."

Take the second chapters of Joel and Isaiah and the fourth of Micah, as an example. It cannot be denied, that these predictions referred to scenes of the day of Pentecost, and that they received a partial fulfillment then. For example, the Spirit was poured out upon that occasion— the mountain of the Lord's house was established upon the top of the mountains—the first dominion came to Jerusalem—the law went forth from Zion, and the word of the Lord from Jerusalem.

*Gen. 12 c; 15 c; 22,c; Isaiah, 9 c: 6; Eph. 3; 15.

†Deut. 18.

‡Ps. 72nd and other Psalms.

But eighteen hundred years have rolled away, and the terrible day of the Lord has not yet come—the idols of the heathen have not yet been destroyed—the glory of the majesty of our God has not yet cast all the devices of man into the clefts of the rocks—nor has the peaceful reign of the branch intervened. But all these predictions have had, as already remarked, a partial fulfillment—the gospel has brought peace, and the terror of the Lord in Jerusalem has brought destruction; but these only typically illustrate the great events yet to be revealed. The feet of iron shall yet become brass, her horn iron; and she shall rent in pieces many nations, and then consecrate the gain and substance to the Lord in a reign of peace from henceforth even forever. Let the reader read the passages referred to, and he will find in them, with this view of the subject before him, treasures of consolation that will confirm his faith, enlist his affections, and strengthen his hope.

But what we have said of these passages, may be said of all those predictions which relate to the coming, character, and glory of the kingdom of heaven. Even that descriptive prediction of Daniel, (ii, 43, 44, 45,) has not yet been fully accomplished. It is true, that in the days of the Roman government, the God of heaven established the kingdom there spoken of, but only in its stone form; only as a stone cut from the mountain of the height of Israel. It is yet to be established in its mountain form—yet to break the image to pieces, and fill the whole earth, That image, with its Assyrian head, its Medo-Persian breasts, its Macedonian body, its Roman legs, and its ten toes, representing the dominion of Rome divided into *ten* kingdoms, with the strength of iron and weakness of clay, stands, doubtless, a representative of all the forms of human government that had, or ever will have connection with the fortunes of God's ancient people, the Jews, or his present people, the Christians. It is a remarkable fact, that no New Testament writer ever refers to this prediction as having been fulfilled in the day of Jesus Christ. The reason, I think, is obvious: it never has been fully accomplished. The Roman government was divided into ten kingdoms A. D. 476. It is still so divided; and among them has since arisen a power of another character, whose destruction is foretold in the seventh of Daniel. Until all these are destroyed, therefore—until the image is smitten upon the toes, (ii, 34,) and the gold, the silver, and iron are broken to pieces, I do not expect the kingdom of heaven to be fully established upon the earth. The first dominion, according to Micah, came to Jerusalem upon the day of Pentecost; but until upon the clouds of heaven (Dan. vii, 13) the Son of Man shall be seen coming to the ancient of days, I do not expect to see the *second* dominion. All human government falls before this, or at this period. Upon the day of Pentecost, the kingdom of heaven was presented to the world, since which time our heavenly Father has been gathering a people out of every nation, kindred, tribe, and tongue. When the day of the glory of the Son of Man shall come, the kingdoms of this earth will fall, and the kingdom, and the dominion, and the greatness of. the kingdom under the whole heaven, shall be given to the saints. Thus, I am taught by Daniel, and by present events, that this period draws nigh. The fortunes of the world have been in the hands of the divided dominion of Rome (the present ten kingdoms of Europe) for 1368 years. The power of the little horn, or Roman papacy, was to continue to afflict the saints for 1260 years—years of the time of the ten kingdoms. All the powers of Europe now slumber, as it were, upon the murmuring volcano—the little horn seems to be making a last desperate effort to extend his dominion. May we not expect, that the stone will soon smite the image, (which, though the dominion of its various parts has been taken away, its life has been prolonged for a season and a time, Dan. vii, 12;) and, as the apostate power of the little horn is allied to the feet of this image, the whole will be ground to the dust of the summer threshing floor, and scattered to the four winds of heaven. For my own part, after a careful examination of almost all that has been written upon the subject, I feel prepared to say, that I am strongly of the opinion that "this generation will not pass away till all these things be fulfilled." I know it may be objected to this, that there are many prophecies yet to be fulfilled. Be it so. May not the very coming of the Master lead to their fulfillment? No man knows the *order* in which the great events of prophecy will be fulfilled. May not the day of the restoration of the kingdom to Israel—the true Israel I mean—be the first event in the great and marvelous series? Has any thing but the long-suffering of God, according to Peter and Paul, hindered the coming of Messiah since the revelation of the man of sin? Let the conscientious examiner of the New Testament, answer.

But I have digressed. The point before me, however, is illustrated, and I have only to remark, in conclusion, that what has been said of the preceding predictions, may be said of all those prophecies which relate to the destruction of Jerusalem, and of the world. The destruction of Jerusalem was typical of the destruction of the ungodly world. Hence, the predictions relating seemingly to the former, only had a partial fulfillment in the overthrow of the Jewish nation, and will have a complete and fulfillment in the overthrow of all nations.

The same may be said of the Babylonian captivity of the Jews, their delivery, and the destruction of their enemies. Christians have been enslaved in Mystery Babylon—will be brought out when the strong angel shall come to destroy her. I will not illustrate these points, as it would be taking from the reader A satisfaction which he can only fully enjoy by examining these matters for himself. Let it be remembered, then, that as two promises were made to Abraham, upon which two covenants, with two kinds of people, have been made; so also, the history of the one promise, covenant, and people, is typical of the history of the other promise, covenant, and people. The origin, fortunes, and destiny of the present dispensation, may be learned from the past.

Perhaps your readers may see something to excite their reflection in the more than common place matters of this epistle; if so, it is at their service. May the Lord awaken his people to discover the time in which they live, and the portion in his government which they occupy! is the anxious labor and wish of one who claims to sign himself, with reference to the present state of things, more than a   LOOKER-ON.

From the Millennial Harbinger. LATE "RELIGIOUS" DOINGS EASTWARD.

"RELIGIOUS" GAMBLING, FEASTING, &C.

[OMINOUS SIGNS OF THE TIMES.—ED.]

I am every day becoming more and more convinced of the great necessity of a thorough reformation in religion—a dissolution of the corrupt sectarian systems of the day, and a restoration of pure, primitive, apostolic Christianity. The different sects and parties, while opposing the progress of the ancient gospel with all their might and means, are themselves filled

*Rev. xviii, 1-6.

with gross corruptions! Practices, most palpably anti-Christian, are openly tolerated and sanctioned by both priest and laity! Some eastern papers have just fallen into my hands, containing notices of "doings," revolting to the mind of every humble end devoted disciple of Christ, forbidden by the letter and spirit of the Christian system, and growing out of the corruption of sectarianism. I will give a few extracts.

"The donation parties which were commenced a few years since, in love and kindness to those who have the spiritual charge of the churches, are now greatly deteriorated in many places, and perverted from their original objects. The annual visits are often, now looked forward to as *scenes of enjoyment,* where large numbers of the parishioners in the respective congregations, the converted and the unconverted, will meet together, not to study the word of God, or inquire more perfectly the way of salvation, but to have a *social chat,* indulge their *pride* in the *munificence* of their *gifts,* and *feast* together on the good things provided. Those most able are emulous to give the greater gift; while those the least able are mortified at the scantiness of theirs. Then follows a *card of thanks* in the various *religious* papers, from the various *pastors* who have been thus honored, which stimulates *others* to like acts of *charity!*

"Even the *children* in the Sabbath schools are *feasted,* and are indulged in their sleigh rides in the winter, and excursions in the summer. Here the *table is spread,* and more of the *dainties* of the season, than spiritual food is given them. These things are temptations to the ungodly who desire to enter, that they may partake of the loaves and fishes, like the Jews, who cared more for those things than for the miracles which the Lord did. John vi. 26.

"These things, however, are small evils in comparison, and would not have been noticed at this time, but for the more gross and disgusting scenes of feasting and revelry which have *grown out* of them, and of which *they* were the *germ*—Church *feasts,* and church *tea-parties,* and church *fairs,* where all the *luxuries* of the day that can please the eye, or administer to the *gratification* of the *appetite,* have taken the place of the old-fashioned church fasts. At these fairs, they have their LOTTERIES; sustaining under the holy *garb of religion,* the very system of GAMBLING which Cesar, in many of the States, has prohibited as *too immoral,* even for him. *Gold rings are* inserted in loaf cake, which is sold at exorbitant prices, on account of the treasure it contains, which will be the portion of him who is so *lucky* as to obtain the piece in which it was inserted. Here congregate the pious (?) and the impious; those that fear God (?) and those that fear him not; the righteous (?) and the unrighteous; the holy(?) and the profane; none are excluded who can pay the *fee* of admittance.

"In all our principal cities, these tea-parties are being held. Several have come off at the late Tremont Theatre, Boston, where the society of Mr. Colver, (Free-will Baptist,) meet; and where a *different* system of *theatricals* are in vogue, but which some believe are none the less dangerous to souls, than those formerly there exhibited. A number of the other professed churches have followed the example, so that even the school children have boasted of the good things and fine times they have at their respective churches. At Lowell, after a round of this festivity, one member remarked in *sober earnest,* that this would be a *grand way* to bring about the *Millennium!*" "The last Zion's Herald (Methodist paper) has an editorial headed, in large letters,   'TEA   MEETING

AT LYNN,' given by the ladies of the South-street Methodist church, in the Town-Hall, which the editor says, 'was filled with a most interesting assembly,' including *six clergymen,* and 'its sociability was untrammeled? Again, he says: 'One of the speakers, who had been acquainted with the sainted founders of Methodism in Lynn, remarked emphatically, that he believed their spirits were hovering with delight over this scene of Christian (?) intercourse among their children. The tables were spread bountifully and elegantly. The hall was decorated with evergreens, and portraits of our bishops and distinguished preachers.' The best of it, however, was, they made *seventy-five dollars* clear of all expenses."

The following advertisement appeared in a New York paper;

"GRAND FESTIVAL, by the Ladies of the 16th street Baptist church, Wednesday evening, January 26th, at the Trivoli Saloon, (the proceeds to go for liquidating the church debt.) *Tickets* to be had at"—

I add another;

"☞ UNPRECEDENTED ENTERTAINMENT at the *United States Hotel,* corner of Pearl and Fulton streets, on Thursday evening, Jan. 25,1844.

'' 1. The Ladies of the Nassau street congregation will commence their Annual Festival in the spacious saloons of the United States Hotel, on Thursday evening, the 25th inst., precisely at 7 o'clock. The festival will close at 11 o'clock. The windows on Pearl and Water streets will be brilliantly illuminated.

"2. Professor Bronson, who, by a happy combination of extensive science, with commanding powers of oratory, is attracting multitudes in other parts of the city, has generously tendered his services for the evening. At suitable intervals he will deliver several of his most entertaining and instructive recitations. He will also give an exposition and exemplification of *ventriloquism.*

"3. Professor Nash, whose vocal powers will bear comparison with any musical performer in the United States, has also consented to be present. Several *duets, solos*, and other pieces, may be expected during the evening. The professor will be accompanied by Miss Dobson, on one of Atnill's grand pianos. The sweet and unaffected vocal and musical performances of Miss Dobson would alone enrich any entertainment. *Tickets,* 50 cents for a gentleman, and 25 cents for a lady, may be obtained"—

"This last," it is justly remarked in a comment by a paper on it, "seems to be but the commencement of a *series of feasts* to be held by this Baptist church, where *ventriloquism,* and not religion, will contribute to the entertainments; and the tickets of which are sold at the *bars* of all the principal *hotels. "*

The following is the advertisement of a fair in Rochester, N. Y.

"LADIES FAIR—ST. JOHN'S CHURCH,—A *rare supper,* at 8 o'clock this (Wednesday) evening. *A splendid Young Deer, fresh from the Alleghenies,* ROASTED WHOLE, will be served up, with *other delicacies.* Tickets for supper, 50 cents." ——

"This feast," it is remarked on this, "was held in the church in charge of Mr. Hubbard, and in which Dr. Lucky of Rochester, preached last year: its ostensible object being to raise money to purchase curtains for the pulpit, and other extravagancies for the church. To raise money for such useless extravagancies—more in accordance with the teachings of HER on the *scarlet colored*

Beast, than with the example of primitive Christianity, it was necessary to appeal to the carnal appetites of the wicked, to tempt them with feasting and revelry, to contribute to the pride of the church!"

The following is extracted from a published letter of Mr. Miller, the father of the "Second Advent" doctrine:

"One of the D. D.'s in Rochester, Mr. Lucky, of the Methodist church, wrote a pamphlet against Millerism, called his lords and ladies in the house of the Lord, (?) made a great feast of oysters, and other picnics, Belshazzar like, drank their coffee and tea, and ate their costly delicacies, and *sold* their ice cream and sweet meats, and his *pamphlet* against the second advent of the dear Saviour. The night before I left, another of the reverend gentlemen had his picnic feast, at a public house or hall, and sold as above his tickets, ice cream, and sweet meats."

But enough of such scenes! They illustrate the great and gross corruptions of the sectarian systems now existing; and show, in language too plain to be mistaken, their rapid approximation to the sensuality, Carnality, worldly pomp and parade, and lifeless form of Romanism! The spirit of genuine Christianity is fast leaving them; and in proportion as it dies away, will it be supplanted by that of the 'Man of Sin!' This, With the rapid spread of Puseyism in Great Britain and this country; the revival of the powers of the Inquisition in Roman Catholic countries; the intolerant and proscriptive measures in religion adopted by the monarchs of Europe, and the courting of Roman Catholic favor and power by them, shows most conclusively that there will soon be but TWO great parties in the religious world: the advocates and holders of pure and unadulterated Christianity on the one hand, and Romanists on the other!

The time has come when the cry must be loudly uttered, and reiterated:— "COME OUT of her, my people, that ye be *not partakers* of her sins, and that ye *receive not* of her plagues."

A time of trial is coming to the Disciples of Christ, when their faith and courage Will be put to the test! For this great crisis, let the "teachers and holders of the true faith prepare, themselves by the cultivation of their powers, by a vigilant purity, by a generous and hallowed courage, for that high service of God and man in which they may so soon be called on to ACT, and perhaps to SUFFER ; and proclaim to all men alike the infinite urgency of redeeming the time before the arrival of a period, that, to the whole world of idolatry, shall come with a civil ruin, of which the subversion of Jerusalem was but a type; and with a physical destruction that can find no parallel but in the inevitable fury of the Deluge." RHO.

Let all our brethren that fear the Lord, and understand the spirit of this present age, avoid luxurious living, both at home and abroad, gay and fantastic apparel, costly furniture, and every species of sensual indulgence. Let them take in their sails; for a storm is coming upon this land, more to be dreaded than the Sirocco or Levanter of more eastern climes. Alas, for the times! when Methodism, and every form of Protestantism, of ancient Puritanism, have so soon run down to the dead level of all manner of conformity to the world. Splendid churches, rich saloons, well crimsoned pulpits, superb curtains, sublime organs, 'elegant preachers,' well read sermons, well feasted hearers, and polite audiences, have gained the day, and triumphed over reason, conscience, the law, and the gospel. A. C.

ANNUAL STATE CO-OPERATION MEETING.

To be held at the large, spacious and commodious brick meeting house called *Friendship,* 9 miles East of Franklin, Williamson county, Tennessee,—commencing on Thursday before the 3d Lord's day in September, 1844.

The Congregations of Jesus Christ in Tennessee, East, *Middle* and West, occupying the Apostolic ground of one Body, one Spirit, one hope, one Lord, one faith, one baptism, one God and Father of all, are urgently and pressingly solicited to represent themselves by letter or *Messengers,* at the above proposed meeting. It is greatly desirable to be presented with information officially, touching the following points:

1. The name, location and Post Office of each Congregation.
2. The date of the organization and present numbers of members of each congregation.
3. Additions during the past 3 years.
4. Names of officers in each Congregation.
5. Names of preachers in your respective vicinities.
6. How often do you meet "to break bread"?
7. What is the order of worship in each Congregation.
8. What sum of money will each congregation contribute to support Evangelists who will devote their whole time, energies and talents to the proclamation of the pure old life-giving word of God through Tennessee?

BRETHREN:—Remember! ye are the light of this community; if Tennessee ever be christianized, ye must do this great work. "Let there be light." We must, therefore, strongly operate and cordially co-operate in spreading the apostolic doctrine. Let us unite our strength—pull all together—and angels will rejoice; hell will mourn; Sectarianism will quail before us; truth will triumph; Jesus will reign; the cause receive a new impetus—Saints will be consoled—and Zion clap her hands! "Preach the Gospel to the whole creation." It must be done. Come up, brethren, and let us mingle in each other's society, refresh each other and be fired with renewed courage.

☞Preaching brethren are especially requested to attend.—Brethren, Wharton, Anderson, Fanning, Hopwood, Speer, Mack, Barnes, Barrett, Curlee, Cantrill. Griffin, McDonald, Osborne, Gooch, Dean, Lee, Hardison, McChord, Hall, Trott, Thompson, Manire,—Howard, Holmes, Gilleland,—all others not named—our Evangelists and Elders generally are all specially invited and entreated to attend without failure. Come up brethren with the answer to this question in your mouths.—What can we do to promote the interests and wide spread of the dear Redeemer's Kingdom at this crisis?

> Fly abroad, thou mighty gospel!
> Win and conquer! never cease!
> May thy lasting wide dominion
> Multiply and still increase!
> 　　　　Sway thy scepter,
> Saviour, all the world around!

Done by request of many brethren; this May 20th, 1844. W. S. SPEER,

Evangelist of the Ch. Church.

N. B. Letters designed for the Co-operation, and letters concerning the above meeting must be addressed to my name at *Columbia, Tenn.,* W. S. S.

☞Bible Advocate, and Millennial Harbinger, please copy.

MR. F. E. PITTS' EXPOSE OF CAMPBELLISM.

Bro. Howard, in his Bible Advocate, asks if Brother F. will not review Mr. Pitts' work on what he is pleased to term Campbellism. Many others have asked the same question, and several essays have already been prepared, by different brethren; but, for the present, I have declined publishing any thing on this matter, and my reasons are the following:

1. It is the ardent wish of the Editors of the Review, to preserve it from low, scurrilous, and profane abuse; but to quote Mr. Pitts' book, or speak of it in terms which it justly merits, this can Scarcely be done.

2. A review of this production is not needed amongst the disciples; for it does little else but excite their pity and disgust; and what we publish is very rarely read by the friends of Mr. P.

3. If there is a review of Mr. P.'s Tracts published, it seems to me, Bro. G. W. Elley would be the most suitable writer. If a review could circulate amongst our Methodist friends, it might be of advantage to them, but doubtless would be of utility to no others.   T. F.

PROPOSALS FOR PUBLISHING A SECOND EDITION OF G. W. ELLEY'S
*Examination of Elder F. E. Pitts' "Book on Baptism, chiefly designed
as a refutation of the errors and infidelity of Campbellism"*

ALSO, a notice of his second edition of slanders against the teaching of A. Campbell, and the Christian brethren, with additional matter against the identity of the "M. E. Church" and the "Church of Christ." The work will contain about 100 or 110 pages of matter, equal to at least the same number of pages of the first edition. The two essays upon the subject of "Remission" and the "Holy Spirit," together with T. Fanning's notice of the Baptist Church, will be omitted.

It will be furnished to subscribers at 20 cts. for any number above 20 copies. The very favorable reception of the first publication among the friends, and the call of many of the brethren for a second and enlarged edition, have induced me to yield to their demands. Elder Pitts' first and second books, have and will be largely circulated in the south, where our periodicals cannot remedy his monstrous perversion of truth. We suggest to the brethren and friends in Tennessee, Alabama and Mississippi, to subscribe for and circulate as many as possible in their regions. In order to aid that object, I have put just such a price upon the work as will pay for paper, printing, &c. Send up, therefore, your orders as early as practicable to J. T. S. FALL, Nashville, Tennessee, (post paid,) in order that I may print to suit the demand. Will the Bible Advocate, Christian Journal, and Millennial Harbinger, publish the above?

July, 1844.   GEO. W. ELLEY.

"THE GENIUS OF CHRISTIANITY"—BY A. G. COMINGS.

Bro. Comings is publishing, in the city of Boston, a neat and able paper, by the above designation; but, for want of patronage and prompt payment, he fears he will be forced to discontinue it. Brethren, for what do we live? To hoard up treasures, neglect the cause of the Saviour, and the without having lived for any valuable purpose? Bro. C. is a most excellent teacher; his paper is a valuable advocate of Christianity, and should be sustained. From my personal knowledge of N. England, I consider it the best field for labor in the U. States. The people are steady in their habits, industrious, intelligent, and religious; and, by proper exertions, immense good might be done. Missionaries should be sent amongst the good old "orthodox" Unitarians, Calvinists, Catholics, Quakers, and Universalists of New England. It is a dark region, in point of Scriptural knowledge; but in most other respects, the Yankee population is the best in the world. Oh, that the Original Gospel were understood in that portion of the earth!

T. F.

MARY STUART AND KNOX.

"You interpret the Scriptures in one Way," said Mary to Knox, "and the Pope and Cardinals in another: whom shall I believe, and who shall be judge?"

"You believe God," replied Knox, "who plainly speaketh in His word; and farther than the Word teacheth you, you shall believe neither the one nor the other: neither the Pope, nor the Reformers, neither the Papists, nor the Protestants. The Word of God is plain in itself: if there is any obscurity in one place, the Holy Ghost, which is never contradictory, explains it more clearly in other places, so that there can remain no doubt, but

such as are obstinately ignorant."

NEAR JONESBOROUGH, E. TEN.,   MAY 28, 1844.

Dear Brethren:—There has been but little said in our Periodicals about the reformation in East Tennessee, though we can count 11 Congregations organized upon the Living Oracles alone, in the following counties:

Counties.	Churches.	Members.	Proclaimers.
Washington	Boon's Creek,	250,	James Miller and J. Hail.
	Kibber's,	39,	J. Duncan.
	Limeston, say	15,	
Carter County,	Buffalo,	121,	T. Wright, D. M'Inturff, G. W. Duncan & J. Wright.
	Mt. Pleasant.	94,	J. Wright.
	Turkey Town,	64,	J. I. Tipton & S. Hendrik.
	Crab Orchard,	24,	
Johnston County,	Liberty,	94,	
	Roan's Creek, 30,		
Sullivan County,		109,	D. T. Wright.
Concord,		43,	

We are gaining some additions for the King in Johnston and Carter. The Congregation at Roan's Creek has been made of new recruits in two or three months passed, and the one in the Crab Orchard was organized on the 12th inst.

There is one Congregation in the edge of Virginia on the North Fork of the Holston River, where we occasionally visit—they number say 200. Dr. Shanklin and J. Counter labor in the word and doctrine. We expect to make a trip to Washington county in Virginia the last of July and return the first or second week in August; and shall spend the most of our time with the brethren in the valley of the N. Fork. On our return we may perhaps give you some account of our success.

J. WRIGHT.

CHRISTIAN REVIEW.

VOL. I.   NASHVILLE, AUGUST, 1844.   NO. VIII.

NOTES ON A TOUR.—No. 1.

Believing the readers of the Christian Review, would be gratified to hear of the progress of truth, and the general condition of the Churches, I proceed to note a few incidents of a tour through the most interesting portion of country, in point of religious intelligence, in the United States. I admit very frankly, at the outset, that a mere visitor of countries, and churches, is liable to be greatly deceived, particularly, in reference to individuals, but as to the general condition of society, there is scarcely any room for mistakes.

Saturday, June 1st, 1844, I left the neighbourhood of Nashville, in company with Bro. G. B. Long of Hopkinsville, Ky., for Clarksville, Montgomery Co., at which place we arrived the same day. The town is a flourishing village of a population of some two thousand persons, with a fine country on the north and west. As is usual in our towns, there are several very respectable churches of partisans. The Episcopalians, Presbyterians, Methodists and Baptists, have meeting houses, and most, if not all of them, have ministers of their respective faiths. The Romanists, I was told, are preparing for a building. The disciples number about thirty-five members, have no meeting house, nor regular preaching. Bro. J. B. Ferguson, however, gives considerable of his time to this place. I was happy to find most of the saints devoted to the cause. They meet weekly, break bread, and, altogether, I know of no church, which, taking all the circumstances into view, is doing more to improve in the truth and advance the Redeemer's cause. Bros. Doctor Young from Illinois, and J. B. Ferguson were with me, and through our labors, three made the good confession, and I left the brethren still laboring in the word.

Tuesday the 4th, I bade adieu to Clarksville, and after a ride of nine miles over a pleasant country, I reached the residence of Bro. Jno. W. Barker, where I spent the evening most agreeably. Bro. B. is an old citizen of the county, and is a man of much practical information, particularly in reference to agriculture; and he has accumulated a large estate. Such men have it in their power to do much to advance the cause of righteousness, and if Christians would spend their means in educating their children, and aiding the cause of education, and in. assisting poor Evangelists, it would be infinitely better than to let their offspring grow up in luxury, and then give a large estate to be squandered. Bro. B. having many of the cares of Caesar to manage, could not accompany me Wednesday the 5th, to my appointment; but his amiable consort finding both inclination and leisure, attended me to Corinth to the neighborhood of Trenton, where I met a large congregation of intelligent disciples, and I was much rejoiced to see my faithful brethren, H. T. Anderson, C. Day and J. Calahan from whom I had been separated several years. After preaching, we spent the evening in the interesting family of Sister Seabry.

Thursday, 6th, with Bros. Anderson and Long, I visited Hopkinsville, in Christian Co.

Kentucky, spoke once and remained a day. At this point there is a church of near two hundred members, and from what I could learn, I could but hope the brethren are increasing in the knowledge of the truth, and are endeavoring to diffuse the light. Bro. Young is their Evangelist, and a very intelligent, firm and faithful brother he is. Four such teachers as Brethren Jesse B. Ferguson, Henry T. Anderson, C. Day and Doctor Young, ought to produce a vast revolution in Society.

Friday the 7th, I journeyed 20 miles eastward to Elkton, in Todd Co., and was kindly received by Brother Ritter and family. At night, and on Saturday morning the 8th, I addressed very respectable assemblies in the court house. There are about 80 disciples in the church at this place, who seem to be fine brethren and sisters. I was sorry to see some engaged in politics, and, evidently, there was too much conversation and feeling manifested on the subject of politics by several.—This is a fatal year to religion.

Saturday the 8th, at "dewy eve," I reached Russellville, and was hospitably received into the family of Sister Edwards. Her son, Bro. J. Edwards, is a young man of good ability, but has given all his talents and energies to the law. Here is but a small company of disciples in the town, but there are several hundred in the county. I preached at night to some twenty persons, and Lord's day morning and evening to about the same number. Such an assembly, in such a place, I had not seen, and I was irresistibly driven to the conclusion the cause had been managed badly by the teachers who had visited the place, or the few disciples did not act worthy of their profession, or that the people were under the strictest code of sectarian tactics, of any I had seen. Upon enquiry, I concluded, the disrespect to the Christian religion was shown, more from clerical influence, than any other cause. Mr. Baker of the Baptist church, and Mr. Stevenson of the Methodist denomination—both men of respectable ability, and indisputable authority in their flock, reside in this village. It will be many a day before much religious light will shine on Russellville. I had forgotten to say, a Methodist woman, during my stay, mounted the rostrum, as is her custom, and delivered a sermon in her denomination's house—of course the multitude exhibited their intellectual culture—as well as their spiritual intelligence, and above all, their good taste, by attending. No people are prepared for the Gospel, while such farces are played off to their admiration.

I must not neglect to say, the few disciples of this place are quite intelligent, and aside from their religion, are much respected. While in Russellville, I was highly entertained by an aged Scotch Brother in Israel—James Gordan. Father Gordan has been twenty-two years in America, and he informed me, that even in Scotland, with a few associates, he had been in the habit of meeting with his brethren weekly, to break bread, and observe the worship of the Lord's house many years before coming to this country. This is another evidence, the religion for which we have pleaded, has not had its origin in this country, or in modern times.

Monday, June the 10th, in company with E. HISE, ESQ., the Democratic elector for the State of Kentucky, I set out for South Union, a Shaker village, fifteen miles distant, which we reached about noon. No sooner was my name announced by Mr. H. to *Friend* Robinson, the Post Master, than he inquired, "Is this Friend Fanning, from Nashville?" On being informed I was the man, and that we would be pleased to spend a few hours with them, he manifested marked gratification, and with the greatest haste ran to the "Centre House," to inform the leading Elders; and it was but a few minutes till Elder Jno. Rankin, who has been on the ground nearly fifty years, and Elder Eades, were seated with us in a snug room, and some half a dozen "sisters's were exerting themselves to prepare us dinner.

We at once engaged in conversation in reference to a book purporting to be "A New Revelation," of which I spoke in a previous number of the Review. My first enquiry was, to know the authority for new revelations at this day, when we have an abundance already to "perfect us in every good work."— "Nay," says Elder Rankin, "if there were no other authority in the Bible, the prophecy of Joel, reiterated by Peter, and recorded in the second chapter of the Acts of the Apostles, is enough." I endeavored to show him, these signs were to attend the preaching of the Apostles TILL "that which is perfect" came—that is, till the knowledge of a perfect man in Christ Jesus, was fully revealed, or fill the perfect law of liberty was completed; and then all these visions and signs were to cease, and did cease.

My next question was intended to ascertain the evidence which they individually had, to prove the truth of the revelation which they had sent me months since, and the reply was, "It is an *inward feeling* of the soul." I showed them very clearly, that all the sects of the land profess to know by the same *"feeling sense,"* that they are Christians, and on their way to heaven; and to admit the feeling sense of one to be true, we must admit all, and when this is done, God becomes the author of confusion, and not of peace. The consequence is, we cannot believe in the thousand and one revelations of the age, and the God of order at the same time. These Friend Shakers, however, speak with great confidence, and they assured me, marvelous signs would soon be exhibited to men, unless they are lying prophets. I hope to live to see the wondrous things at hand.

Mr. Rankin gave me more information in reference to the revival system and camp-meetings, than I enjoyed before. As this is a deeply interesting subject, I contemplate giving a short essay on it, at a future period.

While here, I met with a Mr. Wallis, of my acquaintance, from Alabama, who joined the community a few months since; and knowing he cast his lot amongst them to get direct light without the aid of study, I frankly asked him, if the Spirit had not yet made some communication to him? "Nay," said he; "but I am still a probationer, and expect yet to get it." I have always noticed, when persons doubt not there are hobgoblins, they are certain to see them; and those who look for angels, spirits and new lights, without equivocation, rarely fail getting them. I must not omit one reflection: Long have I believed, and every thing I see confirms me in the conviction, that the whole system of seeking and professing new light at the altar, mourners' bench, and in the Shaker mummeries, is the most successful system of making hypocrites in existence; and now I am driven to the conclusion, its whole tendency is only calculated to deprave and degrade God's noblest work.

But, with all the superstition of the Shakers, they are far in advance of their neighbors in their temporalities. At this place, they own several thousand acres of land, and have several hundred in a very high state of cultivation.— Instead of cropping their land to death, they are constantly improving it. Their wheat, corn, potatoes, and all their crops, are thriving and abundant, whilst the surrounding country, to me, puts on the appearance of poverty and scarceness. The Shakers have fine houses, fine gardens, fine stock, and fine living, while nine tenths of the world can, with great difficulty, get but a few of the comforts which they daily enjoy. If there were no other argument for ASSOCIATION, this one case is demonstrative. After looking at their independence, it is really sickening to behold the miserably dilapidated huts of the country, the worn-out lands, rotten fences, ragged children, and comfortless condition of most of our fellow creatures. I left South Union with an exalted opinion of many of the Shaker practices.

The same evening, I reached Bowling Green, and soon formed acquaintances. At night, I lectured in the Presbyterian meeting-house, upon the subject of Education; and after I closed, I had the opportunity of hearing Mr. Pendleton, of the Baptist Church, Mr. Dickerson, of the Presbyterian Church, and most of the speakers of the town, deliver a few remarks each, in reference to the management of Temperance Societies. Of course, I formed some judgment as to the relative talent and taste of the speakers. I was truly sorry to learn, the Christian religion had but few open, independent friends in this friendly, but sectarian community. Oh! what a shame, that the religion of the Bible should be banished from many of our towns, by the contaminating institutions of modern times!

Tuesday, the 11th, with Brother Sweeney, I crossed Big Barren river, and journeyed along the Louisville turnpike, through a fine country, some fifteen miles, to the commodious residence of Brother Doctor Ford, in Edminson county. I tarried the balance of the day; spoke, in the afternoon, to a few of the neighbors, and an interesting school of young ladies, under the management of Sister M. K. GUFFY, on the "importance and proper manner of searching the Scriptures." I had the pleasure of the company of my acquaintances and highly esteemed Brother and Sister Begg. I found Brother Ford a man of a thousand. He is the doctor, preacher, and emphatically *the* man of the neighborhood. By his zeal for the cause, several churches have been planted in striking distance of him, within a few years. Oh, that we had enough such men as Doctor Ford, of Dripping Springs, Kentucky!   T. F.

(To be continued.)

——————

TO YOUNG LADIES.

In my last, I thought I would say nothing more of the Old Testament, but perhaps it will be best to refer to it again, before we go to the New. It has been mentioned, that it is useless to study the first, in order to learn the practice of the Christian religion. You ask, then, of what use is it to us? I answer, that it is most important to every one who wishes to become intelligent in the great science of Christianity.

In it you see the history of the Jewish religion, which was a type, a shadow of the Christian. There you find the sacrifices that pointed to the great sacrifice of the Son of Heaven's King. You read of its priests, representing the myriads who, in the future dispensation, were to be kings and priests to God.

It had its laver, in which the priests were to wash before they entered on the service of the Tabernacle: a type of the baptism to which we must all submit, before we engage in the service of the Christian Tabernacle. There was the altar, from which sweet incense always ascended to the throne of heaven, indicative of the constantly ascending prayers and praises of the Christians of a future day. It had its light perpetually burning, emblematic of the Gospel light that was to blaze forth in meridian splendor and glory, never to be extinguished, so long as heaven and earth exist.

But, not to be tedious to you, we will go on farther. The prophets, too, pointed to the future. They told of a new kingdom that was to be set up. They spoke of the King that should govern it. Even Moses looked forward to him. "A prophet," he says, "shall the Lord your God raise up of your brethren, like unto me; him shall ye hear in all things." Isaiah, seven hundred years before the birth of this Ruler, in the majesty of God's inspiration, says of him, "Unto us a child is born; unto us a son is given. The government shall be upon his shoulders; his name shall be called Wonderful, Counsellor, the Mighty God, the Everlasting Father, the Prince of Peace." With pathetic tenderness, he goes on to tell of his being "despised and rejected of men; a man of sorrow, and acquainted with grief: and we hid, as it were, our faces from him. He was despised, and we esteemed him not. Surely he hath borne our griefs, and carried our sorrows: yet did we esteem him stricken, smitten of God, and afflicted.— He was oppressed and he was afflicted; yet he opened not his mouth. He was brought as a sheep to the slaughter; and as a sheep before his shearers is dumb, so he opened not his mouth." Notwithstanding his sorrows and sufferings, he was ultimately to triumph; he was to set up this kingdom, the government of which was to be upon his shoulders; he was to rule until all his enemies submitted, and all his laws were obeyed. If you ask *where* this new kingdom was to commence, the prophets will answer. Micah says the law should "go forth from Zion, and the word of the Lord from *Jerusalem.*" Isaiah speaking of it: "And many people shall come and say, Come, ye, and let us go up to the mountain of the Lord, to the house of the God of Jacob; and he will teach us of his ways, and we will walk in his paths: for out of Zion shall go forth the law, and the word of the Lord from *Jerusalem.*"

You recollect, the Jewish religion or kingdom was then in existence; the people to whom it was given, had become corrupt, and a new and pure government was to be established by a risen and triumphant Redeemer. The government was to be upon his shoulders; he was to be lawgiver as well as ruler.

We now go to the New Testament, to see if we can find a fulfillment of the prophecies made in the Old—if we can find the kingdom that was to come.— We open the book, and the first personage therein described, is HE to whom the law and the prophets pointed. He makes his coming as a helpless babe, and multitudes of bright angels appear, praising God, and saying, "Glory to God in the highest; on earth peace, and good will to men. Never before had the sweet anthems of the heavenly host been heard, sounding in melodious strains the unutterable love of God to his fallen creature man.

The child lives and grows. The endearing graces of infancy and childhood gradually pass away. He rises to man's estate, in majestic purity and holiness never before witnessed. He begins to do the will of his Father, amid the sneers of all the religions parties of his age. He is buried in baptism because it became him thus to fulfill all righteousness, or in other words, to

Father's institutions. He goes about doing good to sick and suffering humanity.— At his word the winds and the waves are stilled from their raging, the blind receive their sight, the lame walk, the deaf hear, the lepers are cleansed, the dead are raised to life; the restless demons of the invisible world bow at his command.

Notwithstanding his mighty power, he is as the prophet said he should be, a man of sorrow. "Jesus wept"—"Jesus groaned in spirit"—he wept for the sorrows of those he loved, though there were many hearts he caused to leap for joy.

The Savior finished his mission of love; he ended the work his Father gave him to do; he submitted to the shameful and ignominious death of the cross; he was buried, and rose on the third morning, having conquered death and taken away his sting. He rose from the dead, and was with his disciples for 40 days, giving them a knowledge of the kingdom that was soon to commence at *Jerusalem,* He ascended to heaven, leaving a code of laws for the establishment and government of it; and his disciples, having tarried at *Jerusalem* until they were endued with power from on high to promulgate them, then commenced preaching the Gospel of the Son of God. We will speak particularly of this Gospel the next time we address you.

Your friend,   LUCY.

CHURCH ORGANIZATION.

BEREA ACADEMY, (*near Chapel Hill,*) MARSHALL CO., TENN.

DEAR BROTHER FANNING Permit me to contribute something which may aid in the organization of the churches, so far, at least, as the qualifications of Elders, Bishops, or Overseers may be concerned. I am pleased with the remarks you offered in the June No. of the Christian Review, with one or two exceptions; and, as you close them with requesting the brethren to show wherein you have stated "what is not true," I the more cheerfully undertake the task of pointing out one or two items in the qualifications, as specified by you in that paper, which I deem inconsistent with the Scriptures.

I must, however, premise, that it will appear evident to all, that the Apostle Paul did not command Timothy to require more or less, in order to the appointment and ordination of a bishop at Ephesus, than Titus was to require at Crete. In other words, the same qualifications were requisite to make a bishop at Crete, Corinth, Ephesus, Philippi, or elsewhere. The letter which the Apostle directed to Timothy, was to be *his* guide; the letter to Titus, *his* guide. Those evangelists did not meet and compare directions; Timothy from the letter to Titus adding what was omitted in the letter to himself. They acted each according to his own instructions; and, as "God is no respecter of persons," the instructions were alike. These instructions are not, in every particular, couched in the same words; and the verbal difference may contribute somewhat to the understanding of them: but I think we have no right to increase the number of requisites in either. This, I think, you (through inadvertence) have done. You follow the letter to Timothy in making seventeen specifications; you then turn to the letter to Titus, and give *three* more; thence back to Timothy, and add more: making in all twenty-one distinct items of qualifications. I have doubt that a "second sober thought" will cause you to correct this. I now proceed to offer a few thoughts for your consideration, and for the consideration of the brethren.

1. There are but 16 qualifications prescribed by our Apostle: this number is prescribed in each letter. You place "a desire for the office" as one. No mention is made of any desire, in the Epistle to Titus. Paul's language in the letter to Timothy, does not authorize us to place it as a qualification: "If a man desire the office of a bishop, he desireth a good work," is not the language of requisition.

2. Your 18th qualification cannot be sustained. "Not accused of riot, or unruly," does not refer to the proposed bishop, but to his children, and is evidently intended as descriptive of their character. I dislike to quote Greek in a paper intended for the eye of plain English people; but I must do it now. Titus i, 6, reads thus: "Ei tis estin anegkleetos, mias gunaikos aneer, tekna achoon pista, mee en kateegonia asootias, ee anupotakta." The adjective *anupotakta* qualifies tekna, not *tis.* Besides, the meaning of the word (not subjected, insubordinate, refractory, lawless, or from its derivation, not *reduced to obedience)* determines its application, especially if we compare it with 1 Tim. iii, 4: in this passage, we have *tekna echonta en hupotagee.* This is plain.

3. Your last specification of qualification is, that the bishop must first be "proved." From this I must dissent. 1st, Because the Apostle does not require it. When he says, "And let these also first be proved," he is speaking of *deacons;* for he adds, "then let them use the office of a deacon, being found blameless."—1 Tim. iii, 8-10. 2d, The office of bishop is administrative or executive, and to some extent judicial; this forbids the idea of probation. If an individual possesses the requisite qualifications, he enters upon the office absolutely, and for life. If he should be guilty of malfeasance in office, he is to be tried and cashiered.

4. I am glad to see that you have discovered that Paul does not require that a man's children shall be Christians before he is qualified for the bishop's office. This idea has been presented, and urged with a good deal of zeal, and contended for with much pertinacity. It is not pretended that the letter to Timothy requires it. More could not consistently be asked for in Crete than In Ephesus. The common version is correct in rendering *tekna echoon pista,* in Titus i, 6, "having faithful children." The adjective *pistos,* is frequently used substantively in the New Testament, and then it has the signification of *"believing,"* or "a *believer."* This last is a special and local meaning. In innumerable instances, or in general, it means true, worthy of credit or confidence, firm in adherence to duty.

5. To close. I would cheerfully assent to your list of qualifications for the bishop's office, if you would expunge the 1st, 18th and 21st, and make your 19th end 20th synonymous with some of the others, as they really are.

I am, with much esteem, your brother,   JNO. M. BARNES.

————————

REPLY TO BRO. BARNES.—I am under obligations to Bro. Barnes for directing my attention to the 18th qualification of Bishops which I gave in the June No. as not applicable to the officers themselves but their children. Still I must say his conclusion that the *desire* of the Bishop's office, mentioned by Paul, is not a requirement, and of course, unnecessary, is a very remarkable conclusion. Also, the idea that a man before being appointed to the Bishop's office, need not be proved, is to my mind a strange position. When Paul says let the deacons *Salto be fret proved,"* if he does not allude to the proving of those seeking the Bishop's office, I can see no meaning in part of the expression. I hope Bro. B. will take the second sober thought on this subject. At any rate, I trust not only he, but all the brethren will discuss this subject fully; for I am well assured it has not yet received proper attention.   T. F.

CHURCH DISCIPLINE.

To the Editors of the Christian Review:

BROTHER FANNING:—In *theory,* we profess to follow the Bible, and the Bible alone; in *our practice,* there is a departure, or at least I so deem it, from Apostolic practice, concerning which I wish to ask your opinion. It is in regard to church discipline—I refer now to cases in which expulsion is thought necessary. The practice is, in some congregations, for the bishop or bishops to examine into the charges brought against an offending member, and when they are fully proved, and expulsion considered necessary, to expel him; which event is afterwards announced to the congregation. Now, I doubt whether that was the Apostolic practice, and here are my reasons:

In 1 Cor. v, 4—5,1 read as follows: "In the name of our Lord Jesus Christ, when ye are gathered together, and my spirit, with the power of our Lord Jesus Christ, to deliver such an one to Satan for the destruction of the flesh, that the spirit may be saved," &c. These words, by the unanimous consent of all readers, mean that the offending member must be excluded from the congregation. The question immediately arises, Who, were those the Apostle said must be gathered together? In the 1st chapter, 2d verse, I read as follows: "Unto the church of God which is at Corinth, to them that are sanctified in Christ Jesus, called to be saints, with all that in every place call on the name of Jesus Christ our Lord, both theirs and ours, grace be unto you," &c. Here we learn whom the Apostle was addressing, and very evidently, he did not address the bishops exclusively. A careful examination of the first five chapters, will convince any one that the Apostle does not in the commencement of the Epistle address his brethren, and afterwards direct his remarks to the bishops exclusively.

Again, Paul addresses them as *brethren,* in the 1st verse of the 3d chapter.— Now, this could not mean the bishops; for the next verse declares they had been fed on milk, not being yet able to bear strong food; were carnal, and had envyings, strife, and divisions among them—rather bad characters for bishops. This view is confirmed by the 2d chapter of 2 Cor., 6th verse: "Sufficient to such a man is this punishment, which is inflicted of many," or, as some copies read, "of the majority." Hence, I conclude, those congregations do not follow the apostolic practice, in which the power of exclusion is solely possessed and exerted by the bishop or bishops. If it can be clearly shown, that in the Apostles' time, the bishop or bishops alone possessed and exerted the power to exclude, well and good, say I; all I desire is to invite attention to the subject, in order that the truth may be elicited.

By the way, as I have my pen in hand, and the last verse I quoted has brought it to my mind,

I will say a few words concerning that unreasonable and impracticable "unanimous rule," adopted by a congregation not a thousand miles from Nashville. I laughed most heartily, when I was told it had been adopted, and said to the person who informed me, "It may do well in theory, and will answer in practice, where subjects of minor importance are discussed; but the very moment a proposition of more than ordinary interest is made, the majority will vote the objections of the minority unreasonable, and pass the resolution without paying any regard to the rule." Well, sure enough, shortly afterwards, an interesting proposition was made, and one of the majority arose, and stated that the rule requiring all resolutions to be unanimously passed, was only intended to work when the minority was not factious and unreasonable; he then pronounced the objections of the minority factious and unreasonable, and the resolution was passed, the rule to the contrary notwithstanding. I showed the above-mentioned verse to a strong advocate of the unanimous rule, and asked him, why the Apostle used the word *many,* if not in contradistinction to the few; or, should the other reading be preferred, why should he use the word *majority,* if there was no *minority.* To this he could make no reply at that time. After a week's cogitation, he said to me, "I think, Brother, I can convince you, that the word *many* means *all,* and not what you think it does." "Perfectly useless to try," replied I; "for if you could prove it from the English, there is the original, that is still stronger; there the word is in the comparative degree, which still more forcibly draws the distinction between the majority and the minority; and one who can prove that *hupo ton pleionon,* "of or by the jority," means the unanimous whole, can prove the Bible is not true.

This subject will demand further investigation, in case it should be found that the bishop does not solely possess the power of exclusion; for no offending member can ever be excluded, as long as a relative or a warm friend cannot be made to view matters as they ought to be viewed. Suppose a case is brought before the church; the offending member has warm friends and relatives, whose prejudices prevent their seeing matters in their true light. Now, under the unanimous rule, we must keep him still a member, or violate what we have pronounced the law of God, namely, that all acts should be done by the whole body unanimously, by excluding him by the vote of a majority. Enough for the present.   W.

REPLY TO BRO. W. IN REFERENCE TO DISCIPLINE.

Although I am pleased with the subjects presented and discussed by Bro. W., I cannot heartily approve of the style. The whole church, or all the members at Corinth were commanded to withdraw from the wicked. We have no account in the Bible of a Bishop's expelling any one, but the Bishops have the superintendence of the whole church, and it is their privilege and duty to enquire into and investigate all offences, and report to the church. When a member proves refractory and cannot be reclaimed, the *overseers state the facts to the church, read the law and pronounce the withdrawal.* In all cases, the Bishop is only the mouth of the church, and does nothing to Lord over God's heritage, or independent of the Body. The "church is the pillar and support of the truth," and the officers are only parts of the body.

Notwithstanding Bro. W. seems to laugh at the idea of Christians being required to be of one mind, when he studies the Bible a little more, and sees a few factions formed by one part of a church overruling the other, or the strong trampling the weak under foot, I am persuaded he will change his tone. Bro. W. says if *"the many"* "means the unanimous whole, (I) can prove the Bible is not true?'—We will see. Paul uses the same comparative in Heb. 7. 23, thus: *"And they truly were many priests."* Now I ask Bro. W. does this mean all the priests, or a certain part?

1 declare to all the world, that I believe God has graciously given a perfect law to govern his people, and that when a vote is taken to ascertain what shall be done, it is virtually making law, and that is a sure mode to make void the law of God. Bro. W. intimates that in cases where the friends of the offender will not consent to an expulsion, the majority must *force* the matter. Far from the true plan. Relatives and friends of offenders who cannot see the plain truth of the Gospel in reference to crimes, should themselves be made subjects of discipline. I say to my excellent Bro. W. that he should examine the Bible a little more carefully, before he takes such strong ground.   T. F.

PLAN OF EVANGELIZING.

To the Editors of the Christian Review:—

BRETHREN EDITORS:—I am almost afraid I shall be thought somewhat disposed to find fault. Having said many things of Elders or Bishops, and their character, duties and responsibilities, I will call the attention of your readers to the present system of evangelizing. I think it would puzzle the wisest of our proclaimers, to give a "thus saith the Lord" for the manner in which they are sustained in the field. Did any apostle or evangelist of ancient times, ever engage with any church, or number of churches, for the space of 12 months, and for a certain sum of money? If the record furnishes an example, I have not yet seen it. Therefore, ye evangelists, inform me if you can, on what page of the living oracles, I can find an example for our present practice. I say our practice, for I am practicing on the present plan. I know, however, that the present system is subject to many, and very serious objections, and for this reason I call attention to it.

The apostles and evangelists of primitive times, went forth from the churches; they were not called to the churches. Paul to the Philippians, speaketh on this wise: "Now, ye Philippians, know also, that in the beginning of the gospel, when I departed from Macedonia, no church communicated with me, as concerning giving and receiving, but ye only. For even in Thessalonika ye sent once, and again to my necessity." We have here a fair exhibit of the custom of those pure times. Paul planted a church in Philippi, and when going forth to proclaim the gospel in Thessalonika, these Philippians gave him money, and sent to him once and again, while in that city. The second case worthy of our very attentive consideration, is the conduct of Paul -and Barnabas sent from Antioch. They went, planted churches, returned and gave an account of their labours. After a season they returned to visit their churches, and see how they did. The two cases present us with the true system of evangelizing.

I shall now state the conclusions to which I have come from these. An evangelist when he has planted a church, is not bound by any law of the New Testament to visit that church once each month, or once in two months. But according to the case before us, this church should, instead of calling the proclaimer to preach to them once a month, give him money to bear his expenses; that he may preach to other towns, cities and counties or states. There are hundreds of sermons wasted in these our times on congregations that have heard and refused to obey. Instead, therefore, of being confined to the church or churches, which have been planted, let the proclaimer go to neighborhoods in which the gospel has not been heard, and there abide until he has induced as many to obey as are ordained to eternal life. I have heard it said more than a hundred times by myself and other evangelists, that had we spent some week or ten days more at a place, we should have been greatly successful. This is true in a multitude of cases, as most of us can testify. Here I remark that the result of not remaining in a place, is often disastrous to those who are left. I have known some instances, in which the whole community had become aroused by the preaching of the gospel. The people were left in this condition, because the proclaimers must hasten to another appointment. The people afterwards heard the preaching of sectarians, and were caught in the net of our modern fisher" men, or rather in the modern nets of modern fishermen. The gospel would have saved multitudes of men and women, but the evangelist must leave for another appointment—where it has often happened that no good has been done. I then call on you, my preaching brethren, to testify that the present system of evangelizing, has often proved the loss of many souls. I look on it as a serious evil, which the word of God can easily amend. The selfish disposition of many churches, demands of a proclaimer his monthly visit, to the injury of themselves and the loss of their neighbors. I say the churches are injured by the monthly preaching, because the disciples are thus taught to rely on the preacher, instead of the word of the Lord, to hear preaching instead of attending to the institutions.

The congregations should employ proclaimers to preach to sinners, and not to the churches, unless they would hearken to them, in their efforts to set them in order. The churches need to be set in order; they need officers. It is the duty of those officers to feed the church, and let proclaimers carry the unsearchable riches of Christ to the world. It is the duty of churches to pay a proclaimer, and see that he needs nothing while he is giving to men the word of life.

This 12-month system is unauthorized by scripture or common sense. Let us try its operation. Evangelist X. Y. Z. preachers in a town, county or city, for 12 months. He is not very successful, but has perhaps laid the foundation of a rich harvest for a second year. Some find fault with him, and another must be brought in. X. Y. Z. is dismissed at the end of 12 months, and it so happens that another cannot be gained for some six or twelve months after. Then the community is without a proclaimer, and all that has been done for 12 months, is lost by the whimsies of some discontented spirit. I have known much good labour lost forever by the removal of a proclaimer. To what is this to be ascribed but to the present system? Let the proclaimer remain until the people are divided; to use the emphatic language of Luke, until those who are "ordained to eternal life believe." There are many places where the gospel has gained many persons—has indeed divided the people. The churches in these places should be satisfied to attend to the institutions of the Lord, as they have been taught, leaving to time and their good behaviour, to leaven   the community. But what are the Elders doing that they cannot teach the congregations, and induce persons to obey the gospel? However, I will not say more with respect to them, as evangelists are now under consideration. My sheet is nearly full, and I must reserve some very important objections to the 12-month system, for another essay. In the mean-time let the brethren look to their bibles, and be prepared for true gospel order on this point, and let them determine to sacrifice their selfishness, on the altar of truth, and let the proclaimer go to seek and save the lost. To the law and the testimony, brethren. Yours,   H. T. ANDERSON.

FIRST PRINCIPLES—NO. 2.

In the July No., under the above caption, I endeavored to present such rules of interpretation as would enable the Biblical student to arrive at all truth. In this article, I wish to present a brief sketch of God's temple, or an outline of the Christian institution.

The details of a science cannot become so attractive, without some knowledge of its history and ultimate objects. There is no utility in telling the world to be religious, or become Christians, when those addressed know not the meaning of RELIGION or its intentions. But one theory of religion can occupy the mind at the same time; and if this be erroneous, the correct teaching cannot be received till the old leaven is rooted out. One who supposes religion is what persons *"get"* in excitement, in answer to lamentations, and prayers, or enters our hearts without addressing our senses, is incapable, while in this state, to perceive or believe the truth; and he that imagines men now have keys to forgive sins, or that new lights are promised, can neither see, love or obey the truth of God. The Jews on Pentecost, and the philosophers at Athens were convinced of their error and ignorance, not so much by preaching the Gospel, as by showing the absurdity and contradictions of their systems. The grand secret of educating the young does not consist in filling the heads of pupils with languages and sciences; but in removing difficulties from the mind, and thereby enabling them to think, reason, and conclude for themselves. Success in teaching Christianity consists, not so much in knowing or being amply able to speak the truth, as in being well acquainted with human nature, and in having patience to remove prejudice. This subject might be advantageously pursued to great extent, but I must return to the main point.— As sour, bitter, beauty, and even virtue and vice appear more perspicuous by contrast, it may be, a scriptural description of Christianity in contrast with the religion of the present and past ages, will contribute much to the advancement of truth.

But before proceeding, the reader must be assured, opposition to any religion, must not be taken as an argument, exhibiting the unkindness of the writer. "Whom I love, I reprove," contains a sentiment which actuates me in all controversies with the deceived of the world. From these suggestions, my course must be a negative one. The Christian empire then is not the church of Rome, which cannot be traced within three centuries of Pentecost, and which is dissimilar to Christ's kingdom in every important feature. Neither is it the church of England which sprang from an amorous affair with Henry VIII. and Ann Boleyn; and in a word it can be no protestant

modem origin. It requires truly a discerning man to see many features of resemblance between the church of Christ at Jerusalem and the people of this day professing to be Christians. Without, however, pursuing this branch of the argument further, at present, I must sketch the history of Christianity. As the whole of an edifice can be seen best by a view of its various parts, I will contemplate the Christian fabric

CHRONOLOGICALLY.

Was the kingdom of heaven a subject of conversation with Adam and Eve, Enoch, Noah, Abraham, the Patriarchs, Moses, or the Prophets? Not at all. Why so? It was not in existence. A few rays of light fell upon the prophets, vision, but not in sufficient quantities to give them full and perfect knowledge. Did John, the wisest and best of prophets, live to see the kingdom? He told the Jews it was "at hand" and he was sent to "prepare a people made ready for it;" but the Saviour said, "the very least in the kingdom should be greater than John." Why so? Because John lost his life before the kingdom came, and therefore could not enjoy its light and privileges. Christ chose twelve, and afterwards seventy, and sent them out to say to the inhabitants of Judea, "repent for the kingdom of heaven is at hand."

It requiring a King, Laws and Subjects, to constitute a kingdom; if we can ascertain the first existence of them, we may know when the kingdom of heaven began. While the Saviour was on earth, he was humbled; but he ascended to heaven to be crowned a King. This occurred about forty days after his resurrection. Secondly, subjects had already been prepared, and a hundred and twenty of them were waiting in an up-stair room in Jerusalem for the promise of the Father. "When the day of Pentecost was fully come," the Holy Spirit descended and enabled the apostles to deliver the word of truth in the different languages spoken under heaven, and to give the law for the government of the twelve tribes of Israel, and thus was fulfilled the prediction, that "out of Sion shall go forth the law and the word of the Lord from Jerusalem." Upon the testimony of the Apostle Peter, three thousand believed and were added; and thus, we have the first account, in the world's history, of additions to, or even of the existence of the Church of Christ, at Jerusalem, on the day of Pentecost. I have not only presented the church Chronologically, but Topographically, and now we will contemplate it as a whole.

We view, for the first time in the annals of the world, a multitude of disciples of Jesus the King, bound together by his love, assembling daily for his worship—"continuing steadfastly in the Apostles' doctrine, in fellowship, and in prayers and the breaking of bread." All things temporal were held in common, "and all were together, and were of one heart and one soul." Then it was there was "one Lord, one faith, one baptism;" one body, one spirit, one hope, and one God to guide and direct all. Then it was, Christians loved like brethren, and cared for the things of others as well as for themselves. Then it was, "disciples assembled together to break bread," and spent their Lord's days in singing, prayers, praises, exhortations, and heavenly contemplations.— Then it was, Christians loved the Lord with all the heart, soul, mind and strength, and each other with pure hearts fervently. Then it was, Christians "worked with their own hands," that they might have to give the needy. Then it was, the saints brought up "their children in the instruction and admonition of the Lord." But, oh God! what a contrast do we now behold, between the sects and those ancient Christians? There can no resemblance be drawn between them. None of the features are alike, and but a very faint resemblance can be seen between the ancient church and those who now profess to be the disciples of Christ. Christians of this age can be distinguished by little else than the seats they occupy at the Lord's table on Lord's days. They can scarcely be known by simplicity of dress, manners, intelligence, or spirituality. Thus, it will be perceived, a clear view of the ancient church should now be esteemed an important item in the First Principles.   T. F.

(To be continued.)

CHURCH ORGANIZATION.

Not being disposed to protract the discussion of organization, and believing I have, in previous numbers, brought to view the most important features of a scripturally organized body, I will in this No. endeavor to present the whole at one glance of the eye.

First, let it be remembered, churches never created or planted themselves, and set themselves in order, or ordained their own officers. The Lord's plan was the following, and is still the scriptural mode of propagating Christianity: Christ was God's Apostle to the Jews; the twelve were Christ's Apostles to the world. In the Apostolic day, NO church came into existence without an Evangelist. The Savior's personal Evangelist, planted churches; secondly, the churches were educated by these gospel ministers, and the disciples were convened for the purpose of teaching, exhortation, prayers, breaking of bread, and all that was necessary to perfect the body. Churches continued to worship, and the members to prepare themselves respectfully for the different offices and stations in the body, under the supervision of the Evangelists. When men became qualified to take care of the flock, the Evangelists ordained men of experience, who had proved themselves qualified for becoming Bishops, and others as Deacons. Then these preachers were no longer needed, and they travelled abroad to plant other churches. These organized churches were able to go forward in improvement without an Evangelist, stationed or monthly preachers. The Bishops taught and governed the body, and the Deacons served tables and attended to the poor. These were the daily employments of the officers, and of course their support was from the body. The gifted of the church, when qualified, were set apart by the Presbytery as Evangelists, and were sent out by the church to convert, teach, and organize other churches. For perspicuity, I will repeat the plan. It is short, but correct, and will be effective when adopted. Christ sent his Apostles, as Gospel preachers, to plant, teach and organize churches with the proper officers. Then the Evangelists had done their duty to these churches, and left them to form others. The Bishops took the oversight, and when persons became qualified as teachers, they were ordained by the Bishops, and sent out, by the authority of the churches, to preach, enlist, teach, and organize other churches. Thus, it is evident, the gospel plan, a self-perpetuating system; but with the idea that the Evangelists must convert the people, teach and oversee forever, the work of Christianizing the world must move slowly.

For the present, I will suspend essays on the subject of organization, at least so far as officers

are concerned. If I take up the subject again, I will aim one mighty effort to re-organize Christian society in reference to the world.   T. F.

MATTERS AND THINGS ABOUT COLUMBUS. MISS.

How is it, Brother "Review," that you have several Editors, and but few writers? Where is Bro. J. M. BARNES, whose pen has never failed to make indelible impressions? Bro. A. GRAHAM'S piece in the June number of the Review, has been read with interest; desires are strong that he should contribute more liberally of his *mental means.* Will he gratify? Where is Dr. Raneau, and others in Tennessee who should put their Lord's money out to gain? "Awake! thou that sleepest."

Better, however, have no contributors to the Review, than timid, desponding ones; such will soon debilitate the spirit of any people. It is far better that Zion be surrounded by implacable foes, watching for her destruction, than have drooping dastards within her gates. Religious poltroons are Zion's plagues.— Nothing is so sublime, nothing so powerful, as the concentrated energies of great minds, intent on the completion of any good work. But there is another class of her pretended friends, who are aiming to create and perpetuate the bitterness of party. Upon such the sun, moon and stars will and must look with a lingering scorn. Nothing like union—"United, we stand."

HINT.—"For we preach not ourselves, but Christ Jesus the Lord; and ourselves your servants for Jesus' sake." An old lady used to transpose this passage, in reference to modem preachers, thus: "We preach not Christ, but ourselves; and not ourselves your servants, but your leaders; and that for filthy lucre's sake." And when she was asked, "Why this hard saying?" "Indeed," responded she, "instead of their being as wise as serpents and harmless as doves, they too often have the poison of the adder, and the stupidity of the dove?' But old women are *mighty* tonguey.

The pulpit, in this section, has been so much abused, that it has lost its sacred equilibrium. When one of those catechumen divines mounts the rostrum, and offers to *vend* what he never had—knowledge,—the people look just as if they were uneasy. The under currents of a mighty revolution, are sweeping, in many sections, as with the besom of destruction. Light and knowledge are sought by the intelligent of all parties; and you know that kings and priests of earth do not approve this spirit.

The worst omen I have seen here, was a man whose name is *sorter* like Sea monster, or Sea-horn—came here from Cincinnati, (though he did not resemble those men I have seen from that quarter,) and said he was a Methodist preacher, and was engaged in a benevolent enterprise; and that he had lived on terms of intimacy with most all the great men—and that he lived door-neighbor to several conspicuous men in that city. (I began to think the knowing ones there clustered very thick; or else, his house was of very peculiar shape, to reach right up to so many. In fine, I did not believe half that he said.)— But away went Gilpin, "neck or nought," on his verbose pony. Sometimes, the congregation would roar right out, in "stupendous laughter," (not resembling the *solemn graces* of Christ's house)—but onward the orator—and at last the *hat* became very penitent, and bowed before each and all, and supplicated aid. The citizens of Columbus, though a generous and magnanimous people, did, on this occasion, act *unlike* their former selves.

They gave to this *floating* and *flying* beggar over $200. Query: Wonder if this Sea-monster would have devoured it, if he had known there were many poor and needy in Columbus— children growing up in ignorance of God and rectitude? and who, if the world knows of any greater claimants on the splendid schemes of the Missionary than they, let it speak out in tones of thunder! But he pocketed the funds, and left the untaught bipeds to knife it out! But he can't play a similar trick there.

The Disciples are building a large and commodious house in Columbus; the probable cost four thousand dollars.

I see, in the Acts of the Apostles, that the Spirit did *aid* in the production of faith; but it was by guiding the mind of Peter, Philip, Paul, &c., and they instructed sinners.

If the Methodists send any of your people into the to "get religion," they must send more than one; for one cannot get religion by himself. As many as were baptized into Christ, have put on Christ: there must be the subject and the baptizer.

Query. Does F. E. Pitts's book, or the man, merit as much attention as Bro. Elley is bestowing on them?

Will the publishing Brethren send me a copy of their several periodicals?— The truth is onward here, and there, and yonder.

In hope,   J. A. BUTLER.

Five miles of Columbus, Miss.

POLITICAL STRIFE AMONGST CHRISTIANS.

Will the brethren hear me, while I offer a few reflections on the fearful political excitement of the country? To describe the means employed by both the great parties to ensure success, would be an arduous task, and if I could give a picture to the life, I am not sure but it would endanger my safety. Suffice it to say, the measures adopted are not generally of an intellectual, religious, or moral character; and the exercises are not manly, and are far from exhibiting dignity. Those positions no one will dispute. Now, the question is, Can Christians put "*coon tails*" in their hats, or carry "*poke stalks,*" to convince the sovereign people who should be President, and act agreeably to their sacred profession? That is, can men engage in excitements which all admit are not pure and ennobling, and live the Christian? But alas! there are men who profess the Christian religion, employing their time, their talents and money in electioneering for political aspirants. Can any one do these things, and grow in grace and the knowledge of the truth? Impossible! "Evil communications corrupt good manners," and therefore, it cannot be that Christians can honor their Maker and give themselves soul and body to the cause of any party in politics. I declare solemnly, 1 have never seen it otherwise, than that Christians injure themselves by participating in political strifes. They become lukewarm, next dead to all holy emotions, and finally the mass gives themselves wholly to some vicious practice. Christians are commanded to avoid all appearances of evil, and I doubt not the participation in any of the political companies, as officers or members, or to be otherwise ensnared and led away by the present excitement, is just ground of complaint; and all members so acting, should be sharply rebuked. It is not worth our while to go round the matter; the present excitement is dangerous, and if men will give their hearts to such things, they

should not, by their professions of Christianity, become stumbling blocks to others. May the good Lord preserve the brethren from evil.   T. F.

BIRTH OF THE SPIRIT.

BRO. FANNING.—Will you answer the following questions in the C. REVIEW : 1st. When is a man born of the spirit according to Jno. 3.5?

2d. Was the baptism of the spirit on Pentecost the birth of spirit?

3d. Is that which is born of the spirit, flesh, or spirit? If it is spirit, how can it be done in this life, seeing that which is born of the spirit is spirit?

4th. When and how is a man quickened by the spirit?

JNO. S. WRIGHT.
E. JONES.

REPLY.—If I understand these brethren, they wish to know, 1st. *who* is born of the spirit? 2d. *what* it is? and 3d. *how* it is accomplished? Jesus said, "except a man be born again, he cannot see the kingdom of God." Mind, it is the *man* born of the spirit, and in the 6 verse of Jno. 8 ch. he says, "that which is born of the spirit is spirit. This latter expression is called a "*metonymy,*" that is, the cause is placed for the effect, or *vice versa.* The term spirit is used to designate what is done on man; but the literal interpretation is "What ever is made new by the spirit is spiritual. In other words the man who is under the influence of the spirit is a spiritual being.

2d. The birth of the spirit, to many, is a great mystery, in consequence of the ignorance of the phrase, "*born again.*" To be born is not a creation from nothing, but it is the entrance into a new mode of existence; and to *be born again,* or born of the spirit is to be renewed by the spirit, or to come under the spirit's influence. We are said to be born of God, born of the spirit of God, and to be born of the word of God. These are not three births, but one birth? The man born of God, is made over by the spirit, and this renewal by the spirit is the same as being renewed by the word of God. God is the original agent of all renewals; but he acts by his spirit, and the naked spirit, or spirit without means, that is words and arguments, never convinced or renewed a man, bore witness, or made a prophecy to a human being, or even comforted one of the sons or daughters of Adam, in any age.

The birth of the spirit is indispensable to becoming a Christian, but the baptism of the spirit was never intended for this purpose; therefore, the out-pouring of the spirit on Pentecost, was not the birth of spirit. The birth of the spirit is not even the reception of the spirit, but takes place in order to prepare the man for the reception of the spirit of adoption. The process is, the spirit operates through ideas and arguments,—the soul hears, is enlightened, and quickened by belief of the truth, turns to the Lord by repentance and immersion in his name, and is then said to be born of water and the spirit. These remarks may prepare our readers for profitable reflections on this subject, but at a future time, I wish to define the new birth in all its relations. T. F.

"The Jews scoffed at Christ, and crucified his body; and, by allowing his gospel to become a dead letter, we have crucified his spirit."—CHAS. FOURIER.

FEET WASHING.

BRO. T. FANNING—*Dear Sir:*—As your paper is to give instruction, I deem it not amiss to send you the following questions—it being by the request of the Church where I belong.

1. Did the Disciples of Christ practice the washing of feet in a Church capacity and as a Church ordinance? or,

2. Was it practiced and followed as a family duty to be performed to such as travelled and by chance called upon us for entertainment? OR, 3. Is any of the ways obligatory on us? Please give us a hearing on these questions from some authentic source, in the manner and way it was practiced by Apostles. We want truth—we are in search of truth.

Written by request of the Church.   J. C. DAVIS.

Sparta, Tenn., June 16tA, 1844.

REPLY.—That the Church of Christ, in its congregational capacity, ever washed feet, I cannot believe: or to suppose it was ever necessary to have more than two or three together to comply with the injunction to "wash *one another's feet,*" is most fanciful. Paul to Timothy places *washing* of feet with lodging strangers, relieving the distressed, and other good works; and this is the only place it ever occupied in the Christian institution. In the land of Judea, where sandals were used instead of shoes, and where there was an abundance of sand and dust, feet washing was an every day business, and the disciples could not better manifest their love to one another, and their humility, than by serving each other as feet washers. So should we practice at this day when occasion offers.   T. F.

A CALL FOR PREACHING.

There are a few good brethren about New Lexington, Ala., who are desirous the preaching brethren who travel south, would call and preach for them. Bro. R. D. Randolph, writes "that much good might be done, if an efficient teacher could spend his time amongst the people of that region." Brethren! "The harvest is great, and the laborers are few;" strive to raise up faithful men for this work, and send them out to convert the world.

PROSPECTS IN WEST TENNESSEE.

Bro W. G. ROULHAC, of Rutherford Co., and Bro. S. B. ADEN of Henry Co., both write that the disciples of Paris have succeeded in building a very neat house for worship. This is as it should be, and I should be delighted to spend sometime with the faithful of that region, but when I shall have the pleasure, I cannot tell.

Bro. ROULHAC says the "brethren are attempting to raise funds to support two Evangelists," but he fears there will be a failure. If the Churches would adopt the Gospel plan of contributing, as the Lord prospers them, on every first day of the week, and the preachers would sacrifice all gain for the sake of truth, I think success would attend the effort. While, however, men who make their hundreds per week, satisfy the demands of conscience by putting into the Lord's treasury sixpence per week, and preachers seek fat salaries, I cannot expect to see all things progressing as could be desired.   T. F.

"FRANKLIN COLLEGE."

It was made known to the readers of the Review, in a previous No., that a charter had been obtained, and that arrangements were in progress for the establishment of Franklin College, at Elm Crag, five miles from Nashville, Ten. That the friends of education may be able to form some just conclusions as to the merits of the institution, and of our success in the erection of buildings, and other preparations for opening at the proposed time, I will give monthly notices of what is doing. In the *"Outlines"* published, it was suggested, the system was "new," and, as I have the fullest confidence, when fully developed, it will be an important improvement, I will distinctly state some of the features contemplated.

1st. Special regard will be paid to PHYSICAL CULTURE. By this I mean, that exercise of the physical powers essential to good health and vigorous intellect. For this purpose, grounds will be appropriated for Agricultural and Horticultural exercises; also, workshops will be erected, for the purpose of applying mechanical skill.

The grounds will be so divided, that individuals may have plats of their own, when they are capable of attending to them, or in such a manner that groups may operate together, under the direction of a competent manager. Students will be allowed all they can make, to defray their expenses, or for other purposes, after paying a reasonable amount as interest on the lands, for implements, seeds, &c. In the workshops also, after paying for materials, they will be entitled to the profits of their own labor. Science, as far as practicable, will be connected with all the pursuits. Thus, students will have the motives of sound bodies, sound minds, good morals, good manners, and the whole profit of their labor, to make industry ATTRACTIVE. Is there no improvement presented in this part of the system?

2d. The Intellectual course will be full and thorough. A full course of Languages, Mathematics and Sciences, will be adopted.

3d. For purposes of Moral culture, Franklin College will offer many advantages. It is a retired situation, free from the excitements and allurements of cities, and the exercises are such as to so pleasantly and fully employ the whole time of students, that there will be little or no leisure to adopt vicious practices.

It is the intention of the Trustees to have three departments, viz:

1. THE JUVENILE.
2. PREPARATORY.
3. THE COLLEGE PROPER.

In the Juvenile department, small boys from four or five to ten or twelve years of age will be received. For a class of about twenty pupils a competent teacher will be appropriated, whose duty it shall be to spend his *whole* time with these youths. He is to eat with them, sleep with them, walk with them, talk with them, work with them, study with them, sing with them, and always be engaged in their improvement. On this plan, the whole conversation and lives of youths may be rendered chaste, and boys of ten may have more practical information than men do, on the present plan, generally, at 25 years of age.

In the Preparatory department more advanced youths will be received, and a teacher will devote his time and attention, as with the Juveniles.

In the College proper, none will be received who are not able to enter one of the regular classes. For going regularly through the Freshman, Sophomore, Junior, and Senior classes, four years will be required. It is supposed boarding and tuition can be furnished at from seventy to one hundred dollars per annum, and it is confidently believed, a portion of the students will be able to pay expenses by their industry; particularly those who are mechanics, or acquainted with the cultivation of vegetables, or the management of fruit trees and shrubbery. Others will have to learn how to perform service before they can anticipate much profit; but whatever it is, will be theirs.

I wish to say to the readers of the Review, that but for extraordinary individual enterprise, Franklin College could have had no existence. It may be said truly, we have more Colleges already than are supported; still, the Colleges in existence put it out of the power of at least seven eighths of the youths of the country to become educated, and our chief object is to offer superior advantages to young men who inherit no fortune, but who are willing to depend on their own exertions and merit for success. The colleges of the country are built up and endowed by the States, religious parties, or large subscriptions from the public. Not so with Franklin College. To the amount of fifteen thousand dollars has been vested by two individuals, and we lack yet from four to five thousand dollars. Is there sufficient enterprise in the country to supply this deficit? Fifty men who will give one hundred dollars each, could supply what is wanted. Where are they to be found? A much larger amount than this is paid annually, in Tennessee, to perpetuate the existence of Colleges. We ask not endowments to keep Franklin College alive; but we ask our fellow-citizens, and the friends of *genuine* Christian improvement, to lend their aid, in order to place an institution, just struggling into existence, out of debt.

Have the disciples of Christ, in Tennessee and the South-West, no interest in the education of the rising generation? They have done well in other sections, and in reference to other objects; and I cannot believe they would be indifferent to the interests of Franklin College, if they would enquire into its objects. From fifty to a hundred thousand dollars has been contributed to Bacon and Bethany Colleges, and three times the amount is now asked for endowments. Believing endowments are productive of no benefits; that all Literary institutions should stand on their own merits, instead of a bank of money, and that Franklin College will afford greater advantages than other institutions, we ask Christians to aid in supplying a small amount to finish the buildings.

If our readers should not see an agent, and they are disposed to give a helping hand, they can do so by sending their money, or a memorandum of the amount they are disposed to contribute, to B. Embry & T. Fanning, Nashville, Tennessee. Those who have books which they do *not ready* might do well by presenting them to Franklin College.

For information on any subject connected with the College, address T. Fanning. A list of subscriptions will be published in a short time.

T. FANNING, Agent.

———————

"THE BAPTIST."

The above is the title of a weekly paper which has been commenced in this city, as the organ of the Missionary Baptists in Tennessee. It is edited by the Rev. R. B. C. HOWELL; and to those who wish to know the views of this denomination, I would take great pleasure in recommending to subscribe for this work. Mr. H. is a gentleman of considerable popularity in his denomination, and no doubt he will advocate the peculiarities of his party with ability and great zeal. In the address to the public, the Editor says, "It (the paper) will, towards those who differ from us, cultivate brotherly kindness, and maintain towards all Christian denominations a courteous spirit and respectful bearing? Again:— "To the several contemporary journals, religious, commercial, literary, and political, we offer fraternal salutations." We cordially welcome Mr. Howell into the corps editorial, and we will pledge the Review to support him, when he advocates the principles of Christianity; but if we should find any thing in the Baptist not comporting with sound doctrine, we shall feel it our duty respectfully to point it out for the consideration of the worthy Editor, and the Baptist family in the South-West. In the present No., however, I can only find room for inserting the leading doctrines which the Baptist is pledged to advocate, and offer one reflection for the thoughtful. He says:—"We hold and shall advocate—

1st. That the Lord our God is one Lord; that he hath revealed himself as the Father, the Son, and Holy Ghost, the same in essence, and equal in divine properties.

2d. We hold the total depravity of human nature.

3d. The operation of the Holy Ghost in convicting and converting sinners.

4th. Justification by grace, through faith, and not of works.

5th. The final perseverance of the saints.

6th. The restriction of the bread and wine, in the Lord's supper, to those persons who have received the one baptism.

7th. That the true ministry are called and qualified for their work by God?' REMARK.—Is it not strange we do not find a single one of these seven propositions in the Bible? I may be told, "The precise words may not be in the Bible, but the ideas are there?' The objector is informed, there are Bible words for every idea in the Bible; and if any one has ideas for which he has not scripture words, his ideas are not of God. Is it not a pity the Baptist denomination, with Mr. Howell at the head, should be pledged to support positions which no man can prove from the Bible? In kindness,   T. FANNING.

THE REFORMATION AND SPECULATION.

Our brethren do not need any better proof of the firm hold of their primary principles upon the community, than the fact, that all the mighty effort to connect with them the speculations of a decayed materialism, have not retarded their progressive spread. "That which at one time is a sign of incurable weakness or approaching dissolution, at another seems but the excess of healthful energy and the evidence of unbroken vigor?' Feuds have at times distracted the bosom of some of our peaceful communities—discussions in our midst have partaken of violence; but these proved the strength of the distended nerves of the body, and prepared it for a more extensive and healthy action. The truths which have been elicited by these discussions, will doubtless have a lasting effect upon the character, discipline, and government of the churches.

J. B. FERGUSON.

THE SEVENTH DAY BAPTISTS.

There are many churches of the Seventh Day Baptists in New England and New York, who's most striking peculiarity is that of keeping Saturday as their Sabbath, and not the first day of the week, as other sects do. These Baptists say the Sabbath has not been changed, and the present lukewarm state of religion is evidence, the Lord has withdrawn his face for this change. On this subject all sects are wrong. Neither Saturday nor Sunday was ordained by the Head of the church as a Sabbath; but Christians are authorized to observe the Lord's day, in honor of the Master's achievements.

T. F.

THE CHRISTIAN—BY J. BARKER, OF ENGLAND.

"A Christian is one who believes that Jesus is the Christ—the Messiah; and who, under the influence of such faith, places himself under Christ's instruction and government. In other words, a Christian is one who believes that Jesus is the person appointed by God to be the Teacher, the Governor, and the Savior of mankind, and who, under the influence of such belief, places himself under Christ, that he may learn and do God's will, and so obtain the blessings of salvation.

"'A man cannot be a Christian without faith in Jesus as the Christ, nor can a man be a Christian unless his faith lead him to give himself up to Christ, to be taught and ruled by him; but every one who does believe in Jesus Christ, and gives himself up to him to be taught and ruled by him, is a Christian"

Bro. W. B. RANDOLPH, *Loweville, Ala.,* is informed, that the Post Master is not willing to send books the size of the "Debate" so great a distance. If Bro. R. will examine the subject of church organization, he will find the following land marks: 1st. Evangelists planted churches; 2d. These churches began to worship, and the members began to qualify themselves for ruling, teaching and serving; 3d. When proved, the Evangelists ordained the Bishops and Deacons, and the officers forming the presbytery, sat apart other Evangelists to go abroad, convert, teach and organize other churches.   T. F.

OBITUARY.

Our aged and beloved brother, GEORGE BRANDON, of Rutherford county, slept in the Lord on Sunday morning, the 12th of last month, in the 74th year of his age. After having served his country as an officer in the last war with Great Britain, his family as an affectionate husband and kind father, and the Church as a faithful servant for many years, he died in the "common faith" and peaceful hope of immortality.

J. J. TROTT.

NEWS FROM THE CHURCHES.

DEAR BROTHER FANNING:—As you request information from the Brethren in relation to the progress of truth and the organization of the Churches, I send you the following:

I am preaching for four congregations in Rutherford county, viz: Rock Spring, Spring Creek, Cripple Creek, and Big Creek. We have all the officers required by the Gospel, and are in a prosperous condition. We have accessions nearly every meeting. We number as follows: Rock Spring 130, Bros. Gooch and John Hall, Bishops; Bros. Nelson and Nance, Deacons. Spring Creek about 40, Cripple Creek 130. Big Creek about 60 Brethren; Bros. Keel and Ott, Bishops; Bros. Davies and Gibson, Deacons.

The Camp Meeting at Big Creek, (7 miles South from Murfreesborough,) will commence on Friday before the 2d Lord's day in September. All the teaching Brethren are requested to attend. We hope. Brethren, you will not fail in coming to this meeting, as the Brethren are making considerable preparations, and we hope much good will be done.

In relation to the Co-operation Meeting I know not what to say. We agreed last fall at Rock Spring to meet the 4th Lord's day in September, at Cripple Creek, for the purpose of co-operation. But I see the Brethren have appointed a meeting in Williamson county, for this purpose. Will one meeting of the Brethren for that purpose be sufficient, or will we have two? Please advise us on that subject. I am, with every sentiment of respect, your Brother,

July 7th. 1844.   R. B. HALL.

BRO. FANNING:—I have recently performed a tour of about two months thro' Warren, Wilson and Rutherford counties. Much of the time was employed in preaching to the Churches on the subjects of organization and Christian benevolence, and I am happy to inform you the effort was not in Vain. The Churches at Hickory Creek and Rocky River, in Warren county, after a full investigation of the Apostolic order, came to the solemn determination to meet every first day to keep the ordinances as taught by the Apostles. The Churches in Wilson have greatly improved in the two last years. In Rutherford the Churches are gradually increasing in numbers and Scriptural knowledge. In performing this tour, I had the pleasure of laboring with the beloved brethren, R. Jones, Hooker, White and Hall. Twenty-five additions were made in accordance with the primitive model.   J. J. TROTT.

ROUND LICK, WILSON COUNTY, July 17th, 1844.

DEAR BROTHER FANNING Since I wrote you last, I have had the pleasure of witnessing the power of the Gospel in the destruction of sectarianism and conversion of sinners. Brethren Hooker, Curlee, White, and myself, held a protracted meeting near Woodbury, which closed last Wednesday. One intelligent *Catholic* lady, one intelligent *Episcopalian* gentleman, one respectable *Presbyterian* gentleman, one pious *Methodist* lady, and one *Baptist* gentleman, were persuaded, by the eloquence of Heaven's truth, to abandon the *traditions* of their fathers, and unite on the foundation of "Apostles and Prophets, Jesus Christ himself being the chief corner stone." Truth is mighty, and will prevail. This meeting was held in the meeting house built many years ago for Brother Travis to preach in. His son, B. W. S., with tears flowing from his eyes, made his confession, and was heartily received by the church. Twenty-six were baptized during the meeting, six at a previous meeting.

This church was constituted last fall, numbering at that time about 60—now about 100. The brethren agreed, at the last meeting, to meet every Lord's day. The location of this church is on Stone's River, one and a half miles east of Woodbury, Cannon county. We respectfully invite the preaching brethren to call and preach for us. The name of the house is Liberty, and the brethren and sisters who worship in it Disciples, Christians, &c.

Yours in the truth,   J. J. TROTT.

Bagdad, June 28th, 1844.

BROTHER FANNING—We have just closed a meeting of five days, at the Bagdad Meeting-House, Jackson county, Tennessee. During the meeting, we had twenty-six additions to the church; three of whom were from the Baptist Church, one from the Presbyterians, and twenty-two from the world. Some were immersed every day. Every thing went on smoothly, agreeably, and orderly, during the whole meeting. Nothing occurred, with saints or sinners, to mortify or mar the peace of any. The principal laborer was John N. Mulkey, though he was assisted by brethren Samuel Dewhit and Abraham Sallee. Brother Mulkey gave us a discourse on the duty of the Elders and brethren of the church, and church government in general, which I think excellent, and which came in good time to us. A part of his discourse was entirely new here; yet no body undertakes to condemn it by the Gospel, and all, as far as I have heard, talk about it as being expedient. The part alluded to is this;— He says, that after Elders are elected, or otherwise chosen by the church, that the power is conferred on them to attend to and decide all things relative to the government of the church. That, when dispute may arise between members of the church, or disorderly members may be called before the church, that instead of calling on the church to vote on a motion to excommunicate or restore, that the Elders of the church alone should try and determine all such matters. That the brethren should be subject to the Elders. That the Elders should act as overseers or shepherds of the church, to see that each one performs his duty, and is in a healthy condition. And that if one member fails of attending the church meeting; that the Elders should visit him, as a shepherd would a lost sheep, and ascertain the cause of his absence.

It was a lengthy and good discourse; I wish I had the whole of it to send to you.

Your brother in the Lord,　　　　　　　　JAMES YOUNG.

My *Dear Bro, Fanning:*—I have been thinking for some time that I would give you an account of our numbers and order; but this is the first suitable opportunity I have had.

At Cypress Creek Meeting-house we number about 60. We have 2 Elders, (Bros. C. Wesson and A. Thrasher); 2 Deacons, (Bros. P. Grisham and John Wade.) We meet only twice per month; but I do hope we shall do better before many moons. Bro. James Young and I teach as well as we can. We have joyful little meetings—the Brethren love one another, and our spiritual health is pretty good. Some of our worthy Brethren contribute every time we meet.

We have a little band of Brethren on Blue Water in this county, numbering 13 or 14 members, gathered since last fall, principally by the labors of Brother James Young, (not organized.)

At Bluff Creek, (a place with which you are well acquainted,) there are about 18 or 20 excellent and intelligent Brethren, (not organized.) We have added to the good cause since last fall, at different points, about 25. We direct all our efforts, not at the animal, but at the intellectual powers of man. We are not fond of Brethren created *inn storm,* If we could compensate your labors we would be pleased to have them for a time at Florence and Bluff Creek, this summer. The Review is a good work, may it prosper. Yours in hope, JAMES M. HACKWORTH.

NOTE.—"The Lord willing and I live," I expect to be in Florence, Ala., on Saturday, November 2d, 1844, and remain over Lord's day. Will the friends procure a place for the meeting and let it be known. Besides preaching the Gospel, I expect to present the objects of "Franklin College." As I cannot visit Bluff Creek, I hope the Brethren Will meet me in Florence.

T. FANNING.

MERRIVILLE, KY., 20 JUNE, 1844.

Brethren Fanning, Wharton and Anderson:—Bro. S. E. JONES and myself have just closed a meeting at Lafayette, Ky., at which we organized a congregation of 19 members and obtained 17 additions. Seven of these additions were from the Baptists, five from the Methodists, and five from the world. The

Brotherhood rejoiced, and the cause of Christian Union greatly promoted. I do not know that I have ever witnessed an organization under more favorable and promising circumstances. May the Lord continue to bless their efforts to promote his glory in the region of Lafayette.

There were four immersions at Clarksville, Ten., during our last meeting there. Brethren Day and Anderson obtained 9 additions at Street's Schoolhouse, Christian county, a few weeks since, three of which were Presbyterians, and one Methodist.

Although the people are drunk with the wine of political ambition, yet there are some, you discover, who are willing to submit to the institutions of the Redeemer. May the good Lord keep us from Idols.

As ever your brother in the hope of the coming of the Lord,

J. B. FERGUSON.

P. S.—Since writing the above, Bro. Jones, Anderson and myself have closed a meeting at Cadiz, at which five were added to the saved. Among these was a Methodist preacher of the most respectable character. Some 18 months since I had a public discussion with this gentleman, since which time he has been engaged in examining the principles we teach. The result was a full conviction that we occupy the only ground for a rational Christian Union, and a hearty obedience to the initiatory law of the King. I believe the Lord will make Bro. J. J. HARRISON a blessing to us all. More anon.   J. B. F.

TRIANA, 15 miles S. of Huntsville, Ala. }
JUNE 20th, 1844. }

Messrs. *Editors:* I have by accident attended a meeting here of some days, with Bro. D. G. Ligon a part of the time, which has resulted in 13 valuable additions, and the removal of much prejudice on the part of many, although our teaching has greatly excited some of the religious people as usual. Contrary to all my expectations, when I left Columbus, Miss., the first of this month. I have been compelled from a sense of duty to yield to the calls of the brethren here to remain in this beautiful valley some 7 or 8 weeks, in order to aid the cause of the Bible and truth. The Lord willing, I shall endeavour to scatter the good word of truth as fast and as thick as possible. When I leave, I desire to visit Murfreesborough, Lebanon, Hartsville, Gallatin, &c. in Tennessee.   Yours truly,   GEO. W

To the Editors of the Christian Review:

BELOVED BRO. FANNING:—The day after we parted, brother and I commenced preaching at Stanford, Ky,—11 or 15 converts were made—3 amiable Presbyterians.   A. KENDRICK.

Lexington, July 1844.

MACEDONIA, KY., JULY 16TH, 1844.

BRO. J. T. JOHNSON and T. SMITH, have just closed a meeting at Republican, Fayette Co., with 14 additions.   A. KENDRICK.

P. S. BRO. CAMPBELL, is expected at Georgetown the 11th of August, and at Lexington the week following.   A. K.

QUERY.

BELOVED BRO. FANNING:—Permit me, through the C. REVIEW, to ask my Methodist, Baptist, and Presbyterian friends in Tennessee, whether, when they speak of "the witness of the Holy Ghost, or evidence of pardon, they mean that God actually favors them with new revelations concerning remission of Sins, on which to build their hopes of Pardon and of Heaven—or do they mean that the Spirit bears testimony in the language of the Bible, on this subject. I am sure you will give them room in the Review, to Answer this question.—Many think they, or some of them, discredit the Bible and its blessed Author, in reference to remission of Sins, and it is but right they should be understood.

In much love,   A. KENDRICK.

CHRISTIAN REVIEW.

VOL. I.   NASHVILLE, SEPTEMBER, 1844.   NO. IX.

NOTES ON A TOUR—No. 2.

Wednesday morning June 12th, I left the residence of Dr. W. FORD, in *Edminson County Ky.,* for the purpose of visiting the "Mammoth Cave." At 8 o'clock, A. M., I found myself at the entrance of this subterranean world, with a "guide," lamp, and other preparations necessary for a journey in the earth. A full description of the cave, could not be given without considerable space, Indeed, no accurate description has ever been given; and I am much surprised that *Dr. Croghn,* the talented and enthusiastic owner, has not had an accurate survey made of every department. A scientific gentleman could give minute details in a month or too, which, might be published in a small book, and visitors would have much more satisfaction, in their excursions, and, the proprietor would find it greatly to his interest. Poets and fanciful persons who have written of the cave, have failed very much giving accurate accounts of this greatest wonder, of the kind, in the world.

I travelled ten hours in the cave, observed most that was interesting; but can find room for only two items. First, distances have been greatly augmented. A few years since it was said the cave had been explored to the distance of 18 miles, but when I reached the most distant point, it was said by the "guide" we were only nine miles from entrance. Second, the formations most important, are "compact limestone," crystallized carbonate lime, sulphate of lime, (*Gypsum*) in abundance, and sulphate of soda. There are fish in the "river Jordan," almost transparent, and entirely destitute of eyes.—Eyes are useless where there is no light.

I must not forget to say, when I had travelled about seven miles, I met with a brother preacher—a Baptist by the name of Eaken, and we had been together but a few moments, till we forgot the scenes about us, and were closely engaged in discussing religious matters. The controversy was in reference to the comparative merit of the Baptist Church, and the church of Christ. Mr. Eaken is a considerable revivalist, of great flesh and blood powers, who attributes all his success in making partisans to some secret agency of the spirit. With such men neither an intellectual nor scriptural debate can be conducted.

Thursday the 13th, I left the Mammoth Cave with the determination, if ever convenient, to make not only a survey of it, but the surrounding country, and endeavor to ascertain the course of this vast cavern. I directed my course eight miles east to Dickeys—about mid-way of the great turnpike road from Nashville to Louisville. To-day, I passed Munfordsville, on Green river, and reached Elizabethtown, in Hardin county. In this town I learned there was a small congregation of disciples, but they are much opposed, and exert but little influence on the world.

Friday the 14th, I travelled near fifty miles to Louisville, and spent the night with Bro. James Trabue—merchant of that city. Saturday the 15th, I spent the day in visiting the city, renewing

acquaintance with old friends and forming new ones. Amongst the rest, I became acquainted with Dr. JOHN THOMAS, who is, at present, publishing the "Herald of the Future Age," in Louisville. As Doctor Thomas has been the cause of some difficulty amongst the disciples of Christ, both east and west, I hope a few reflections on his course and the course of others towards him, will not be considered derogatory to the objects of a Religious journal. I found the Doctor a pleasant gentleman of about forty-five years of age, much devoted to the study of the Bible, and one who thinks very intensely on all subjects which engage his attention. My own opinion is, Doctor John Thomas wishes to do right; but he labors under considerable embarrassments. Although he is an intellectual man, he is certainly very speculative,—is an abstractionist in the fullest sense—is devoted to his friends, but has no mercy on such as he esteems his enemies. I shall not pretend to enter into the merits or demerits of the Doctor's religious career. Suffice it to say, he may be an *injured man,* and he has in turn, *injured,* in my judgment, every one who has come under his influence. His position in reference to the necessity of persons understanding the nature of baptism to enjoy its benefits, IMMORTALITY being a subject of promise in the New Testament, and the anti-Christian character of Sectarianism, may doubtless be sustained by the Bible. Still, on all these subjects, his language is generally too strong, or rather of a character to embitter those who love it, more than pious instruction. His notions of the non-resurrection of infants, idiots, and pagans, and annihilation of the wicked, are certainly subversive of all the benevolence of God, and contrary to the Scriptures of truth; but yet, he *admits* these things constitute no part of the Gospel of Christ, and I regret, with the admissions, the doctor persists in such unprofitable speculations. From the Doctor's peculiar organization and temperament, and the unmerciful opposition which some of his views have met, he has become emphatically a man of war, and always uses dangerous weapons. In the heat of conflict, he not unfrequently knocks out the eyes, and commits other damages on his best friends. Hence the idea that "his hand is against every man" and every man's hand is against him. The evils resulting from his course, have not been so much from *what* he has pleaded as from the STYLE of his teaching. His admirers generally possess the same spirit of the Doctor. While I blame Doctor Thomas, I can but love him, and regret that his organization, and the circumstances which have governed him have been such, as to render his best efforts worse than useless in the cause of Christ. I separated with the Doctor with the conviction, if he could forget Alexander Campbell, would quit studying and *writing* upon his speculations, and could be thrown into *pious* society, where he would be told plainly his errors, by genuine friends, he might become a good and useful man.

Lord's day, June 16th, I delivered a discourse in the "Christian Chapel" to a very respectable assembly. At night I spoke in the same house, and three or four successive evenings I addressed small assemblies. There are some excellent disciples in Louisville, but it will require some time for the church to learn the whole truth. This church like many others, has been troubled with leaders who have regarded their own aggrandizement more than the intelligence of the flock or the prosperity of the cause. The consequence is, there now exist in Louisville the seeds of two or three factions. Several men have studied for years to ascertain who should be greatest, and while they thus continue, it is almost useless to preach the Gospel in that fashionable, luxurious city.

would not dishearten the brethren. They have to contend against worldly pride, foolish show, love fashionable preaching, and pestilential factionalism, still the word of God is powerful, and will yet work wonders. Were it not for my unlimited confidence in the Gospel, I should despair of much good being done any where. The brethren seemed much distressed at the loss of their preacher,—Bro. D. S. Burnet, who had recently left them; but I was sorry that they seemed not to have learned their own progress in knowledge, and growth in grace, did not depend half so much on eloquent preaching, as their constant devotion to the cause of truth.

Wednesday, 19tb, I left on the Mail packet for Cincinnati, at which city I arrived on the morning of the 20th. I spent several days in the city, and made many observations which may be of utility to the readers of the Review.— Cincinnati contains a population of from 65 to 70 thousand souls, and what strikes a southerner with most force is the fact, that this is a business population. Every man, woman, and child, has something to do; and a more prosperous, happy people I have rarely seen. I have been told they are a *"picayune people."* Be it so. If the business of many is small, they attend to it, instead of *loafing,* and these many little streams make one great current of commerce, manufactures, and prosperity.

The cause of the superior prosperity of Cincinnati over more southern cities is in consequence of the industry and economy of the population. They are literally a working and prosperous people; but this, alas! cannot be predicated of all southern towns. There are religious denominations in Cincinnati almost past enumeration. Jews, Romanists and Protestants are here in considerable abundance. There are also five congregations of Christians. Bro. D. S. Burnet preaches to the congregation on Sycamore St.; Bro. J. Challen preaches for the brethren on Lower Vine St., and Bro. Moss, is the preacher in Jefferson Hall on Upper Vine St. As I could not attend all the places of worship, I did not learn who were the teachers at the two other places. I had the pleasure of preaching in Sycamore meeting house and Jefferson Hall, and I must say, in justice to the brethren, I was not only pleased with the city, but much more with the intelligence and zeal of many of the saints, and was most happy to know the truth had achieved a great deal since the year thirty-five.— I thought I saw in the churches a disposition to seek popular preaching, and rather an "itching of the ears" of many, for false eloquence. It was said the preachers had made some discoveries on this subject, and had taken their *salaries* in proportion to their oratorical powers. If I am not mistaken, the present system of paying large salaries to men who proclaim to congregations weekly, to keep them alive, is opposed to the practice of the Apostles, and the whole genius of the Christian institution.

While at Cincinnati, I became acquainted with most of the educated men, and I was gratified to see there were many devoted to the study of Natural History, Geology and Mineralogy. I made known the objects of Franklin College, and the people, generally, were pleased with the system. I feel most grateful to the friends of science and religion in Cincinnati for their kindness,

Monday 24th, I left Cincinnati and reached Louisville on the morning of the 25th. On the trip down the river, there were several distinguished politicians from the South, and I am sorry to say I saw but little love of science or sound morals in most of our pleasant company—party politics was the all engrossing topic the whole time. I delivered a discourse at night on the *"Christian Union"* to a much larger and more intelligent congregation, than I had been in the habit of addressing in Louisville.

Wednesday, 25th, in company with Bro. A. Kendrick, I travelled 32 miles to Frankfort, and was kindly received in the family of Bro. Moore. At night I addressed a small, but, I supposed, an intelligent congregation on the *"power of the Gospel"* in a very neat little meeting house, which the brethren have recently erected. While here I had an interview with Bro. W. M. Brown, and Bro. P. S. Fall, at whose residence I spent Thursday the 27th, most agreeably.

Friday the 28th, I journeyed by Versailles to Lexington, and met my old friends Dr. B. F. Hall, A. Kendrick, W. M. Brown, J. T. Johnson, Doctor Pinkerton and many other esteemed friends. At night I lectured in the brethren's magnificent meeting house, on the subject of Education, to a very fine audience. Lexington has a population of about eight thousand; of this number, there are some four or five hundred persons who profess to have taken the Bible alone as a government in religion, and doubtless they have made great advancements towards the truth. It was suggested, however, the *steeple* of their fine meeting house was rather tall and showy for the humble followers of the Lamb, and that there was full enough confidence in pretty little sermons for their growth in grace and the knowledge of the truth. The disciples, however, were exceedingly kind, and for aught that I could tell to the contrary, the truth has triumphed gloriously in that city.

Saturday, 29th, and Lord's day 30th, I spent with Bros. Hall, Morton, Kendrick, Rousee and other ministers at Macedonia, 8 miles from Lexington.— The congregation was immensely large and remarkably attentive. In the evening of Lord's day, I returned to Lexington and addressed the congregation on the *"cause we plead."*

Monday, July 1st, I visited Nicholasville, where I spent the time to the 3d, with my friends and relatives. I delivered but one discourse on the subject of Christianity, while at this place.

On the 3d, I visited Danville, and reached Harrodsburg at night, and addressed a respectable congregation.

Thursday, the 4th, I attended the examination of Bro. Mullin's Female Institute, and preached again at night. I was led to conclude this was one of the best managed Schools of the kind I had seen. "BACON COLLEGE," under the patronage of the disciples, is also in this place. The college building is quite a handsome edifice, and from the zeal manifested in the subject of education, this institution ought to do well. Bro. Shannon—the President, is a good scholar, and an excellent man, and the Professors are all men of fine ability, still all complain that the institution lingers. A large amount of money has already been raised, and yet it is argued, unless an ENDOWMENT of fifty thousand dollars can be raised, the college must go down. Why is this the case? Education will be a burden to states and the public, so long as large amounts of money are contributed to furnish high salaries, and educate the sons of the more opulent in *idleness* and *luxury.* The system is more at fault than the men who manage the colleges of the country. It is a lamentable truth, there is not a self-supporting college on the continent, and if the most of them depended on their own merit for support, they could not live a day.

Labor must be the basis, before education can become general, and thorough. I would to God the brethren would study this subject. No one is of paramount importance.

Bro. Shannon's hospitable mansion was truly a home to me while I remained in Harrodsburg. While here, I became acquainted with *Bro. McChesney* who was formerly a Lutheran clergyman, but was convinced of the truth of Christianity by the arguments of Bro. Campbell, in the debate with Mr. Rice, and was immersed during the discussion. Bro. M. is now preacher for the brethren in Lexington, and a most amiable young man he is; still if he is susceptible of injury, flattery may steal a march upon him. Bro. M. bids fair to become a most efficient and useful minister of the Gospel.

Friday, the 5th, I left for Glasgow, 90 miles distant, in Barren county, at which place I arrived on the 6th, after a very tiresome travel, through a quite uninteresting country, and took lodgings in the family of my good brother *G. Trabue.*

Lord's day I addressed the brethren twice upon the subject of Christianity, and once on the subject of education. Bro. Doctor W. D. Gorden of this place is an efficient and able teacher of the Scriptures.

Monday, the 8th, I journeyed to Scottville, and addressed the people on the subject of Education. Bro. Evans of this village, is an intelligent and excellent man.

Tuesday, the 9th, I travelled from Scottville to Elm Crag, a distance of 58 miles, after an absence of more than two months from home.

In my tour I had two objects supremely in view. 1st. I wished to ascertain the progress the Churches were making in the truth; and 2dly, I wished to make known the objects of Franklin College and collect funds for rearing the buildings. After careful observation, I was almost irresistibly led to the conclusion, the disciples as they get strength and influence, incline much to the corruptions of the age, and become too well satisfied with mere conversion. In reference to the College, I wish to state, that I found enthusiastic admirers of the plan, but it was almost offensive to speak to religious people about funds. A couple of SCEPTICS, however, subscribed a hundred dollars each, and one wealthy old brother put down ten dollars.   T. F.

FIRST PRINCIPLES.—No. 3.

The great Apostle to the Gentiles defined the principles or beginning of the "doctrine of Christ" to be,—1st, *"Faith toward God;"* 2d, *"Repentance from dead works;* 3d, *"The doctrine of Baptisms;"* 4th, *"The laying on of hands;"* 5th, *"Resurrection of the dead;"* 6th, *"Eternal judgment."*

In the order here presented, I will proceed with the discussion, till enough shall have been written to enable enquirers after truth to see what God requires in order to eternal life. The first subject presented is

FAITH.—"Without faith, it is impossible to please God; for he that comes to God must believe that he is, and that he is a rewarder of them that diligently seek him?' Again, the same says, " Whatsoever is not of faith is sin." As no man can love or serve God without faith, or anticipate joys beyond the grave, we must consider it of the first magnitude in religious discussion. The following order of presenting it, may answer a valuable purpose: 1. What is faith?

faith?

2. How do we get possession of it? 3. How many faiths are there? 4. What is the effect of faith on the heart?

1. "Faith," says Paul, (Heb. xi, 1,) "is the confidence of things hoped for, the evidence of things not seen." All the theological writers of the world, have failed to improve on this definition. Persons whom we have not seen, but of whom we have heard, may be objects of our faith. Thus, we believe such men as Alexander, Napoleon, Washington, and Franklin lived, because we have read reports of them which cannot be resisted. We believe there is a God who upholds the earth and skies, not because we have seen him, or could infer his existence from the wide volume of nature; but because he has been kind enough to reveal his existence and immaculate perfections to the world. We believe in Jesus is God's son, because of the character reported, and the indubitable evidence of the truth given by his Apostles. Remember, Paul does not allow a mere admission of these heaven-born truths to be faith, but says, "it (faith) is the *confidence* of things hoped for." A firm reliance on the Savior, as being able and willing to exalt his followers to the skies, is indispensable to the existence of faith. The greater portion of those who have the Bible, and who "profess religion," do not rely on the promises of the Lord for consolation in distress; and therefore, these cannot come under the head of believers. The true believer is one who receives every word and every promise of the heavenly Father, as important to his salvation, and who is influenced by this faith to purity of life, and is always happy in the contemplation of the joys beyond this mode of existence.

2. Faith is given of God just as our food, raiment, and all our knowledge of science are given. We have the means in nature to clothe our persons and furnish ourselves with provisions, and to become learned in science; but if we neglect our privileges, we must perish of cold and hunger, and languish in ignorance and disgrace: and we have the means in the Bible, to gain the knowledge which invariably produces faith; but if we slight this privilege, destruction must be our portion. Paul informs the world, "faith comes by hearing, and hearing by the word of God." Faith was produced anciently by the preaching of the word, and no one in this age can enjoy the faith of the Gospel, who has not the privilege of reading or hearing the word of life. I need not stop here to say what will become of the ignorant and unbelieving heathen: "The God of all the earth will do right." Heathens and the unbelieving in civilized nations, are not prepared to enjoy happiness, and therefore cannot associate with the humble disciples of the Lamb.

3. In the Bible, there is but one faith for Christians. The understanding of the same words, will produce the same ideas in all; and the same ideas must constitute the same system of belief for every nation, tongue and tribe under the broad heavens.

To speak of Romanistic, Calvinistic, Arminian, and Universalist faith in the Bible, is transcending reason and revelation. "To us, there is one God, the Father, and one Lord Jesus Christ, the son and offspring of the Father, full of grace and truth," and one Holy Spirit, which "guided the Apostles into all truth," by direct communications in words, and which still guides us by the truth in the Scriptures. The belief of these great and fundamental truths in the Bible, constitutes the basis of all Christian hope and consolation.

4. The belief, of the facts of the Bible, changed the hearts of the Jews on Pentecost, when Peter

preached from Solomon's portico—the multitudes which daily flocked into the fold, of Jewish laymen and priests; it changed the hearts of the Samaritans, Simon the Magician, and the Ethiopian nobleman, Saul of Tarsus, and all persons who were induced to own the authority of Christ in the days of primitive Christianity. It is belief in the promises of God which at this day melts and renovates the hard heart, and takes the affections from what is gross, wicked, and devilish, to embrace God, and all his precious promises.— Faith is that active and powerful principle which induced Abraham to forsake his country, his kindred, and all that was dear to him on earth, and become a "wanderer in a strange land;" and it is the same faith or confidence in the promises of Jehovah, which induces men to deny themselves, take up the cross, and follow Christ.

So much for the nature and power of faith. On this inductive system, we next call attention to

REPENTANCE.—This is the second step in becoming a Christian, and without it all sinners must perish. Repentance embraces contrition of heart for the past, a cessation of hostilities against the Creator of all, and the actual turning away from all sin. No sorrow alone, is the repentance required in the New Testament; but, in the language of Paul, "Godly sorrow works repentance unto salvation, not to be repented of," or regretted. No offender repents towards his neighbor, who does not confess his fault, and turn from it; and no one repents before God, who does not deeply and heartily regret his wrongs, confess and turn from them to the service of the living God.

These are matters understood and taught by no party in Christendom, and few of the saints have given them proper attention. Hence the skepticism, hypocrisy and rebellion of the great mass of professors. Gospel faith and gospel repentance are unknown to the sectarian world; and hence the impurity and unspirituality of all human institutions.

In the next No. I expect to introduce, for the first time, in the Christian Review, the subject of Baptism; and as it is but imperfectly understood, I earnestly solicit those who think we err, "not knowing the Scriptures," to send in their objections to our teaching on this subject. Paul places it at the beginning of the teaching of Christ, and to give you a clear and comprehensive view of the whole subject of Christianity, this theme must not be omitted. This proposition we make to all sects, and it is a challenge which we will take from no one.   T. F.

(To be continued.)

SPIRITUAL INTOLERANCE.

Long have I believed, the bitter opposition to the Christian religion originated from the Ignorance and deep depravity of its enemies. A highly cultivated gentleman cannot condescend to a mean thing. These thoughts have been suggested by a little occurrence in Giles county a few weeks since.

I visited *Pulaski,* for the purpose of making known the objects of Franklin College, and while in this town I was earnestly solicited to preach in a neighborhood about eight miles distant, on my way to an appointment at Robertson's Fork. I informed the gentleman I would do so, if the arrangement could be made. They sent a messenger to accompany me, but on arriving at the place, I saw there was some little confusion, in consequence of another appointment; but

meeting house was called *Bethel, (the house of God,)* and that it had been built by the neighbors free for all, I imagined I should be treated at least with civility. After being seated near the house a few minutes, I saw a pert looking young man approaching the house, with a book under his am, whom I took to be a preacher. I followed him into the stand, to ascertain if he had an appointment. To which he replied, coarsely and abruptly, he had. Said I, "There shall be no interference; but if there is time when you are done, I will say something." He made no reply, but made arrangements to consume the day. First, a long song or two had to be sung, then a long prayer was said, and then came the text, "The greatest of these is charity." Said the dark visaged young man, "This charity is the love of God in the heart, or the Spirit— But (said he) I have often heard it said, *this book (the Bible) was the Spirit of God.* How (said he) would you like to hear the book groaning in one's pocket?" This seemed to fill the hearers with much joy, and the preacher seemed to gain much strength by the utterance of these reckless falsehoods. This is a pretty fair specimen of the preacher's labored effort. At the close, he called *"the mourners,"* and there were three miserable looking creatures made their appearance. The preacher commanded all present "to get down on their knees, and pray for God to come down and convert these sinners." Being a little alarmed at such presumption, I stood up. The prayers were made almost as long and loud as those of the prophets of Baal; but their God did not appear. Finally, the preacher dismissed, to try it again at night. I rose and stated that I regretted being there under the circumstances, but if there were no objections, I would address the people a few minutes. There rose up a desperate looking man, who I understood was the assistant "class-leader" of the region round about those hills, by the name of *Willis Portrice,* but who could neither read nor write, and said, "This house is on my land, and you cannot speak in it."— "Very good," replied I, "we will go to the shade." "But" said he, "this is my land about here, and you must not preach on it." I was compelled to tell the man he was not only *mean,* but extremely ignorant; for he had as well insultingly tell gentlemen they should not travel across his land. However, as it was necessary to his spiritual welfare, I went on to another's land, and addressed the people about an hour.

I spoke of *Mr. Cates,* the self-conceited, ignorant Baptist preacher's course as being desperately wicked, having told several down right falsehoods, to gratify his own wicked heart and the hearts of his brethren, and especially the class-leader. After portraying the malignity of the behavior of these men, I expressed to them what I now believe, viz: Neither the character nor person of a Christian is safe in the hands of ignorant and desperate sectarians of this age. I then preached the gospel, but most of the persons present were unprepared to receive it. A woman or two accosted me, full of rage, but with a determination to sustain the preacher, and one affirmed that she had often heard Mr. Barrett (Bro. W. Barrett) say the Bible was the Spirit. This wicked falsehood of the woman, was another evidence, party preachers could have witness to prove any thing they might affirm. Others gloried aloud in their ignorance, and rejoiced that they had the spirit *then* in their hearts to guide them. Although there were some *gentlemen* present, such religionists I have rarely had the misfortune to meet, and I pray God that I may never be caught under similar circumstances.

My whole object in mentioning this affair, is to suggest, that I presume this is a pretty fair specimen of the behavior of the lower order of partisans generally, and my entire misgiving that such people can ever receive the Gospel.—This whole "get religion" and "direct inspiration" system, to cloak lying and carry on desperate designs, must be destroyed, before the great mass of our contemporaries can believe or obey God. Now the question is, the best plan of accomplishing this object.

There are many individuals, members of party churches, who would not knowingly do a mean act; but the tendency of *all modern human establishments, is to corruption, and to utter opposition to Christianity.* Lord, teach us moderation in all things.   T. F.

A SHORT DISCOURSE ON CHARACTER.

One important thought is enough for a single sermon, and if I can offer in this discourse one idea which will cause useful reflection, my labor will not be lost. My chief design is to call up the living nations as they now exist, and learn, if possible, how the race of Adam presents such contrariety of character. In other words, I wish to ascertain from Scripture, and the best philosophy of which I am master.

To WHAT EXTENT MAN IS THE CREATURE OF CIRCUMSTANCES—That my views may be perspicuous, I will vary from the common beaten path—that the whole world is composed of but two classes, saints and sinners. It may be literally true, but as there are different kinds of sinners, another classification of the world will better answer my present purposes. I assume the position, then, that the whole race of man is composed of—1st, *Natural or Animal men;* 2d, *of Moral men merely or those of mixed character;* 3dly, *of Spiritual persons*— All the world may be grouped under these heads, and my first object will be to define the Natural, Moral, and Spiritual man; and in the course of the investigation, it will of necessity devolve upon me to show why mankind are thus classified.

1. THE NATURAL MAN.—Perhaps, on no subject has there been more false teaching, than on this. Generally, the religious world pronounces all men who are sinners, or those who are not members of an orthodox church, merely natural men. Presuming all who are not church members are in a state of nature, we are thrown into great confusion from the language of Paul. He says: "The natural man receiveth not the things of the Spirit of God, for they are foolishness unto him; neither can he know them, because they are spiritually discerned." But is it true, the things of the Spirit are "foolishness" to all who are not professors? Why then preach the Gospel to them for the whole Gospel was given by the Spirit. It is a truth of the Spirit, that there is a God; that his Son died for sinners: but why preach these things of the Spirit to the wicked of this country, if they are all men in "nature's darkness," and are consequently incapable of receiving or believing these truths, upon which salvation depends?

Not to be tedious, most of the religious world has done nothing but darken counsel on this subject.

The (*pscuhikos*) animal or natural man, is he whose knowledge of God, himself the world about him, is circumscribed by nature. It has not been long since the Siamese and other eastern nations were in a state of nature, "having no hope and without God in the world." The Australians, at this day, approach a state of nature. Men and nations whose knowledge are limited by nature, and who, like the beast of the field, are ruled by appetite and passion, are in a state of nature. Such know not their origin or destiny. In this condition, mankind is not capable of receiving the Gospel. It is foolishness to a savage to say, "Jesus Christ died for sinners, and will save his people in the eternal mansions." It thus becomes obvious, a savage state is made by the *peculiar circumstance* of the case, and neither by inclination or disinclination to be a natural man. Now, the question is, can such men be Christians—be converted by the Gospel? In other words, are savage tribes prepared to receive the Gospel? Does the history of the world exhibit an instance of a savage tribe being Christianized by the Gospel? Romanists and protestants have all failed. What is the reason? The circumstances surrounding savages are so unfavorable as to preclude the possibility of Christianizing them in this state. Missionaries, however, to some extent, have benefited savages, but not by preaching the Gospel. The very degraded of all countries, and the very opulent, are in circumstances most unfavorable to Christianity. *Civilization* is indispensable, before an individual or nation can-receive the Gospel. How is this to be accomplished. God has ordained *Agriculture, Horticulture,* and the *Mechanic Arts* as the means of civilizing the degraded of the earth, and preparing them to receive and practice the truth. No people ever did become Christians, and act worthy of this profession, without personal acquaintance with the *industrial* and *responsible* pursuits of life. By these, God teaches man dependence and humility, and without their influence no community can be truly pious. It is utter folly to talk of savages, and the lazy, indolent portions of the earth, being Christianized.— Their state must be greatly exalted, by the means God has appointed, and their circumstances materially changed, before they can possibly act the Christian. It is casting pearls before swine, to preach to such. Am I asked what will become of men in a state of nature? I know not: God will do right; they cannot enjoy heaven, in consequence of disqualification. God will send them to their own place, and they will experience, in the world to come, according to their qualifications. Enough on the first division of the world.

2d. THE MORAL MAN.—The merely moral man is one whose outward conduct is in obedience to moral government, but whose heart is not influenced by the grace of God. Piety has reference to the purity of the heart, and the pious man is not only moral, but also spiritual. The moral man, is the honest gentleman and good citizen merely. Any one civilized, but who is not under the economy of favor, may be considered a moral man.

The great question, however, is to ascertain what makes the moral man. It may be answered, MORAL GOVERNMENT. But what is moral government? Any government which is not exclusively spiritual. All moral governments are mixed, and consequently, those who live in conformity to them can have but a mixed character. *Most civil governments* are moral institutions, and those who conform to them closely, have the character the government imparts. It is not for want of honesty in the subjects, that mere civil governments do not make pious men, but it is owing to the Circumstances that govern. No stream can rise above its fountain; and therefore, to have more than a moral character, we must have more than a moral government. TEMPERANCE SOCIETIES are moral institutions, fraught with a good deal of worldly wisdom; but the temperance cause cannot make a pious man. Although it is a good institution, it is a worldly one, and men of the world should conduct it without the aid of others. Am I asked why I am not a member of this society, which I call good? I answer, if I were to join every world establishment to do good, I would have no time nor means of doing good by higher authority. God commands me to be "temperate in all things;" and if the Bible fails restraining me, I admit the greater influence of human wisdom over me, and I thereby detract from the dignity of my Christian profession, and from the sacred authority of God. A greater insult cannot be offered to a king, than for a subject to refuse obedience, from the word of the king; but to conform by the advice of a servant. The Christian who puts his hand to any thing human to perfect him in usefulness offers marked insult to the authority of God. All that is good in the Temperance Society, is in the Bible, and if the same money had been expended on Christian principles, and the same talent and zeal brought to bear, to make men temperate from the authority of God's word, a thousand more benefits would have been the result. Let merely moral men manage the temperance cause—I say amen to it, Christians have a higher and more holy calling.

FREEMASONS AND ODD-FELLOWS, have moral societies. Their governments are mixed and so must be their character. These are amongst the best human institutions of the world; but they are merely human—are not of God, nor countenanced by him, and therefore Christians need them not. Whatever is good in either, is in the Bible, and if pious people will not be influenced by the word of God, it is greatly detracting from the Christian profession, to resort to other means to form the most perfect character. Freemasonry will not make a pious man, yet it has relieved many an orphan and widow. The Christian needs not any auxiliary society to perfect his character. Indeed the way to heaven, is a high, open, straight road, and when professed Christians are in any of the little by ways, dark ways, and side cuts, they are liable to wander clear away from the open road. But to men of the world, I say go on with Freemasonry, for aught that it is time, and do all the good you can with your merely moral institution; but to the Christian I say, all such establishments are useless, to say the least.

Mohammedanism, is a mixed institution, and comparatively, it is a good establishment. The Alcoran is composed of the laws of Christ, laws of Moses, Jewish fables, and Heathen philosophy, consequently it is mixed, and those who conform to it can but have a mixed character. A Mohammedan cannot live under the law of Christ and the Alcoran at the same time.

Roman Catholicism is a moral institution and has done some good in the world, and in consequence of the mixed government and mixed character of the subjects, it has done a great amount of evil. The Romanist's government is taken from the law of God, and the wisdom of men, and is a new compound. Permit me here to state, that the law of God taken out of its connection and combined with any thing else, is no longer the law of God, or even truth.— Combine alkali and oil, and we have neither alkali, nor oil; but a new substance. The Pharisees neutralized, or made void the law of Moses by combining it with the traditions of the fathers, and Romanists paralyze the law of the Almighty, by combining it with the fables of the dark ages. Hence, according to my definition, this may be a moral government, but is mixed and consequently imperfect, and it is physically, intellectually and morally impossible for a Romanist to have a pure character.

His system is mixed, and his life must be defective.

Romanists may be honest, prayerful and zealous, but pious, in my definition, they cannot be. The circumstances with which they are surrounded forbid a spiritual, or any but a mixed character. They cannot obey God, though they become the most zealous persons in the world, till their position is changed; and keep in mind, reader, all civilized nations and individuals are responsible for the circumstances in which they act.

ALL PROTESTANT ESTABLISHMENTS, are moral institutions; and it is probable most of them have been beneficial in some respects to man; but the governments are mixed, and it is impossible for a defective government to forma pure character. Men under the influence of Calvinism, Arminianism, or Universalism, may have the characters which these respective *isms* impart, but to talk of any mixed government, such as Mormonism, Shakerism, or any human law, making a pious mart, or constituting the full Christian, is perfect folly.— This is not for lack of honesty or religion on the part of Protestantism; but the failure in forming purely spiritual characters, is owing to the unfortunate *circumstances* with which they are surrounded. The whole territory of sectarianism must be abandoned, before the purely Christian character can be fully exemplified. No system of religion made by men is spiritual, and consequently it is impossible for any defective system to give spiritual life. I want it not to be forgotten, that I class Romanism, Protestantism, and all human establishments as merely moral systems; and now I say, in the face of all men, no one of them, nor all of them combined, can make such a character as God will accept. God must have the honor of exclusively governing such as he will approbate. So much for moral government and moral character.

THE SPIRITUAL MAN.—I am aware it is the opinion of many, that all our effort at reform consists in ascertaining a better way of *becoming* a Christian than others; but I must take the liberty of stating, if we could have believed men could have had the characters required by God, by the popular systems of the age, we should never have made war upon them. We have attacked them because we love the people under their influence, and because we ardently desire their salvation. But who is the spiritual man? All whom the Spirit directly governed, anciently, were spiritual, "and needed not that any one should teach them; for they had an unction which taught them all things." There are but two theories now in the world on the subject. The majority of religionists, particularly in this country, profess to be governed by direct revelation. Shakers, Calvinists, Arminians and Mormons, say they have inward lights or feelings produced by the Spirit, which teach them they are the servants of God, and on their way to heaven. They do not profess these revelations come through the sense of seeing, or hearing, or the Bible, but through the sense of *feeling.* The disciples of Christ on the contrary say, God, in no age or country, ever made a revelation by feeling; that all *these feeling* and not *speaking* spirits, are delusive, and those under their influence are under too unfavorable circumstances to believe or obey God; and that the New Testament is to us what immediate inspiration was to the Apostles and first Christians. The Bible is the voice of God, the sword and language of the Spirit, and all who are governed in heart and life by the truth, are strictly spiritual persons. None are spiritual whose hearts, lives, and states have not been changed by the Spirit. Jesus, in illustrating his government, put a change of

position first. Said he to the laborers, "Go into the vineyard and work." From this we conclude the work of God can only be performed under favorable circumstances. It cannot be performed in the kingdom of Satan.

But after persons are converted to God, circumstances must be of the proper kind to enable them to form the purely spiritual character. Men cannot live the Christian alone, and scattered over a large territory, where they have more of *worldly* than *spiritual* society, The Jews, while they continued in their respective sections of country, and with their brethren, could obey God; but as they commingled with the surrounding nations, they lost the spirit of their institutions, and fell into the current of pagan philosophy. While they remained in these separate tribes, they had a beneficial influence on strangers who came amongst them; but when Jews went amongst the world, their light went out, and they lost their influence. They were obliged to conform to the corrupt regulations of society with which they associated, and therefore, as a distinctive people their character was lost.

While Christians took cognizance of each other in all things, they were a pure and spiritual people; but as they introduced the customs of worldly society, and conformed to the fashions of their neighbors, they became corrupt, and the spirit, power and beauty of Christianity disappeared from most parts of the earth.

At the present day, we as a people have in fact taken the Bible as our government. This has not been done by others. Still, we confess ourselves unorganized under the Bible, and therefore the circumstances under which we act, prevent us from being purely spiritual. The Gospel contemplates spiritual society, but still, we see the most favored conforming to the world. Christians need not be exhorted to abstain from show, dress, and the fashions of the world; they cannot help themselves, without a change of circumstances. They must either have Christian manners and Christian maxims and modes of doing every thing, or continue to conform to the world. Amongst the brethren, we have had essay after essay and number after number on "*Organization of churches* but still there is either a stand still position, or an inclination rather to retrograde. What is the matter? The brethren have not studied the subject, and therefore know but little about it. We need light, but it is in the Bible, and I confidently believe it will be seen soon. I conclude this subject by saying, man, to be spiritual, must have spiritual society; and no society can be spiritual, which is not organized by the Bible. Is the Bible sufficient? If so, brethren, let us seek the truth. This subject will bear profound investigation.

T. F.

THEMES FOR DISCUSSION.

Will our brethren furnish essays on the following topics—Reflect before you write, brethren.

1st. What is the Biblical idea of DEATH? of LIFE? of IMMORTALITY? of ETERNAL LIFE? of HADES? of DESTRUCTION? Speculations are not wanted, but the teaching of the holy spirit. T. F.

☞ The Review of Campbell & Rice's Debate must be deferred till the next Number.

THE FEAST OF PENTECOST,

Probable evidence that it was kept in commemoration of the giving of the Law, as well as the dedication of the first fruits of the harvest.

This feast was so called among the Jews, because celebrated upon the *fiftieth* day, (*e Pentecoste emera*) counting from the second day of the festival of unleavened bread, or Passover; that is, seven weeks after the sixteenth of Nisan. There were three great Jewish festivals, in which all the males of the children of Israel were obliged to repair to the temple, to commemorate three distinct events in their remarkable history; the feast of the Passover, the feast of Pentecost or of weeks, and the feast of Tabernacles. The Passover, the signification of which is *a sparing,* was instituted in commemoration of the sparing or immunity granted the Hebrews, when God by his angel of distraction destroyed the first born of the Egyptians, and was celebrated on the 14th day of the month Nisan, which began with the new moon of April. The Pentecost, in commemoration of the giving of the Law, which I think can be shown to have taken place on the fiftieth day after their coming out of Egypt. The feast of Tabernacles was celebrated in commemoration of the 40 years' wandering of Israel in the desert, where they dwelt in booths of boughs and leaves, and was kept for eight days from the 15th day of the month of Tisri.

It is with the second festival that we have to do in this article. We propose to show that it was kept in commemoration of the giving of the Law upon Sinai, fifty days after the deliverance of the children of Israel; and affording a striking and beautiful type of the giving of the Christian Law upon Mount Zion, fifty days after a deliverance from sin was consummated in the death of Jesus Christ for all who believe through his name. This is probable,—

First, Because the feast of the Passover was kept not only as a season of thanksgiving for present blessings, but in commemoration, as already remarked, of a great national event. So also, with the feast of Tabernacles, which was kept not only for the purpose above described, but also as a season of thanksgiving for the ingathering of the harvest. The feast of Pentecost has been understood, by those who oppose the above view, as intended to celebrate simply the offering of the first fruits of the harvest. Now, it is true, that the first fruits were offered at this feast; but that they were the occasion of the feast, cannot be shown, no more than the *ingathering* of the harvest can be shown to have been the occasion of the feast of booths. It is the more probable opinion, therefore, that the offering of the first fruits was an exhibition of the gratitude of the nation, presented at this festival as a most fit and solemn occasion—rather an effect of its institution than the occasion of the institution itself. The other national feasts were instituted in commemoration of signal and never-to-be-forgotten events in their history as a nation, and were incidentally periods of thanksgiving. So, unless Pentecost is an exception in the history of all nations, it also was established in memorial of a notorious and national event, and became a season of thanksgiving, which was presented in the offering of the first fruits of the harvest to the Lord. What event could it refer to, unless to the giving of the Law, which occurred as we shall show presently, exactly fifty days after the event that occasioned the Passover; and this was the order in which they were kept throughout the whole Jewish age.

Secondly. The day of Pentecost has been called among the Jews, from time immemorial, the "day of the giving of the law;" and, if their own authorities are to be accredited, they kept this festival in commemoration of that event.—The Jews, it must be acknowledged, are the best exponents of their own customs.

Thirdly. I think it is fully established, when we prove that the time that elapsed between the deliverance of Israel and the giving of the Law, was exactly a week of weeks. It is admitted that the feast of Pentecost was kept exactly fifty days after that of the Passover; so that, if we establish the period of time between the event the Passover was intended to celebrate, and the one now in dispute, the case will have been made out. The whole investigation of this part of the subject depends upon the proper exposition of Exodus xix, 1, and the phrase "same day" in that verse. "In the third month, when the children of Israel were gone out of the land of Egypt, the *same day* came they into the wilderness of Sinai." There are three opinions entertained by the learned with reference to this day:

1. The same day has allusion to the fifteenth day of the third month, which was the same day the children of Israel departed from Egypt. This being admitted, it will make sixty-five days to the giving of the law.

2. The *same day* signifies the same with the number of the month—*third* month, third or *same day,*

3. By the *same day* the first day of the month is intended.

The last View must be correct, because it corresponds with the history and with all the allusions to those times and feasts. It corresponds with the allusions, because the feast of Pentecost was celebrated exactly fifty days after the Passover. It corresponds with the history thus: The Jews left Egypt the fifteenth day of the first month, Abib. The second month was wholly spent in the pilgrimage. If, then, we make the "*same* day" refer to the first day of the month, we have 45 days to this time. Moses went up into the mountain on the second day. Three days were given to the people to purify themselves, which added to two make five, and which together make fifty—thus:

From 15th Abib to 2d of Sivan or 3d month,   45 days,

From the 1st to the 5th of 3d month, inclusive, (i. e. 2 days for
   Moses in the mount, and 3 for purification of people,)   5 "

From the deliverance of Israel to the giving of the Law,   50 days.

[It was upon the 3d day of the purification, the 5th of the month, that the Lord came down in the sight of all the people—11th verse.]

The view here taken, is the one taken by all the Jewish Rabbins, the best exponents, in such cases, of the manner in which the Jews understood this matter. And Hebrew critics say that the Hebrew word *chodesh,* month, is put for *new moon.,* which is with the Jews the *first day of* the month; which to my mind furnishes conclusive confirmation of the view here taken.

And when we take into consideration, that the Jews kept the feast of Pentecost in commemoration of the giving of the Law, as well as the offering of the first fruits; that this view alone corresponds with the nature and character of the other feasts, and was called by the Jews (*schimhath torah*) "the joy of the Law;" and most of all, when we know that there is an exact correspondence between the giving of the Law and the descent of the Holy Spirit upon Pentecost, fifty days after Christ, our Passover, was slain for us,—this view carries with it the force of a demonstration.

In the ordering of the ages preceding the coming of the Lord, the Author of our holy religion seems to have had in view, in all his arrangements, a typical illustration of the gospel dispensation. At the Passover, the Israelites were delivered from Egyptian bondage, in commemoration of which they eat the Paschal Lamb on the night preceding. Upon the very same day of the same month, Jesus Christ was sacrificed for our sins, and on the night preceding, the Lord's supper was instituted to celebrate the event. Fifty days after the Passover, God gave the Law on Sinai, accompanied with thunder, lightning and tempest. Fifty days after our Passover, the Holy Spirit was shed forth, with a sound of a rushing mighty wind—tongues of fire sat upon the Apostles, and the Law of the Spirit of life went forth from Jerusalem. When the Law of Sinai, gendering death, was given, 3000 were killed; when the Law of Zion was given, the same number were delivered from condemnation, and introduced into the life of the gospel. Thus we have a perfect analogy. Their deliverance from literal, our deliverance from spiritual slavery; their baptism into the sea our baptism; the giving of the Law our Pentecost. The first, as it was a fleshly system, was but a mere shadow——a rude draft of the good things to come—the spiritual blessings in Christ.

The feast of Pentecost is so called in the New Testament, because the Greek word *Pentecost* signifies *fiftieth.* It is called the feast of weeks, because it is celebrated after a week of weeks from the Passover—Exod. xxxiv, 22; of harvest, because the barley harvest, which ended at that time, began at the Passover—Exod. xxiii, 16; the day of the first fruits, because upon that day a new meal offering was offered—Num. xxviii, 26; Lev. xxiii, 16. It was upon this day that the Priest waved the offerings with the bread of the first fruits before the Lord. [How beautifully this also corresponds with the antitype! for it was upon the day of Pentecost that the Apostles first presented Jesus as raised from the dead—the first fruits of the rich and full harvest of believers that shall yet be gathered and reared before the Lord.] But this day was called also, among the Jews, the day of the Law, because it was and is the constant opinion of the Jews, that upon this day, the fiftieth after their deliverance, the Law was given. St. Augustine among the ancients, and Honbigarnt, Stackhouse, Clarke, Horne, *cum mul tis aliis,* all concur in speaking of Pentecost as a feast commemorative of the giving of the Law; and, unless it can be supposed that the whole nation of the Jews could be induced to keep a feast in commemoration of an event that never happened, we must admit that their interpretation is correct.

Are we not, then, prepared to say, in conclusion, that never in the history of God's dealings with the human family, has there been such a concentration of circumstances to one point, as in the history of the last authorized Pentecost of the Jewish nation, recorded in the 2nd chapter of Acts? 'Twas then the gospel was first preached in its facts—'twas then the kingdom came to Jerusalem—'twas then the Law of the Lord went forth—'twas then a divine pattern of all things necessary for life and godliness was shown us. Let the transactions of that day never be forgotten; for remembered, they afford a key to all the treasures of life, peace and joy, contained in the blissful reign of Messiah, the prince and Saviour of man.	J. B. F.

Merriville, Ky., July, 1844.

HOPKINSVILLE, KY., JULY 31st, 1844.

BRETHREN EDITORS:—In my last communication, I considered the evils of our present system of evangelizing to some extent. The choosing of evangelists, their time of service, their remuneration, their qualifications, are all subjects of great importance, worthy of the most serious consideration, and now demanding the attention of the brotherhood. On the proper organization of the "corps evangelistic," if I may use the phrase, depend the well-being and purity of the churches. It is a proposition that requires no argument, that properly trained officers are absolutely indispensable to the well-being of an army. Our evangelists are objects worthy the attention of all the faithful. Their character fixes the character of the churches. The evangelist finds himself reflected by the churches, under his care. The old proverb "like Priest, like people," is entirely applicable to the teachers of modern times. Purity of doctrine, sound speech, fidelity, faithfulness, righteousness, sobriety, gravity, are the indispensables in the formation of the character of a proclaimer. Where we find a proclaimer possessed of these virtues, we find the churches reflecting the same like polished mirrors. None should be permitted to go forth in the proclamation of the word of the truth, who is not possessed of these. No church that fears the Lord, will ever employ or give countenance to men in the absence of the above character. The choice of evangelists should always depend on the exhibition of the virtues which have been specified. The choice should never depend on the wayward dispositions of the unlearned and badly taught, but on those virtues known, and approved by men of sobriety, wisdom and godliness. To subject the qualifications of evangelists to the judgment of inexperienced and unqualified men and women, is unknown to the whole college of inspired apostles, bishops, pastors and teachers. Some persons must judge; but let those persons be such as are known to be capable of judging. Had I any matter of importance to decide, I should never ask the opinion of the young and unlearned, but of the aged and sober. Know then, ye younger, that it is one of the excellencies of youth to yield to the judgment and discretion of age. There are instances, however, in which men have grown old without knowledge or discernment; I wish it distinctly understood, that I always couple wisdom with age.

As there is no authority human or divine, no law enacted in all the realms of reason or common sense, by which an evangelist can be elected for the space of twelve months, or any particular number of months or years, I shall not pretend to offer any remarks by which the practice may be disproved; but shall say, that an evangelist possessed of the character drawn by the Spirit, is a minister of the Lord, and is as much the object of the church's care as was an apostle or evangelist of primitive times. The churches are bound, by the highest considerations, to sustain and assist such, as long as they remain faithful to their Lord. When a church rejects a proclaimer, it should be done because of unfaithfulness on his part, or some departure from the character required by the Master. Great indeed have been the evils arising from a change of teachers. The churches acquire the reputation, unenviable indeed, of being fickle-minded and hard to please. The community around looks on them with doubt, not knowing why they should dismiss a man of piety, virtue, sobriety, and sound knowledge. They sometimes are so unfortunate as to lose their own reputation and injure that of the evangelist; thus, the salvation of many   is   lost   by   the   loss   of   reputation   by

many   is   lost   by   the   loss   of   reputation   by both the evangelist and the church. God designs the churches to act the part of conductors of his grace; when they cease to *act* this part from any cause, God no longer regards them as his, and they are plucked up by the roots.

The sects keep their preachers many years, and often for life, and flourish under their government. Should not the brethren learn a lesson from this fact? When the community become acquainted with a man and have confidence in his honesty and goodness and capacity to teach, it is most strange that anyone should ever think of a change. Some, however, will not be satisfied with & man unless he can affect much at once—that is, baptize multitudes in a few days. The character of evangelists now is estimated by the numbers which they baptize, not by the correctness and soundness of his teachings and his faithful exhibitions of the truth to the churches. I fear that some churches of mine acquaintance are worthy of the character which Paul has drawn. They have itching ears, and heap to themselves teachers. Nothing, in my estimation, so strongly exhibits a corrupt taste, as the disposition to change the proclaimer every year. It proves that the truth alone is not sufficient, but something more is necessary to satisfy a depraved taste.

I might enumerate the numerous evils to which a proclaimer is subjected, in this constant removing to and fro. With no certain home, he can never be comfortably situated. His wife and children are often neglected, and endure many privations. The family of a proclaimer is necessarily subject to privations, from his almost constant absence. His children are sometimes left destitute of education. His frequent removals require many expenses, so that nothing can be laid by for times of misfortune. The mere support a proclaimer for a certain term of months, is as much as most churches think of. They do not consider what may become of him when his term of service is out, and what may be the condition of his family, when the sum which is allowed him has been paid him and expended in the support of his family. I am persuaded that the present system is more expensive than any that the law of our King would require. Let the proclaimer be chosen for his good character; let him be put in possession of a home, and when this is done the contributions of the brethren could easily sustain him at a less expense than that now incurred. Many families of the evangelists could be sustained with ease by the churches, by a contribution of the necessaries of life, without an expenditure of money. The articles of food and raiment would be very inconsiderable, when the proclaimer once becomes settled at home. Six or seven hundred dollars annually, could be much reduced. When a home is once gained, the expenses would be much less than they now are. But under the present arrangement, many hundreds are required which could be more profitably expended. Instead of the support of one, the churches could have two, if they would adopt the plan suggested. Money would be saved, and a double amount of good effected. Seven hundred dollars would purchase a comfortable home for a small family. The evangelist in possession of a home, could be sustained by the churches for one half of this sum, provided he would be willing to live as a Christian should live. Let the churches select their proclaimers, give them homes, and they will find their expenses much lessened. Let them learn to be satisfied with the truth, and never dismiss a man unless he is guilty of bad conduct. The order of heaven leads to good, and that continually.

Bishops who have the qualifications, are

chosen for life, and are better beloved as they become better known; then let some person who is wiser than I, say why proclaimers should not enjoy equal advantages. I have known persons occupy the office of bishop who had no qualifications; and I have known evangelists dismissed who were possessed of every qualification necessary for the conversion of the world and the building up of the church. May the churches look to these matters and do better, is my sincere wish.　　　　　　　　　　Yours,　　　　　　　　　　HENRY T. ANDERSON.

LETTER FROM G. C. METCALFE.

ATHENS, TEN., AUGUST 1st, 1844.

DEAR BRO FANNING:—I have delayed writing to you thus long in the vain hope, that some of our Nashville brethren would feel sufficient interest in the upbuilding of the good cause to come to our assistance, to aid us in rearing the broad and glorious banner of Gospel truth, and primitive Christianity.— But we have not been idle; already from our mountains and valleys, the joyous sound has gone forth, and here and there a little band is rallying to the onset. The *Bible* "alone" is our watchword—and "*The Union* of Christians" and the "conversion of the world," our motto—and built upon this foundation—"Jesus is the Christ—the Son of the living God," we Stand firm as our own everlasting hills, bidding defiance to the storms of envy, malice, and misrepresentation, which burst in *harmless fury* at our feet, and though we are but few, we look forward to the happy time, when thousands shall flock beneath the standard of our King, and go forth in the strength and beauty of holiness, "conquering and to conquer."—It is a glorious cause, my brother, and one in which we should all fight valiantly. In the strength of Israel's God, let us go on.

Near five years ago, I attached myself to the Baptist Church in Talladega, Ala. But I will frankly confess, I knew little of what it took to constitute a Christian—and I can only now look back with heartfelt regret upon my course of life, for the three succeeding years, wandering from place to place.—I was often thrown into the midst of scenes and society, which alas, often proved too seductive. But I trust in God, such scenes are passed forever. Then adieu to vain regrets—let my course henceforth be onward and upward. While residing in Marion, Ala., in the summer of '44, I received intelligence that Bro. Jas. Shannon, on his way to Georgia, had immersed four persons in this county—two my own brothers—the others, relations. You will not be surprised when I tell you that my Baptist vanity was not much flattered by this—true I desired to see them Christians—but as I should have said, at that time, *not Campbellites,* At the same time I was informed of the debate between Bro. Campbell and Rice, and I determined to attend and hear for myself.

Previous to my departure for Lexington, I requested a letter of dismission and license to preach from the Baptist Church in Talladega.—I heard every word of the debate, with the exception of two hours, on creeds; what effect it had on others, I cannot say, but to my mind, Bro. Campbell fully established every proposition—not by bold assertion, but by proof—still I thought I could do more good by reforming the errors of the Baptists, while in their midst, than by leaving them; and having on my return from L. received my letter, and License from the Talladega Church, I offered it for the acceptance of my Baptist brethren near this place—asking admission into their body on two conditions; 1st. that I might be allowed the liberty of taking the Bible and the Bible alone, as my rule of faith and practice——-and 2d, of partaking of the emblems of the broken body and shed blood of our Lord, with all *immersed* believers, whose faith and conduct proved them to be Christians—to which some objections being made, I withdrew my letter. This was in the first of April. On the 3d Lord's day, I delivered a discourse from 4 Eph. 1-6; and on the 1st. in June a sermon on Christian Union—we then organized a congregation of nine members—(including the four above mentioned.)

Brethren Jon. T. Johnson and Jon. W. Payne of Ky., arrived on the second Lord's day in June, and preached for us during the week. On the 3d, they ordained our church officers, 2 Elders, one Evangelist and Deacon; 12 more were added during the stay, making in all 21—5 or 6 were from the Methodist Church. May the God of all goodness reward them for their labour of love in our behalf. Bro. E. A. Smith of Danville, Ky., is now with us, but owing to the weakness of his eyes, he is unable to undergo the labors incident to the proclamation of the Gospel. However, he has delivered several discourses, much to our own gratification—and well calculated to lead others to the knowledge of the truth as it is in Christ Jesus. We meet every Lord's day for the purposes of breaking the loaf, prayers, &c. There are several congregations of the Brethren in this part of the State—as to their condition I am not at this time well informed, but will endeavor to be so before the general meeting in September, which, the Lord willing, I hope to attend.

You know, doubtless, something of the fiery ordeal through which the truth is destined to pass, ere it can prevail—more especially in such circumstances as those with which we are surrounded. As an instance, it is said we deny the operation of the Spirit—Elder Cunningham, to prove it true, and to convince his brethren that he knows all about these things rises, and under the guidance of Elder F. E. Pitts' work, &c., of precious memory, proceeds to show the people that he so, ever and anon quoting from the aforesaid work, adding some sage remarks of his own, to season it with all—proceeds to prove (so he will tell you) that A. Campbell of Virginia does deny the aforesaid doctrine— ergo, all the Disciples do—"like premises, like conclusions." But time would fail me to tell of all the battles fought and won by these mighty men of valor; I must close. Bro. Smith will remain with us until the last of the month. We expect to be in Nashville before the General Meeting.

Your brother in the one hope,

G. C. METCALFE.

RABBAH TAKEN;
OR

The Theological System of Alexander Campbell examined and refuted, by Robt. W. Landis, Pastor of the Presbyterian Churchy Bethlehem, New Jersey.

While in Cincinnati, a few days since, I saw in one of the morning papers, *"published this day,"* a work of the above designation; and without delay, I walked to the book store of Mr. More and purchased the book. The work is a neatly executed pamphlet, of 155 octavo pages; and the publisher, thinking it a profitable undertaking, has stereotyped it.

On examining the title page, I saw the words, "I have fought against Rabbah, and have taken the city of waters," which was the language of Joab to David, when he had destroyed one of the cities of Ammon; and the thought occurred, that if Mr. Landis had as completely demolished A.

Campbell as Joab did Rabbah, I had better be fleeing for "parts unknown." However, I opened the book, and examined it closely; but found nothing new. The old charges of " water salvation," "no Spirit," &c., were reiterated and refuted; but in the whole work, I could see nothing argumentative or reasonable, and the style is by no means of a manly bearing. The charges made by Mr. L., were once fashionable and popular, but they are now too gross—are stale; and any one who will repeat them, must subject himself to the indignation of honorable men.

As evidence of the author's recklessness, I will give a few extracts. On the tenth page he says, what we teach "Has no more valid claims to be regarded as the religion of the cross than Mormonism," and on the ninth page he says the Mormons are certainly as "sincere and respectable'5 us ourselves. He says pa. 10, we "keep our sentiments concealed." On pa. 13, he says: A. Campbell "Condemns the doctrine of justification by faith" &c. &c.

If Mr. L. would come west, the children and negroes could tell him, he was either extremely ignorant or desperately wicked to utter such slanders. It is too late to speak thus. The most amusing point of the whole affair is, Mr. L.'s attempt to give a history of the brethren, when lo! and behold! all his authority is from Doctor Fishback, who has acknowledged the error of his course years since, by coming out and uniting with the disciples in Lexington, Ky. Mr. L., is really ignorant of what is doing in the world—is too far "behind the times" to write, and is too reckless to tell the truth, if he could imagine the slandering of one of his fellow citizens, would give a little brief notoriety and conspicuity in the world. Most of the "Reviews of Campbellism" I have noticed for some years, only prove their authors are seeking fame in the eyes of an ignorant, prejudiced and sectarian people. This is evidence of a degraded age. These pseudo slanderers will not prosper much longer in their offences before High Heaven.   T. F.

"BAPTISM OF REPENTANCE AND CHRIST A PRIEST BEFORE HE ASCENDED."

A brother asks the question, "Was the repentance preached by John, before or after Baptism?" He answers by saying *"it was after baptism;"* but may I ask a question, "why did John tell them to bring forth fruit worthy of repentance" if the baptism came first? Reconcile this, and I will remove all the rest of the difficulties.

2d. If Jesus Christ was not made high priest, before he ascended into heaven, how could the high priest under the old institution be typical of him, seeing he was not made high priest in the holy place, but made without in order that he might enter within?

This is the way all difficulties come into existence. They are imagined and oftentimes a little reflection, would remove great darkness. Suppose Bro. L. had just taken time to reflect, that Christ was a priest after the order Of Melchisedec, and not after the fashion of Aaron, would not the difficulty have vanished?   T. F.

Bro. Geo. W. Horn of Pennsylvania is directed to remark in the last number on *"feet washing"* for answers to his questions. If his views differ, I should be pleased to have his objections, on this, or any other topic.   T. F.

A SUGGESTION TO THE WHOLE FAMILY.

Dear Brethren, we all are aware the word of truth is greatly obscured by "the traditions of men," and that it is our duty to do all in our power to enlighten the world. In view of this important matter, I would respectfully suggest that, teachers and the churches, generally, agree to issue a large quantity of short essays, discourses or tracts, upon all the leading points of discussion of the day, and that these tracts be distributed gratuitously to the world. Let brethren of ability be selected for writing those tracts, and let the expenses be defrayed by the churches. One might be written, on the sufficiency of the scriptures; another on the manner of searching them; one on Faith; another on Repentance; three on Baptism; one or two in answering objections and removing difficulties; one or two on Sects; one on the church of Christ, &c. &c. Might not much good be done in this way? Will the brethren give their views?   T. F.

THE MAJORITY GOVERNMENT.

Bro. W. has written a lengthy essay to prove the majority in a church should govern, and that a word of *comparative* import cannot mean the whole. Although the production I found in type, I do not think it expedient or profitable to publish it. I can admit most of the criticisms and conclusions, without violence to my own position. The Greek comparative *Pleioon,* literally, means a part; but it must be recollected Rhetoricians all admit, that in every language a part is frequently put for the whole, and sometimes words ordinarily implying the whole, denote only a part. Paul in the 7th of Hebrews, uses the word which implies a part, to designate all the Jewish priests.

Not wishing to protract this controversy, I wish to say when an example can be found in the New Testament of a majority's ruling the minority, I will yield the point. "The whole church" at Antioch agreed before there was any decision.   T. F.

Bro. Fanning:—Suppose an infidel should say to you, "Mr. Fanning, there is one difficulty that must be removed, before I can believe; I have proposed it to several believers, but have not received a satisfactory answer. It is this: Your Bible plainly teaches, that the one Lord whom you worship is unchangeable; and from the belief of that fact, you derive more pleasure than from any other; for, though you might believe Christ died for sinners, unless you believe the Lord will continue to pardon through his blood, you will derive no pleasure from the belief of that fact. You will also readily admit, the New Testament teaches that to one man, only one wife is allowed, and any thing like polygamy the Lord holds in abhorrence—in fact, so strict is the law, that a man cannot even divorce his wife, except for one cause. Well now, here is the difficulty: In the Old Testament, we find that many of the characters who are said to have been servants of the Lord and acceptable in his sight, had two or more wives; and even the Savior (I admit, for the sake of argument, that what you believe is true) declares that it was on account of the hardness of their hearts they were allowed more than one wife. I wish you to reconcile the two positions. *Note,* the Lord looks on one who takes a second wife as an adulterer, and will not hold him guiltless; *formerly,* be sanctioned it: has he not changed? I have had repeated to me the words of the Savior, "on account of the hardness of your hearts," &c; but I contend that this, instead of reconciling the difference, in reality makes it worse; for it admits he has changed, and assigns the reason for it: to my mind this is any thing but a reconciliation. As for myself, I cannot place any confidence in a book thus contradicting itself and must still doubt." How would you meet his objection *fairly* and *fully?*

ANSWER TO THE INFIDEL.

To say God changes because he "winks at" things in a dark age on which he can look with no allowance, with an enlightened people, is to say the least, a manifestation of very little thought or discrimination in any one. At the times of certain ignorance "God winked at;" but now that he has developed all his will concerning man, he commands all the creation to believe or be damned.

T. F.

LETTER FROM GEO. W. ELLEY.

To the Editors of the Christian Review:—

MESSRS. EDITORS:—I have just closed a second meeting at this place, with 20 more additions—making 33 added to the church in Triana since my stay in this region. At other places there have been gained 8—making 41. Among the above number, there were 4 Methodists, 1 Baptist, 1 Episcopalian, and 1 Cumberland Presbyterian. I also had the pleasure of congregating 13 brethren and sisters at Sommerville, in Morgan county, with fair prospects of doing good.— I am grateful to my heavenly father for the acquaintances which it has been my good pleasure to make in Triana, Morrisville, and Somerville, and generally in North Alabama. I have never met with a more hospitable and interesting people; and their attention and kindness shown us, and especially to my afflicted wife, while our sojourning among them, will long be remembered with gratitude. In the above number, there are many who are among the choice spirits of the land.

The whole valley of North Alabama, from Huntsville to Florence, is a delightful country, highly cultivated, and filled up with a population of much intelligence and moral worth. With one or two exceptions, I have found the people every where anxious to hear our teaching; and I must specially invite the attention of our teaching brethren to that part of Alabama. I have never seen a more interesting field for doing good, and the cause we plead demands that special attention be given to that region. The few brethren and sisters we found at Triana, acted their part with great devotion to the cause. I was also greatly aided and refreshed by the continual company of Bro. N. Hackworth, who conducted all the singing—truly an important work. In a day or two I leave for Kentucky.   Yours truly,   GEO. W. ELLY

Triana, North Alabama, Aug. 6, 1844.

Merriville, Ky., July 23, 1844.

DEAR BRETHREN:—Our meeting at Street's school house, resulted in 8 additions—one Methodist, whom we re-immersed, not being satisfied with his former immersion. One from the Baptists in Hopkinsville; 5 at Elkton. Brother P. G. Young had 7 additions at Lafayette, a few days after the meeting referred to in my last. He and Bro. S. M. Scott were with me at all the places referred to.   Yours as ever,   J. B. FERGUSON.

☛ We call special attention to the remarks of Bro. Anderson in this No., on the subject of supporting the Gospel. Will the brethren study the Bible, on this matter? But after studying, they must have more confidence in God's plan than their own opinions of expediency.

For the Christian Review,

APPEAL TO SINNERS.

What more could your Redemer do,
Your guilty soul to save?
He bore the cross to sinners due;
What more can sinners crave?
Though he was rich, he looked on us,
And for our sakes was poor;
He bore our sins upon the cross,
And opened mercy's door.
He's now ascended, where he pleads
The merits of his blood;
For sinners vile he intercedes,
Who hearken to his word.
Come sinners, then, obey the Lord,
Who for your guilt was cursed—
O! listen to his gracious word,
"Reform and be immersed."
Reform! reform without delay;
For life's a fleeting breath:
 O! come and wash your sins away;
Obey the gospel faith.
And though your sins like scarlet are,
As white as snow they'll be;
No more your guilt you'll ever fear,
When Christ has made yon free.
And now we ask you, in his name,
Will you to heaven go?
Accept his proffered mercy, then.
Or sink to shame and Wo.
The Savior stands, with outspread arms,
To call the sin-oppressed—
Cries, "Come to me, O! flee from harm!
And I will give you rest."
O come unto the gospel feast,
Ye heavy laden, come;
Come all ye wanderers and oppressed,
Here seek a heavenly home.
The happy gates of gospel grace
Stand open free to all,
And God will all their sins erase
Who hearken to his call.　　　　　　　R.

N. Y.

ERRATA.—Page 156, 5 lines from bottom, after "Israelitish," read Page 158, five lines from top, after "general" read *expectation,* instead of "preparation;" four lines below, for "has been unfolding," read *have been;* two lines below, after whole, read/ace, instead of "force." Page 159, eleventh line of poetry, for "rock" read *book.* Page 160, ten lines from top, after same, read or. Page 161, nine lines from top, after shall, read *rend,* instead of "rent." Page 162, four lines from close of article on Prophecy, for "portion," read *petition.*

CHRISTIAN REVIEW.

VOL. I.   NASHVILLE, OCTOBER, 1844.   NO. X.

CHURCH ORGANIZATION.

BEREA ACADEMY, (*near Chapel Hill,*) MARSHALL CO., TENN.

DEAR. BRO. FANNING:—I make another effort to set the qualifications of a Christian Bishop clearly before the brethren. The prosperity of the churches depends upon their having Bishops properly qualified for the office. I feel in no mood, this morning, for disputation; nevertheless, a few thoughts candidly and calmly submitted, may do good. I hope that we shall agree when we understand each other, although one of your remarks is a "very remarkable" one.

I shall begin now as I began in my former communication, with the remark concerning the Epistles to Titus and Timothy. I am led to the conclusion that you did not see their force, from the circumstance of your not noticing their correctness or incorrectness. But I substantially repeat them.

1. Each of those letters were intended by the Apostle to be the guide of him to whom it was addressed.

2. They either contain (as far as the offices of Elder and Deacon are concerned) the same requisitions or different ones. If the same, either Epistle is a safe and sufficient guide to us as it was to Timothy or Titus. If different, then the Apostle was a respecter of persons, and we are perplexed to know which set of qualifications to require. You will not consent to this; you must therefore contend for the first supposition.

3. Take each Epistle separately, and we are fully agreed, excepting two ideas—"a *desire*" for the office, and "*the proving*" of the Elder. Let us see— If the Apostle says to Timothy, "A bishop must be, 1, blameless; he says the same to Titus. To the former he says, 2, "the husband of one wife; to the latter the same direction is given. In this manner might we go through the list of qualifications, findings similar one in the other. That I may be fairly understood, I copy the sixteen requisites from Timothy: 3, Vigilant; 4, Sober; 5, Of good behavior; 6, Given to hospitality; 7, Apt to teach; 8, Not given to wine; 9, No striker; 10, Not greedy of filthy lucre; 11, Patient; 12, Not a brawler; 13, Not covetous; 14, One that ruleth well his own house, having his children in subjection with all gravity; 15, Not a novice; 16, Having a good report of those without.

4. With respect to a "*desires,*" I conclude that it is not a requirement, and therefore not necessary. This, you say, is "*a very remarkable conclusion.*"— Now, you will forgive me, or make some excuse for me, when I say that I cannot understand your meaning in this remark. When the expression "very remarkable" is not used ironically, it is indicative of something worthy of particular notice and remembrance. I admit that it would be "very remarkable." if we could find a man in this office-seeking age, who did not desire some office. "A very remarkable" circumstance it would indeed be, to find a man, within the last fifteen years, holding the Bishop's office, who had not *desired,* and never electioneered and intrigued for it.

But my objections to it *as a requisite*

are, (1,) That it is not mentioned in the letter to Titus. (2.) Those who are best qualified, know too much of its responsibilities to desire it. (3.) Their modesty would prevent them from mentioning this desire, if they entertained it. (4.) Their qualifications are all moral and intellectual, and to desire the office is certainly no mark of intellectual attainments, and a man may desire the office for his own advantage. You will probably not find a man in our Union qualified for the office, who will say *he desires it.* (5.) The Apostle does not say he *must* desire it, but *if* he desire it. He does not say, "If he desires it he must have it"—but, "he desires a good work;" and this we all say—it is a good, a noble, a glorious work. (6.) Would you reject a man possessing the qualifications above named, and who was willing to serve the church as one of its Elders, but who could not say that he *desired* the office. I now leave this with the brethren. (7.) I have taken, you say, "a strange position" in reference to the "proving" of the Elder. Although I am nothing but a country schoolmaster, I see that my Bro. Fanning will soon bring me into notice of some sort, if he makes me come to "very remarkable conclusions'1 and take "*strange positions*," and tells the people of them. Well, however strange it may be, still I cannot give it up. "Let these, also, first be proved," I cheerfully admit refers to Elders as well as to Deacons. But what is this "being proved1'? In what does it consist? All the qualifications laid down by the Apostle are dependent upon the individual himself. Here is one in the imperative passive—he is passive in it; others are to act. The word "dokimazesthoosan," may be, and indeed is, translated variously in the common version. Let them be proved, tried, examined, judged, or, as Demosthenes used it, admitted, as fit for office. A man ought not to be permitted to exercise the office until he is judged to have the qualifications for it—I only object to a church saying to some brethren—two or three—"Do you *act* as Bishops till we can ascertain whether you are qualified"—in other words, "If we are pleased with you, we will make you Elders." If they *desire* the office, they will be careful to suffer each to do as he pleases. Do we make Judges, or Governors, or Presidents in this way? The world (according to the fable,) was once set on fire by putting the reins of the chariot of the Sun into hands not qualified to hold them—and that only for a Single day. The "being first proved," is the strict and solemn scrutiny into the character and attainments of those the church would make her Bishops. Adieu.

Your Brother,   JOHN M. BARNES.

FRATER FRATRIBUS.

"Only with renunciation," it has been observed, "life, properly speaking, can be said to begin."

This is true; but elsewhere is originally expressed thus:

"He that findeth his life shall lose it; and he that loseth his life for my (Christ's) sake, shall find it."

An admonition is here conveyed: how fearful it is to hesitate between the Finite and the Anti-Finite, the infinite; to yield to the temptations and blandishments of the world, which are ever conflicting with the dictations and requirements of Heaven! Brothers, calmly (if you can) bethink yourselves. How many days *have* you to yield to the temptations and blandishments of the world? how many to expiate the criminality of so doing? What is Time? Who can answer ere it

is gone, ere it is not? Can you tell what is ETERNITY? Ultimately, you shall; in Eternity that is, and through Eternity. Oh! Brothers, know that you must make a venture! Chafes around you a huge, tumultuous ocean, whose fierce, devouring waves are agitated by evil spirits as by wild winds, and which you must buffet strenuously and triumphantly, or perish. Divest yourselves of all hindering trammels; pluck from your hearts, old affections, inordinate desires, and longings after that which is behind you, which is vanity or deception; renounce your wonted sensual life; then, when like bold swimmers you have attained the haven you pant for, a new, spiritual life begins, will dawn upon you.

Again. It is written:

"Whosoever shall exalt himself shall be abased."

What is man, that he should be proud? Of few days, and full of trouble. He springeth up like grass, and like the flower of grass—withereth. What is your "great" man, that he should be proud? Faint sounds from the remote, accomplished past, may ever and anon reach your ears: some "hero" of destruction has been busy with slaying a number of his fellow mortals—reaping with malignant folly the grass which the sultry season had already blasted, and you account it enviable "fame" that his name (mis-spelled and mis-pronounced) should be dimly remembered by you—aye, by you, who (as is most likely) will be utterly forgotten of men: had you not heard of him, his fame, his posthumous nominal vitality, had been less, in some sense not at all! Brothers, Brothers! it was a miracle of humility when Messiah vestured himself in humanity.

"He that shall humble himself shall be exalted."

Alas! how many there are who let their left hand know what their right hand doeth; how many in their lowest humility, highest exalt themselves—not in God's view! Here is the shoal whereon divers that founder are lost. "Like other plants, Virtue will not grow unless its root be hidden, buried from the eye of the sun. Let the sun shine on it—nay, do but look at it privily thyself—the root withers, and no flower will glad thee." Pharisees and hypocrites yet live who are not Jews!

"He that shall humble himself shall be exalted."

Such is the fiat of the divine Architect of the Universe, who hath pledged his Godhead his promises shall be of effect. Meek Christians, who endure the spitefulness of evil and cleave unto whatso is good, who walk in the shadow and valley, and are soiled with dust while on earth, in heaven you will be clothed upon by royal robes of white, will sit in high places, and see a reconciled Creator!

For of yourselves and without God, what are you, Brothers? With God, what are you not? Let each take his cross and follow in the heaven-road— Take his cross; learn patiently, and with hope and fortitude to *bear* the ills which in this world, in these unjointed times, and in reference solely to these, oft are consequences of following in that road.

Yet not merely by endurance or forbearance; not merely by confession or other lip-service, is a citizenship to be earned in the kingdom. In all kingdoms, they that work not enjoy not, or should not enjoy. "Faith, if it have not works, is dead." To work is to worship. Is the very Devil content with less than *deeds (of* sin) from his followers? Boldly and earnestly work, then, in the true spirit, and with what talents God hath endowed you withal. Consider yourselves well, O brothers!

Behold the FUTURE of this life circumbound by that eternal Ocean whose surges already wash the sand of Time from under your feet; conjecture what may be your DESTINY, which you are wholly empowered to shape; See how that the fair verdure of earth but decorates sad, still GRATES, where sleep millions of beings like you who now breathe; look into the melancholy, inarticulate Firmament, jeweled by God's hand with innumerable pendent Worlds, and linked Solar Systems—the incorporate thoughts of God's mind, which, circling harmoniously through immensities and infinities, in the thunder-notes of the Melody of the Spheres, hymn his everlasting praises,—and say, O Brothers, what are you to do but, with deepest gratitude and profoundest reverence and devotion, to mark these indications, and join in this glorious WORK CONCERT OF THE UNIVERSE!

Another quotation here, apparently episodically, yet tributary to the tenor of this discourse, is meet to be written with all emphasis:—

"This is my commandment: that you love one another, as I have loved you." So spoke He who died to prove his love.

It is proper to know *what it to love.* Is it the ebullition of wind from the larynx upward, articulated by the tongue and *membra oris* into words, to please or deceive the ear? Verily, no! Or, at least, this is love in word and in tongue. "My little children," writes the beloved Apostle, let us not love in word, neither in tongue; but in deed and in truth." Something is to be done, then, not all spoken. Feed the hungry; appease the thirsty; clothe the naked; heal the wounded; comfort the distressed; inform the ignorant; upbraid not your enemies, or others; envy not: on all occasions, refrain where you are forbidden— do where you are commanded. What call you that? That is love, love to God and love to man: that is also duty to God and duty to man.

Brothers, this is the work concerning which you have been spoken to: that you keep the faith and love one another. *God is lore.* Whatso, therefore, is of God, or God-like, or God-ly, is loveable and lovely. Love is the conservative principle of the universe. For is not *God* omnipotent? "Whither," sings the Psalmist—"Whither shall I go from thy Spirit? Or whither shall I flee from thy presence?" Even dull matter is subject to a kindred influence. Has not dull matter its *tendencies* and its *attractions?* Man was created in the image of God; let him, by loving his brethren, imitate him in his actions!

In respect to this duty of loving: How many love in word and in tongue merely; how many in deeds—that halt this side of Christian charity! For there are those who cast in God's treasury out of their abundance, yet give not so much as they who, like the poor widow, of their want cast in all they have.— Brothers, Brothers!

CAST IN ALL YOU HAVE.

Have you not seen, O brothers, that only with renunciation can life, properly speaking, be said to begin? Know you not that this world, which will ere long pass phantom-like away, into inane nothingness, is *not* the sphere of man's exaltation; is not the treasure-house where abiding riches are eternally to be found; on the contrary, that they who humble themselves on this earth, who *bear,* as a great cross, the opposition and contumely of this earth, in God's cause and his Son's, shall be exalted in the high Heaven of Jehovah? Are ye not aware there is a task to be done, the doing of which, in the true spirit, alone is acceptable worship? Oh, Philanthropy! Behold you not millions of beings like you dying of hunger, of thirst, of cold, of disease, of sorrow, of ignorance?

Ay! cast in all you have, ye immortal souls, posting rapidly to eternity! Can you carry aught you have, except your immortal souls, with you into eternity?— Furthermore: Is it possible to serve God and Mammon? Leave one, and wholly cleave to the other! Think you, like Ananias, to bestow a part of your possessions, and privily to reserve the rest for Mammonish sacrifices? Like Ananias! Rather like CHRIST, give all, even a life's labor *and* life.

And here—as the previous digressions, their object being in some sort attained, begin now to converge, and the scope and design of this essay begin to foreshadow themselves—a brief summary of what hath been said, and a few assumptions, will be recorded.

Time is fleeting, the world will be consumed, but Heaven and Hell are everlasting. For the last to be your goal, it is necessary that you forget it has an antipodes, to make the world and its ways your pleasure, and time subservient thereto. For heaven to be your goal, it is necessary that you be transformed, to make the word and its ways your abomination, in so far as they conflict with the dictations and requirements of God. This you may readily say, but really to *do* demands deeds of testimony. These deeds are not undefined, but clearly specified in the holy Revelation; they are the exercises of Christian charity or love.

It is assumed: No religious body has reached perfection; no religious body imagines it has reached perfection. On all sides, complaints are heard concerning the present state of religious society; on no side is approbation or contentment expressed. It is therefore assumed: The present state of religious society is susceptible of improvement; according to your temperament, it will appear susceptible of improvement in a great or less degree—at all events, in *a* degree. Perhaps this question may attract attention: If a plan of religious organization, which had been tested, and during the attestation of which it was discovered Christians approached nearer the true standard than under the adoption of any other plan; could such a plan of religious organization now be proposed, would it meet with careful consideration, would it be adopted? Suppose farther: If the APOSTLES had sanctioned, by their adoption of, this plan; would that circumstance, considering the deteriorated state of religious society, its susceptibility of greater or less improvement, (according to your temperament,) —would that circumstance of the Apostles having sanctioned this plan add another motive to, another reason for, its adoption now? O Brothers! Would that circumstance of the Apostles having sanctioned, by their adoption of this plan, add to its merits a demonstration of its meeting with the approval of God? Remember this.

In deepest earnestness, one word to this "Reformation." At *what place* under the sky does it avow its origin springs? The question need not be perverted: Where were its seeds first sown; its doctrines—itself, if you please—first proclaimed? AT JERUSALEM. Methodism, of every species, with its independent miraculous divine influences and interpositions, may occur sporadically, (like Cumberland Jerks and other epidemics,) or spread fiercely by contact and infecting breath of windy Puritanical eloquence. God (it is asserted) reaches forth his almighty hand, and from among the foredoomed multitude leadeth out in safety his Presbyterian elect. Catholicism, with fond credulous love, looks for its source to the coasts of Caesarea Philippi. No religious denomination, save the Christian, claims Jerusalem for its birth-place. Christian preachers make Jerusalem the constant climax of their sermons. The hills of Jerusalem are elevated above Gerizim piled on Sinai, above all hills and mountains The Pentecostian scene is upraised to the world's view; its basis resting on *Hell* its apex penetrating Heaven. And why? Very reasonably. For hereto pointed the finger of prophecy: "Many people," said Isaiah, rapt in the vision which he saw concerning Judah and Jerusalem—"Many people shall go and say. "Come ye, and let us go up to the Mountain of the Lord, to the house of the God of Jacob; and he will teach us of his ways, and we will walk in his paths: *for out of Zion shall go forth the law, and the word of the Lord from Jerusalem."* So, Micah, using the same language. In Luke's narrative, it is recorded that Jesus, just before parting from his disciples for the last time, said to them: "Thus it is written, and thus it behooved Christ to suffer, and to rise from *the* dead the third day; and that repentance and remission of sins should be preached among all nations, *beginning at Jerusalem.* And ye are witnesses of these things. And, behold, I send the promise of my Father upon you: *but tarry ye in the city of Jerusalem until ye be endued with power from on high?'*—Be silent about this grace of God, the remission of sins, until endued with power, when ye shall begin to testify. What imported this power? In the commencement of the Acts, it is found Christ, after having commanded them *"that they should not depart from Jerusalem,* but wait for the promise of the Father,"* said to his followers, the Apostles whom he had chosen: "Ye shall receive power, *after that the Holy Ghost is come upon you;* and ye shall be witnesses unto me, both in Jerusalem, (Jerusalem first in connection, mark,) and in all Judea, and in Samaria, and unto the uttermost parts of the earth." These are emphatically the last words the Savior spoke in this world. The interrogation is answered; the "power" was to follow the impartation of the Holy Ghost. When was the Holy Ghost imparted? Listen, and you shall hear: *"When the day of Pentecost was fully come,* they wore all with one accord in one place. And suddenly there came a sound from heaven, as of a rushing mighty wind, and it filled all the house where they were sitting. And there appeared unto them cloven tongues, like as of fire, and it sat upon each of them; and they were all filled with the Holy Ghost, and began to speak, as the Spirit gave them utterance." When was the Holy Ghost imparted? WHEN THE DAY OF PENTECOST WAS FULLY COME. Therefore, is it Jerusalem, and the deeds done there, properly enough, form the chorus of Christian exhortations, for which praise should be awarded, and for this: that only they, of the thousands who profess to proclaim the Gospel, seem actually striving to fulfill the prophecy of Isaiah, viz: that the mountain of the Lord's house should be exalted above the hills: the others seeming to lower it, at all events to prevent the true significance of the scene of Pentecost.

Thus, O Brothers! do you not perceive the infinite significance of this Pentecostian scene? All religious denominations, save this Reformation, are independent of it. This Reformation is built (in part) upon it. For thereon was first exhibited the Divine Commission, containing the terms whereby alone the guilty race of mankind can be saved: Faith, Repentance, Baptism for the Re- mission of sins, the reception thereafter of the Holy Spirit, and the exercises of charity. Considering now, all that hath been said, is not this, though unspeakably surprising, equally true:

There is not on the earth one Church organized like the Primitive Church, the Model Church, the Apostolic Church of Jerusalem, composed of Pentecostians?

"All that believed were together, and had all things in common, and sold their possessions and goods, and parted them to all, as every man had need.— And they continued daily with one accord in the temple, and breaking bread from house to house, did eat their meat with gladness and singleness of heart, praising God and having favor with all the people."

Thus acted the Pentecostians of the Apostolic Church at Jerusalem. And this is Christian Association. A joint-stock association of disciples, where each could follow the impulse of his own passion, guided however by the holy word of God; where perfect equality reigned; where Love dwelt—love to the Creator and his creatures; where the follies and extravagant fashions of the world had no place, where economy, co-operation, union, dignified and attractive labor, and not wasteful expenditure, counter-operation, disunion, degraded and repulsive labor, were the adopted system. Oh! who can calculate the Good that might be effected by such an association of disciples of the Lord?

Have Christians attained to perfection? Are any content with the present state of religious society? Is not Christian association beautiful in theory? Was it not fairly tested by the Apostles and Pentecostians? Are not the advantages it proffers, both of a spiritual and religio-temporal character, paramount to those of any other organization? Therefore, if it were possible, would in not be your duty to adopt it? And, judging by the past, may it not be affirmed that it is possible?

Faith, Repentance, Baptism—these are true, have been acknowledged to be true in all ages since they were divulged; these are necessary, absolutely necessary: but these are not all, only the beginning. These are the portal entrance into that magnificent palace, whose walls are adorned with pictures of the scenes of Palestine, of Jesus' humiliation, of his benevolent deeds, of his ignominious death, of his glorious resurrection, and of his ascension; of the travels and Acts of his Apostles—on the margins of which representations, engraved in golden characters, are lessons recorded, inculcating love to God and love to men: the church of the Holy One, wherein dwell the blessed, whose existence, as they journey gladly together from earth towards heaven, is continual mutual help and affection, and adoration of the great Builder, wherein harmony hath supplanted discord, and the passions of man, having a proper channel, are as rivers to his happiness. O Brothers! dwell ye in such a tabernacle?

HADEES.

The word Hadees is compounded of "a" privative, and "eidoo" to see. Its meaning is "*not seen,*" literally. Schrerelius gives it thus. Hadees; Pluto, Oreus, inferi, mors. These are its meanings in the Classics, The word Orens, though of Latin use, well expresses the meaning of the word Hadees. Orens is State, House, place, or receptacle of the dead. The Greek word Katachthorioi answers well to the Latin inferi. They both signify the persons under the earth. I do not remember a place in either testament where Hedees means Death. There is one portion which I have seen in which the word death occurs, where the word is Hadees in the LXX. But the reading in the LXX is I suppose different from the Hebrew. Job 38, 17. Have the gates of death

been

opened unto thee? or hast thou seen the doors of the shadow of Death. In the last sentence Hadees is in the Greek. But I should read the sentence thus, from the LXX. Have the gates of Death, (thanatou) been opened to thee from fear? or have the keepers of the gates of Hadees been afraid when they saw thee? We have the Greek word Thanatos rendered Death, Taphos a Tomb, mneema and mneemeion a sepulchre, and Hadees, which has been rendered graro, pit Hell. The word properly rendered Hell is Gehenna; that rendered pit is lakkos.

I shall from the above draw the conclusion that Hadees means the place of departed spirits. Its composition given above, forbids us to translate it by the word *grave.* Its meaning I shall also endeavor to ascertain from its use. I remark again, however, that as it denotes something or some place that is not seen, we cannot translate it by the word grave; because the grave is something that is seen; its width, length, breadth and depth are known and seen by men. Hades represents some place the depth of which is unknown; the depth of which is contrasted with the height of heaven. Job. xi, 7, 8, read thus: Canst thou find out the Almighty to perfection? As high as heaven; what canst thou do? deeper than Hadees; what canst thou know? We see; in this instance, Hadees in depth is contrasted with heaven in height. Who would think of contrasting the height of heaven with the depth of a grave or sepulchre, which would not exceed six or ten feet? Hadees is found Isaiah xiv, 9; the prophet is speaking of the king of Babylon: "Hadees from beneath is moved to meet thee at thy coming. It stirreth up the dead for thee, all the chief ones of the earth; it hath raised up from their thrones all the kings of the nations? Hadees here represents the place of the dead where all are assembled. The reader is forced to think of beings with powers of perception. The kings of the nations rise to address him as he descends. They are moved to meet him. No person could think of the dead bodies of the kings of the earth thus moved, and thus speaking to one coming among them. But the following language makes a very clear distinction between the bodies of those kings and the place of the bodies, and their spirits and their place: "All the kings of the nations, all of them be in glory, every one in his own house; but thou art cast out of thy *grave* like an abominable branch." We see here the honorable burial given to the bodies of the other kings; but this king of Babylon is cast out of his grave, or "on the mountains," as the LXX has it. He was not buried at all; but he descended to Hadees, where were all other departed spirits. Again, (verses 14, 15,) the king of Babylon is represented as saying, "I will ascend above the heights of the clouds; I will be like the Most-High." Yet, says the prophet, "thou shalt be brought down to Hadees, to the sides of the pit." For the expression, "sides of the pit," the Greek has "foundations of the earth;" which "foundations of the earth" must be much lower than the grave. But in this place the height of heaven is again contrasted with the depth of Hadees.

Whatever men may be disposed to say respecting the Witch of Endor, the circumstances very clearly are against the idea of Samuel's body's being raised out of the grave. "Bring me *up* Samuel," said Saul. "Why hast thou disquieted me, to bring me up?" are the words of Samuel. We cannot suppose that Saul had any idea of bringing up from the grave the body of Samuel. The whole affair proves clearly that there was something more than body there, brought from some other place than the grave.

The Apostle Paul speaks of being in heaven, on earth, and under earth. The Epouranioi, or heavenly inhabitants, are contrasted with the Katachthorioi, or those under earth. These Katachthorioi are the Inferi of the Latins. Nor will it answer for any one to say that those Katachthorioi are the buried bodies of men; for they are spoken of as being of understanding and perception.

The case of Lazarus and the rich man, is another in point. "The rich man lifted up his eyes in Hadees-"—"He died and was buried." Now, any one knows that he could not lift up his eyes in the grave; nor could his body be tormented. The Savior says that God is able to destroy both soul and body in Gehenna, Hell—not in Hadees. Lazarus was carried by angels to Abraham's bosom.— There' was a gulf between them, that could not be passed. One was comforted, the other tormented. This case shows Hadees to be not only the place of all the dead, but that there is a separation between the dead, the just and unjust. I think that portion in which the rich man was, is the prison of which the Apostle Peter speaks, wherein are confined the souls of the antediluvians, with the souls of all the unjust, until the judgment of the great day.

The Psalmist David said of Christ, that God would not leave his soul in Hadees, nor suffer his flesh to see corruption. The flesh of Christ was in mneimeion, a sepulchre, his soul was in Hadees. That portion of Hadees called Abraham's bosom, was the abode of his spirit during his death. This is too plain to require argument. The distinction which Peter makes between the flesh and the soul of Jesus, presents the case so strikingly, as to leave no room for doubt on the subject. Hadees, then, is demonstrated to be the abode of the spirits of the dead.

Unfortunately for the English reader, the words Hadees and Gehenna have been rendered, by the king's translators, *Hell,* There is a wide distinction; In the 20th of Revelation, we are told that Death and Hell are cast into the lake of fire. We understand that Hell is a lake of fire. Then Hell is cast into Hell. But Hadees is cast into the lake of fire. Here the place containing the dead, is put for the dead whom it contains—a very common figure of speech. In Rev. vi, a pale horse is seen; Death sits on him, and Hell (Hadees) follows. How very fit the representation! Death kills the bodies of men, and Hadees, the place of the departed spirits, is represented as following, as if in readiness to receive them as soon as they have put off their mortal tabernacles.

Thou Capernaum, which art exalted to heaven, shalt be thrust down to Hadees. Here the contrast again takes place. The expression is figurative here, as in Isaiah xiv, 14, 15. Let every one know, however, that figures are borrowed from literal things. Heaven is very high; Hadees is very deep: though Capernaum had been exalted very high, it should be brought down very low.

The word abyss is sometimes used in the sense of Hadees. Romans x: "Say not in thy heart, Who shall ascend into heaven? (that is, to bring Christ down) or, who shall descend into the deep? (Greek, abyss) (that is, to bring Christ again from the dead.) Now, to speak of the grave as the abyss, is without example. The word abyss is also applied to the ocean, as being of unknown depth.

I remark on the word Hadees, that it is never used to signify many places, but one place, the place or receptacle of the dead. There may be innumerable mneemata, (sepulchres,) taphoi, (tombs,) but only one Hadees. I have heard it said that the Jews learned their ideas about Hadees from the Chaldeans, during their captivity. This I think without foundation; for we see the word used by the patriarchs, by Moses, and the prophets. Whence the idea originated, I am not able to say, unless we conclude it was a matter made known by him who alone could have a knowledge of it. I think that man could hardly have originated the idea. The Latins and Greeks have, I think, borrowed it from the Scriptures, and added much to it. Why the spirits of the dead should be supposed to be under the earth, I know not. This idea does not, however, constitute an objection to the idea of such a place as Hadees. Because we are not able to give an account of the locality, we should not therefore reject the idea of such a place. I am persuaded, that if a man should be called on to say where what we now call heaven is, he would be as much puzzled for its locality as any one would be for the locality of Hadees. No one thinks of rejecting the idea of heaven because of this difficulty. Let each one act thus with respect to this subject. These remarks must suffice for the present.

HENRY T. ANDERSON.

EXTRACT OF A LETTER FROM T. CAMPBELL.

To the Editors of the Christian Review:

The following is an extract from a reply to a letter addressed to Brother T. Campbell, in regard to praying for the Holy Spirit. Believing its contents would be read with interest, and profit, by many, I have procured the consent of the writer for its publication.   R.

"Into what were you baptized? Was it not into Christ? Gal. 3, 27. Into one body? Cor. 12, 13. And if so, are we not divinely authorized to pray for the enjoyment of the Holy Spirit of promise. See Luke, 11, 13. And does not the Apostle pray most earnestly for the believing Ephesians, "that they might be strengthened with all might by the Spirit." Eph. 3, 14, 21. Indeed, without his indwelling presence, and influence, we can do nothing spiritually good; so that "if any man have not the Spirit of Christ, he is none of his;" and it is only as many as are led by the Spirit of God, that are his acknowledged children. Rom. 8, 9, 14. Therefore we are baptized, into the name of the Holy Spirit, as well as of the Father, and of the Son. For as our baptism is, on our part, the divinely appointed act of confessing our belief of the Gospel; soon the part of Heaven, it is the divinely appointed means of acknowledging our new relation to the Father, as our Father;—to the Son, as our Redeemer;—to the Holy Spirit, as our sanctifier. So that our adoption into the family of God;—our redemption by the blood of Christ;—and our sanctification by the Holy Spirit, are signified and sealed to us in our baptism. Thus by one Spirit are we all baptized into one family; and so become sons and daughters of the Lord Almighty:—into one Body of Christ; and so become Christians:—into one Holy Spirit; and so become Saints; that is holy persons. For we have all been made to drink into one Spirit. 1 Cor. 12, 13. And are thus made partakers of the love of the Father, of the grace of the Son, and of the fellowship of the Holy Spirit.

Now this is the very Gospel, the good news, into which we are scripturally baptized, if so be the Gospel is duly exhibited and realized. For it was the love of the Father that sent the Son to seek and to save the lost. John 3, 16. And it was the love of Christ, which passes knowledge, that induced him to give himself for us, that he might redeem us from all iniquity, and purify to himself a peculiar people, zealous of good works." Eph. 3, 19. Titus, 2, 14. And it is this love of God, and of Christ, shed abroad in our hearts by the Holy Spirit, that fills our souls with the blissful assurance of sin-pardoning mercy, and sanctifying grace. Rom. 5, 5. Thus causing us to rejoice in hope of the glory of God. For which blissful purpose the Apostle ceased not to pray for the believing Ephesians, "That the God of our Lord Jesus Christ the Father of glory, would give them the Spirit of wisdom and revelation in the. knowledge of him, &c. Eph. 1, 16, 17.

Now, surely, the divine declarations, invitations, and promises; and the recorded prayers of our Lord and his Apostles for his people, are our directory, to teach us for what we ought to pray. And also, that what we truly desire and ask, we should ask in faith, not doubting the divine goodness or veracity; having the blissful assurance, "That if we ask anything according to his will, he heareth us," and, if so, "that we have (granted) the petitions, that we desired of him." Consequently, that we shall surely receive them;—that they shall be accomplished. See 1 John, 5, 14, 15. We would just observe here, that as many of the things for which we are authorized to pray, stand connected with the use of certain means, we ought, therefore, in all such cases, never to neglect the proper use of the appointed means, "knowing that our labour shall not be in vain in the Lord;" "For without faith it is impossible to please God."

Upon the whole, "Salvation is of the Lord." "We are all by nature "dead in trespasses and sins." "There is none righteous, no, not one." But God, who is rich in mercy, for the great love wherewith he loved us in this wretched, guilty, perishing condition, hath quickened us together with Christ, and hath raised us up together, and made us sit together in heavenly places in Christ Jesus. For by grace are we saved by faith, and that salvation not of ourselves, it is the gift of God; not of works, lest any man should boast. For we are his workmanship, created anew in Christ 'Jesus to good works, which God hath before ordained, that we should walk in them. Eph. 2, 1, 9.

Now, these Gospel declarations are the sole and adequate foundation of the believer's confidence, and blissful hope of an inheritance, incorruptible, undefiled, and unfading, reserved in heaven for all such characters, who are kept by the power of God through faith, unto a salvation, ready to be revealed in the last time. 1 Pet. 1, 2, 5. Paul in like manner addressed the believing Philippians, See, chap. I, 6. "Being confident of this very thing, that he, who has begun a good work in you, will perform it till the day of Christ." Thus, the believer's confidence is divinely sustained by the divine immutability. See Rom. 8,28 -39.

Having then, dear Brother, such a foundation of confidence, the believer of the blessed Gospel has nothing to fear, in the due use of the divinely appointed means of enjoyment. "For every one that asketh, receiveth;—our heavenly Father giveth the Holy Spirit to them that ask him." Are we then convinced of the heinous nature, ruinous effects, and terrible consequences of sin, so as to be sincerely desirous to be delivered from the love and practice of it? And have we been led by the Gospel, to look to, and to rely upon, the blood and Spirit of Christ for deliverance from the guilt and practice of it?—To the former for our justification:—to the latter for our sanctification. If so, we are authorized to believe, that He who has begun this good work in   us,   will   enable   us   to perfect it. May the good Lord enable us so to do."   THOMAS CAMPBELL

JAMESTOWN, OHIO, 1st SEPT., 1844.

Herewith you have Eld. Thomas Campbell, on praying for the Spirit.

I should like to know whether it be not skeptical to pray for that which we have already received? Did any who received the Spirit, in ancient times, pray for it afterwards. The promise of the Spirit to the Apostles was on this wise. "He shall abide with you forever." Would it not be as rational for a man who had received remission of Sins, to ask God to forgive him a second time, as for one who had received the Spirit to ask for it again, and again?   W.

EDUCATION.

To talk of reforming society by merely preaching the Gospel, and baptizing believers into Christ, is futile in the extreme. The mass of professors of religion are as anxious for the wealth, glitter and honor of the world as those who openly avow infidelity. The young are generally devoted to dress, gaiety and the fashionable amusements of the country, still they *"break the loaf"* on Lord's day, and "hear preaching" with the impression they are heaven-bound.

The evils in religious society are too many for enumeration, and too enormous to mention— Will religion as now practiced insure the joys of heaven? What shall be done? The secret consists in reforming the Education of the times. I do not mean, a change with teachers, or some minor improvements for the young while at school. Society—old and young must be educated— To accomplish this. Physical, Intellectual and Moral training must become the daily pursuits of society. No system of education or religion can reform or permanently improve society unless industry—daily labor, is made the basis. This is God's order, and education and religion must fail in any organization of society where this plan of Heaven is not regarded. A community of people who will live economically, and cooperate to each other's advantage, can make bountiful supplies for themselves, have to give to the needy, and grow rich by a few hours daily, and well directed labor. Another portion of time should be devoted by old and young to the cultivation of the mind. From four to six hours might, and should be given, every day to the study of science, languages, history and the acquisition of all useful knowledge. Old and young should also spend a few hours daily in religious science and exercises.—Where, at this day, is an industrious, intelligent and pious church of God? Who will answer this question, or tell how such society can be formed? There are truly intelligent and pious individuals, but for want of organization, their efforts are but feeble, and their influence is circumscribed.

T. F.

FEMALE EDUCATION.

Glad I am to see that Bro. W. S. SPEER has taken a wife as every young man should do, and that he and his "sister wife" intend to devote themselves to the training of young Ladies. Sister

S. was a diligent pupil of the writer several years, and I hope success will attend this laudable undertaking.   T. F.

EXPLANATION OF EPHESIANS II—8.

" For by grace are ye saved, through faith; and that not of yourselves, it is the gift of God. "

To what does the adjective pronoun *that* refer in this passage? This question has been answered three ways: 1, to Grace; 2, to Faith; 3, to Salvation, (included in the verb saved.)

The last is unquestionably the correct answer. I support it in two ways: 1st, the analogy of the English language; 2dly, the gender of the pronoun in the original.

1. The analogy of the English language. "He collected a hundred dollars, and *that* after much trouble." What does *that* refer to here? To dollars? No; to the action of collecting. Again, take a passage from the Bible; turn to 1 Cor., vi, 6: "But brother goeth to law with brother, and *that* before the unbelievers." To what does *that* refer in this verse? To the action or process of going to law.

2. The gender of the original pronoun. If the foregoing is not satisfactory, what I am about to offer will settle the matter beyond the possibility of contradiction.

The original for *grace* is *char is,* placed here in the dative, *chariti,* a noun in the feminine. The word for faith is pistes, placed here in the genitive, *pisteoos,* also feminine. Now, it appears that the original for this little word *that,* about which there has been so much controversy, is *touto,* neuter! Is there any law for a pronoun in the neuter referring to a noun in the feminine? But can *touto,* upon strict rule, refer to salvation? Yes. Turn to the Greek lexicon, and you will find *sootaerion* (salvation) neuter.

But, to lay aside the grammatical criticism on this passage, let me ask the friends who resort to it in order to sustain their doctrine of mystical spiritual influence, a question or two. Let us admit that faith is the gift of God—how does God give it? How does he confer all his favors on man, in nature and in grace? He gives him food and clothing. Does he prepare his diet for him and then open his mouth for its reception? Does he prepare the cloth and put it on his back? It would be an insult to the meanest mind, to give an answer to such queries.

Dear reader, has not a kind and indulgent God adapted himself to man in the system of grace, upon as rational principles as he has in the system of nature? Has he not sent his son in order that man might live? And did not the blessed Savior present himself to the world lying in sin, as the great object of faith? Did not the Apostles proclaim the crucified, buried and arisen Son of God as the only being by whom salvation could be secured? Yes, they did. And what was necessary on the part of man? I answer, briefly, *Faith* and *obedience* of the Gospel. But how comes Faith? *Faith comes* by *hearing,* and *hearing by the word of God.* Now, all this is in truth the gift of God. He has given us minds capable of understanding his holy word—minds capable of appreciating the value of eternal truth—capacities for hearing the word, believing it, and obeying it; and if we sit still and expect God to infuse faith into us by an immediate agency of his Holy Spirit, we are just as unreasonable as the man would be to stand still naked and hungry in the open air, and cry out to God to feed and clothe him.

He that hath ears to hear, let him hear.   W. J. B.

TO YOUNG LADIES.

I promised to address you on the Gospel of the Son of God—given for the salvation of a dying world. Paul in a few short sentences presents its leading principles. Moreover, brethren, he says, I declare unto you the Gospel, by which you are *saved,* if you keep in memory what I preached to you. I delivered unto you, first of all, that Christ died for our sins, according to the Scriptures; secondly, that he was buried; and thirdly, that he rose from the grave, according to the Scriptures. To prove his assertion, he adds, that he was seen of Cephas, then of the twelve, then *of five* hundred brethren at once, of whom the greater part remain unto the present, but some are fallen asleep. These few items contain the Gospel, by which Paul says you are to be saved.

Matthew, Mark, Luke and John are more diffuse. They give not only the facts aforementioned, but also a minute account of his life. You ask how this Gospel is to save you? You will find information on this subject by reading the directions given before the ascension of the Lord. To his disciples he says, "Go ye into all the world, and preach the *Gospel* to every creature: he that believeth and is baptized shall be saved, but he that believeth not shall be damned." Luke tells, that repentance and remission of sins should be preached in his name, beginning at Jerusalem. Have you ever noticed in what part of the Bible this beginning is recorded? Read through the 2nd chapter of Acts. Pardon of sins through a crucified Redeemer, is there for the first time set forth for the acceptance of the human family. Peter is the man authorized to proclaim it, and in the majesty of one commissioned from on high, he stands forth and announces that Christ had died, was buried, and had risen from the dead to save the world. At first you see that his hearers are mocking and deriding him; but as he progresses in his discourse, he convinces them not only that Jesus died, but that they were his murderers. He produces in their mind a strong faith that these things are so, and as proof of it, they cry out to know what they must do. It is not necessary here to give you his answer, but will only enquire what caused so great a change in their conduct? You will not hesitate to reply, that it was their faith. You know if they had not believed, nothing he said Would have had any effect. We will then first talk a little about faith. In order better to understand it, we ask your definition of faith. Any of you will say, faith simply means belief, I have faith in my mother, when I believe that she in all cases speaks the truth. When she affirms any thing, I believe it.— Just so, and it is exactly the same exercise of the mind when you believe that God speaks the truth to you. If we ask how faith in God comes, Paul answers that faith comes by hearing, and hearing by the word of God. If this be true, is it correct for you to PRAY for faith? You have heard there is such a place as Paris, or London; you don't pray to believe it, I imagine. No, in this case you exercise good common sense. Your faith rests upon testimony—testimony that cannot be contradicted. It did not come from praying, then it came from hearing, and hearing from the word of man. Now, you can receive and possess unshaken faith in the word of your fellow creatures; but when the word of Heaven is presented for your belief you say, Lord give me faith, make me believe. Is it not equivalent to saying, Lord, I have not confidence in the truth of thy word, make me believe it? You may offer this prayer until the loud clangor of the last trump bursts upon an astonished and God-forgetting world, and it will never be answered. God has not promised to *make* you believe his word. He has given you the New Testament, containing the history of the Saviour, who lived, died, and rose again for your salvation. He has given you intellect to comprehend it; and if you wish to have faith in this Saviour, you have to study its sacred pages, and learn of his love, his wondrous power, his sorrows and sufferings. When you understand and believe what is there recorded, you have all the faith a mortal can have. The first four books are given to make you penitent believers. You see then faith, as Paul tells you, comes by hearing, and hearing by the word of God. Never insult the throne of Heaven by praying to believe his word, as though it were not worthy of all confidence. We will go farther, and see what was next commanded the Jews, after they had faith. In hopes you will study the word of life,

I remain your friend,   LUCY

FRANKLIN COLLEGE.

The land, dwelling houses, &c., connected with Franklin College, has cost from 12 to 15 thousand dollars, and the College buildings will cost from six to eight thousand dollars; making in all, at least twenty thousand dollars. To the amount of fifteen thousand dollars has been raised by two individuals, but there is a deficiency to complete the building of five thousand dollars—perhaps more. Of this amount about fifteen hundred dollars has been subscribed by the friends of learning, and one thousand has been taken in stock; but yet we lack from three to four thousand dollars to complete the improvements. This amount has to be paid January 1845, and January 1846, and I can scarcely conclude the public will not this debt hang over an Institution which of all others in the country promises most benefits to the rising generation. Subscriptions at the times specified would be gladly received. But we have the most favorable proposition over made to present. To any one who will pay to the Treasurer of Franklin College ONE THOUSAND DOLLARS, the Trustees will grant the privilege of sending one Student forever free of cost for boarding and tuition, and to make the investment sure, a lien will be given on real estate. To any one who will give five hundred dollars the privilege will be granted of sending a Student forever free of cost for tuition fees. A less amount may be owned as stock, or given as a donation. One Methodist gentleman has taken a scholarship at a thousand dollars, and I appeal to the friends of knowledge, while I affirm this is the best investment a man can make for his family, his relatives or for posterity. Who will do likewise?

T. FANNING, *Agent.*

"CO-OPERATION MEETINGS'."

The readers of the REVIEW no doubt have observed that a Co-operation meeting has been appointed by Bro. W. S. Speer at Friendship, Williamson County, embracing the 3d Lords' day in Sept, and another has been appointed at Cripple Creek, Rutherford Co. for the 4th Lords' day in Sept. In reference to those meetings, I am not prepared to say which will prove the co-operating assembly, but as brethren have promised to attend both, I hope each will go on, and the brethren will exert themselves to the utmost of their ability to advance the Redeemer's Kingdom.   T. F.

FUNDAMENTAL ERRORS.

To the Editors of the Christian Review:

We have heard much in our day of fundamental truths, essential truths, &c. But are there no fundamental errors? We will specify two or three.

1. The Pharisean Scribes taught the Jews to expect that their Messiah would be a Martial Deliverer, who would come riding upon the clouds of heaven, with power and great glory, and who would break the Roman yoke from off their necks, and who would lead them to conquest, to feasting, to merriment, to sensuality and universal monarchy, and that Jerusalem would be the metropolis of this splendid monarchy, and that all the Jews would share in its blessings. This one fundamental error was the rock of offence—the stone of stumbling against which their vessel stove and sunk to rise no more. The whole institution of Moses, all the prophets, and the Psalms, taught a different doctrine, taught that the Messias must suffer, that he must be low, despised and rejected of men—Isaiah 53. He must be led as a sheep to the slaughter—see Psalm 22, and all the Psalms. See Luke 24th chap., Daniel 9th chap. This one error proved the ruin of that nation, of their eternal overthrow, in despite of all that their own Moses, the Prophets and Psalms—in despite of all the miracles and sermons of our Saviour and the Apostles, they crucified him and his Apostles. Miracles will not remove prejudice. This prejudice was *their unpardonable* sin. Their traditions nullified and rendered powerless the law and the prophets. Let Christians beware that they do not shipwreck on the same rock.

A second fundamental error. The whole Catholic institution is built upon one *religious lie*— the misinterpretation and perversion of one single passage of Scripture,—Thou art Peter, thou art Prince of the Apostles—thou art the vicegerent of Christ, I will build my church on you, Peter,—we are your successors. This is the cage of unclean priests,—the tap-root of the Papacy, —the den of those hissing and poisonous vipers,—the mint of the Papal wealth, the golden mine of all her glory, the perennial fountain of all her corruptions. This assumption is contrary to Scripture, history and fact.

Saint Peter sat by the celestial gate. His keys were rusty, and the lock was dull, so little trouble had been given of late; not that the place was by any means full, but since the Gallic era, "eighty-eight," the devil had taken a longer, stronger pull, and a "pull all together," as they say at sea—-which drew most souls another way. What arithmetician on earth or angel in heaven can calculate the evil, mischief and ruin that has accrued to the world during the last twelve centuries, by the belief of this one lie? Who can tell how many souls will suffer the vengeance of eternal fire through all the countless ages of eternity, by believing this lie? The effect of that Jewish delusion clings to them to this day, and will while time endures hang upon them like an incubus; and so will this other fundamental Catholic error remain while there are hearts susceptible of error as well as of truth. Both these errors originated with men, and have been propagated by men, and both for the sake of present advantages. The spirit of God did not originate these errors.

Having named the Jewish and Catholic fundamental error, let me name one or two Protestant errors. First, the idea of man's being mystically regenerated before faith in order to faith, without knowledge, without the use of any of his rational powers—without this regeneration or revelation, he cannot read, hear, believe, nor act understandingly. What mischief and ruin has this one Protestant the effected! How many worthy and fine men and women have been deprived of the benefits and enjoyments of Christianity in this life, and have died in their sins, under its influence, during the three last centuries—who can tell? This is the foundation of corrupt Protestantism—of all Protestant sectarianism. Many, very many are now living under its blasting influence, who are under sectarian influence, and beyond our reach. This do-nothing system, waiting for grace to fall upon them as dew and rain fall from the heavens, and as the Lord rained manna upon the Jews—this law-making, or putting the finishing hand to God's work, is another capital error—one of the first magnitude. I might have stated that the devil ruined our race by one lie—he first spiritualized the Scriptures—he substituted his word in the place of God's—he put a lie in the place of truth. O Lord, banish and consume all these lies from the earth!   J. CREATH, JR.

ELDER AND BISHOP SYNONYMOUS.

LIBERTY MEETING HOUSE, JACKSON CO., ALA.,
JULY, 1844.

BRO FANNING:—In your last No. of the Review, you say, "Who will undertake to prove that Elder and Bishop are synonymous?" I do not, by any means, think myself qualified to give you instruction on this grave subject; but allow me to present a few words for your consideration, touching this question—will you hear me?

I am not going to try to make it appear that Elder and Bishop are synonymous in their usage, in Scripture, at all times; but I do think it certainly is obvious to any close observer, that they sometimes signify the same. For a proof of this, let's notice Paul's letter to Titus, 1st chapter, including the 5th, 6th, and 7th verses. Says Paul: "For this cause left I thee in Crete, that thou shouldest set in order the things that are wanting, and ordain Elders in every city, as I had appointed thee. If any be blameless, the husband of one wife, having faithful children, not accused of riot, or unruly. For a Bishop must be blameless, as the steward of God; not self-willed, not soon angry, not given to wine, no striker, not greedy of filthy lucre," &c. Now, if Elder in this case signifies "old members of the church," what does the word ordain mean, or for what purpose is it used? Inasmuch as the word ordain means to appoint, to what I ask, were they appointed, but to the duties of the office? Now, Bro. Fanning, you too well know, that Bishop, in the foregoing example, could be substituted for Elder, without violating any good rule, to entertain one single doubt about the matter. Then it reads, or should read, thus, "and ordain Bishops in every city," &.c.

1 know quite well, that there can be, and are, many old members in churches who are not Bishops, though Elders or Seniors, and I know just as well, that it is impossible to have gospel qualified Bishops, without said Bishops being Elders or old members of the church; but all this does not, by any means, prove that Elder and Bishop are not synonymous, sometimes at least. Then, if they can be substituted one for the other, why not "talk about the Elder's office"? This is an important subject, and I feel my inability.

Yours in hope,   W. B. RANDOLPH.

REMARKS—The term Elder is an adjective, or descriptive, and is employed to designate a qualification. Elders, or Seniors, could be ordained or set apart to be Bishops; but how one can be ordained to be an *old man,* I cannot so well understand. To supply Bishop for Elder, makes nonsense of the whole subject. To talk of ordaining a Bishop to the Bishop's office, is extremely preposterous. We might call a lawyer a judge, but to say therefore the terms are similar, is childish; and it is right to say Bishops are Elders, but then to affirm the terms are of the same import, is confounding the different

parts of the Bible.
　　Read again.

 The Value of the Bible.

THE VALUE OF THE BIBLE.

Suppose a person, compelled to quit a foreign Country, were invited to return home to receive a large possession which his father had promised him. Suppose he were entirely unacquainted with the road he had to go, but knew that it was often rugged, difficult and dangerous; that there were also many false guides to mislead him, and many enemies to encounter; and that thus he would be exposed to the loss not only of his promised possession, but of every thing he had and even of life itself; what would be such a person's first enquiry? where can I get a sure direction? Is there any one who will defend me from my enemies? With what delight he would hear, "your Father has given you a plain, full and particular direction, and an all-sufficient Protector." How diligently he would look at this direction as he went along, and how entirely he would trust his Protector!

Gentle reader, this journey is the Christian's life: God is his Father; Heaven is his home; eternal Bliss is the promised possession; Christ is the all-sufficient Protector, the Captain of our Salvation, who has himself gone the road, and conquered every enemy, and who now guards and defends as many as commit themselves to him; and *the Bible* affords a sure direction to Heaven and everlasting bliss. "The testimony of the Lord IS *Sure,* making wise the simple."

By means of the Bible, God himself condescends to direct your path. In all important points, it is *so plain.,* that "he who runs may read." It is also *so full and particular,* that you will find in it something adapted to remove your most perplexing doubts, and to guide you aright in your greatest difficulties. Its fullness speaks its divine Author.

Some, perhaps, may say, how am I to know that the Bible is *true?* I will tell you how. Bad men could not write a book so plainly condemning all sin. Good men would not have deceived mankind by pretending that an invention of their own was a divine revelation, especially when they were likely to get nothing by this deception but reproach, imprisonment, torture and death. Its doctrines and precepts are evidently superior to all human wisdom. It gives you an account of various *miracles* which were wrought in the midst of vast multitudes. There are also various *prophecies* in the Bible, such as those respecting the fall of Babylon, the dispersion of the Jews, and the appearance of the Messiah. These, and many others, are all well known to have been written long before the events which they relate could have taken place; and their manifest accomplishment is abundantly sufficient to satisfy every sincere enquirer respecting the truth of the Bible. These evidences have convinced good and wise men, in all ages, that *it is true.*

But the Bible is not only true—it contains a revelation of the will of God.— It is expressly declared, that "all Scripture is given by inspiration of God." "Holy men of God spake as they were moved by the Holy Spirit." By inspiration is here meant, "such an immediate and complete discovery to the minds of the sacred writers, by the Holy Spirit, of those things which could not otherwise have been known, and such an effectual superintendence as to those matters which they might be informed of by other means, as entirely to preserve them from all error in every particular which could in the least effect any of the doctrines or commandments contained in their writings."

As all men have sinned, the Bible is above every thing valuable, since it is addressed to sinners, and discovers to us the person, character, and offices of Christ the Saviour. It is this discovery which throws a peculiar splendor on the pages of the Bible. That important question, What must I do to he saved? is here alone satisfactorily answered. Forgiveness of sin, through the name of Jesus Christ, reconciliation with God, peace of mind, and a solid ground for the Hope of immortality and eternal life, are clearly set before us in the Scriptures, and freely offered to our acceptance, through the mediation of a Savior.

Finally, the Bible is the only unerring standard of religious truth, the source of all religious knowledge. It has "God for its author, Salvation for its end, and Truth without mixture of Error for its contents."   BICKERSTETH.

TO THE READERS OF THE REVIEW.

The present No. is the last but two of the first Volume of the REVIEW, and we take this occasion to return our grateful thanks to many friends for their kindness in circulating our work, and we wish to remind our readers, that the Publishers in establishing the REVIEW, incurred considerable expense in purchasing new Type and Press, and again call upon every Subscriber we have, to use her or his influence in its further circulation. We have a considerable lot of Back Numbers to send to each new subscriber, and we most respectfully ask our friends to send in their orders for them, as fast as possible, at only $1 per Volume. Calling upon our Teaching Brethren, and Evangelists to use their exertions in their several meetings, to procure new Subscribers. Will you rally to our aid, and give the REVIEW an extensive and wide circulation. Please take these matters into serious consideration, as we wish to promote your interest, by placing the work in the family of every neighbor we have in the South West.

Those of our readers who wish the REVIEW for 1845, would do well to send in their Dollar, before the close of the year—as our terms are cash in advance. We earnestly entreat our brethren to solicit subscribers.

THE AGRICULTURIST ALMANAC, FOR 1845.

The above ALMANAC, highly illustrated with Engravings, and containing much valuable and interesting matter for the Farmer, Gardener and Poultry Raiser, can be found for sale at the Agriculturist Office, the Bookstores and several other places in our City. Having been highly complimented by many of our Editorial friends and neighbors, we respectfully ask the encouragement of the public. To Country Merchants we give a fair opportunity of freely circulating the above work, having put them down at a low price.

CITY BOOKSTORE, NASHVILLE.

We take the present opportunity of saying to the readers of the Review, that should they wish to purchase Books, Stationery, &c. the present season, to call on MESSRS. BEERY & TANNEHILL, of this City, where any amount of Law, Theological, Miscellaneous. School and Blank Books, can be procured at the shortest notice; with a large and splendid assortment of new and rare works daily expected. We earnestly request our friends to give them a call, knowing, every possible exertion will be made to render entire satisfaction.

INTERESTING.—TO receive a communication of three pages of manuscript for the Review, and have to pay 50 cts. Postage.

ON THE DEATH OF A. Q. CRIHFIELD.

I ask'd the winds that around me blew,
    The zephyrs and breezes and storms,
If aught of a land of bliss they knew,
    Where sickness nor sorrow alarms?
        The zephyrs fainted, the breezes sigh'd.
    The storms, in the grandeur of wo,
        As passing the circuit of earth, replied,
    "No! mortal disconsolate, No!"

I ask'd the moon, whose pale teary face
    Shone darkling, night's sister and queen;
1 ask'd all the stars to point the place.
    If aught of that land they had seen?
        The moon beam'd dubious in tears of blood,
    And shed her dim mantle below,
        And stars that encircle the throne of God
    Said, *"Mortal disconsolate, No!"*

I ask'd the sun, as he rose at morn,
    I ask'd him at noon and at ev'n,
If those his bright beams a land adorn
    Where rest to the weary is giv'n?
        He veil'd his visage while Jesus died,
    And gave dying mortals to .know,
        He claimed not the glory, and, veil'd replied,
    "No! mortal disconsolate, No!"

I ask'd the earth if an isle she own'd,
    In Eastern or Western domain,
Where man in his majesty enthron'd
    Reigns monarch of death and of pain?
        I heard her answer in sighs and tears,
    In anguish and travail and wo,
        As heavily rolled her ling'ring years, .
    "No! mortal disconsolate, No!"

I ask'd Philosophy if she knew
    Where those happy regions appear.
What portals we enter, who bears us through,
    Or what is to hope or to fear?
        She hung her head and her doubts express'd.
    Nor farther than doubting could go,
        Then lifting her dreamy eyes confessed,
    "No! mortal disconsolate, No!"

I ask'd the BIBLE if IT could tell,
    Or teach me the way to the place?
And all the great works of Immanuel
    In peace to my soul answered "YES!"
        "I am the Way, and the Truth, the Life,"
    Said JESUS, almighty to save:
        Farewell, then, vain world of sin and strife,
    I'LL ENTER THAT LAND THROUGH THE GRAVE!

NASHVILLE BOOKSTORE, COLLEGE STREET.

We would call the attention of our readers to the above Establishment of Messrs. EICHBAUM de SMITH, where they keep constantly on hand a large and varied stock of Law, Medical, Religious, School, Miscellaneous and Blank Books, of all descriptions, and should our friends wish to procure the writings of A. Campbell, they can easily do by calling at the above concern. Will our friends give them a call, assuring them all satisfaction will be rendered.

NEWS FROM THE CHURCHES.

ROUND LICK, SEPT. 11, 1844.

DEAR BROTHER FANNING:—Last month I performed a tour in the hill country of Tennessee, through the counties of Overton and Jackson. We have many more churches and brethren in those counties than I was aware of. In the month of July, I was informed that the brethren at Livingston had requested me to visit them. Being unacquainted with any one of them, I addressed a letter "To the Church of God at Livingston, Overton county, Ten." When I arrived, I learned that the Post Master, a *Baptist* brother, had delivered the letter to our brethren! Meeting commenced at Livingston Friday night before the second Lord's day, and continued till Tuesday night. I soon became acquainted with many interesting brethren, and citizens of this pleasant village and its vicinity. Brother Clarke of Kentucky had labored here some eighteen months previous, with much success, and will long be remembered by many won to the truth by his preaching. The church numbers about 50. The Elders are brethren Grace, Cash and Allen. Six members were added during my stay. This church, as most others, has had some severe trials, but is in a tolerably prosperous condition. According to the information I received, there are eight churches in the county, numbering, upon an average, about 70 members, making, in all, about 560. I had the pleasure of forming an acquaintance with several preaching brethren. Brethren Louis Stover, Willis Huddleston, Nathaniel Fisk, Wm. Stewart, Allen Scott, Jesse Sewell, Stokely Huddleston, Louis Stover jr., John Hill, and Levy Morgan, live in Overton. I had the pleasure of hearing Father Stover and Brother Fisk.

From Livingston I traveled north to Obed's Rivet, thence down the river to the Cumberland, thence down the Cumberland, through Jackson county, to Bagdad. In Jackson, I was informed, there are 9 churches, averaging about 100 members, making about 900; making in the two counties about 1500. I held four protracted meetings in these counties. The last meeting was held near Fort Blunt, by Brother John N. Mulkey and myself. Bro. Mulkey is a son of Father John Mulkey; who is still living to see the fruits of many years labor. Brother Newton is an interesting and very efficient evangelist. By his zealous and persevering efforts some 60 additions have been made to the churches in Jackson, during the two last months. I had the pleasure of spending about one week with him, during which time we had some 15 additions. I left him in the midst of a very interesting meeting, which, I have since been informed, resulted in the conversion of many persons. Overton and Jackson constitute an interesting and very important Held for Evangelical labors, and much good might be done by experienced and competent workmen. The brethren, though in moderate circumstances, are liberal, and would, no doubt, sustain an able Evangelist. Brothers Stover, Fisk and others of Overton, are able and most excellent Teachers; but age, infirmity and the care of families, prevent them from devoting as much time as is necessary to carry on the good cause. The brethren are anxious to receive the assistance of those who labor in word and doctrine. Some thirty accessions to the truth, was the result of my tour.— "The Bible, the whole Bible, and nothing else but the Bible," is triumphing gloriously. Baptists, Methodists and Presbyterians, are giving up their traditions, and uniting with us on the old foundation, inconsiderable numbers, in different sections. During my visit to the hill country, one Presbyterian, four Methodists, and two *Baptist Families,* were redeemed in Cannon county, Brother Jones and others held a protracted meeting on Brawley's Fork, which resulted in the conversion of 38 persons, among whom were several Presbyterians, Baptists, and Methodists. I am now on a tour of protracted meetings in Wilson county. Last Friday night about ten o'clock, I buried one Presbyterian gentleman in the waters of Smith's Fork. His wife was a Baptist, but with her husband took up the line of march out of Babylon. Let us thank God and take courage. The weapons of our holy warfare are spiritual—the truth, the whole truth, and nothing but the truth—but mighty through God to the pulling down of party strong holds. The signs of the times are favorable—never more so. Last Monday Mrs. Johnson, of Alexandria, a Presbyterian lady, was baptized according to the ancient pattern Shown in Mount Sion. On to-morrow a protracted meeting (if the Lord will) will commence at Bethlehem, in this county (Wilson), where we had last fall between 70 and 80 conversions at one meeting. Since that time the brethren have built a large frame meeting house, recently finished, and now ready to be occupied as the Lord's house. I hope we will have a good meeting.

Since writing the above, the meeting was held at Bethlehem, and resulted in the conversion of 21 persons. Brethren S. E. Jones, White, Dill, and myself, were the laborers.

In the lively hope,   J. J. TROTT.

BRO. "REVIEW:"—Tell the brethren, that Brothers Dean, Curtis, and myself have just closed a protracted meeting at Sand Creek, 16 miles of Columbus. Eleven united; two from the Baptist Church, and of her brightest ornaments— one, a standard work, sister Skinner, from the Methodist. Brother Campbell's exposure of the corruptions and humanisms of this society, together with her own internal feuds, and broils, and divisions, are paralyzing their influence.— Methodism has had its day in this government, and is destined to sleep with its fathers, in the sepulchres of forgetfulness.

The good old Baptists are coming to their "second sober thought." The recent debate between Messrs. Campbell and Rice is achieving more for the good cause of Messiah than all anterior efforts in this reformation. It will give an impulse to truth, whose fluttering agitations will not cease until Zion becomes convalescent. The Literati of my acquaintance understand the conundrum policy of Mr. R.; but it is too late in the intellectual day for such quibbles upon subjects of such magnitude as those debated. It seems difficult, with some, to class and locate Mr. R.'s powers. Some think he would have made a first rate second rate "limb of the civil law;" others think him altogether unqualified for the sacred functions of the pulpit, because of the deep bias of his mind, produced by a too long scholastic, Calvinian race o'er the turf of Westminster; others, that his mind is not sufficiently balanced for a successful logician; and others, that he would have appeared to much better advantage had he not been so unequally yoked. I opine that there are but few who believe that he is near the equal of McCalla. But, in my judgment, his *greatest* opponent was Divine Truth. Who can successfully, combat divine truth. A man of Brother Campbell's gigantic mind and unrivaled skill in debate, and of his ripe age and experience, together with an inexhaustible fund of Biblical knowledge, connected with general literature and a methodically systematized mind, and above and still better than all, Almighty

Truth on his side, must, must win

and conquer, when the issue is between truth and error.

The Disciples of Christ, or the Christian Churches, in this section, are onward in their efforts for comfortable preaching houses. There are three or four within a short distance of Columbus going up. Praise to the brethren and liberal hearted friends.

All that is wanting here, to roll the car of gospel victory through the land, is sacrifice—sacrifice of world, time, effort—to contribute our substance, and time, and effort, and then to live out Christ in our families and neighborhoods, Church and state, is to triumph-over error, sectarian opposition, this world, the flesh and the devil, the grave, its gloom—over doubts, trials, troubles, afflictions, persecutions.

HINT. If you have any energetic men, who wish to labor for the cause of Christ and do extensive good, tell them that North Mississippi is a goodly land. The soil is fertile, the clime salubrious, rivers navigable, country densely populated—and that too by a warm-hearted, enterprising and highly intelligent people. Come and cast your destiny among us; we will do thee good, and not harm. Will Brother JOHN M. BARNES visit us? There are many here who are anxious to hear his voice on the theme of Jesus Christ and the resurrection.

In hope of eternal life, JAS. A. BUTLER.

LITTLE ROCK, 24th Aug., 1844.

BROTHER FANNING—DEAR SIR:—I have waited long for a fair breeze to set out for the columns of the Review; but as yet nothing favorable has offered. Left this place on the 5th July,. on a tour to Louisiana, to preach and attend what is called a co-operation meeting. In Claiborn Parish, La., we met on Thursday before 3d Lord's day of July. The meeting continued until Monday, during which we had a fine opportunity to speak, in the name of the Master. Every ear was open; not a word was lost. It may be said that the gospel is fully laid before that people. The public mind has been disabused, mountains of prejudice removed, the field fully prepared for the seed of the word to be sown. But alas! there is no one to labour, who can devote his whole time to it. Six made the good confession, and two were reclaimed and restored to the fold again.

When the co-operation affair came up, I felt timid, expressed my fears, and declined having any thing to do with it. The reasons were given, which satisfied the brethren. The co-operation of the apostles was governed by the law of love—no penalty attached. While churches are in love, there is no need of any other rule; but when love ceases to move, other laws become a resolve, or "be it ordered." These laws are generally enacted while love is in full exercise; they lay harmless and useless as a sword in its scabbard, until the law of heaven begins to fail, and then they are brought to bear—the sword is taken from the scabbard, not by the band of love, but by a well known gentleman with the compound name, *Order Rule,* whose footsteps have been marked with blood, pains and penalties from the days of Cain to the present. A law without a penalty, is no law at all. If we order or resolve a brother or brethren into obligation to do, they must be punished if they neglect to do. Is it not a fact, that brethren sometimes resolve an Evangelist into the field of labor, and then leave his family to starve? There is no court to punish this offence; for the churches cannot err. But suppose the Evangelist should receive one, two or three hundred dollars in advance, and then refuse to preach, Mr. *Order Rule* find show to reach the delinquent. Order is beauty, but love alone can give heavenly life to order. Love to God, love to Jesus, love for the Holy Spirit, love for the body and members of Christ, leads to the love of the poor and perishing, and to the love of money to be used in the fear and love of God, for the good of mankind.

You may expect to hear from me once a month, for some time to come.   W. W. STEVENSON.

To the Editors of the Christian Review:—

BELOVED BRETHREN:—Bro. C. Curlee and myself have just returned from a tour through the counties of Bedford, Lincoln and Franklin. We held a protracted meeting at Cross Roads, Bedford County, including the 2d Lord's day in July. The meeting continued 7 days. We had 9 immersions, and one added who had previously been immersed.

On Saturday preceding the 3d Lord's day, we commenced a protracted meeting at New Hermon, Bedford County. Meeting continued 4 days—10 additions. Bros. Hopwood, Griffin and M'Donald were in attendance.

We then proceeded to Lynchburg, where we staid a day and night, and gave the citizens of that village three addresses on the subject of Christianity.

We then went to Bean's Creek, Franklin County, where we also continued 4 days, Bro. Hopwood being with us. We had 9 additions, 4 by immersion and 5 from the Baptists.

At all of the above-named places, we had large and attentive congregations. I do not think I have ever witnessed a more general manifestation of interest on the subject of Christianity Heaven's cause *will* triumph.

AUGUST 1st, 1844.   B. W. WHITE.

OBITUARY.

DIED, on the evening of the 27th September, in the vicinity of this City, after an illness of ten days, and in the seventy-sixth year of his age, Our venerable and good brother ROBERT C. FOSTER, an elder of the Church of Christ in Nashville, and for more than half a century a citizen of Tennessee. When a good man dies, it is said, all the world should be mourners; and truly, the departure of this time-honored Patriarch, sinking down into the shades of death, surrounded by more than forty living descendants reaching to the fourth generation, has awakened in society a deep and mingled feeling of sympathy and of sorrow seldom witnessed among us. Eminently prospered throughout a long life, and blessed in all his domestic relations, at peace with his fellow-men and with his God, to whom he had been reconciled in Christ Jesus for upwards of forty years, his whole history is one of marked purity of purpose, of fervent piety, and of incorruptible virtue. During the entire period of his last and only sickness, the patient resigned spirit of unmurmuring and ready submission to the will of God which he manifested, his unwavering faith in the Gospel of the Kingdom, which but a week before his illness he had proclaimed to others, and the joyful calmness with which he met the last enemy, and which remained fixed upon his features even in death, testified to all who beheld him in the final struggles of nature, that the Gospel was indeed 'the power of God unto salvation to all them that believe?

*Here is the patience of the saints: here are they that keep the commandments of God, and the faith of Jesus. And I heard a voice from Heaven, saying unto me: Write—Blessed are the dead which the in the Lord from henceforth: yea saith the Spirit, that they may rest from their labors; and their works do follow them?   W.

CHRISTIAN REVIEW.

VOL. I.   NASHVILLE, NOVEMBER, 1844.   NO. XI.

NOTES ON A TOUR.—No. 3.

When I finished my notes on a tour through Kentucky, I thought I should publish no more, for the present year at least, but from the anxiety of the brethren to continue them, I have concluded to give a few observations on religious matters in Tennessee, and other sections which I may visit. Though I am very sure this is not a pleasant employment, and but for the beneficial results anticipated, I would adopt a different course. Unfortunately, religionists generally suppose, if they do not merit praise, it is the province of no one to make public their faults. If there had been no sin in the world, the Saviour would not have visited our earth, and if there were no sin now, no reproof would be necessary. But in all my little peregrinations, I have seen much to commend, and some things which richly merit reproof.

Lord's day, Aug. 25,1844, I left *Elm Crag* for *Murfreesboro,* in Rutherford County, Ten., at which place I arrived by 11 o'clock A. M., and hastened to the humble little meeting house in the suburbs of the village, where I found a congregation of some forty persons assembled, listening to a sound discourse from *Bro. S. E. Jones,* on the subject of *"Justification."* I remained through the day, and delivered two discourses, to the disciples and a few friendly aliens.— The people of Murfreesboro are generally religious; but many of them are much opposed to the Bible as an exclusive government in religion. Consequently, there is considerable partyism, and 1 fear it will be many years before the Christian religion can have deserved countenance. There are some twenty or thirty *enlisted* soldiers of Christ in the town and vicinity, and some of them very capable of teaching worldly matters, and politics in particular; but alas! the weekly worship is neglected, and growth in grace and the knowledge of the truth can scarcely be anticipated. The Lord has in reserve a rod for some of these good brethren; and I pray it may not fall upon them in an unexpected boor. These are kind and excellent brethren as far as they have gone, but the Savior requires greater advances in his cause.

All the disciples are remarkably fond of good preaching, but they should reflect preaching alone will not convert the world. If the churches universally would honor the ordinances, and the members could be induced to teach and admonish each other, and thereby correct every fault, pleading with the world to become united with such, would be delightful employment. There are five or six churches in Rutherford county, and some six hundred disciples, and amongst this number there are many talented brethren; but I sincerely regret to know there is much more zeal to propagate political opinions than the doctrine of Christ, with some of them. Several of the brethren are able orators in Whiggery and Democracy, and no doubt considerable of the Lord's funds go to the support of these respective causes. I doubt very much whether any of the Apostles or primitive disciples, made political speeches, were honored with seats in worldly councils,   or

contributed a shilling, only by way of taxation, to make governments for the "lawless and disobedient."

If the talents and other means in Rutherford county were brought to bear upon the Christian institution, the whole country might be leavened and revolutionized. Oh! Lord, how long before thy poor, erring, frail people will learn wisdom?

Monday, the 26th, I journeyed to Woodbury, in Cannon county, and delivered a discourse at night on Christian character, in connection with education.—Our Brother *J. J. Trott,* whose praise is acknowledged by many of the churches, resides in this town, and there are some hundred and fifty disciples in the neighborhood. How they are improving in their Christian deportment, I am not prepared to state.

Tuesday, 27th, I visited McMinnville, in Warren county, and finding no Christians, (though there are a goodly number in the county,) I lectured at night in the Presbyterian meeting house, upon the subject of Education in general, and Franklin College in particular, and left next morning, the 28th, for Sparta, in White county, which place I reached on the 29th, and remained in the vicinity till Sept. 2d.

On Saturday, the 31st, I preached with Brother Hooker, near Sparta, to a congregation of disciples, and on Lord's day, the 1st of Sept., I preached three times in Sparta, to a number of anxious enquirers after the truth. Three made the good confession, amongst them one who had been some time a class leader. In Sparta and vicinity, there were some 10 or 12 immersed.

On Monday, 2d, I travelled 22 miles, to Smithville, in DeKalb county, in the forenoon, and gave a lecture on education. In the afternoon, I travelled 11 miles, to Liberty, where I expected to deliver a discourse, but there were no brethren at this place, and as the Methodist meeting house was the only one which could be used for public meetings, and the gentleman who kept the house could not see the propriety of any thing being taught but Methodism, the house was not lighted, and I was prevented from carrying out my purpose. 1 am sorry the Methodists are such uncompromising partisans. They should remember the opposition Mr. Wesley, the father of their religion, met. Some of the Methodists of this generation may live to see the day, when they will consider themselves peculiarly fortunate to hear the religion of the Bible, (and not their modern fanaticism) taught, in its ancient simplicity.

Tuesday morning, the 3d, I preached in Alexandria, and at night in Lebanon, Wilson county, to large congregations. The people at Lebanon are, many of them, disposed to hear the truth; but this is the seat of *Cumberland Presbyterianism,* and the location of Cumberland College, the only institution of learning under the influence of that sect, and as the preachers are amongst the bitterest opposers to what we teach, all their influence is directed against what we consider the truth. There is a small, but intelligent and worthy congregation of disciples of Christ in Lebanon. The brethren meet weekly, and study and teach the Scriptures, and keep the ordinances. To do this, members of churches must disregard the pomp and show around them, and have more love for the worship of the Bible than for the gratification of the flesh.

The 4th, I reached the "Crag," after an absence of ten days, and remained till Saturday, the 8th, when I joined the company of Bros. Wharton, Sledge, and others, for a meeting eight miles from Murfreesboro. We reached the place of our destination on the evening of the same day, and remained till the next Tuesday morning. During our stay, there were some 21 immersions. The preachers in attendance were Bros. Hopwood, Jones, Hall, Curlee, McDonald, Thompson, Hooker, Barbee, Wharton, Dill, Cane, Runnels, and W. Speer, and the love and zeal manifested by preachers and brethren were truly encouraging.

Tuesday, the 10th, I journeyed with Bro. Hopwood and others to Shelbyville, in Bedford, and spoke at night on education. This place is very much addicted to sectarianism, but I hope the Lord "has much people" in it notwithstanding.

Wednesday, the 11th, I visited Fayetteville, in Lincoln, and preached at night in the Cumberland Presbyterian meeting house.

Tuesday, the 12th, I travelled thirty miles to Huntsville, in Madison county, Ala., and finding my appointment had not preceded me, I slept free from the cares and anxieties of life. I remained during the 13th, and preached at night in the Baptist meeting house, to two ladies and six gentlemen, and a few colored people round the doors, and I think it was one of my happiest efforts. Huntsville is a beautiful town, with a population of about 2000 persons, who are intelligent and no doubt excellent people with reference to worldly matters; but most of them are prejudiced against the Christian religion. The professors are under the influence of imaginary revelations, and where this is the case, the Bible is little respected. There are a few noble friends of the truth, and I trust the time is not far distant, when the day star will dawn on this village.— At present, the people are, through the influence of their preachers, afraid of the truth. Bros. Caldwell, Putnam and Malone, should hold up the light to their acquaintances.

Sat. 14th, I travelled some fifteen miles to Triana, a pleasant little village in Madison county, and found a very excellent congregation of disciples of Christ. At this place I preached day and night till Tuesday, the 17th; and although the beloved brothers and sisters were much encouraged and strengthened, there were but two additions. Notwithstanding most of the members are young in the cause, they are generally intelligent, and I trust they will grow fast "in grace and the knowledge of the truth." *Bro. J. J. Ward* is a young man of promise, and I hope he will direct his talents and energy to the Lord's honor.

On the 19th, I visited Moorsville, in Limestone county, and. addressed quite an attentive congregation at night, and on Wednesday morning. Few of the good people in this section are as willing to trust the great truths recorded in the Bible as they are the "*new* revelations" for which they pray at camp meetings. Our venerable *Bro. Hunley,* a few miles distant, I am persuaded will exert a happy influence on the surrounding country. On the 18th, I crossed the Tennessee and reached Somersville, in Morgan county, and preached at night and next morning, to a respectable congregation, many of whom love to hear the truth. Still not all the people are capable of hearing the truth, and of this Mr. P., the clergyman, evinced his conviction, by forewarning his flock to keep at a respectable distance. While describing the modem process of "getting religion," a Baptist man, finding it a little too hard for him, left the house, and casting my eyes over the assembly, I saw a Methodist gentleman who I thought, from his *appearance* would not be able to bear the whole at once, and I therefore invited him or others in the same situation to leave, and it was scarcely said till the man was gone. If ever these good friends should   chance   to   see this notice, they, I trust, will profit by the reflection, that they should be ashamed of themselves to the day of their death, for taking offence at the exposure of a practice, (*"getting religion"*) for which there is not the shade of authority in God's book, and which only becomes a dark age and an ignorant and degraded people. Shame upon you, gentlemen, for advocating such superstition in the nineteenth century!

On the 20th of Sept. I visited Oakville, in Lawrence county, and delivered .one address. There are several good brothers and sisters in the vicinity, and I look for considerable increase in numbers.

On Saturday, the 21st, I began to preach at Moulton, and continued day and night to the close of the month. *"Grove worship"* was carried on for several days, by the Presbyterian and Methodist friends, in hearing of the town, and at the close of this fruitless effort, the people were invited to another grove in the opposite direction, a little further from the village. It is presumable, the friends had better success in the latter grove, as I was informed there was less intelligence in that direction; and as ignorance of the true God has been favorable to that kind of worship, since the children of Israel "left all the commandments of the Lord their God, and made a grove" in which to worship Baal. (2 Ki. xvii, 16.)

However, the Lord was very kind to us, and although every means was employed to prevent the people from hearing, there were FIFTY-TWO noble additions to the cause of the Blessed Master. In this company there were many of the most intelligent; and amongst the rest there were *ten* Presbyterians immersed, several Methodists, and six Baptists added—two or three of whom were immersed into Christ on a confession of their faith, although they had been put into the water, "on account," as they supposed, "of the remission of their sins," in order to join the Baptist Church. This was a matter they determined between themselves and their God, after solemnly investigating the truth. I am not certain but most of our friends who are immersed at this day *"because they are Christians,"* as the preachers require them to say, will have yet to confess the Messiah, and be baptized into him in order to the remission of sins, before they can enter the kingdom of Christ. But as this is narrative, and not the place for investigation, I must proceed.

The church at Moulton was planted at the close of the controversy in June, '43, between the champion of New School Presbyterianism, Mr. Edward McMillon, and the writer; and it is not to be forgotten there has been much boasting on the side of our party friends in consequence of the triumph of their doctrines during the discussion. I rejoice in such triumphs no little myself; but oh Lord, to THEE, and thy precious word, I am indebted for all that I have witnessed in Moulton. The brethren are strong in numbers, talent and influence, and I pray God they may be kept humble.

Oct. 1, crossed Tennessee river, with the vivid recollection that on that day fourteen years since, I bade an affectionate mother, Who now rests from her labors, adieu, and crossed the same stream for the purpose of preaching the Gospel for the first time.

On the third of October, I reached my humble, but sweet home, much rejoiced, and was no little refreshed with the reflection it was not good "for man to be alone," and that in future, if I travelled abroad to preach the Gospel, I would endeavor to have "an help mete" along.   T. F.

FIRST PRINCIPLES—NO. 4

Baptism stands, in the New Testament, amongst the first principles of the oracles of God. Yet by the great mass of professors of the various religions it is deemed an unimportant matter, and of very mysterious import, as relates to its action, subject, and design. Faith, repentance, prayer, &c., are thought to be plain subjects; but baptism, which is enjoined on the wayfaring and fools, is treated as an incomprehensible non-essential. Believing as I do, that the commandments of God are not only given in literal language, but have been presented in a style not easily misunderstood, I will endeavor to exhibit the teaching of the Scriptures on the subject of Baptism, and knowing that most of my readers are not critics, and that critical disquisitions are not necessary to teach the Christian religion, I will depend mainly on the common version of the Bible, and on the plainest passages of God's word.

1. THE ACTION.

Does the word Baptism denote any specific action? Faith, repentance, prayer, the Lord's supper, &c., all denote certainties, and it would be a strange conclusion to suppose baptism implies no particular performance. The king's translators had a distinct idea of the original word, and always where it occurred in the Old Testament, they were careful to give its import in an English dress; but in the New Testament, they scrupulously adopted the original, but never translated the word. I need not tell the intelligent, that King James prohibited the translators from giving ecclesiastic words, such as church and baptism, in plain English. This was a, relic of the darkest days of Popery, when it was supposed, as is at this day, by many, to be unsafe and unwise in the priesthood, to let the common people have the Bible in their own vernacular. Popery has thus cheated a large portion of the world out of the idea, practice and benefits of one of God's plainest and most forcible ordinances. The Romish church and all her daughters still refuse to let the world see what this ordinance is; but the true Christians, in every age and climate, have acted differently. In the language of the learned ALL, "All Asia, all Africa," and all the rest of the world, except the "Western" or Romish church and her offspring, have ever practiced a specific action in Baptism.

As premised, the King's translators knew well the meaning of the word in the Old Testament. 2 Ki. v, 14, where Naaman was told to go and wash in Jordan, it is given by these translators, that he DIPPED himself seven times; and the reader must not be surprised when I tell him that the word is BAPTIZO in the Greek. In the New Testament, however, when the ordinance of baptism was mentioned, the word was kept in its original obscurity. However, the circumstances connected with the ordinance are unerring criteria in arriving at the truth. The unprejudiced man who reads the New Covenant, will find more than enough to satisfy him that IMMERSION is the one baptism of Paul. I will mention a few of the passages which criticism will ever fail to subvert, and which will, to the day of eternity, convince honest enquirers after truth, whenever they permit the Holy Spirit to speak for himself. Amongst the rest, the following are some of the plainest scriptures: John baptized "in Jordan" "in Enon, *because there was much water there,*" and when Jesus was baptized, he "went up *straightway out of the water;*" "*Buried with him by baptism into death, that like as Christ was raised up from the dead by the glory of the Father, even so we also should walk in newness of life:*" "*Having your hearts sprinkled from* washed with pure water." Now, gentle reader, have you ever gone down into the water and been baptized, as was the Eunuch, and come up out of the water as he and the Savior did? have you ever been buried with Christ by baptism? or have you ever had your heart sprinkled from an evil conscience, and your body washed in pure water? If not, how can you assure yourself that you have obeyed the Lord in this ordinance? The objector may say, persons frequently have water poured or sprinkled upon them, and are satisfied. I might say with as much truth, that more than half the world have not the Bible and are as well satisfied, and many indeed are satisfied to reject the word of God in lands denominated Christian. Being contented, in no condition is proof that one is a servant of the Lord. A man's feelings always coincide with his education, and if he be taught error, he will live and die without promise, and falling into the ditch will perish. Omnipotent truth alone can free the sinner from his transgressions, and fit him for society in heaven.

2. THE SUBJECT.

Jesus said, "Go teach the nations, baptizing them into the name of the Father, Son, and Holy Spirit." This is Matthew's version; but Mark says, "Go into all the world, and preach the Gospel to every creature. He that believes and is baptized shall be saved." The person must be exceedingly blind who does not see, that to be taught, and to believe the teaching are indispensable to baptism. As a preparation, the people on Pentecost were "pricked in their heart," at hearing the words of Peter, and "gladly received the truth," before they were baptized. Read second chapter of the Acts of the Apostles. The second city visited by the disciples was Samaria, and when "They believed Philip preaching the things concerning the kingdom of God and the name of Jesus Christ, they were baptized both men and women." Simon believed and was baptized, and the Ethiopian nobleman before descending into the water confessed, "I believe that Jesus is the Christ, the Son of the living God." The Corinthians "hearing, believed, and were baptized."

But why need I quote more Scripture on any one point? A single clear thus saith the Lord should satisfy any honest enquirer after the truth. Will any lover of the Bible affirm that there is evidence in the word of God for baptizing any but believers? Where is the passage, or even the inference? No one can find either. Who will show it? We will publish it.

Further argument certainly is unnecessary. I will only add, that the doctrine of original sin, and infant damnation without baptism, is the foundation of the practice called baptism, to infants and all who are not actual transgressors. Thus, Catholics and Episcopalians call baptism regeneration to infants, and even Mr. Wesley says, "Baptism washes away the guilt of original sin." See Doctrinal tracts, under the head *Baptism.* Infants are not totally depraved, and hell deserving sinners; and therefore, they need no baptism. Jesus said, "of such is the kingdom of heaven," and I infer all that keeps them out of the mansions of rest is the resurrection into life from the grave. Not so with sinners.

3. DESIGNS OF BAPTISM.

Commemorative institutions stand pre-eminent as evidences of the truth of Christianity. The Lord's Supper will remain a living monumental evidence of the crucifixion of the Savior till he comes; and Baptism will remain as long the great monumental evidence of the burial and resurrection of Christ. By it, sinners put off the old man with his deeds, and put on the new man.

Hence Paul says; "As many of you as have been baptized into Christ have put on Christ." Gal. iii, 27. It is the "answer" or (*Eperitoma*) "the seeking of a good conscience towards God."

Jesus said, "He that believes and is baptized shall be saved." Can one, according to the commission, be saved from his sins, who does not believe the Gospel and is baptized into Christ? The first commandment ever given to believers by the authority of Christ, was "Repent," and the second, "Be baptized for the remission of sins." Acts ii, 38. Can this be misunderstood by a sincere and intelligent person? John indeed "baptized the people in Jordan, confessing their sins." With these scriptures before the mind, believers can submit to baptism, with perfect understanding; but without the knowledge they impart, darkness and confusion pervade the whole transaction; and the person who is put into the water ignorant of the teachings of the Bible, mocks the ordinance of God, and woefully deceives himself. To be baptized to join a sect, because one hopes he has got religion, resembles not the obedience of faith.— A man had as well be put into the water while asleep, or with his eyes and ears stopped, and call it baptism, as to be immersed in ignorance of its designs and call it obedience to God.

The men who brought forth fruit, "some thirty, some sixty, and some an hundred fold," were such as received the truth into honest and understanding hearts."

In these brief statements, I have not pretended to stop and answer objections; still I feel not unable to do so, and would not shrink from answering every objection, and removing every difficulty either real or imaginary, if the opposers will present them. Light is my object, and I will "buy the truth" at any sacrifice, and would not sell it for the world. I will close with a plain, frank and friendly proposition to the partisan world. If these are not truths of God, and anyone will show the error, I will publish it to the world, and frankly confess I have taught what is not authorized.

T. F.

REGENERATION.

This is a: subject, perhaps, on which religionists differ as widely as any that has agitated society. To give all the different speculations of theologians, would be an arduous undertaking; but to present the single notion of its import, according to the most popular religions, is an easy matter. When through with this, it will require but little space to pen what the scriptures say. I will give the views of some of the respective denominations numerically.

1. REGENERATION *of Romanists.* According to Wall, all the Catholic fathers used the word Regeneration as synonymous with baptism; and it is still the teaching of the Mother sect.

2. EPISCOPALIANS teach that the baptized are thus regenerated.

3. THE METHODISTS. Mr. Wesley taught (Doc. tracts, p. 249), "By the water of Baptism we are regenerated and born again."

4. PRESBYTERIANS. Mr. Rice taught, as will be found in the debate with A. Campbell, p. 704, that "Regeneration is by the special agency of the Spirit before faith," and in order to produce faith.

5. BAPTISTS. *Mr. Howell,* the pastor of the Baptist church in Nashville, taught, in the sixth No. of his Baptist, p. 83, that regeneration is an act of God by his Spirit, in which man is passive." On

the 84th page, he teaches that Regeneration produces faith, and that faith is one of the evidences of regeneration.— From these declarations it is not difficult to ascertain, there are differences of opinion with regard to regeneration. According to Romanists, Episcopalians and Mr. Wesley, it is not difficult to be regenerated; but according to Presbyterian and Baptist views, if Messrs. Rice and Howell are authority in their churches, it is rather a difficult matter for a man to be regenerated, (even admitting this is correct phraseology.) They both place it before faith, and give faith as one of the evidences of it. If regeneration be remission of sins, and the salvation of the soul, and man is merely *passive,* no one should be blamed for not believing, and turning to God. Jesus, to be sure, said "believe," or "you shall be damned;" but the sinner might reply, "Lord, I am passive, tell me not to believe, so long as faith is the result of regeneration, and the work is in thy sovereign power." But not to be prolix, the doctrine of these gentlemen renders man irresponsible, and contradicts the whole Bible. Neither do I believe Catholics, Episcopalians or Methodists, ancient or modern, teach the scriptures on this subject.

REGENERATION OF THE BIBLE.

The word *regeneration* occurs but twice in the Bible, Mat. 19: 28, and Ti. 3: 5, and from its connection the proper meaning is easily deduced. The Savior says in Matt. 19: 28, "Ye who have followed me (that is in my trials) in the regeneration, when the son of man shall sit in the throne of his glory, ye also shall sit on twelve thrones judging the twelve tribes of Israel." The passage may be transposed without doing violence to the original, or to the sense, and the true idea will be much more forcible. Thus we might read it, "Ye who have followed me, shall sit in the regeneration on twelve thrones, judging the twelve tribes of Israel, when the son of man sits on the throne of his glory" From this reading no one can doubt that regeneration is truly a state, and not the act of entering into it, or becoming a Christian. The Greek word PALEGGENESIA is from *palin* again, and *genesis* creation, and denotes a new creation, in contradistinction to the creation of the world. God made the world, and Jesus Christ made a new world, or the regeneration.

In reference to this passage, DR. CLARK says, "The regeneration is thus referred to the time when Jesus shall sit on the throne of his glory, and not to the time of following him, which is utterly improper. The *Syriac* gives it *"the new age,"* and Calmet says, "This perfectly agrees to the phrase *the age to come, the age of the Messiah."* Others render the word the *renovation,* or *new state* which commenced at Jerusalem on the day of Pentecost. The whole passage forces this meaning upon us. When were the disciples to sit on thrones? Jesus said "when the son of man sits on his throne." Did he not sit on his throne when he ascended to heaven? The disciples will not sit on thrones at the day of judgment, for this the son of man is to do; but the thrones denote the authority with which the Apostles were clothed, when they were commissioned to pronounce the laws to the nations. From all this argumentation, it is obvious the *regeneration* is synonymous with *new creation, new church, or kingdom of heaven.*— Luke records the same, (Luke 22: 28, 29, 30,) in these words, "Ye are they which have continued with me in my temptations, and I appoint unto you a KINGDOM, as my Father has appointed unto me. That you may eat and drink at my table in my kingdom, and sit on thrones judging the twelve tribes of

Israel.” Matthew says “they shall

sit on twelve thrones, in the *regeneration;"* and Luke says, they shall sit on twelve thrones in the *kingdom* of heaven." Now I ask the candid reader if *regeneration* and *kingdom,* are not used by two inspired authors to denote the same state?

The word is found again in Titus 3: 5. Paul says "He has saved us, by the washing of *regeneration,* (or of the new institution, church of God, or kingdom,) and the renewing of the Holy Spirit." The washing of regeneration is no more the regeneration, of which it is affirmed to be merely the washing, than the fruit of a tree is the tree itself. The washing, all the world agree, is baptism; but the new institution or *regeneration,* is the state into which enter by this baptismal washing and renewing of the Spirit. Jesus speaks to the same effect, when he says "Except a man is born of water and the spirit, he cannot enter into the kingdom of heaven," or the church, or regeneration. The idea, then, that coming into the *regeneration, new creation,* or *church,* by this new birth of water and spirit, or washing and renewing of the spirit, is the regeneration or state itself, is most preposterous. It is usual for preachers to speak of being "regenerated;" but it is equally good sense to say, when a man becomes a Christian, he is churched. To be sure, we do sometimes say a man is housed, when he is merely in a house; but we never call the man the house, or the act of going into it, the house. It would be equally as good sense to affirm the act of entering a door into a house is the1 house, as to assert, the act of entering the *regeneration* or kingdom, is the kingdom itself.

An objector might say, "if the washing of regeneration is not the regeneration itself the renewing of the Holy Spirit is not the holy spirit." Who pretends to say the renewal of, or by the spirit, is the spirit? The spirit is the instrument, but the work done is a different matter. The axe cuts the tree, till it falls, but the wound made by the axe is not the instrument itself. God enlightens the mind, by the Spirit, through the word, and the man is thus enabled to turn away from his sins and obey the Gospel, and so is made new, by the bath, that belongs to the new institution, and this enlightening and renewing of the Spirit. "Because he is a son then, God sends forth the Spirit of his Son into his heart, crying Abba Father." Who will gainsay these things?   T. F.

CHRISTIAN REVIEW.

We rejoice to know the CHRISTIAN REVIEW has been well received by the brethren generally, wherever it has been taken. Not only so, but many of the world have been favorably disposed towards the truth by reading this journal. The circulation of the Review is quite extensive for the time it has been published, and if the brethren will exert themselves, it may be much more so.

The character of the essays so far, has not been such as to give offence, and indeed it has been the study of the Editors to give no just cause of complaint to Jew nor Greek, nor to the church of God.

We are now more than satisfied, where the Review circulates, a good influence will be exerted. Therefore, brethren, and friends, we ask you to extend its patronage. Let each subscriber determine to obtain *two* new subscribers, (a thing only requiring a little effort) and the Christian Review will be on so permanent a basis, as to place it out of danger.

Let every friend to free religious discussion exert himself, and our list will be more than quadrupled by the first of January '45.   EDITORS.

CAMPBELLISM IS IMPROVING IN NASHVILLE.

The above is the style adopted by Mr. R. B. C. Howell of Nashville, in his "Baptist" to sneer at the disciples of Christ in this city. I mention the course of Mr. H. not because I am anxious to engage in discussion with him, or any other individual; or because I am unkindly disposed towards him, or his church; but because I wish to say to him and his friends, such a course is unmanly, and unchristian. While we profess, not Campbellism, but the religion of the Bible, it is not treating us as he would be treated, to attempt to throw odium upon us by an approbrious and very offensive name.

Moreover, the cause which Mr. H. is pleased to call "Campbellism," cannot be put down by sneers. Stronger and sharper weapons must be used. But what is the cause of Mr. H.'s unkind course towards the Church of God? If I am permitted to state my conviction, it is Mr. H.'s greatest pleasure, to find something which seems wrong to him in reference to any single member of Christ's body, and then charge the whole church with the sin. Hence, because our beloved Bro. Wharton felt it his privilege to deliver a lecture or two against the corruptions of Society, and in favor of any association by which Christians, in his estimation, can live more devoted to God, Mr. H. seized upon the opportunity as capital by which to charge us with error. Mr. Howell knows, or ought to know, this subject has produced no more excitement in the church of God, indeed, not half so much in the United States, as in the Baptist denomination.

If Mr. Howell will examine closely, if I am not mistaken, he will find some of his own members favorable to Association. Why then should he charge the act of one man, even admitting it is a sin, as a crime upon the whole body. Bro. Wharton can, no doubt, defend himself; but Mr. H. should not attack the church of Christ by sneers, or by publishing the slanderous documents of others, unless he made good his charges. Whenever he shall feel himself prepared to expose our errors, not by sneers, but by manly argument, he will find his equal. But while he pursues the plan he has commenced, the intelligent and unprejudiced, can but hold his efforts against the truth, in merited contempt. While we live in obedience to the laws of Christ, it will ever remain an evidence of the Scripturality of our course, to have the opposition of Clerical bigots, and men who attack by sneers suited alone to the vulgar, rather than come out in open day to assail us. T. F.

PRAYER.

The Christian, though alone and separated from all earthly associations, in the most arduous and distressing situation, may have recourse to a friend and adviser, whose ear is open to the cry of the poorest and most distressed of his people. He may kneel and pray with fervent sincerity; and although he may not receive a special answer "borne in upon his mind" to his earnest petition, yet laying open his doubts and his distresses in prayer, with proper feeling, will necessarily, in the act of doing so, purify the mind from worldly passions and interests, and bring it into that state where the resolutions adopted are likely to be selected rather from a sense of duty, than from any inferior motive. Ah! nothing can so fortify the heart to endure afflictions and face difficulties, as the state of the mind thus produced. J. B. F.

NAMES IN RELIGION.

THE following excellent and judicious remarks arrested my attention a few days since, in the *"Medical Recorder,"* conducted by Dr. A. Curtis of Cincinnati. Having formed a pleasing acquaintance with this distinguished Reformer in medicine and advocate of the moral and intellectual freedom of man, I am much gratified to see that his independent method of thinking upon medicine, frequently directs his mind free from sectarian shackles to spend a thought or two upon Christianity as it is. And, although, if I am correctly informed, he has attached his *name* and influence to one of the last developed limbs of the Calvinian tree, I trust his own views of propriety will lead him to the same practical independence indicated theoretically below. His remarks are certainly founded in right reason and are worthy of the candid consideration of all those who are now teaching the faith and "fear of the Lord by the precept of men." Were the Dr. to carry out his views upon this subject, I apprehend he would have occasion for as much forbearance among his religious associates, as he has now amid the misrepresentation, ridicule and contempt of many of his redoubtable opposers among the Sons of Esculapias. Still, I yet hope to see all such men maintaining the truth upon every subject, *"invitis omnibus"* and for the truth's sake.

I am often times at a loss to account for the tenacity, with which men of penetration and reflection, hold on to the senseless and contradictory nomenclature of an age when popular religion was but little more than a singular and mysterious mixture of Heathenism, Judaism and a few of the great truths of Christianity. The confusion of tongues and ideas, created by the unmeaning Shibboleths of the schoolmen, has almost as effectually prevented a correct, consistent and scriptural knowledge of Christianity, as could have been effected by a non-intercourse with the Christian Oracles themselves, to which in a great measure they have indeed led; and as a consequence, our deferential respect for names and Sectarian designations, has destroyed much of the mental independence, peace and happiness of individuals and societies. To abandon forever the unmeaning names of Calvinism, Presbyterianism, etc. etc. as designations for Christianity, and to return to the Scriptures to learn what it was before these assumed their Babylonian authority in the church, while such a course would secure to all the Reformers the honor due to their names, it would at the same time pioneer the extirpation of the schismatical and persecuting character of Religion so called and greatly advance the spread of that true and primitive Christianity which breathes good-will and peace to our race. Human authority and superstition would lose their almost uncontrollable away. The tenacity of which we speak, however, is so great with some, that no man can be recognized as a Christian, no matter what his pretensions to Scriptural knowledge, piety, and morality may be, who will renounce the venerated names of Luther, Calvin or Wesley, or the *isms* of presbyters and Bishops whose authority in the church is equal to the *Juie Divino* of Despots over the inalienable privileges of free born men. If an independent thinker arises among them, they cither tie up his tongue or throw him from their midst if he dare speak against the authority of the Elders. Camden, the celebrated antiquary, relates that certain Brittainnes (Britons) going over into America, and taking wives from among the people of Normandy, *"did cut out their tongues"* through fear that when they should become mothers they would teach their children some other than the sacred language of the old Welch. The proscription occasioned by adherence to our present Theological nomenclature is often times similar.

A brighter day, however, is dawning. Thousands of the most talented and worthy are throwing off the shackles and delusions of great names, as well as the decisions of those who have assumed the judgment seat over our consciences. The deep interest now exhibited in the examination of truth, irrespective of the authority of the misnomers of the systems of past ages, indicates a greater change from the crude and fantastic ideas and feelings created by the early associations and fostering habits of the straight-laced and tyrannical hierarchies in Religion. A more liberal spirit will necessarily ensue; and it will be found that goodness and worth are not limited to any single form of the religious observances of Sectariandom; and whatever truth may be discovered by those who are not denominationally associated with us, we can say to them without fear of consequences, ,

"If thou hast *somethings* bring thy goods—a fair return be thine
If thou art *somethings* bring thy soul and interchange with mine."

J. B. FERGUSON.

"What's a name? Ans.—Something that indicates something else. A sound or succession of sounds, or a combination of letters which represents some person, place or idea. In the adaptation of names to things, the world has ever been committing gross errors, particularly in their application to principles. These are very improperly designated by the addition of the termination *ism* to the name of the person who teaches the doctrines, whatever they may be; as Calvinism, Lutherism; or to the principle intended to be signified, as Methodism, Transcendentalism; and it always means the doctrine of the man, or of the method, or of the principle, and nothing else. Thus Calvinism, Lutherism, Wesleyism, mean the principles and practices of Calvin, Luther and Wesley, and no others.

Methodism means the doctrines and practices of method, but does not say what method, and is therefore just no name at all. It designates nothing. It does not say whether the principles and practices are those of the church or the world. It only designates some kind of a system, and transcendentalism means the doctrines and practices of the transcendentists, which we leave it to them to explain.

Now, if Calvin, Luther and Wesley, had been infallible men, and the first to discover and teach the principles and practices they recommend, and had taught every thing about those principles and practices, so as to leave no room for new developments or further illustrations; and if there were but one Methodism in the world, this system of nomenclature would be perfectly correct. But, were the principles of those men never known till they divulged them? Was there no method of doing business in the world till the days of Wesley, and have those principles and practices continued from their days to this, *as they were?* If not, then the terms are better calculated to mislead than to lead; to chain the enquiring and benevolent mind, than to direct it.

The fact is, that men calling themselves Calvinists, Lutherans, Wesleyans, &c, &c., believe and do, now a days, things not a few, which never entered the brain of those renowned worthies; and, at the same time, reject, in toto, many of the principles and practices for which those men were distinguished. Witness the opposing principles and conduct among the divisions of those who profess to follow each of these distinguished leaders, and now we see persons attempting to give to Mesmer the honor of discovering and developing principles and practices which never entered the brain of that mysterious operator. All this is as unjust as it is erroneous. Think you, reader, that these distinguished men would be willing, were they alive upon the earth, to father all that is now taught and practiced in their names? We think not.

Another method of nomenclature is still more objectionable than the one which adds the *ism* to the name of the person or idea. It consists in adding the *ism* to the name of the followers of the founder; as Lutheranism, Arminianism, Thomsonianism, Episcopalianism, &c., which mean not the *ism* of Luther, or Arminius, or Thomson or a bishop, but that of a or any follower of those men, or believer in that form of religious worship. Here the enquirer is led still farther from any definite impression, for it is possible for him to find out what one man taught and practiced, and to receive or condemn it; but to find out and decide on, the *ism* of all the followers of all the *isms* of the principal founders of *isms,* is a task that no man who fears a straight jacket, will attempt.

What is the remedy for all these evils? Ans. Simply to adapt the name to the principle, instead of the man who teaches it. For example: let religion be called Christianity, a name which signifies the doctrines and duties taught in the scriptures, with which every man can compare his own principles and life, and by which he can ascertain whether he is or is not a Christian. What —and forget all the Fathers and great reformers of religion? No: honor them in exact proportion to the evidence they gave of their adherence to these principles and practices, and their efforts to persuade others to do it.

So of medicine. We have never been pleased with such teems as Cullenism, Brunonianism, Rushism, Thomsonism, &c., nor with Botanic or reformed medicine. The only true name for the *science* is *medicine* and for the *advocate* and *practitioner,* is *physician;* and the only way to find out who is best entitled to it, is to ascertain who develops best the laws of the human economy, and succeeds best in preserving its integrity and functions, and in rectifying its derangements."

OUR CAUSE.

BRETHREN:— Permit me, through the columns of the REVIEW, to offer a few suggestions for the purpose of arresting the attention of such of our brethren as have not taken the trouble to examine for themselves the extent of their responsibilities, and the important part they are called upon to act. We are engaged in a glorious, and, no doubt, finally triumphant reformation; but my honest convictions are we do not pursue that course best calculated to ensure the most speedy consummation of every Christian's desire.

Our labors in the heaven-born cause for which we plead, are directed to the making of proselytes rather than "building up in the most holy faith," those who have enlisted under the banner of King Emanuel. Too many of our preaching brethren seem rather desirous to excel in beautifully rounded periods of declamation and in numbers initiated. The consequence is, multitudes hear, believe and obey—churches are planted, but often left without the requisite and qualified officers; while the labors of the teachers are directed else where. Not unfrequently, without Bishop or Deacon they meet probably once a month, ignorant of many of the plainest and simplest duties of a Christian. An apathy and cold indifference takes possession of the members.— They commemorate the broken body and shed blood of the Savior two or three times annually! Their efforts are paralyzed—their interest diminished in the Redeemer's cause. They pine away for want of spiritual food and languish, clogs and burdens upon the wheels of Zion.

Brethren, it should not be so. It is wrong, and retards our cause in its onward march. Evangelists should take more care in organizing churches upon Heaven's plan. They should not leave a congregation till they have fully unfolded to the members their relative and absolute duties, and set in order the things in the house of the Lord. The faithful discharge of duties on the part of the preachers, is not all that is necessary to the rapid advancement of our cause. The members of many congregations should be more prompt than they arc. Let us all arouse from our lethargy—awaken our slumbering energies— equip ourselves with all the armour of heaven, and victory will be ours. Our Captain is unrivaled in skill, invincible in war. The proclamation has gone forth, calling for true and valiant Soldiers; and will you, my brethren, after enlisting under such a Captain, and in so glorious a war, act the part of cowards or traitors? The world is destined to be the trophy of our Redeemer's conquest; and there are but two principal weapons to achieve the victory; the gospel with its arguments and Christian deportment. We have the first, keen, sharp and brightly gleaming, "mighty and powerful even to the dividing asunder of soul and spirit," but O the humiliating thought! where is the second? In many congregations it is dull, rusty and frequently thrown aside as useless or concealed in the scabbard of human tradition, manufactured in some clerical shop.

In many instances the line of distinction drawn broad and deep by the God of Heaven between the deportment of those in the world and Church of Christ, is scarcely discernible. The Bible with all its heavenly inspired lessons, is neglected, often too, for the sake of boisterous political reveling. Elections are necessary, we admit, but does the *rostrum* to which all parties often go, savor much of the truly Christian character? Not only so, but practices dear to the brethren when of the world are retained by many, though contrary to the spirit of the religion they profess. Vulgarisms—foul language—vain and idle conversation—evil reports—slanders and all this sort of thing belong not to the Christian. Brethren, let us reflect, we have engaged in the cause of Heaven.

The religion of the meek and lowly Jesus we profess; then for its sake—for the sake of the eternal destiny of those who are bound to us by all the endearing ties of friendship and common kindred; let us "act worthy of the vocation wherewith we have been called."

Much more is, and ought to be expected from us than others, yet it is a lamentable fact, we are behind all the denominations of the day, as far as conformity to system is concerned. Others may conform to the requirements of *their* religion, but are we as faithful in the performance of every duty enjoined by the religion we profess? Do we assemble together on every Lord's day to break bread and partake of the cup in commemoration of the sufferings and death of our Redeemer, and to "teach and admonish one another in psalms and hymns and spiritual songs"— Do we pray for and with one another? Do we read in our families daily a portion of our Heavenly   Fathers'   will and offer in humble prayer, our petitions before the throne of His all-bountiful grace"—Do we "love one another with a pure heart fervently" as children of the same Father and joint heirs to the same blessed inheritance of immortality—Do we labor for each other's good and deal justly, honestly and candidly with our brethren and strangers? Are we careful of our brother's reputation? Are we disposed to forgive a repenting brother who has often offended against us, as to conceal his offence from the world till we find in him no symptoms of repentance? Are we at all times disposed to reason with and persuade, in the mild and gentle spirit of a Christian, a brother that we may reclaim him from errors into which he may have fallen, rather than upbraid him for willful disobedience? If we are lacking in these things, "we are blind and cannot see afar off, and have forgotten that we were purged from our old sins." Let us examine ourselves, and wherever we find error detect it. The religion of Jesus is not designed to give us long faces and sanctimonious deportments one day in the week, and license us to act any way the balance; but it is intended to regulate our conduct, chasten our manners, and purify our minds at all times and in all the pursuits of life. Let us then individually resolve that we will act up to the requirements of our confession of faith, the Bible, notwithstanding the sneers, scoffs and derisions of all the world beside. Such a course would be an argument in favor of the great truths of the. religion for which we plead, that would soon overcome all opposition of the religious world, and disperse the gloomy doubts of skeptics. The unchristian like conduct of professors has made thousands of infidels. How often do we hear it said "I would become a Christian if I thought it would benefit me, but I am much better now than many of your members." The theory is often judged by the practice. We know we have the best and only perfect theory;—One originating in the mind of Deity himself. If we would successfully recommend it to the world, let us prove its divine origin by our conduct. Peace, joy, comfort and the necessary things of this world, will be ours, during our pilgrimage below, and crowns of never fading glory, immortality and eternal life at the right hand of God.

King Institute, *Warren Co., Ten.* S. W. OWEN.

SCEPTICISM.

The Skeptics of this day, or at least those of them with whom I am acquainted, oppose Christianity upon three counts:

1. The late period at which it was introduced into the world.
2. Its partial propagation.
3. Its inefficiency to secure the ends proposed, at least so far as numbers are concerned.

I propose a few thoughts upon each of these; and although I believe that the most successful method of addressing skeptics is to present the provisions of the Gospel, in their primitive simplicity, and with these make appeals to their moral susceptibilities; demonstrating what God has done and what in the nature of things man should do, I will nevertheless notice the above difficulties, confident that unless skepticism is a disease of the mental organization, they can be removed, to the satisfaction of all.

In answer to the first difficulty, it should be observed, that the objection lies with equal force against the designs of God in the physical constitution of things as in the religious. Contemplating an eternity past, may we not with equal propriety ask why God delayed the creation of the heavens and the earth, as why he waited for four thousand years to develop the system of salvation for man? True, by the delay of creation no physical suffering was occasioned, though by the delay of Christianity much more suffering occurred. And the objector continues—If Christianity be a perfect scheme, and absolutely necessary to the salvation of man, why should man be allowed to live in all the sufferings of his probationary state thousands of years without, that which is absolutely necessary? To which it has long since been observed, that perfection and necessity are words which when applied to the divine government, must have a relative meaning. What God has done it was necessary should be done; and to think that only one purpose was gained or had exclusively in view in the moral government of man prior to the Christian era, is contrary to the general analogy of the physical as well as the spiritual world. The annual revolution of the earth secures, as a great and paramount object, the regular rotation of seasons; but how many thousand objects are secured by that revolution beside this one! In the vegetable kingdom, we have first the germ, then the blade, and then the ripe corn in the ear. In the animal, we have puling infancy, advancing childhood, and vigorous manhood in the full and ripe development of its powers. Each stage and period have their uses, their objects, as well as their preparatory adaptations to an ulterior end. So, in the moral government of God, we have a patriarchal administration for an infant state of man; a national administration for an associated or childhood state; and a universal or Christian administration for a manhood state of our race. What was done in the patriarchal and Jewish ages, was necessary to be done, and what was omitted was not necessary; and all the schemes of each, although they looked forward to an ultimate end were nevertheless had perfectly fitted to gain other ends which Jehovah proposed. And whilst those other ends were gained, the great end proposed by Christianity, viz: the redemption of man by the blood of Christ, has a retrospective as well as a prospective influence. So, we are taught by the Christian Scriptures. But we have a more summary way of settling this difficulty. Who is prepared to assert that in the divine mind, there is a past, a present and a future? The objection, therefore, like most others formed against our faith, is founded upon a presumptive knowledge of all the divine perfections, which is of course nothing short of the most presumptive ignorance.

Again. It is impossible to answer the question why moral evil exists; yet we can justify its existence, without invalidating the character of the moral Governor of the universe. If, then, the existence of sin does not invalidate the glorious character of God as revealed in his word, who is prepared to say that the gradual instead of the instantaneous extinction of sin, invalidates against it? For aught that the Bible reveals to the contrary, ages upon ages may continue to succeed each other, whilst the race of man may run on in the succession of generation after generation, so that the time which elapsed before the advent of Christ, may prove a very small part in comparison with that which shall have elapsed after it; and the knowledge, holiness, and bliss that may result from the introduction of Christianity at the time in which it was introduced, may dispose us to admire the ways of God as much as we now, in our ignorance, are disposed to complain of them. I reserve the two remaining objections to another paper.   J. B. F.

Graysville, Ky., Oct. 18, 1844.

THE DELUSION OF THE AGE.

Perhaps every age, and every clime, has its peculiar superstition and delusion. In the nineteenth century, there is an all-prevailing delusion which, for grossness, far excels all others, and it is to be fondly hoped till the Lord comes, it shall have no equal. It is the notion THAT THERE IS SOME OTHER AGENCY TO COMMUNICATE TO MAN THE TRUTH OF GOD BESIDES THE BIBLE. All sects from Romanists to Shakers and Mormons, zealously contend for direct revelations by the Spirit of God; and most of the converts of the age, profess communications directly from above, teaching them that they are Christians. All the ridiculous exercises of Shakers, and of other sects during camp meetings and other excitements, are said to be prompted by the Spirit of God. But a sober man can but be astonished that these great spiritual operations and out-pourings take place only with and by the influence of some preachers of great animal powers.

With the more intelligent, it is a question of sober thought to determine, whether a man can believe in direct revelations and the Bible at the same time. He who confides in the Bible, devotes himself to it for knowledge; but he that looks for light from direct influences, without the dull slow processor studying, resorts to the secret grove, or some other doleful place to converse with an unrevealed, mysterious and unknown God. T. F.

LIGHT ARISING IN DARKNESS.

It has been stated to me on good authority, that two of the leaders of a modern sect which rose in Tennessee, (and one of them, perhaps, is the strongest man of the party) have learned that the mystical religions and influences of the day, are nothing but *Mesmerism!* If these men are sincere they will learn much more, but it is said they are going or are gone to another sect of equal darkness, because she promises more money. Many men have their prices and obviously gold is the God not of a few of the mystical preachers of this degenerate age. Esau sold his birthright for a mess of pottage, and I fear Messrs. S. & O. will swear to support Calvinism, and mystical religion, neither of which can they believe, for a few more hams of bacon, and a little more sectarian honor, than they could have as Cumberlands. Honesty is a jewel.

T. F.

CORRESPONDENTS.

CHURCH AT BAGDAD, SMITH COUNTY.

Of this congregation Bro. James Young says, "We number something over one hundred members. We have regular preaching on every fourth Lord's day by Bro. Dewhit, and occasionally preaching by some others. We had a five days meeting in August, at which eleven additions were made to the church. We have agreed to meet every Lord's day, except some preaching interposes. (If I understand the brethren, they have really promised to obey the Lord unless there is preaching in striking distance. Some of the Sectarians in these parts, particularly the Baptist and Methodist, are beginning to bold up the Bible and contend for the Bible in preference to anything else, and to recommend it to their hearers, to read and judge for themselves. Yet they hold us at a distance, not willing to break bread with us or suffer us to break bread with them." Most Baptists and Methodists have to be born again before they can act like Christians.—ED.

LETTER FROM JAMES A. BUTLER.

We the humble petitioners do, in behalf of a young man in our midst, ask a deck passage on your new but swift steamer, The "Review," believing that those who sail under her pennon are safe.

By granting this our petition, we will ever pray.

You will readily discover, from the youth's own petition, that sad penury lingers around him. Thus follows his wants: Rufus C. Burleson of Hickory Grove, thus writes to "The Baptist," mainly under the Editorial of R. B. C. Howell, D.D.:

"We (I) desire that you should give us in "The Baptist," as soon as your leisure will permit, an illustration and exposition of the doctrine of Depravity, Faith, Repentance, Remission of Sins, and Regeneration. In this part, our churches are filled up with young members, and our ministry, qualified to instruct, is not sufficiently numerous.

"☞The *Campbellites* are exerting themselves to sow the seeds of heresy and division, and unless promptly met with truth (baptist traditions), they will unsettle the faith of some, and perhaps *destroy* them. Instruct us in these great *doctrines* of the Bible, *and we will use them with the more efficiency,* not in the form of *controversy,* but by pouring them upon the minds of our people, as the clouds do replenishing showers upon the springing grass."

Now, to show' that the Dr.'s mental sensibilities were touched, hear, O hear the response: "We (I) promise (Jas. i, 5) bro. B. to give an essay, under the head of "Minister's Department," in consecutive order, upon each of these topics named, which we (I) trust the brethren will employ to the best advantage."

1. "In this part, *our churches* are filled up with young members," &c. What think you is meant by the word, "churches"? Meeting houses, I suppose, unless the phrase *our* (baptist) churches, refers to the many divisions of the Baptists, each of which claiming to be the "Old fashioned Baptists?'

The latter must be the meaning. It cannot refer to the meeting houses, for the young members and the old, and the poor gentiles included, do not often fill their synagogues. As to those minors alluded to—neither "many" nor few have been made in "this part of Mi., since my acquaintance here. I came in January, 1843. True, there have been great efforts made to proselyte, among all parties;' but Achan has not yet confessed his sin against the Lord God of Israel. He has brought into Israel's camps Babylonish garments, and two hundred shekels of silver, and a wedge of gold, &c. Joshua 7.

That is, the mourning bench—feelings for, or in place of, obedience, and *deliverance* before *birth,* and has transferred the *pangs* of the *mother* to the *child!* There is a voice of *noise* from the city, a voice from the temple, crying—behold! Before she travailed, she brought forth, before her pain came, she was delivered of a *male* child. Who ever heard such a thing? Who hath seen such a thing? None. But when Zion travaileth, then she bringeth forth her children, Isa. 66.

2. "The Campbellites are exerting themselves," &c. It is a fact, bro. B., that there are some Christians here, who are doing vigilantly what their hands find to do. But if you have strewed the gospel seed upon good ground, I cannot see how the words of *heretics* can root them out, unless their words be stronger than the gospel—Rom. 1 : 16. And do you not recollect when you pour Gilead *juice* (Jer. 8: 22) into your predestinated, elected "young members," you tell them,

“that

neither life nor death, nor principalities, powers, things present, nor things to come, shall ever separate them from the love of God," &c. Then, if none of the foregoing can separate your *elect* from the love of God, you need not fear Fanning, Elley, Curtis, Dean, Carrington, Hill, Butler, Usery, Estis, &c., &c.—all is safe, and their little skiff shall outride the storm, and safely anchor on the banks of everlasting deliverance!

Bro. B. forgot one *little* matter, viz: that the minds of many of his baptist brethren, of full age too, had been delivered from the shackles of baptist traditions, and are now active members of the Church of Christ.

3. "Instruct us in the great *doctrines* of the Bible," &c. Who? Why, bro. Howell. No. If any of you lacketh wisdom, let him ask of God, who giveth to all men liberally, and upbraideth not; and it shall be given him. But let him ask in faith nothing wavering. Jas. 1: 5, 6. And if bro. B. had asked Paul upon the word *doctrines,* he would have informed him, that when used in its *plural* form, it appertained to the *notions* of Demons, at least not to Christ, for that is always in the *singular.* Col. 2: 22; 1 Tim. 4: 1; Heb. 13:9.

4. "Not in the form of controversy," &c. Poor soul!!   J. A. B.
13th Oct., 1844.

N. B. Brother Howell hopes that his essays will be used to the best advantage. Amen. Acts 19: 19.

POLITICS.

Great anxiety and unhappiness are felt by many of the Disciples of Christ, at seeing their brothers and sisters take so active a part in the Politics of the day. Numbers are so engrossed by it that they seem almost to have forgotten their God. Their minds are so engrossed by the bustle and distraction inseparable from the spirit of Whiggery and Democracy, that the worship of the Lord is but a dry and lifeless business.

Society they formerly avoided as deleterious to their growth in grace and the knowledge of the truth, is now eagerly sought. Where blasphemy, drunkenness and all wicked conduct abound, there do we find the professed disciples of the pure and lowly Redeemer; and if not actually engaged in those vices, they at least encourage them by their presence, and participation in the soul-destroying systems of politics that so much encourage their growth and universal spread. Evil communications will corrupt good manners, and if we engage with pure hearts and hands, a very short service will be sufficient to defile and corrupt. Many know and *feel* the truth of this.

But to come to the point. I intend to talk a little to my sisters, if they will not think me presumptuous. I was led to think of this by visiting some who arc so deeply interested in Politics, that Clay or Polk engaged all their thoughts, or at least all their conversation. Can we, my sisters, with all our hearts, serve two masters? Are we as much devoted to the Lord as before we commenced our exertions to elect these men? Are our thoughts as often raised to him, and is our conversation as much in Heaven, while we are carrying and making banners, dressing in uniform, and screaming hurrah, hurrah, as the Christian religion requires?

I have no doubt, when many try to pray, their thoughts are more filled with Coons and Poke stalks, than with the goodness of God. This may seem hard, but I judge from actions. I cannot see how a *really zealous* Whig or Democrat can at all engage in the things of Eternity. Ah!—

Eternity, Eternity is a sober word. All political excitement will be allayed, so soon as we breathe its solemnizing atmosphere.

The names of Clay and Polk will have but little influence there, except to cause deep anguish in the hearts of many who are undone forever, undone by giving up the service of the Lord for the sake of these two poor mortals.

My sisters, while we are engaged in earthly politics, the footstep of time is gliding noiselessly away. Death and judgment are coming apace. The politics of a spiritual world will soon be forced upon our attention. In view of this, are we making ready? Do we say that our conduct has a proper influence on our families, or have we forgotten that some entrusted to our charge are not reconciled to God,—have not submitted to the Saviour! Are we going to Barbecues and political gatherings, forgetting, and teaching others to forget, we have a God to serve! Perhaps young men of our families are encouraged by our example to attend these places, and join in the excitement, to associate with those who scoff at virtue, and blaspheme God, and are thus by degrees led to taste and love the destroying wine cup, when a proper influence exerted by mothers and sisters might have save them from evil. We may say this excitement will soon be over, and then we will all get into sober habits again. Perhaps, some may come out of it unscathed, but no doubt the hearts of many parents will in future be made to bleed. They will have to mourn over the ultimate ruin of many promising sons, from having suffered them to associate this year with the idle and vicious. I would not be far wrong were I to say that its effects have been felt before this time. Many young wives have had this year to weep at the neglect of those who are as dear to them as their own life.

But to return to these gatherings. Have any of us learned to be better Christians by attending them? Have we felt our own hearts more warmed with the love of God? Had it increased our love of secret communion with our Heavenly Father? Have we exerted ourselves more to promote his cause; or rather did not every one we went to, have a tendency to wean our hearts from serious reflections? We do not so much wish to examine ourselves.— Prayer is more troublesome, and we scream hurrah! to drive away thought.

If we serve the Lord, we are commanded to lay aside all superfluity of naughtiness. And certainly, as there is a great amount of wicked spirit displayed at these places, we should not only now, but forever forsake them.

We are told to put on the whole armour of God; to be sober and watch unto prayer; to let the word of Christ dwell in us richly in all wisdom; teaching and admonishing one another in psalms, hymns, and spiritual songs, singing and making melody in our hearts to the Lord.

Some of us are very fond of badges and uniforms to distinguish the party to which we belong. Would it not be better to wear the uniform appointed by our king? You know we cannot well wear both at once. They don't suit together. The Lord's uniform is not made up of plaiting of hair, wearing of gold, or putting on of apparel; but it is the ornament of a meek and *quiet* spirit, (not a hurrahing one) and is of great value in his eyes.

Its banner is kindness, and the other parts of the dress are made of humbleness of mind, meekness, long suffering. After we put it on, Paul says we had better be keepers at home, good, and discreet. These injunctions carefully obeyed, would I think, prevent all undue interference in politics, and we would have more time for the proper discharge of our duties. These lines are submitted to the consideration of my sisters, with a more earnest desire that we may all be devoted to the Lord, who died for us, and may at last hear the delightful approval of "well done!"

With affectionate regard, LUCY.

FRANKLIN COLLEGE,
FIVE MILES EAST OF NASHVILLE, TENNESSEE.

THIS INSTITUTION, which is the first of the kind that has been attempted in America, will commence its first Session on Wednesday, the first day of January, eighteen hundred and forty-five.

FRANKLIN COLLEGE was chartered by the Legislature of Tennessee, January 30th, 1844. Since which time a Kitchen 24 by 20 feet, a Dining Room 60 by 30, and a College Edifice 120 by 40 feet, three stories high, containing a large hall, rooms for societies and recitations, and fifty rooms for students, have been erected, and will be in readiness by the time specified. The buildings are of brick, and the workmanship is of the most substantial character. The 'Trustees believing confidently this Institution will be a decided improvement on the present plans of training youth, and a permanent benefit to the country, avail themselves of this means of presenting to the public, a synopsis of the system which will be adopted, the names of the Faculty, costs of the establishment, &c. The charter contemplates a combination of PHYSICAL, INTELLECTUAL, and MORAL CULTURE, and the Trustees and Officers are of the opinion, this is the only plan upon which an energetic, intellectual and Moral race can be reared up.

1. PHYSICAL DEPARTMENT.

To secure health, vigorous constitutions, sound minds, and good morals, a sufficiency of Agriculture to teach the properties and improvement of soils, the proper cultivation of the different grains and grasses, and the management of farm stock, also Horticulture and Orcharding in all their branches, and the Mechanic Arts, will be introduced. Each student, as an indispensable part of his education, will devote from two to five hours per day, to some one or more branches of physical industry. The profits accruing from the labor, after paying for materials, and rents, will belong to the students. This is the system which has been adopted in the best colleges of Europe, and it is fondly believed no department will be more pleasant than the Physical in the United States, when properly understood and put into practice. Thus, the rich will be taught the value of property, and indigent and aspiring young men, will acquire the means of paying for their education.

2. INTELLECTUAL DEPARTMENT.

As full a course of English and Classical literature, Mathematics and general science will be adopted as at any College of the United States.-—A list of books will be given, with the laws of the Institution, so soon as the Faculty can convene.

3. MORAL DEPARTMENT.

Under this head will be introduced Sacred History, Music, Discipline and personal accomplishments. The Bible, Ancient Geography, History and Dictionaries, will be the only books employed in Sacred History. Music will be a daily exercise of the College. The discipline will be firm but parental, A plain and cheap uniform will be selected so soon as circumstances will justify, and the greatest pains will be taken, to improve the manners of students.

In addition to the regular College department of Freshman, Sophomore, Junior and Senior classes, there will be a Juvenile and Preparatory department. Boys after arriving at the age of five years will be taken into the Juvenile department, and a teacher or teachers will spend the whole time with them.

In the Juvenile department the first principles of English Education will be taught. In the Preparatory Department, students will be made ready for the regular classes of the College.

The Collegiate year will consist of one Session of ten months or forty-two weeks, and no student will be taken for a less time, or from the time of entering to the close of session, and if the entry is made within two months of the opening of the Session full price will be charged. One day in each month will be set apart for visiting. Half the expenses will be required when students enter College, and the balance will be due the first of June in each year, and if the fees are hot paid at the appointed time, interest will be charged.

CHARGES.

Plain, substantial and wholesome fare, comfortable rooms and fire wood will be furnished at SIXTY DOLLARS per annum.

Tuition fees in the Juvenile Department will be $20 00
Tuition in the Preparatory class, ...$30 00
Tuition in the College proper, ...$40 00

Five dollars will be required from each student as a matriculation fee, for the purpose of purchasing books, and apparatus.

Thus it will be observed the whole cost of boarding, room rent, fuel, and tuition will range from 80 to 100 dollars per annum. Students will furnish their own rooms, and pay for their washing, also the Professor of Music will be entitled to a small extra fee.

FACULTY.

TOLBERT FANNING, *President and Professor of Intellectual and Moral Science, Natural History, Agriculture and Horticulture,*

I. N. LOOMIS, *Professor of Mathematics, Chemistry, Mechanic Arts, and Assistant Professor of Horticulture.*

JOHN EICHBAUM, *of Tenn., Professor of Ancient Languages, and Assistant Professor of Agriculture and Horticulture.*

E. CHANDLER, *of Ohio, Professor of Music.*

A. J. FANNING, *of Mississippi, Principal of Preparatory Department.*

P. R. RUNNELS, *of Tennessee, Principal of the Juvenile Department.*

B. EMBRY, *Steward, and Principal of the Boarding House, under the advice and direction of the Faculty.*

TRUSTEES.

T. FANNING.
JNO. W. RICHARDSON, *Stewartsborough, Tennessee*
GEO. W. MARTIN, *Nashville.*
JAMES H. FOSTER, *Nashville.*
EDWARD TRABUE, *Nashville.*
B. EMBRY, *Nashville.*
W. H. WHARTON, *Nashville.*
TURNER VAUGHAN, *Ladago, Tennessee.*
JNO. SIMPSON, *Sparta, Tennessee.*
JNO. A. GARDNER, *Gardnersville, Tennessee.*
THOMAS MARTIN, *Pulaski, Tennessee.*
D. G. LIGON, *Moulton, Alabama.*
DAVID KING, *Russellville, Kentucky.*
JNO. SHELBY, *Nashville.*
ANDREW EWING, *Nashville.*
BEVERLY NELSON. *Mt. View, Tennessee.*
JNO. R. WILSON, *Nashville.*
FRANK McGAVOCK, *Nashville.*

A limited number of Students will be taken, and applications may be made through the President or Secretary, B. EMBRY. Persons who have indulged their Sons inhabits of idleness and extravagance, will please not apply for situations, and it is the request of the Trustees that none shall attend the Institution, who are not determined to be educated, and who cannot bear the strictest government.

Papers throughout the country favorable to this mode of educating youth, will please publish this Circular.

NEWS FROM TEXAS.

JACKSON, MISSISSIPPI, SEPT. 30tb, 1844.

To the Editors of the Christian Review:

DEAR BRETHREN:—Since my arrival in Texas about the first of last April, I have not had the opportunity of a regular reading of the Christian Review. I have learned that my letter is published, and also a desire is expressed to know where I am, and what I am doing. I regret that I have not been able to get the number containing my letter, which would enable me to give the information called for. However, I will do the best I can. On my arrival in Texas about the first of last April, I found the fields white already to harvest. Brethren Weaver, M. W. Mathews, E. D. Moore and others, had been labouring with success in the counties of Bua, Red River, and Lamar and different Churches were in a state of organization. After having laboured among them for some two months, and as I thought was upon the point of starting back to Illinois, I reflected upon the state of the Christian Churches in Texas, a number of them newly converted to the Gospel faith, and protracted meetings for some six weeks arranged to come on in succession at the different places, I determined to forego all other considerations, and continue until fall. We have just cause of thankfulness to God for his blessing in view of the success that crowned our efforts. Brethren Moore, McCluskey, Matthews and myself, were the principal labourers, but Bro. John McCluskey laboured more abundantly than we all. Our most successful meeting was hold near Dangerfield, southern division of Red River county, during a protracted meeting of five days, we had the pleasure of witnessing sixty additions, some fifty-five of whom were immersed, and on the next Sunday at the same place seven more were added, and five of them were immersed; our five days meeting was the two last days of August and three first days of September. I never have in any country seen the Gospel wield an influence so universal as it does in this part of Texas.

The Churches in Texas need the Gospel government, and discipline exercised among them, in order to their permanency and growth. I hope our preaching brethren will not forget Texas. I am now in Jackson, Mississippi, with James E. Matthews; but it seems to me that the people are nearly run wild on politics, professed Christians and all. I intend returning to Texas so soon as I can go to Illinois, and arrange my business. I have been unable to do anything for the Review in Texas. The great uncertainty in the conveyance by mail to that government is in the way, money is scarce in Texas, and your invariably in advance is in the way where the conveyance is so uncertain, and the brethren there, some of them, are taking the Christian Messenger when they can get it. But those who have subscribed and paid, cannot get the paper regularly as yet. I am going from here to Illinois by Railroad and Steamboats. When I have leisure, you may expect to hear from me again.

Affectionately yours in the bonds of Christian love,

ABNER HILL.

————————

Bro. EUBANKS, of Glasgow, Ky., has sent us some very good remarks on the New Birth; but in as much as there other suggestions which we do not so well comprehend, for the present, we have declined the publication of the essay.

CANNON COUNTY, SEPTEMBER 2d, 1844.

To the Editors of the Christian Review:

For the encouragement of your readers I write to let you know, we have just closed a meeting at my house, the result of which was as follows:—Thirty-one persons were immersed, three of whom were from the Old Presbyterians, four from the Cumberlands, one from the Methodists, and four from the Baptists. One Methodist lady united who had been immersed. One of our brethren who had been out of the way, came back, made a noble confession, and was received. There were many persons in attendance. During the whole of our meeting, to their credit he it told, they honored the Author of the Bible and themselves by hearing what was spoken.

Brethren R. B. Hall, S. E. Jones, Y. W. M'Daniel, B. White and Wm. Dill, laboured with us. The Gospel is rapidly obtaining in my neighborhood.— We have persons from all the sects to hear us, and much prejudice is put to rest.

On my last Circuit at Flat Creek, Bedford County, we immersed eight, and two on Boon's Creek. In all we added 14.

Your brother in the Lord,   C. CURLEE.

———————————

Cedar Grove, White County, Tenn., Aug., 1844.

DEAR BRETHREN OF THE CHRISTIAN REVIEW—Seeing the interest taken in the news from the churches, I proceed, in compliance with your request, to make a statement of a few facts connected with my labors.

Since the first of June, I held a meeting at Antioch, White county, with Bro. R. Jones, at which place we had 16 additions; 6 from the Baptists and 10 from the world. I also held one meeting in Sparta, and two at Bethlehem, 5 miles below Sparta, at which meeting we had 13 noble additions—some from the Methodists, I know not how many; but amongst the additions at Bethlehem were our old friends, Col. Lowry and his excellent old lady, and Gen. John W. Simpson. We also held a meeting at Ivy Bluff, Warren county, where we had 20 additions, and the prospects were good for many more—but I was compelled to leave. May the Lord bless you, and prosper the truth, and your very excellent paper.   Yours in hope, W. H. F

A THOUGHT.

Are there not in the providential government of man, presentiments of misfortune? I have often been harassed by oppressive and indistinct fears that all was not right, immediately preceding the greatest calamities of my life. I remember one wherein those fears created a sickly sensation of my whole frame. The effect of those fears and the succeeding calamity, have never forsaken me —have been the ruling events of my life. May not this state of the mind oftentimes be mistaken for religion!   J. B. F.

GOOD NEWS FROM OXFORD.

Nine Theological Students have recently been expelled from Oxford, for denying special influences of the spirit without the word of God. Light is spreading.   T. F.

CHRISTIAN REVIEW.

VOL. I.   NASHVILLE, DECEMBER, 1844.   NO. XII.

NOTES ON A TOUR.—No. 4.

Tuesday, Oct. 29th, 1844, I left Nashville, in company with *Mrs. F., Bros. S. E. Jones, P. R. Runnels, and Jno. Eichbaum,* with a view of preaching the Gospel in the States of Alabama and Mississippi a few weeks, and the first day we reached *Franklin,* in Williamson county. In this place, there are some forty disciples, who meet weekly and keep the ordinances. Bro. Jones delivered a discourse at night. Our excellent Brother, Dr. Barbee, who is a man of good education and most amiable disposition, is residing in Franklin, and is conducting a school for young ladies. Brother B. richly deserves patronage.

Wednesday, 30th, we journeyed to Columbia, in Maury county, and at night we had meeting in the Masonic temple. While at Columbia, we gave ourselves the pleasure of visiting the Female Institute, under the superintendence of the Rev. Mr. Smith, of the Episcopalian religion. The building is the most spacious and superb edifice that has been erected in Tennessee, or the West, so far as we have been informed, for a Female school. Mr. S. is a polite and courteous gentleman, and we should think admirably calculated to preside over such an institution. There are some two hundred pupils in the Institute, and from all the facts presented, we conclude there is no school for young ladies in the West, of higher repute. The Rector has been at considerable pains and expense to collect books, Philosophical and Chemical apparatus, Minerals, and organic remains, for the use of the establishment.

There is a congregation of about thirty disciples of Christ in Columbia, who meet weekly, and most of the members are devoted Christians. We were deeply afflicted, however, to learn, political excitement and other species of *dissipation,* have well-nigh destroyed a few of the members. What a shame that Christians, who should be the "salt of the earth and light of the world," do not keep themselves unspotted from the world! Brethren, "let your light so shine before men, that others may see your good works, and glorify your Father who is in heaven."

Tuesday, 31st, we travelled 30 miles, to Lawrenceburg, in Lawrence county, and held meeting at night in the Methodist meeting-house. It would require great patience, and considerable time, to introduce successfully, the Christian religion in Lawrenceburg.

Friday, November 1, 1844, we journeyed to the neighborhood of Florence, in Lawrence county, Ala., and spent the night with our faithful friends in the family of Jno. Chisholm, Esq.

Saturday, Nov. 2d, we reached Florence, where we met our brethren, Ligon, McDonald, Dunn, Hackworth, Young, Houston, and many others of our brothers and old acquaintances. The Methodists were kind enough to open their house of worship, and we addressed the citizens for three days, on the first principles of Christianity. The men of the world listened attentively, though few partisans were inclined to know the truth. There was much prejudice against the church of God, mainly from the influence of the party preachers, and the unbecoming conduct of *false* friends. One maneuver I can but mention: From various circumstances, it was obvious the members of the Presbyterian church were either forbidden by the pastor, or had mutually agreed not to attend. They were evidently fearful to trust themselves in hearing of the truth. But a Rev. gentleman, Mr. Slack, D. D., who was supposed to have great learning, and who felt himself well grounded in his traditions, attended and heard for all the rest, and reported to the timid lambs of Mr. Vancort's flock, as seemed to him best calculated to satisfy them with their sect. I heard one of the members say, "Dr. S. knows all about it"—meaning thereby, that he understood all we teach, and was better capable of judging of the truth than the common people, and his version of the matter was to satisfy all who were not to be trusted to hear for themselves.

A word or two in reference to this course. In the first place, it was not true the Doctor had investigated the subject of Christianity, and understood our teaching, as was supposed; and in the second place, he acted as no independent man, who knows the truth, will act. We frequently and respectfully invited those who had objections, to make them known, and we pledged ourselves to answer them; but this he sternly refused to do, yet he insinuated to his brethren, and other gentlemen in private, that the "doctrine was very bad," even "worse than he had before thought." Thus, it will be seen our opposers are covert, and such as will not show themselves in open day. May the Lord enable us to bear opposition as good soldiers of Jesus Christ!

While at Florence, we had the opportunity of presenting a great amount of truth, and we doubt not fruit will be seen in the good world. But one, however, had the nobility to confess the authority. Mr. and Mrs. Jon. Simpson were most kind in their attentions to Mrs. F. and myself.

Tuesday, the 5th, we travelled twenty-four miles, to Russellville, in Franklin county, and spent one day with the beloved disciples. At this point we left Bros. Jones and Dunn, to labour a few days. There are about 160 disciples at Russellville, and taking all the difficulties into consideration with which they have had to contend, we have confidence to believe they are doing well. A few, however, have joined the company of Bacchus, and are dead to all godly influences. Still there are many truly pious brothers and sisters in Russellville, whom we hope to meet in better climes, when the ills of life shall have ceased.

Thursday, the 7th, we set out in the stage for Columbus, in Lawrence county, Miss., a hundred miles distant, and arrived safely on the 8th, and remained till Monday, the 18th. In Columbus there are about 150 disciples, many of whom, in point of intelligence, are seldom equaled. Some difficulties were in existence amongst the members, when we arrived, and we labored most of the time in endeavoring to settle them; and we think our labor was not in vain. This church was planted in '41, and for about a year the disciples met and attended to *their own* worship; but unfortunately, they finally employed preachers to worship for them a good portion of the time; since which, they have not done so well. The best preacher in the world, preaching three times on every Lord's day, to keep the saints alive, will kill them spiritually; and without great care, eternally. Preachers should plant churches and set them in order, but permit the

to their own worship. If the disciples in Columbus will study the Christian religion carefully, and particularly *study and cultivate the meek and lowly spirit of the Savior,* they will save themselves, and many of the good people of the South. *Brother Green Hill* has been at great expense to build up the cause in Columbus, and the Lord will reward him richly for it. The brethren have a first rate meeting-house in the progress of erection, and when finished their means of benefiting the public will be still greater. May the Lord preserve the church in Columbus in the Spirit.

Monday, the 18th, we left Columbus, and journeyed to Colbert, on the Tombigbee river, a distance of twelve miles, and delivered a discourse to some twenty persons, in a cold old house, on the outskirts of the town, after which we travelled to Aberdeen, in Monroe county, a distance of 18 miles, where we spent the night. This is a flourishing village, but like most of the Southern towns, it will, most probably, in a few years, have reached the zenith of its glory. It however has a good country on the West, and may flourish much longer than other Southern towns. The people were most kind and obliging in Aberdeen, and we would have been much pleased to have given a few discourses on the Christian institution, but time would not permit.

We left Aberdeen Tuesday, the 19th, and journeyed across the country in a North-Western direction about a hundred miles, to Holly Springs, in Marshall county, at which place we arrived Friday, the 22d. We spent but one night, and delivered but one discourse in Holly Springs. There is a pleasant church at this place, and the brethren need help and encouragement. The disciples have contended with great difficulties, but not half so much injury has been done them from the world and partisans, as from false brethren. They have been cursed with several preachers who were bad men, and who have left a stain on the cause which will require much time to deface. We left on Saturday, the 23d, with regret that circumstances would not permit us to remain longer. Bro. Davenport, the Evangelist, is about leaving this country, but we hope the brethren will raise up preachers amongst themselves. We tarried the first night at Bro. Curlee's, and gave a discourse to some thirty persons, and reached Bro. Matthew W. Webber's, in Shelby county, Tenn., Lord's day, the 24th, and delivered a discourse at Bro. W.'s dwelling on the 25th, Bro. W. is an intelligent and energetic brother, from the old Virginia school of Baptists, who has thrown off the shackles of party and is contending boldly for the truth in the country round about him. There is a congregation of some forty disciples in the neighborhood, and from all we could learn to the contrary, they are generally excellent persons. Still there is something wrong amongst them, they only meet twice a month, and that to hear Brother Webber preach. Christians should be cautious that they lose not their reward, in listening to good sermons instead of studying the word and attending the worship for themselves. I do earnestly hope the time is not far distant when churches will be devoted to the Christian practices, and when the preachers will spend all their time in converting the world and putting in order the converted.

Wednesday, the 27th, we left the residence of Bro. Leake, for Jackson, in Madison county, a distance of sixty miles, at which place we arrived on the evening of the 28th. There is no church of God in Jackson, though there are people of every other calling, perhaps, from Romanists down. If correctly informed, there is but one brother who is a professed disciple in the place, and he

happened to be from home. But for this fact, I suppose, I should have remained several days. There is a church of Baptists, who have been taught many leading principles of the Christian religion, by Jon. Finley; but I fear there are few who have the independence to acknowledge the whole truth.— Mr. Finley is decidedly the ablest Baptist preacher I have heard in the West, and yet he has no independence, but is a bond slave to his and his sect.

On reaching town, I learned Mr. G., of the "Star" of Universalism, Cincinnati, was to preach that night, at the Court House; so I and my company determined to attend. Mr. G.'s text was, Prov. 18: 13: "He that answereth a matter before he heareth it, it is folly and shame unto him?' It was his object to show that all men would be happy in the next world, *"being children of the resurrection."* He answered with much adroitness many of the party objections to his system, and concluded by exhorting the people to receive the truth; "for," said he, "I assure you your eternal weal or woe depends upon it." Although this was rather a strange sentiment from a Universalist, yet Mr. G. was much more noble than most partisans; for after concluding his sermon, he invited any one present who desired, to answer his arguments. His proposition was so fair, that I could not, as an honest man, feel myself at liberty to leave the house without entering my solemn protest against the doctrine of the heavenly enjoyments of the finally impenitent. In this matter I spent some twenty minutes, and concluded with the declaration of Paul, (2 Thes. 1:6,) "That Christ shall come from heaven in flaming fire, taking vengeance on those that know not God, and obey not the Gospel." Mr. G. replied in a discourse of about an hour's length, and I gave a second reply of about ten minutes. Mr. G. spoke again, but as the hour was late, the people did not listen quite so kindly. In conclusion, he proposed debating the question at some future period. In reference to this matter, I would respectfully ask the teachers of the Christian religion, if it would not be well enough to have a full discussion of Universalism some time during the next year, at Louisville or Cincinnati, and let the arguments go forth to the world?

The Universalists boast of their numbers being over a million of souls in the U. States, and it occurs to me the rewards and punishments of the Bible could be set forth in a very clear and forcible manner by a discussion of this kind.

I was not a little amused at my own position with Mr. G. Although I had had many discussions with religionists; this was the first time in my life, that I found myself *"orthodox"* with most parties. The denominations seemed well pleased at my arguments against Universalism, and I was emboldened to make an appointment for the next day, to introduce to the consideration of the citizens of Jackson the Christian religion; but alas! there was more alarm at this than the rankest Universalism. However, a few attended and listened with much respect.

In the afternoon of the same day, we left for Huntingdon, in Carroll county, and found ourselves safely stored at the tavern of the Rev. Mr. Woods, in the destined village, on Saturday evening, the 30th. I preached at night, and twice on Lord's day, Dec. 1st, to small but very attentive congregations. From the respect paid the truth in Huntingdon, I am persuaded the seeds are already sown for a rich harvest in that region, at no very distant day. "Parson Woods" proved himself a most hospitable gentleman, and from my soul I can wish him no greater harm than to know the truth, and become the Lord's freeman by it.

Monday, the 2d, we set out for Franklin College, a distance of 110 miles and arrived safely on

Wednesday, the fourth, after an absence of near six weeks.

But one reflection more, and I close "Notes of Tours," for at least ten moons. Through all the parts of Alabama, Mississippi, and Tennessee we passed, there is great lack of Godly intelligence, and Godly piety. The people are generally intelligent on other matters, add friendly disposed; but the blessings of the pure and spiritual religion of the Bible, are but imperfectly enjoyed. A hundred able and humble preachers are needed where there is one to be found at present. Preachers of the cross should be diligent.											T. F.

UNIVERSALISM & C. F. R. SHEHANE.

Notwithstanding I have been teaching the Christian religion some fourteen years, during which time I have had many discussions, both oral and written; yet 1 do not recollect to have had the charge of misrepresentation of sentiment before alleged against me. My motto has ever been, "If I cannot meet an opponent in all his strength, I desire not to meet him at all." My object through life has been to learn the truth, and live according to its mandates.— I have not been particular Who the teacher should be, so he knew and taught the truth; and living in what is called an "enlightened age," I have ever felt it my privilege, and a duty I owed myself and my contemporaries, when I heard or read any thing opposed to the pure and wholesome doctrine of the Apostles, to publicly tender my dissent. I have met men as they presented themselves, great and small, and I ever expect so to do. Bui to give the reader some idea of the charges made against me in the "Messenger of Glad Tidings," published at Wetumpka, Ala., edited by S. J. McMorris, and occasionally assisted by C. F. R. Shehane, who formerly professed to be a member of the church of Christ, and who was for a considerable time one of my old school fellows, I will give a few extracts. Mr. Shehane speaks of me as being "ungenerous," "censorious," "ignorant of universalism;" but the Editor says I "indulge in the common slang against Universalists, that they make no discrimination between virtue and vice, or the righteous and the wicked, regardless of their good or evil conduct." Again, this Editor of pretended universal benevolence, makes a serious charge for not sending him the Christian Review, in which I speak so *"harshly and unjustly;"* and again, he pronounces myself and my brethren *"a servile set of Campbellites."* More of this style, would be offensive to good men, and I will spend a few moments in noticing the charges.

These benevolent gentlemen assail me as an enemy to righteousness, for communicating the idea that Universalists send the abandoned, the filth and offscouring of the earth, rejoicing to heaven, to be seated with the patriarchs. Prophets, the Apostles, and all the sufferers for Christ and martyrs for the truth. Is this misrepresentation, gentlemen? We will see. In the Messenger of Nov. 15, the Editor says the *"Universalists contend the whole human family shall be finally saved."* To be brief, I take the liberty of stating the doctrine a little more fully, in my own words. Universalists contend that the wicked get all their punishment in this life, and that, in the world to come all will be happy; that is, those who die in wickedness, as well as those who die saints. They quote many scriptures to prove all the resurrected will be saved in heaven.— Mark, they do not say men will be sinners in heaven, but they admit men in their sins, and they suppose   there   will   be   a

suppose   there   will   be   a cleansing of sin somewhere on the road from death to the heavenly Jerusalem. They do not use the word purgatory, but I see no reason why they should not. I ask the candid Universalist, if this is unfair? I will offer but two objections to the doctrine. 1. IT IS UNREASONABLE. The idea of putting Paul, who suffered so much for the truth, and did so much to promote piety in the earth, with ouch men as Jon. A. Murrell, in the world to come, whose example was contaminating, and whose life was rebellious against God, to me, is most absurd.

2d. The Bible teaches the condemnation of the wicked in this, and the next world. Mark 16: 16; 2 Thes. 1:6.

It is, however, my humble opinion, the horrific pictures drawn of hell-fire, brimstone, clanking of chains, deep groans of the damned, &c., by the preachers, has been the cause of driving many sincere persons into the doctrine of the final and perfect happiness of all men. To be sure, "knowing the terror of the Lord, we should persuade men; but we should not transcend the limits of the Bible/in threats calculated to alarm the ungodly. It is quite enough to say God "will render to every man according to his deeds. To them who by patient continuance in well doing, seek for glory, and honor, and immortality, eternal life," will be rewarded. "But unto them that are contentious, and do not obey the truth, but obey unrighteousness, indignation and wrath. Tribulation and anguish, upon every soul of man that doeth evil, of the Jew first, and also of the Gentile."

Of Mr. McMorris, I have but little to say. He may be a clever man, but it will be very difficult for him to convince good men that he is sincere in his assertions in reference to myself. Of C. F. R. Shehane 1 wish to speak a few words in kindness. I could once call Mr. S. *Brother;* but the day is passed.— My reasons, I wish particularly to give him, and I hope if the disciples do not treat him with the cordiality they formerly did, he will not call it persecution, but conclude we have just grounds for saying he is either desperately ignorant, crazy, or a traitor to his God. I insinuate not these things, solely because Mr. S. professes to believe God will save all men. It may be in the range of possibilities, a man may be mistaken with regard to the character of the punishment of the wicked, and still practice many of the wholesome precepts of the Gospel; but a man cannot, in fact, deny the cause of his God, and still serve him. This, I have little hesitation in saying, Mr. S. has done. Once he professed to believe, a man, to be a Christian, was required in the Scriptures to believe with all his heart on the son of God, repent of all his sins, and be immersed into the name of Jesus Christ, for the remission of sins; that these persons constitute the church of God, and not a sect; that Christians should be governed by the Bible alone, and honor the Master by wearing his name. But alas, without disproving one of these propositions, or denying the least of them, so far as I have been informed, he has united himself to a professed sect, (that is heresy,) and a sprinkled one at that, and gone through the solemn mockery of being ordained a preacher in it, and now glories in being a "Universalist," and takes great pleasure in sneering at the disciples of Christ, as constituting *"this sorry reformation."* Such a man I look upon as being untrustworthy, and unsafe even as a friend.

To tell what drove this young man into such desperate extremes, would be useless, were one capable; still, I esteem it not ungenerous to say to Mr. S.,

I have seen others besides himself, who attempted to become distinguished, by poetical effusions, great effort to recite Scriptures, without connection or common sense, to be eloquent, and to excel others in writing, and because they failed in all, and were consequently less noticed by their friends than their self-importance imperiously demanded, yield themselves dupes and servants of causes most abandoned. All I have to add is, I am not disappointed at the course of my quondam friend, and I must be indulged in the opinion, if any man experiences hell in this life, (which is the doctrine of Universalists) C. F. R. Shehane must be the individual.

I know not that I shall ever speak of these friends again; but if I should ever see an opportunity of exposing the speculations of this modern sect, I shall certainly feel it my duty to do so. I have many personal friends who are Universalists, and most of them I blame not for their sentiments. A full expose of Universalism should be given to the world. If true, we should all adopt it; but if untrue, the consequences will be disastrous indeed. T. F.

ZEAL FOR GOD.

The Apostle recommends "zeal in a good thing;" but the Jews had "a zeal for God, but not according to knowledge; for they being ignorant of God's righteousness, were going about to establish their own righteousness," and could not, therefore, submit to the righteousness of Christ. Those at Corinth who were zealous for Paul, Apollos, and Cephas, were pronounced "carnal;" but those who were in profession and fact, for Christ, were the true servants of God. There are many liberal minded men who look upon all professions as merely sectarian. Not long since, a highly respectable gentleman of the bench stated to me, that the disciples of Christ were a sect, for "see," said he, "how zealous they are of their teaching." To such, I wish to state, a sect is a heresy or faction; but those who plead for the Bible alone in religion, for the Church of Christ, the "one Lord,, one faiths one baptism, one body and one spirit of Christ," cannot be merely fragments of the one church, and their ground is evidently much higher than all the sects, who say in fact, the Bible is not a sufficient government, and who love party names much more than the name of Christ.— But this was not exclusively my object. I Wish to remind Christians that their lives must be zealously devoted to God and his institutions, to be prepared for the heavenly rest.; It must be acknowledged there is great indifference to reading, meditation, prayer, singing, and Godly conversation, with not a few professors.

Brethren, what are we doing to improve our own temper and manners, and advance the cause amongst others? The whole building is made up of "*living* and each member is a king and a priest to God." Are we preaching by example, in conversation, or publicly to the world? Do we consider the earth the Lord's, and the fullness thereof? Do we remember we "are not our own, but have been bought with a price, and should therefore glorify God in our bodies and spirits, which are the Lord's?"

Alas! too many have their hearts more upon bodily decorations, and pride to see their children excel in dress and lightness, than upon intelligence or Christian meekness. What can be more offensive to Heaven, than to see those devoted to politics, fashions and general levity through the week, attempt to mock God, by going through the forms of his service on the Lord's day? It is possible for a church to become intelligent in the Christian Scriptures, and to become so pure in life, that the members can say to their friends, "See, here are people who, like Zachariah and Elizabeth, 'walk in all the commandments and ordinances of the Lord blameless? "The yoke of Jesus is "easy, and his burden light," but the way of transgressors is hard. It is a great cross to serve the Lord one day, after serving the devil six. Let each brother and sister enquire of him or herself, "What is lacking to the character to make it perfect?" Few can lay their hand upon their heart and say, they have done all in their power to advance the cause of the Blessed God.

In the whole State of Tennessee, there are perhaps but two Evangelists who devote their time to teaching the word, and it is with difficulty they can be supported The Christians in Tennessee gave enough during the late Presidential canvass, to keep at least ten preachers in the field for a twelve month. Shall we, brethren, give our substance to sustain every other cause than the cause of Christ? The fields are ripe to the harvest, and laborers are few.— More faithful men should be SENT to the work. These we cannot have, unless we educate them, and rear them up in the instruction and admonition of the Lord. Unless, too, we support the teachers, they will continue to turn their attention to the professions of law, medicine, agriculture, &c. It is a great apostasy for a man to leave the Gospel for any worldly profession; nevertheless, all seem to quote stern and grim necessity as an apology. But why protract these remarks? Brethren, if we use not all the means within our power, "to perfect holiness in the fear of God," and save our fellow creatures as "brands from the burning," the Lord will require it of us in the day of judgment.

T. F.

MORMONISM.

Recently, I took time to look into the pretensions of Mormonism so far as to read the book of Mormon, and several numbers of their paper published at Nauvoo, and as a part of the news of the times, I give the following as some of my serious convictions.

1. The book of Mormon is the dryest and most uninteresting document, by a hundred per cent., I ever attempted to read. Mohamed contended there was a kind of sublimity and power in the Alcoran which proved its divine authenticity; but such cannot be affirmed of the book of the *"latter day saints."*— Brazen impudence and unpardonable stupidity are deeply engraved on every page? The whole book is intended to be a kind of imitation of, and commentary on the Bible. There are many absurdities taught, such as "life and immortality of the Gospel, six hundred years before Christ, and long before Prophets or Angels could have a glimpse of such things. I do not know, however, but I have learned something useful in reading the "Book of Mormon." I had thought bad men would not write a book purporting to be a revelation from God, which would condemn themselves; but I think I have been mistaken. These authors condemn hypocrisy and lying, and still there is little doubt they have fabricated the whole matter, to suit the times. From their papers it seems, there is considerable difficulty amongst the leaders, since the death of their founder. Sidney Rigdon was sent to Pittsburg not long since, with directions to raise a church, and while there it seems he received many new revelations, and

among the rest, some revealing the great secret that Joseph Smith Jr. had really hoaxed his followers, at least in many respects. Upon

Sidney's returning to Nauvoo, he was brought to trial for his rashness, and many witnesses testified that his "revelations were all of *the devils* and the chief, Mr. Young, on whom the mantle of Joseph is supposed to rest, in a flaming speech against poor Sidney, said he (Sidney) "had been SOFT-SOAPING the people, to get himself a great name." A Mr. Amassa Lyman, that I saw a few years past in West Tennessee, a cunning fellow, has stepped in Sidney's shoes. Rigdon, however, has friends, And I hope their present commotions will be the means of divulging the truth to the community. It cannot be that Sidney Rigdon will live under the charges, without exposing the superstition. A man of intelligence who will read their writings, can but feel holy indignation at their ignorance, arrogance and vulgarity.　　　　T. F.

SCEPTICISM—CHRISTIANITY—No. 3.

To the objections that Christianity has extended its influence over a comparatively small proportion of the human family, and has failed to eradicate the irreligion and profligacy of those nations among which it has been most successfully propagated, we base our reply.

FIRST—Upon analogical grounds, as we have our replies to the preceding objections. We may ask with triumphant propriety, what remedy for the physical diseases of man has proved of universal efficacy? What medical prescription has, in all the cases to which it has been applied, been found to be a successful catholicon? Does not every remedy for the ills of our shackled constitutions prove ineffectual even in the same disease when applied to different persons? The truth that we have no El Dorado—no panacea to apply for the relief of all the sufferings "to which flesh is heir," is considered no objection to the many remedies which Nature and Art afford for the alleviation of our various distempers. Why, then, should we object to the Gospel, because there are many who profess to receive it who are not benefited by it; or because there are many whose moral diseases are of such a character that it can afford them no immediate or individual relief? There are some diseases which under some conditions of the human constitution even the proper remedy cannot cure. So there are certain stages of the moral world —the Paganized for example— which the Gospel as such cannot relieve. Christianity belongs to civilized man; and if men cannot by its reflex or indirect influence be to some extent civilized, they cannot receive it. It is like casting pearls before swine, or giving that which is holy to the dogs, to offer Christianity to many individuals and nations of mankind. But assuredly this argues nothing against either the truth or the value of the system itself. The sublime science of Astronomy is not proven a fable by the failure of a Hottentot to understand or appreciate it.— The demonstrations of Euclid, are not shown to be absurd because the infant, the idiot or the unenlightened Pagan cannot solve the problem. Nor are all the great and useful discoveries and improvements of Science, Literature and the Arts rendered visionary and vain by the truth that all the Hindoos and American Indians know nothing of their value. I will not tax the pages of the "Review" or the patience of its readers by the application of these analogies. Still, I would suggest that every man who rejects Christianity upon the ground that universal man has not received it, must by parity of reasoning reject all the

discoveries of all the good and great of our race for five thousand years; all that has served to ennoble and adorn human nature, or to relieve the ignorance or advance the happiness of mankind. Until, therefore, we shall adopt the chimera of the Sophistical Rosseau respecting the superiority of the savage over the civilized state—as long, in other words, as civilized man would not be a savage or a savage a brute, men informed upon these moral and intellectual capabilities will not reject Christianity because it is a progressively developing system.

SECONDLY.—But we may affirm with strict propriety, that Christianity is, when properly examined, an universal remedy. There is nothing narrow, local or necessarily exclusive in any one of its precepts. It makes no barriers by which to separate the interests of mankind. It is not the religion of a sect or a nation; and any who thus consider it, abuse and misrepresent its cardinal features; but it is emphatically the religion of universal man. Prior to its establishment upon the resurrection of its divine founder, some of its provisions may have been suited only to the peculiar state and circumstances of his first disciples; but these are, by no one thoroughly read in the system, made a part of it. From its proper commencement—the day of the last authorized Pentecost of Judaism, no regulation can be found in it that is not as comprehensive as the race and as immutable as the nature of man. I defy the Skeptic to produce one precept of a local, political or temporary nature—any one that is not suited to the ever-varying exigencies of human existence. The innovating and corrupting hand of man may domesticate it to suit the political complexion of Italy, England or St. Petersburg; but its true features will appear again, and its free-born spirit will break all such restraints, so that commensurate with the temper, disposition and character of man it will shed abroad its enlightening and enlivening influence. The laced jacket of Roman Catholicism, or the many-coloured coat of divided Protestant Christendom cannot confine it to any local centre, for it will dwell only in a temple as extensive as the wants of man, and it cultivates afield as wide as the exigencies of suffering humanity. It breaks all chains that can be put upon it—abrogates all sectional claims. Neither "in this mountain" nor in Jerusalem, nor yet in Rome or London, does it acknowledge an Imperial Residence. In a word, it esteems no individual, or association of men, as possessing any exclusive claims to the knowledge or blessings it imparts; and in this sense, it is essentially and emphatically universal.

THIRDLY.—As it respects numbers, the Christian Scriptures have never assured us how many or how few will be saved. The question was once asked the Messiah—Are there few saved? But the separation of his religion from the gratification of all idle curiosity and the practicability of his teaching, gave it no other reply than "seek to enter in, for many shall seek to enter in who shall not be able." The aggregate amount of the saved or lost, has not been determined by any Prophet or Apostle of the government of God under either Old Testament of New. And just at this point, by the same authority that the Skeptic claims in making the objection, I claim the right of making a suggestion. We are taught prophetically by Daniel, and positively by the Savior, that in the coming age all nations shall be placed under the dominion of the Saints, who shall reign over them by the authority of the King of kings.— Now it is a question unsettled either by the captive prophet or the Lion of his tribe, for what purpose they shall be thus placed. Shall they reign over them for salvation or condemnation? Will the great King make his people the Saviors of those nations? Will the benefits of his death in that age be extended to them by the Saints, as they are to us by others in this? Is there any thing in the Christian Religion that would be forfeited, were we to say that God will at the coming of the Messiah, and the downfall of the present political and hierarchical governments of the earth, raise up all those nations who have never had an offer of life; and placing them under the dominion of his purified people, make the latter emphatically the Saviors of the world. There are many sayings in the prophetic word which seems to favor such an idea; and as it is more pleasing to consider celestial happiness more in connection with humanity at large, than with ad infinitesimal minority of mortals; and as the universal reign of the royal family which our Heavenly Father by his Son has been gathering out of every nation, kindred, tribe and tongue certainly has some object; and as we cannot well conceive that their happiness would be much accelerated if that object be the damnation of those over whom they are to be placed, I have concluded that the reign of the saints is to extend the offer of Salvation to those who have never heard the joyful sound. Of course, however, the finally neglectful and impious—the cowards, the unbelieving, the abominable of every age, past, present or to come, who will not know, or knowing, despise the Gospel, must share an everlasting banishment from the presence of the Lord and the glory of his power, with the Devil and his angels. No truth is more clearly insisted on than this, and as no opinion should be made known that subverts a plainly revealed truth, I only make the suggestion that the dominion of the Saints is a reign of Salvation, for the reflection of the thinking, and not as in the least invalidating the final condemnation of the willfully neglectful and disobedient.

In conclusion, may I not with confidence ask the Skeptic to examine Christianity as it is—as it appears in the doctrine and precepts of its authorized teachers—the Apostles? Let no imaginary objection divert you from a candid and careful examination of the messages of love, glory and Immortality— They appeal to the common sense of mankind; and their worthiness of the Creator, Preserver and Benefactor of man—their consonance with the dictates of reason— their friendship to the dignity and improvement of intelligent beings—their measures of genuine comfort, delight and glory;—by which they enable man to weigh in the equal scales of truth, the frowns of fortune with the felicity of an eternal inheritance—the loss of friends with the more intimate, tender and lasting associations of the refined and purified of heaven—the fluctuations of all external things, with the endless and immutable felicity of the innumerable company of the blood-washed throng, who have gone up through much tribulation—the mortifications, disappointments and insults of the conflicting pursuits of man, with the Heaven-born honor of being a Son of God, emphatically so by the resurrection—in a word, by which they enable us to weigh time with eternity, earth with heaven, and death with the everlasting joys and exquisite happiness of the New Jerusalem,—are to be determined by their own weight of evidence, and not by the cavils and apparent difficulties, that man in his ignorance or presumption may suggest.

Graysville, Dec. 1st, 1844.   J. B. F.

DEFICIENCY IN JOY.

I hear Christiana at times complaining of a deficiency in their enjoyments. 'To what is it to be attributed? Evidently to deficiency in obedience. Old Israel rejoiced even under the rigor of the bondage of the old Sinaiatic Covenant. Festivals of rejoicing before the Lord were held for days together, when they were diligent to keep the law and bring their offerings, their choice gifts and their vows to the place where the Lord had recorded his name. Hence says Deut. 12: 5,7,12, "You shall come to the place which the Lord your God shall choose out of all your tribes, to put his name there and to dwell in it, and you shall offer in that place your burnt-offerings and your victims and your tithes, and your vows and your gifts, and the firstborn of your herds and your flocks, and there you shall eat before the Lord your God, and *rejoice* in all you put your hands into, you and your households wherein the Lord your God has blessed you. * * * And you shall rejoice before the Lord your God, ye and your sons and your daughters, and your men-servants and your maid-servants and the Levite that dwelleth in your cities." Obedience was the cause of their feasts of joy; for they brought their sacrifices and their gifts, and their chosen vows to the place where the Lord caused his name to dwell, v. 11. The name of the Lord now dwells in his holy institutions; and were we to bring your sons, daughters and servants with our gifts and vows every first day of the week before him, we, too, would rejoice with a fullness of joy. How many of us, my brethren, can, in the midst of earthly tribulations, say with old Habakkuk, "Although the fig-tree shall not blossom, neither shall fruit be in the vines; the labor of the olive shall fail, and there shall be no fruit in the vines; the flock shall be cut off in the fold, and there shall be no herd in the stalls, yet I will rejoice in the Lord, I will joy in the God of my Salvation," Heb. 3: 17,18, 19. Paul, on account of our citizenship in the Heavens, exhorts us to rejoice always; and surely with every justified man "tribulation will work patience, and patience approbation, and approbation hope, and hope makes not ashamed because the love of God is shed abroad in our hearts by the Holy Spirit, which is given unto us." Alas! many rejoice not, because they bring no gifts to the Lord, pay no vows in the assembly of his Saints; but make the world their God;   its appetites their shame; who mind earthly things. "But our citizenship is in the Heavens, from whence we look for the Lord Jesus."

Joy has its fountain in the purified heart; it is a spark from the "throne of God where there are pleasures forever more;" it is the homage of holy sympathy; the link between human worms and choral angels; it is the mainspring of Nature's harmony; and it leads to a triumph over the cares of life and the surfeiting of pleasure, by waving its banner of glory, honor and Immortality over the shattered vaults of Death.

"Drink sweetly of Joy's holy spring. While standing on time's falling rivers;— Look to the Heavens and to their King, Where Joy abides forever!

Bear this life brothers—bravely bear— Bear this life for a better one!

See yon the Stars? A life is there, Where the reward is won!"

Graysville, Ky., Nov. 29th, 1844.   J. B. F.

SKEPTICISM—No. 2.

A second objection of the Skeptic is, the partial propagation of Christianity. At no time has it extended over the whole race of man; and at this present period, six-tenths of the whole family of man are in midnight darkness of a superstitious, cruel and absurd Paganism. Admit it, and what then? Christianity should be examined with reference to its natural and supernatural evidences; and if upon these it should be found to be true, receive it, for then all cavils are at an end. If the All-wise Disposer of the blessings of his Providence has entrusted us with an inestimable treasure, will we despise and contemn it because he has not entrusted it to others? As well might we say, because he has bestowed intellect and reason upon me, and not upon the "midnight Idiot," I will not use my gifted powers; I will neglect and scorn the priceless trust. Or because the indolent and filthy Hottentot starves for food, I will not eat of the abundance that industry and frugality have showered upon me. Reason would rather say, eat and send if possible, to the wants of the destitute. Again: If it were consistent and proper (as we have shown in a former article) in point of *time* to progressively develop the light and glory of the gospel to those who first received it, why may it not be so to the whole world of mankind? The state of the world was considered in its first propagation, why not in its continued advances? The spread of the gospel is committed to human agency; and all persons who raise such an objection as the above, should be careful lest they, instead of assisting in its onward triumphs, should be found hindrances in its progress, and thus justly deserve its condemnation. For if they are not so to others, they certainly are to themselves.

But if the objector is not satisfied, let him ere he reply against the God of the gospel, look abroad upon the distributions of Nature in its physical administration and see if his objection does not weigh with equal preponderance against those very things that daily come under his observation. Let him compare the physical and mental organization and geographical situation of the frozen Esquimaux, with the situation and nobler specimens of the Anglo-Saxon race. Or if he dislike a national, let him make an individual distinction. Let him contrast the man of robust constitution and uninterrupted health and vigorous intellect, with the pale, sickly hypochondriac who drawls out a pitiable existence amidst all the lavish beauties and abundance of nature's wide-spread tables. In short, we can find every variety in situation, condition and circumstances obtaining with reference to the physical as well as the moral man. Differences of climate and region produce differences in the species; and in this view apparently manifest partiality characterises all the arrangements of Providence. But perhaps were we to make ourselves fully acquainted with the world's situation, we would find everything directly under the disposal of Providence more equal than at a short sight we imagine. Still a difference exists —in appearance, in stature, in physical and mental ability, wherever we view our race—whether in the frozen regions of Iceland, or in the spicy Islands of eternal Summer, or in any of the intermediate belts of the earth. He had as well complain of this as of the variety and difference in the spread of the gospel. Besides, as already hinted, it is a part of our probationary trial whether or not we will send out the treasure committed to our hands; and as much of the physical suffering of men may be attributed to their fellows, so may much of the moral, and Christianity requires us to relieve both so far as we have means and opportunity. Perhaps the truth that many individuals and nations have not now the enlightening and happyfying influences of the gospel, may be laid to our charge; and if so, how will we meet the account? If Christianity be truth—and its truth depends upon evidence independent of the cavils we are examining, there can be no doubt that every man who has been made a recipient of its enlightening blessings, will be held accountable for the manner in which, as a Steward, he has held the sacred trust.

The objector must see that there is no point upon which to place his feet between Christianity and absolute Atheism. For every objection which he forms against the moral administration of an Infinitely Holy and Just God, can be formed against Nature with equal effect. And as with an Atheistical philosopher there is an end of reason, we will close our answer here, satisfied that any man who can deduce the present Heavens and Earth, from a casual reencounter of atoms, can deduce a conclusion from any premises. Atheism in absurdity, and when an objection runs into it, all reasonable men draw back.

J. B. FERGUSON.

CONFERENCES.—To remedy the effect of religious errors, to settle controversies, and allay the fervor of angry dispute, men sometimes assemble in Councils, Synods or Conferences. This expedient has been compared to that of a physician who placed in the region of some contagious pestilence, instead of using all the means in his power to allay the disease and stop the contagion, takes his patients into a populous assembly of physicians and others that they all may determine upon the nature and effects of the disease and adopt some method to destroy it. Any one can imagine the effect. Each person becomes inoculated and returns to his home only to spread a calamity which ostensibly he was seeking to prevent. It is only adding fire to the flame —patients to the disease, to assemble *divines* (?) to allay it. To correct errors, meet them where they originate.   J. B. F.

ERRATUM.

MESSRS. PUBLISHERS:—In my article in the last number of the "Review," on "Names in Religion," you present me to your readers as locating ancient Normandy in America, instead of America. An *o* instead of an *e* in this case makes considerable difference in the Geography of the globe. There are several minor errors, but the reader will correct them. By the way, permit me to say to your readers that my chirography is more to blame than your compositors; and that it has been a question with me for some time, who is most to be blamed, he who never writes, or he who writes so as never to be read. But for my deficiency in this useful mechanical Art, I shield myself behind the names of Byron, Parr, Buonaparte (and if Madame Fame is correct) A. Campbell, whose illegible chirography more resembles Stenography, or Egyptian Hieroglyphics than intelligible characters. I will try, however, to do better, and should I fail, I hope your readers will substitute what I Should have said, instead of what your compositor makes me say. I have been rebuked and jeered enough to have reformed long since.

Scrallingly yours,   J. B. F.

THE AMERICAN AND FOREIGN BIBLE SOCIETY.

The above is the name of a Society formed by our Baptist brethren in the year 1837, for the translating, printing, and distributing the Sacred Scriptures, at home and abroad.

We think it due to the Baptist brotherhood to state, that, in the estimation of many who stand decidedly opposed to a majority of the religious enterprises of the day,—believing that they are fitted to the fostering of existing party divisions and strifes—this Society is such an one as justly merits the joint co-operation of all who desire the spread of Scriptural holiness over this and all other lands. It is "founded upon the principle, that the originals in Hebrew and Greek are *the only authentic* standards of the Sacred Scriptures; and that aid for the translating, printing, or distributing of them in foreign languages, should be afforded to such versions only as are conformed as nearly as possible to the original text; it being understood that no words are to be *transferred,* which are susceptible of being literally *translated.*"

Prior to the organization of the "American and Foreign Bible Society," the Baptist Church, in common with various other religious denominations, was a member of the "American Bible Society." Of this Society they would have remained a member, but for the odious, and we may add, *disreputable* conduct of their pedo-baptist allies. In order to securely guard the citadel of pedo-baptism,—*i. e. sprinkling*—its supporters virtually rejected the originals in the Hebrew and Greek, as the only *authentic* standards of the Sacred Scriptures, choosing to adopt the common English Version in their stead. Accordingly, in 1836, they adopted the following Resolution, viz:

"Resolved., That in appropriating money for the translating, printing, or distributing of the Sacred Scriptures in foreign languages, the Managers feel at liberty to encourage only such versions as conform in the principle of their translation to the common English Version; at least so far that all religious denominations represented in this Society can consistently use and circulate said versions in their several Schools and communities."

The above resolution is but a servile imitation of the spirit and tone of the Papal hierarchy. The annals of Romanism is filled with such. Take a few examples:—"The Council of Trent, in 1563, declared that a Latin translation, called the Vulgate, was "authentic, and to be refused by none," which decree was confirmed by Pope Pious IV. in solemn consistory the following year; and the Rhemish Testament was translated from the Vulgate into English in 1582 —the translators declaring that the Vulgate "is not only better than all other translations, but than the Greek text itself in those places where they disagree?" Again; at a theological discussion held at Nantz, about the year 1524, between the Reformers and the supporters of the papacy, one of the latter party exclaimed "Ah!" cried the curate of Dintzen, as he glanced at the books the two Zurichers (Sebastian Hofmeister and Jas. Amman) held in their hands, "if the Hebrew and Greek languages had never obtained entrance into our country, there would be fewer heresies among us." Vide D'Aubigne, p. p. 324, '25. Protestant pedo-baptists will not exactly say that the originals of the Old and New Testaments are sources of heresy; but, in language lees intelligible, though designed to express virtually the same thing, *they "feel at liberty to encourage only ouch versions as conform in the principle of their translation to the common English Version"!!*

Who does not know our "Common English Version" is an incomplete translation? *Baptizo,* with all its cognates, are almost uniformly *transferred,* instead of being *translated.* And yet, this Version is to be made the *authentic* standard, to the principles of whose translation all other versions, foreign and domestic, are to be made to conform!

Languages are the scabbard in which the sword of the Spirit is securely kept; the casket that holds the precious jewels. When they are abandoned, as the repositories of Inspiration, and imperfect translations substituted in their stead, protestant christendom will soon find herself hurled back into the thick mists of papal darkness.

Sprinkling, pouring, &c., are so completely identified with the existence of the pedo-baptist fraternity, that we do not think it evinces a want of true charity in us to say we believe that, in order to the maintenance of these unauthorized usages, they would even dare to suppress, if not openly violate the sense of the original words, expressive of the proper action of Christian baptism. In some of their foreign versions, they have rendered *"baptizo"* by the word *"moisten!"*

It is with feelings of more than ordinary solicitude that we commend the "American and Foreign Bible Society" to the liberal patronage of all such as desire that all nations may read and understand the Bible "in their own languages wherein they were born." This Society sends out the Bible without note or comment. It is gratifying to learn that many of our brethren in Kentucky have nobly begun a co-operation with the managers and supporters of the "American and Foreign Bible Society." Their contributions are said to be quite liberal. With them we may also mention the congregation at Bethany, Va.   J. H. JOHNSON.

Commerce, Ten., *Nov.* 15tA, 1844.

ROMISH ANECDOTE.

The following singular circumstance is recorded by D'Aubigne, in his History of the Reformation of the 16th century, and will be read with interest.

J. H. J.

"A Saxon gentleman had heard Tetzel at Leipsic, and was much shocked by his impostures. He went to the monk, and inquired if he was authorized to pardon sins *in intention,* or such as the applicant *intended* to commit? "Assuredly," answered Tetzel; "I have full power from the Pope to do so." "Well," returned the gentleman, "I want to take some slight revenge on one of my enemies, without attempting his life. I will pay you ten crowns, if you will give me a letter that will bear me harmless." Tetzel made some scruples; but they struck their bargain for thirty crowns. Shortly after, the monk set out for Leipsic. The gentleman, attended by his servants, laid wait for him in a wood between Interlock and Treblin,—fell upon him, gave him a beating, and carried off the rich chest of indulgence-money the inquisitor had with him.— Tetzel clamored against this act of violence, and brought an action before the judges. But the gentleman showed the letter signed by Tetzel himself, which exempted him beforehand from all responsibility. Duke George, who had at first been much irritated at this action, upon seeing this writing, ordered that the accused should be acquitted." p. p. 223-4.

Little Rock, October 25th, 1844.

To the Editors of the Christian Review:

Bro. Fanning: *Dear Sir:*—In my note of the 24th August, I promised to write monthly—this I have not done—the cause of failure, was long absence from home—left on the 2nd September and did not return until 21st inst. My tour was to the extreme North West corner of this State. I stopped on my way and spoke five times at a small town (Lewisburg) and immersed one person, a young lady, in the Arkansas river, near the Hull of the Steamer Cherokee, which blew up in 1841, with a terrible loss of life and property. Near Fayetteville, attended a Cumberland Presbyterian Camp-meeting, where I met the Rev. gentlemen who some ten years ago, in honor to the good cause Orthodoxy, expelled me from their body as a Schismatic and Heretic. I attended two days, to learn what improvement had been made in religion-getting in this age of improvement. The *sorrowing stools* seemed to be the chief reliance and most favorable place for the Lord to "come down and give faith."

I opened a course of Lectures in Town, where two of the Revd. gentlemen reside. Exposed the humanism of such appliances as had been used at the late meeting, with a hope to draw one or both of them out. One of them did take notes, but neither of them responded. Such was the will of the Heavenly Father, that I fell sick and could only deliver a few of the intended Lectures., The last one was on Regeneration—this was given out several days. In the mean time, a New School Presbyterian, a man of good sense and learning, came to town: him these gentlemen induced to expose the dangerous tendency of my teaching. He anticipated my Lecture; but the brethren are of opinion he will never be caught in a similar net. No one made the good confession, but much good was done by way of removing evil reports. Our very intelligent Brother Strickland resides a few miles from town. There are many Disciples who are slowly progressing; there is much need of the "*second teaching.*"— There is a defect in relation to "living for Christ"; indeed this defect is too general, and requires steady and efficient teaching to remedy it this should be done by the Bishops. It is their duty to teach the Disciples.

With this you will receive several articles for the Review; they are not finely written, but sufficiently plain to be understood. The topics are important, and should be calmly and in the love of truth examined. As there is but "one body and spirit." The spirit is the active, efficient principle in the body, not only on a small, but a large scale. To secure a proper organization, congregations must be fully set in order and taught to live for him who died for them. This time serving conformity to a wicked world must give place to "*love, self-denial, and dying daily.*" Think you that the spirit of, Christ will dwell in the fashionable Belles, Beaus, loud and merry lovers of the present day? Immersed they may have been, but not into Christ. Indeed, it is to be feared that but too many of the late Disciples are like the twelve whom Paul met near Ephesus.	Sincerely yours,	W. W. STEVENSON.

CONGREGATIONAL ORGANIZATION.

Little Rock, Oct. 25th, 1844.

To the Editors of the Christian Review:

Order and congregational organization has for some time past, attracted much attention, and drawn forth many valuable essays from the brethren. But nothing satisfactory has as yet been presented; the question is yet open for discussion, and will be perhaps for years yet to come. Indeed, it is not easy to determine whose plan shall be adopted. Even should one State adopt any particular system of organization, there is no rule by which it can be made the order in other States. Those who desire a political organization, had better begin at the only practicable point, which is to first form a head upon some plan from which their rules *organic* may emanate, and become obligatory.— This head may be formed of one man, or ten, or any given number by way of delegation, who may after due organization with moderator, clerk, &c. &c., proceed to consider any and every plan of organization,, and adopt that one that seems best to accord with their understanding of the whole matter. If it be objected that such convention would be unscriptural and dangerous, I answer that such conventions being an essential part of the system of organization upon any other plan than that of mere ecclesiastical organization clearly defined in the word, then the whole must be unscriptural. It is better to fall short of the divine mode, than to go beyond it; men can be more easily induced to except of power than to part with it. The body of Christ is the entire family of believers, of which Christ is the head; the cement of the Temple is the Holy Spirit. But what is said of the whole congregation of the faithful is said of a particular (Ecclesia) congregation, "Jesus is the chief Shepherd or Bishop." The love of his Kingdom is one that is the general love of Ecclesiastical intercourse.

If we refer this matter to the divine record, we will not find any thing that will answer to a general organization, except upon the plan of mutual obligation, governed by the law of love. The objects of such plans seem to be but two, the first is to avoid imposition by feeble and unworthy Evangelists, and the second to secure more efficient cooperation in support of the Gospel. If I am not wholly mistaken, the first can be secured and *only* secured by individual congregations; a church and not conventional tribunals, can make Evangelists. There is no question at all, that a congregation of believers with their Bishops and Deacons, is the highest ecclesiastical power on earth. Such a body and such alone, can lawfully send out Evangelists, which are without doubt the moist important offices in the Kingdom of Jesus, and should never be conferred on a man, who does not combine all the qualifications specified by Paul, which amount to nearly twenty. No congregation not fully set in order, can lawfully send out an Evangelist; and again, it is more than obvious to all, that none should be sent out except those who are fully qualified. To have the moral requirements is not sufficient; but *with* these, to be able to teach the word, and set things in order. Such men are strictly responsible to the congregation that sends them out, and from the apostolic example should report to the brethren at the expiration of each Evangelizing tour. No man is an Evangelist except he who has authority from a congregation. Men may go forth and preach, and preach in right of their character; but to do the work of an Evangelist they may not. To act in good faith, a congregation should have some oversight over their Evangelists, and should recall them if they should stray off beyond their appointed bounds, and revoke their letters if they do not the work of an Evangelist; this they owe to themselves, as well as the whole family of the faithful. And brethren who may have been imposed upon, whether through design or ignorance, and have been organized by one not lawfully set apart as an Evangelist, should seek such an official, and be properly set in order by a legally authorized Evangelist.

In my next, if the Lord will, I will notice the second object insisted on by those who seem to desire *"Organization,"* and say a few words further illustrative of the work and office of an Evangelist.

W. W. STEVENSON.

WORK AND OFFICE OF AN EVANGELIST.

LITTLE ROCK, OCT. 25TH, 1844.

To the Editors of the Christian Review:—

In a former No., there was an attempt to point out the mode of making Evangelists. It was then intimated, that none but congregations fully set in order, can lawfully authorize men to set others in order, and that no man should be invested with so high an office, but one *fully qualified.* Men may teach the Christian religion in right of their citizenship; they may also administer the ordinances, and any number of Disciples may, and of duty, ought to meet and keep the ordinances; but they can neither set themselves in order, nor send out men to set others in order.

A second object of organization is the support of Evangelists. That real Evangelists need support, is sufficient evidence, that while they may exercise that office, some one must feed and clothe them; and if such *"entangle themselves with this world"* (and such entanglement does not incapacitate for the office) then the wife and little ones must also be fed and clothed; no man is bound to labor unless the brethren feed him; of this there can be no doubt.— If he has a desire to preach on his own account, not sent, let him do so; but if the brethren send him, they are bound in sight of Heaven and Earth to support him, unless   he voluntarily chooses to wave his right. Indeed, it is difficult to imagine that a Disciple who owes every thing to the Lord, who is not his own, can feel content, not to lay up a small amount of treasures in heaven, by giving a small pittance of what we have to support the good cause of persuading men to be saved. If this support is to be from a joint contribution of several congregations, and this regulated by fixed laws, then these congregations have a right to vote who shall go, and where, and participate in setting him apart. This cannot be done except by a conventional power. Such mode of Evangelizing may be well defined in the Sacred Records, but I must say it has escaped my notice. The congregations of Corinth, Macedonia and Galatia, made contributions for the poor saints; this was a voluntary thing; Paul gave orders as to the manner of doing it. But this is quite another matter. Here, there is no law commanding this duty as to how much or little each shall give, but that of love; and surely no man's soul can love the Lord if he love his goods more. Not only the church sending out the Evangelist, but even other brethren should "bring the servant of their master on his way. The rule of raising revenue in the Kingdom of Messiah, is neither by a capitation, nor ad-valorem tax; it is by free-will offerings, and that too weekly. How can the love of God dwell in the house of that mother or sister, who has never given a dollar to support the Kingdom of the Master.

I have seen more worthless books and toys on the mantel-pieces and center tables of Disciples, than would fit out the servant of the Lord with a good suit of *Kentucky Jeans,* Alas for the Christianity of the age! We have a *Christ, but he has no cross.* Sarah will never own for her Daughter, those slaves of fashion and vain show. But I have wandered from the topic. It is possible that much of the caution felt on this subject, is unbecoming, and should be abandoned. To organize congregations is right; to induce the whole family to walk in love and live for him who died for them, is also proper; but as to general organization, to say the best of it, if it is taught, perhaps the 15th chapter of Acts could be made to squeeze out such a thing as will suit our purpose; it has done wonders already, and may do more for aught I know.

If the Lord will, in my next something will be said respecting Evangelists and others, on the subject of doing, &c. &c. W. W. STEVENSON.

EVANGELISTS.

LITTLE ROCK, OCT. 25TH, 1844.

To the Editors of the Christian Review:
The Office of Evangelist, being the most important in the Kingdom of Jesus, requires the most important talents to fill it. Be an example to the believers in "words, in behavior, in love, in faith, in chastity." 1 Tim iv, 12. Take heed to yourself and your doctrine—continue in them;——16 v. These, with many other similar passages, leave the conviction strong that the Evangelist is to be no common man in piety and knowledge. Indeed, he should be the impersonation of godliness—pleasant, kind, affable, eating whatever is set before him. None but holy congregations can either educate or appreciate such men. Are all who go forth to Christianize the world, of this sort? It is to be feared they are not. As my remarks are not mere theory, I will present a few facts. Evangelist arrived at and must preach—spoke a few minutes, reciting what he had memorized—"forgot the rest," and sat down. Bro. — followed—told the people to watch the preachers—many of them were not to be trusted—with many similar sayings. So, the people set a mark on him. Evangelist——spends much time in adjusting his hair and cravat in presence of those to whom he is to speak. He affects French politeness—talks loud, laughs boisterously. Evangelist — has a small blank book for notes; this he keeps in his hand while in the congregation, placing a fancy kerchief in the book at the place where his notes are—this done in sight of all. Bro. Evangelist — introduces foreign words, French and Latin in his discourse, and at the same time violating every rule of Grammar. Bro. speaks against text preaching, and plunges into a confused jargon of generalization, so as to have neither head nor point. Evangelist   is young, but very wise in his own estimation; treats senior— as inferiors. Evangelist—must dress fine, must "appear as a *Gentleman*"—visits the wealthy brethren only—requests the service of one or two servants. In the stand declaims

loudly against Sectarianism—uses many

quaint sayings. Bro._______________ is very different from these—he looks pleasant— is dressed very plain—evinces deep thoughtfulness—reads closely—converses pleasantly—is much in prayer—treats the old women as mothers—the young as sisters, with all chastity. He eats what is placed before him. In preaching, shows reading and study—argues much from inspired authority. These pictures are not mere fictions, but real. The congregations are responsible to God and the world for those they send out and permit to preach.!!

W. W. STEVENSON.

CHURCH OFFICERS,

With the exception of what has been published in Nashville, and a few essays by H. T. Anderson, in the C. Journal, I have seen nothing so forcible and scriptural on the subject of Church Officers, as an essay in the "Genius of Christianity, published by Bro. Comings, in Boston.

"There are now two official stations which I can discover in the Christian church; and these are, first, that of bishops, or overseers, and second, that of deacons. The first of these are executive officers, having charge of the *spiritual* health of the particular church of which they are members. Observe, they do not possess one particle of *judicial* or *legislative* authority. All committed to them is *executive,* either by express commitment or inferentially, from the nature of the Christian system, of their station, or their qualifications specified. The second, that of deacons, is more strictly *ministerial,* having charge of the *temporal* affairs of the church, and acting by its direction in the divinely appointed duties of the station. Both grades of officers are to be chosen out of the eldership of the church. There is no such thing as the elder's office in nature or Christianity. Elders are men of age and experience, of wisdom and prudence, on whom, collectively, devolves the care of the *infant* church, (see Paul's charge to the elders of the church at Ephesus, Acts 20,) and from among whom, *when proved,* officers are to be chosen for this very work. They are still, however, to exercise an eye of vigilance over all their affairs, and to correct any abuse which may intrude itself, either from want of vigilance, or by the consent, of the officers. *Elders,* not *minors,* are entrusted by the Saviour with the conservation of the peace, holiness, happiness, and prosperity of his church.

But I will now attend particularly to that portion or the subject embraced 1 in the appointment of overseers or bishops, and the qualifications essential to the office as delineated by Paul, in his letters to Timothy and Titus.

The Qualifications are of *three* kinds, which fact must be seen in order to understand the matter in all its force. They are as follows:—I. *Positive,* 2. Ac*tive.* 3. *Negative.* A little attention to these distinctions will open the matter to our apprehension better than any other manner I know of. But in order to impress it upon the mind, I will endeavor to address the eye by the following arrangement:—

Positive Qualifications.

1. He must be the husband of one wife.
2. Must be blameless, as the steward of God.

Active Qualifications.

1. Must have faithful children.
2. Must be a lover of hospitality.
3. "   "   "   good men.
4. "   "   prudent.
5. "   "   holy.
6. "   "   temperate.
7. "   "   just.
8. "   "   vigilant.
9. "   "   patient.
10. "   "   of good behavior.
11. "   "   fit, or apt, to teach.

12. "   "   one that rules well his own house.

13. "   "   hold fast the faithful word, in teaching, as he has been taught.
14. "   "   have a good report from them without.

Negative Qualifications.

1. Must not be riotous.
2.   "   "   "   unruly.
3.   "   "   "   self-willed.
4.   "   "   "   soon angry
5.   "   "   "   given to wine.
6.   "   "   "   a striker.
7.   "   "   "   a money lover.
8.   "   "   "   a brawler.
9.   "   "   "   covetous.
10. "   "   "   a young convert.

The above list, of twenty-six specifications, plainly exhibit the three classes. Any person, to be suitable for the office of bishop, must possess the positive qualifications, perfectly; the *active, to* a degree; and the *negative,* must also be to perfection. There are no degrees in negatives. A man must *not* be "*self-willed,*" another cannot be *more so.* But of the *active,* one man may be "patient," and yet another may be *more so.* So of all the active. One may possess, or entertain, them all, yet another may excel him in them. To be a bishop, a man *must* be "vigilant;" but he who is more so, would, in this particular, be better; and so with each item— so also with the whole collectively. There is no possibility of excelling, or improving in the negatives—all improvement is in the actions. No one can be properly appointed to the office of an overseer of a Christian church who does not answer to all and each of the above specifications—of the *active,* to a good degree; and the *positive* and *negative,* his answer must be complete—perfect. A failure in any one respect will forever disqualify one for the discharge of the duties of the office, although he should (if it were possible,) possess all the others. Should a man be "self-willed," or should he be *not* "vigilant," divine wisdom says he is not a suitable person. And let all the people say, amen.

We often hear it suggested, that if churches have not persons in them who answer to the apostolic requisitions, then those coming *nearest* should be appointed. I admire both the spirit and the practice of compromise, in all matters of human experiment and management, but must now and forever protest against any compromise affecting any of the divine appointments or arrangements. This plea of being satisfied with something *near* the truth, (that is, something else than the truth.) is like making a breach in the walls of the city, while the enemy is at hand and the guards are slumbering. Destruction is the *only* consequence that can follow, as the result of such conduct. "Pouring" is *nearer* immersion, than "sprinkling."

In the appointment of overseers, see to it, that they possess "all and singular" the qualifications enjoined by the spirit of inspiration. Make choice of those who have them in the highest degree, not of those who come nearest, but do not possess them.

It will, undoubtedly, be asked, what then must be done when there are no suitable persons to fill the station of bishops? My answer is, do not appoint *unsuitable* ones—make no appointment, but await the providence of God, trusting that in due time suitable persons will be provided.

Again, what must be done when there are more persons than are needed in the office of overseers, possessing the requisite qualifications, in one church? The answer is easy, select a sufficient number of those who are endowed in the *highest degree.*

There is a great fondness for office common to the American people, and I do not know but the world over. This has, in a great many instances, been brought along with individuals into the Christian church; and should the church be so indiscreet as to appoint any such person to office, he is soon seen to be puffed up. And if he has ingenuity enough, he may presently be found contriving some scheme of greatness. His little soul is seen swelling under some great project of consolidated councils; or he is heard to talk much (and hard if opposed,) upon the *powers* of his office. The term *power* is always a favorite one with him—seldom, or never, is he heard to say any thing about the *duties* of the station. This kind of character should especially be guarded against.

Such persons, by care and watchfulness, may become good Christians, but never good officers. This same fondness for office frequently urges people to premature appointments. Appointments are made before it is possible for any of the brotherhood to be proved. I have known some instances where all were but "babes in Christ"—where not a week of weeks had elapsed since any of them had put on Christ according to the gospel,—and notwithstanding the injunction "not a young convert," they have proceeded to the appointment of overseers—and I have known two instances in which the overseers constituted two-thirds of the brethren in the body. Premature appointments always indicate an unhealthy or weak state of the body. Some have insisted that the appointment of officers is "Me organization" of the body—or, in other words, that without officers there can be no organization, and without such organization, no church! No comment is necessary. To avoid making injudicious appointments, let all take time to know one another, the scriptural character, and the duties, not powers, of the office. At some future time, I may undertake to amplify the foregoing remarks, but cannot now promise when.

At the commencement of this article, I thought to say something of qualifications, calling, and duties of deacons, but have concluded to cast that matter for a future day.

Let me entreat the brethren in "the reformation" to look well to these things. Remember, brethren, our motto is, "the truth, the whole truth, and nothing but the truth" of the gospel; our aim is, the character, the whole character, and nothing but the character of Christians; and that our standard is, the bible, the whole bible, and nothing but the bible.   A. P. JONES."

ADVICE TO YOUNG SISTERS.

Will the sisters read attentively the remarks appended, and determine to be governed by the sacred precepts introduced? EDITOR.

CLARKSVILLE, OCTOBER 3, 1844.

BROTHER FANNING:—If you think the remarks below worthy of a place in the Review, 1 shall be pleased to see them.

Dear young sisters in Christ, have we not reason to conclude, when we compare the multitude of young Women who profess to be the disciples of Christ, with what the word of God requires, that there are but few Christians among us? In love I would ask you, if we can with any propriety claim to be the disciples of Jesus, while we live in constant disobedience to his commands?— I fear we too much neglect to examine ourselves by the word of God. What avail will it be to us, that we have done as well as others, if others have failed to obey God? O! my dear sisters, we must stand as single creatures before the judgment seat of Christ, and a mere profession of Christianity will not screen us then. Eternal life is promised to them who, by patient continuance in well doing, seek for glory, honor, and immortality. We are exhorted not to be conformed to this world; but are we not greedily following the customs of the world, even in opposition to our great lawgiver, to say nothing of our daily deportment in other respects? I fear that in following the fashions of the world as we do with reference to dress, we trample upon the precepts and examples of the New Testament more than we are aware. Let us attend to the language of inspiration: "In like manner, that women adorn themselves in modest apparel, with shamefacedness and sobriety; not with broidered hair, or gold, or pearls, or costly array, but (which becomes women professing godliness) with good works." 1 Tim. 2: 9, 10. Also 1 Pet. 3: 3. And now, sisters, are we not spending much money, and not only money, but time, to do what is here forbidden, and in this manner preventing ourselves, to a degree at least, from doing what is enjoined, that is, good works? If the money that is spent to adorn our persons in a manner God disapproves, were spent to support some faithful evangelist, or many, would they be compelled to retire from the field, or

suffer their families to be deprived of the comforts of life? Were it given to the poor, how many would be relieved from the sufferings of cold and hunger? Were it spent for Bibles, how many might have the word of life in their hands, who have not the means of obtaining them? I think these are important interrogations. Let us look into the matter. Have we not both precept and example for feeding the hungry, clothing the naked, and enlightening our fellow men, as we have opportunity? And shall we deprive ourselves of the means of so doing, by spending what we possess for that which God disapproves? He who was rich, for our sakes became poor, that we through his poverty might be rich; shall we refuse to deny ourselves of those things which will do us no real good, in order to please him and benefit our fellow men? If we will do so little to please Him who gave himself up to suffering and death for us, while we were his enemies, have we any reason to think we love him? Let us listen to the words which fell from his lips, while on earth. "If any man will come after me, let him deny himself, and take up his cross daily, and follow me. Our Savior, while on earth, went about doing good, being despised and rejected of men, a man of sorrows and acquainted with grief; and shall we not better follow Christ, imitating his example, by spending more of our time visiting the sick and attempting to alleviate human sufferings, and less of it in preparing and placing ornaments upon our bodies? Can it be otherwise than that we wound the feelings of our brother, whom we call upon to teach ourselves and others the word of truth, when they see that we spend much in sinfully adorning our persons, while their families are in want? Is this loving our brother as ourselves? Certainly, we can be under no less obligations to our brother than our neighbor. Do we consider that in thus injuring our brethren, we injure our Savior? "In as much as ye have done it to one of the least of these my brethren, ye have done it unto me." Perhaps, dear friends, I have already wearied your patience, but I wish to say a few words in reference to conversation. Do we suffer unkind words to fall from our lips, and thus reproach the cause of Christ? And oftener do we not indulge in vain conversation? O that we might each remember the exhortation of the Apostle, not to let foolish talking and jesting be named among us as becometh saints; but rather giving of thanks. Also, let your speech be always with grace, seasoned with salt, that ye may know how ye ought to answer every man. O that we might give head to all the admonitions of the word of the Lord, that it might indeed be a lamp to our feet and alight to our path, and guide our feet in the way of peace. Let us remember, my dear sister, that we are each exerting an influence on our fellow travelers to eternity, and O that the influence might be holy. Time is hurrying us on to eternity. Death is often admonishing us.— May its voice be regarded. We have but a little time at the longest. It may be we are spending our last hour; and may we live as we shall wish we had when we come to the day we so live that with joy we may stand before our judge. Let us remember that he who soweth to the flesh, shall of the flesh reap corruption; but he that soweth to the spirit, shall of the spirit reap life everlasting. With a great desire that we may sow to the spirit, I bid you adieu.

A SISTER.

Brother JAMES COLLINSWORTH, of Athens, Ala., held a meeting at Green Hill, five miles from that place, in the month of Oct., at which fourteen were added to the faithful. Brother C.'s letter would have been given in full, had I been at home in November.   T. F.

A GOOD MAN HAS FALLEN.

On the covering of the Oct. No. of the Christian Messenger, published at Jacksonville, Ill., and edited by B. W. Stone and D. P. Henderson, the Junior Editor writes, "Please say *to Mr. Fanning that B. W. Stone sleeps in Jesus. He died on the 9th inst., (Oct.) Particulars hereafter.*   *D. P. H.*"

The history of Brother Stone would be the history of the most important religious movements in the U. States, for nearly half a century. He was educated and ordained a Presbyterian preacher; but about the beginning of the present century, he became satisfied, obedience to the Westminster Confession of Faith was not obedience to God. and therefore he, as an honest man, was compelled to change his ground. In his new position, his motto was, "the Bible alone, is the only creed for Christians;" and although at the time, he was not extensively acquainted with untrammeled Christianity, his motto freed him from speculation after speculation, till he became one of the ablest and most faithful defenders of the faith in America. To be sure his talent was not, perhaps, quite so brilliant as some others; but his acquaintance with the Scriptures was extensive and critical, and a more humble, conscientious and pious man cannot be found. If justice is ever done to his memory, he will be regarded as the first great American reformer,—the first man who, to much purpose, pleaded the ground that the Bible, without note, commentary, or creed, must destroy antichristian powers, and eventually conquer the world. Although I

Dr. J. R. Wilson, Nashville, Ten.	$100	T. J. M'Daniel, Oakland, Ala.	40
F. M'Gavock, Esq "	100	Hardy Hightower, Florence, Ala.	50
A. Fall, "	100	E. W. Bennett, Colbert, Miss.	50
E. Trabue, "	100	Dr. W. M. Bennett, "	50
James Woods, "	200	A. B. Duling, "	40
A. &N. Anderson, "	50	Green Hill, Columbus, Miss.	50
R. Stewart, "	50	John B. West, Nashville,	10
Berry & Tannehill, "	100	M. W. Johnston, "	10
James A. Woods, "	100	O. E. "paid	50
Josiah F. Williams, "	100	Robt. C. Foster sen. " paid	25
Andrew Ewing, "	50	Dr. D. W. Mentlo, Gallatin,	25
W. A. Eichbaum, "	100	Peter Brison, "	10
Dr. D. T. M'Gavock, "	50	Elcanah Bush, "	5
John Beaty, "	100	John W Hall, "	10
C. Conner, "	25	James Fulgham, Fayetteville, Ten.	10
P. W. Maxey, "	15	John Goodrich, "	10
Maj. G. W. Martin, "	100	W. Dickens, Elkton, Ky.	10
Mark R. Cockrill, Esq. "	100	A. Randall, Cincinnati, in Books and Apparatus,	100
Benj. Litton, "	50	Jno. W. Campbell, Louisville, Ky. in Books,	40
J. J. Corley, "	10	M'Nairy & Hamilton, in Paints,	25
Dr. T. Wells, "	20	W. W. & J. B. Berry, in Paints,	25
L. L. Shreve Esq., Louisville, Ky.	100	D. W. Bodenhammer. Louisville, Ky., a splendid Herbarium.	
Jno. M'Gavock Esq., Franklin, Ten.	50		
Jacob Wright, Readyville, Ten.	50	Thomas Martin of Pulaski, Ten. and	
G. N. Newman, Millersburg, Ten.	20		
Caleb Toney Esq., Triana, Ala.	100		
J. J. Ward, " paid	20		
John W. Looney, "	20		
Dr. J. B. Coons, "	10		
B. F. Harris, Somersville, Ala.	20		
D. G. Ligon Esq., Moulton, Ala.	200		
W. Alexander, "	20		

J. Moore and R. Preuitt of Moulton, Ala., gave their obligation for $1000, which will entitle each to the privilege of sending a student forever free of cost for boarding and tuition.

have heard Father Stone slandered, and his views grossly perverted, yet never did I hear mortal man utter a syllabic derogatory to his moral worth. A man more devoted to Christianity, has not lived nor died, and many stars will adorn his crown in a coming day.   ED.

DONATIONS TO FRANKLIN COLLEGE.

The amounts subscribed are made payable January 1st, '45 and January 1st, '46.